RED WINGS OVER THE YALU

TEXAS A&M UNIVERSITY
MILITARY HISTORY SERIES
80

Red Wings over the Yalu

China, the Soviet Union, and the Air War in Korea

Xiaoming Zhang

TEXAS A&M UNIVERSITY PRESS COLLEGE STATION

The paper used in this book meets the minimum requirements
of the American National Standard for Permanence
of Paper for Printed Library Materials, z39.48-1984.
Binding materials have been chosen for durability.

Library of Congress Cataloging-in-Publication Data

Zhang, Xiaoming, 1951–
      Red wings over the Yalu : China, the Soviet Union, and the air
war in Korea / Joseph G. Dawson, general editor.
            p. cm.— (Texas A & M University military history series ;
no. 80)
      Includes bibliographical references and index.
      ISBN 1–58544–201–1 (cloth)
      ISBN 1–58544–340–9 (pbk.)
         1. Korean War, 1950–1953—Aerial operations, Chinese.
      2. Air power—China—History.   I. Dawson, Joseph G., 1945–
      II. Title.   III. Series.
      DS920.2.C46 Z46   2002
      951.904'248–dc21   2002001763

To my father, a veteran of the PLAAF

Contents

Illustrations

Maps

Acknowledgments

I could not have completed this book without the assistance of many people. My thanks first go to Noel Parsons, former editor-in-chief of Texas A&M University Press, who encouraged me to start the project and continued to motivate me to finish it in a timely manner. My mentor, Lawrence Gelfand, not only helped me with the basic craft of being a historian during my study at the University of Iowa, but also continued to offer me encouragement and advice throughout my writing of this book. Conrad C. Crane, Stephen L. Sewell, and William W. Stueck read the entire manuscript, and I am grateful to them for thoughtful comments. Numerous individuals have helped me develop the Soviet side of my story. In particular, Sewell provided translations of many Russian-language materials and shared his knowledgeable insights on the Korean War records of Soviet Air Force units. Mark O'Neill and Frank G. Rozendaal were most generous in supplying me with their own works and Russian materials that initiated my earlier understanding of Soviet involvement. Chen Jian and Zhai Qian never tired of sharing Russian Korean War documents translated into Chinese and newly available Chinese materials. Peggy Hardman, a friend and former colleague, read an earlier draft of the manuscript and offered me useful suggestions. Kathryn Weathersby and anonymous readers for Texas A&M University Press also took time to read the manuscript and suggest revisions.

The staffs of several libraries offered essential assistance in my efforts to exploit their holdings. These institutes are the U.S. Air Force Historical Research Agency, the University of Texas at Austin and Texas A&M University libraries, the Nanjing University and Liaoning Normal University History Department libraries, Nanjing City library, the Nanjing City Party Academy library, the Jiangsu provincial archives in Nanjing, and the archives of Dalian city. Texas A&M International University provided funding for this study. I am also grateful to Jerry Thomson, dean of the College of Arts and Humanities, for his inspirational support throughout this project. Members of the Texas A&M University Press editorial staff deserve great credit for their assistance in publishing this book. Dale Wilson, a freelance copy editor, did a superlative job, saving me from more mistakes than I can enumerate.

This project was expanded from an article published in the *Journal of Military History* (October, 1998). I am grateful to the journal for permitting me to reuse previously published materials in this book.

Among those in China who helped me with this project, I would particularly like to thank Su Bingyi, an old friend, for translating a large portion of the Russian language materials I used. I would also like to thank Larry Bland from the *Journal of Military History* for supplying me with one of the maps. John R. Bruning, Jr., and Alfred W. Dymock, Jr., deserve thanks for supplying me with photographs.

I owe a great deal to my children, Michael and Connie, and my wife, Fang Shengli, who supported me with their tolerance of my absence and inattention during the years of research and writing that have gone into this study. I could not have completed it without them and their understanding of how much this book means to me.

Finally, my greatest debt is to my father, a veteran of the People's Liberation Army Air Force. Despite his advanced age and poor health, he helped me collect Chinese source materials and arrange interviews with many of his former colleagues and acquaintances who participated in the Korean War. I dedicate this book to my father in honor of his devotion to the Chinese air force and the unfair treatment he suffered during the political turmoil in China.

A word on orthography: I employed the *Pinyin* form of romanizing the names of all Chinese persons and places with the exception of Sun Yat-sen. Apostrophes are used occasionally to help with pronunciation. The spelling of Korean personal and place names follows the commonly accepted forms used in English-language literature on Korea (e.g., Kim Il Sung, Syngman Rhee, Pyongyang, and Seoul). I employed the standard system adopted by the Joint Research Service for use by the Foreign Broadcast Information Service for the transliteration of all Russian names except those already widely available in English-language publications (e.g., Joseph Stalin).

Abbreviations

AAA: Antiaircraft Artillery
AAD: Antiaircraft Artillery Division
APRF: Archives of the President of the Russian Federation
ATD: Aviation Technical Division
BAD: Bomber Air Division
CCP: Chinese Communist Party
CMC: CCP's Central Military Commission
CPV: Chinese People's Volunteers
DPMO: Defense POW/MIA Office
DPRK: Democratic People's Republic of China
FEAF: Far East Air Forces
GCI: Ground Control Intercept
GIAP: Guards Interceptor/Fighter Air Regiment
GMD: Guomingdang (Nationalist Party)
GSAP: Guards Searchlight Air Regiment
IAD: Interceptor/Fighter Air Division
IAK: Fighter Air Corps
IAP: Interceptor/Fighter Air Regiment
NEBDA: Northeast Border Defense Army
NKPA: North Korean People's Army
PLA: People's Liberation Army
PLAAF: People's Liberation Army Air Force
PRC: People's Republic of China
PVO: Soviet Air Defense Forces
ROK: Republic of Korea
SAP: Searchlight Air Regiment
SHAD: Ground-Attack Air Division
SHAP: Ground-Attack Air Regiment
VVS: Soviet air force
UN: United Nations
USAF: U.S. Air Force
USAFHRA: U.S. Air Force Historical Research Agency

RED WINGS OVER THE YALU

Introduction

The implications suggested by China's growing military and economic capabilities concern today's policy makers, strategists, and scholars as they consider the future security of Asia. Airpower proved a dominant factor in the 1991 Gulf War, more so than in previous conflicts, and China, like many other nations, has subsequently placed more emphasis on developing airpower to fight what Chinese planners refer to as any "modern local war under high-tech conditions." Current Beijing leaders anticipate that the Chinese air force will be able to "bear the brunt of, and play a sustained, independent role" in such an event.[1] While making a domestic effort to modernize its air force, China has also, since the early 1990s, purchased a significant number of long-range fighters and anti-aircraft missile systems from Russia. Russian technology has also been imported to improve China's own military industry. The growth of Chinese air and naval power is of less concern to Western nations than how China might use that new military strength. In the fifty-year history of the People's Liberation Army Air Force (PLAAF), the only air war it fought was in Korea against United Nations forces led by the United States in the early 1950s. Understanding the PLAAF's performance in Korea and the lessons learned seems essential to gaining insight into the importance of the PLAAF to the People's

Republic of China (PRC) and better comprehension of the role airpower plays in Chinese thinking today.

The Korean conflict constitutes an important experience for the PLAAF, not only as a test case for this fledgling service but also as a formative experience for the later development of Chinese airpower. During the Korean War, it expanded from virtually nothing to one of the world's largest air forces (after the United States and the Soviet Union). China, however, has never been regarded as a formidable player in the global balance of airpower. It was not until the collapse of the Soviet Union and the apparent end of the Cold War that China's airpower came to pose serious concerns for regional security and world peace. Yet, our knowledge of the Chinese air force remains limited. No institutional history has been written to detail the organizational culture of the Chinese air force or reveal the PLAAF's full identity.[2] In retrospect, it is evident the Korean War significantly affected the Chinese air force's strategic and doctrinal thinking, structure, performance, and capabilities. The development and growth of the air force serve as concrete examples of China's ability to develop and use modern technology in warfare. The PLAAF became a symbol of China's political aspirations, at home and abroad. A scholarly study of China's involvement in the air war in Korea is certain to shed new light on any contemporary discussions of the "China threat" in the Asian-Pacific region and beyond.

When the Korean War broke out on June 25, 1950, the newly established People's Republic possessed an armed force of five million soldiers, but few planes or pilots. Nevertheless, Chinese intervention in October, 1950, and the subsequent appearance of Communist jet fighters over Korea, stunned UN forces and U.S. leaders in Washington. General Douglas MacArthur, commander of the UN forces, responded by escalating the air war to "deter" or limit "any intervention by Chinese forces" in Korea.[3] One result was a new type of aerial warfare as the UN and Communist air forces skirmished with jet aircraft. Although the reality was much more complex than any one side's account would indicate, pilots from all belligerents found an opportunity to show their ability, pursue glory, and claim triumph for their side. The young, inexperienced Chinese pilots were no exception despite the U.S. Air Force's (USAF) air superiority.

The story of the Chinese ground war has been studied at length for the past fifty years, but the Chinese air war in Korea has been virtually ignored.[4] Most existing analyses have assessed Communist air operations from the American perspective, and have given short shrift to China's participation in the air war.[5] Robert F. Futrell's *The United States Air Force in Korea, 1950–*

1953, (first published in 1961), using sources from the USAF archives, provides the most authoritative account of USAF operations in the Korean War. However, the author had little access to Soviet or Chinese sources, and relied on U.S. intelligence analyses and eyewitness accounts of pilots. His depiction of Communist air involvement in Korea is one-sided, even misleading, as he alleges Korea was an easy adversary for the Americans and their sleek fighters, which achieved an astonishing 7:1 kill ratio over their Communist adversaries. This central theme has dominated the American interpretation of the air war in Korea. Documentation about the PLAAF tended to be ignored or dismissed because American analysts have a tendency to view the other side's story through their own myths and values. Communist accounts and sources were neither comprehensive nor fully candid, and thus have had little credibility.[6] Scholars have only recently begun to revise the history of the air war in Korea, acknowledging that there was no "walkover" in the skies of Korea, and that American pilots "probably highly inflated" their victories.[7] This new interpretation emerged with recent revelations of Soviet participation in the conflict. The new evidence shows the Russians and Americans, in terms of technical and psychological quality, were actually more evenly matched, and that the Americans might have grossly overestimated enemy losses.

America's knowledge of Soviet involvement in Korea first came from the UN's interception of Russian language transmissions from MiGs around the Yalu River.[8] Not until the collapse of the Soviet Union in the early 1990s, however, did the West come across the first authentic accounts of Soviet involvement in the Korean air war. Relying primarily on interviews with a small number of former Soviet pilots who participated in the Korean conflict, and on articles from Russian journals dating from 1989 and 1990, the accounts offer an excellent beginning to a chapter that for too long has been only a minor point of speculation in the larger body of Korean War historiography. Human memory is flawed, however, particularly forty years after the events. Without any archival references to refresh or sharpen those memories, the recollections of the pilots' combat experience provides little insight into why Soviet leaders decided on limited intervention in Korea, or how Soviet air involvement affected the Communist war efforts on the ground.[9]

With Soviet archival materials increasingly available since 1995, there have been a handful of attempts by Russian scholars to shed light on the Soviet participation in the air war over North Korea. The most significant ones are Askold A. German and Igor A. Seidov's *Red Devils on the 38th Parallel*, and Vitaliy P. Naboka's *NATO's Hawks in the Sights of Stalin's Falcons*.[10] Both authors conducted their research at the State Archives and Military Archives for Air Defense Forces (PVO) in Podolsk. The former book draws material from the summary after-action reports of the LXIV Fighter Air Corps (IAK), which awards claims to different pilots than those who originally made them, based on after-action studies of gun-camera film and correlation with observations and wreckage. The authors also couple their narratives with interviews of the pilots that may not quite track with the events of the time. The latter offers a detailed study of the pilots' combat reports, yet covers only the period of war from June, 1950, to July, 1951. Although these two books provide a reasonably good picture of the Soviet experience and their overall claims and losses in Korea, they are only accessible to Russian readers.[11] Mark A. O'Neill's dissertation, "The Other Side of the Yalu," presents the first English-language scholarly treatment of Soviet air efforts in Korea. Drawing sources primarily from the Central Archive of the Ministry of Defense, he furnishes an illuminating account of Moscow's decision making and the daily combat of Soviet pilots during the first year of the war.[12] A significant limitation of his study is the coverage of Soviet involvement solely in the earlier months (November, 1950—April, 1951) and too much detail on daily combat activities. Perhaps this is largely due to the nature of his sources.

While there may be nothing new to say about Soviet pilots flying in Korea, a systematic examination of the employment of Soviet airpower in the Korean conflict is still needed. Particularly, questions of how the Soviet air involvement in Korea actually unfolded and about the Russian perspective of the air war need to be explored. In addition, the air operations on the Communist side involved not only Soviet pilots but also Chinese and North Koreans. Although revelations of Soviet participation suggest the Chinese role may only have been a sideshow, the story of China's involvement in the air campaign is actually far more complex. At least three interrelated elements were involved: (1) China's notions of airpower and its efforts to build an air force, (2) the peculiar nature of Soviet assistance and involvement, and (3) the character of Chinese air operations.

First, Chinese Communist concepts for the deployment of airpower derived primarily from Mao Zedong's plan for the invasion of Taiwan in 1949. Chinese political leaders and generals were ground war veterans, and therefore had no experience or conception of air warfare. Lack of airpower, however, became critical for Beijing when the question of intervention in Korea arose. A combination of historical, strategic, political, and ideological considerations dominated the country's war-waging capabilities. China entered the war without air cover, and the lack of air support had an immediate and significant impact on Chinese ground operations. The leadership in Beijing responded with a hasty effort to build an air force and carry out an air campaign in support of Chinese ground forces. Hence, one central focus of this book is to examine the conditions, events, and incidents that influenced Beijing's decision making, its views of airpower, the PLAAF's organizational structure and preparation, and ground operations. This will be preceded by a narrative explaining how the Chinese Communist Party (CCP) derived the idea of a Communist air force from its revolutionary experience and how efforts were made to train aviation personnel during its struggle for power prior to October, 1949. Those were difficult years for the CCP, but it laid foundations and prepared its peasant soldiers to earn their wings. When the Korean War began, those trained by the Chinese themselves became the first pilots of the PLAAF to engage the Americans over the Yalu.

Despite the CCP's determination and effort to build an air force, the newly established PRC possessed no aviation industry and lacked access to Western aircraft and assistance. Obviously, as the USSR and the PRC had just formed a political and military alliance, the buildup of a Chinese air force had to depend on Soviet equipment and training. Thus, any analysis of the air war from a Communist perspective involves an examination of the complex relationship between China and the Soviet Union. The second primary dimension of the book deals, therefore, with Soviet assistance to the PLAAF and its role in the war. Comparison will be made between Beijing's and Moscow's war policy and involvement in Korea. Although the war brought the two Communist countries into an alliance, senior leaders in Beijing and Moscow maneuvered as best they could to use the conflict to serve their separate national interests. While transferring modern technology and a massive military system to the PLA, Soviet leadership restrained its involvement in Korea to avoid direct confrontation with the United States. The concomitant role played by Soviet MiG pilots had, meanwhile, limited effect on the ground war. In due course, the Chinese and Russians—supposedly acting as cobelligerents fighting with the same objective—displayed different aspirations, attitudes, beliefs, and perceptions about the war. Nevertheless, Soviet pilots demonstrated the utmost fighting spirit, dedication to duty, and a willingness to perform feats of heroism in the pursuit of national goals, international brotherhood, and comradeship. Their side of the story thus facilitates a more balanced examination of the history of aerial warfare in Korea.

The Chinese air force did not engage in combat with American planes until September, 1951. The third focal point of the book is on Chinese pilots—their organization, their planes, ground crews, and exploits—in Korea. Although they were flying advanced machines, Chinese pilots were poorly organized and poorly trained. Unlike the Americans and Russians, whose operations were limited mainly by political restraints, the PLAAF's operations were handicapped by their inexperience. They took their losses, scored successes, and suffered astounding defeats. In the end, these young men endured, becoming the bulwark of the Chinese air force. Little is known in the West about Chinese action and life on the northern side of the battle line. Whereas, numerical and technical superiority, or the right correlation of both, guaranteed good morale among the Westerners, the young PLAAF pilots' capability to challenge a tried and tested foe also came from their high spirits and superior morale, conditions encouraged and sustained by the Communist Party's relentless political oversight. Raised according to Chinese traditions, the PLAAF pilots displayed almost blind obedience. It was no simple thing for young men who had only recently been infantry soldiers and civilians to be hastily trained to fight a high-tech war against much better trained and skilled adversaries. This aspect of the study is an attempt to tell the PLAAF's side of the story, assessing its training, operations, strengths, weaknesses, and motivations. Some historical events chronologically related to air operations in Korea and drawn from Chinese primary sources are offered to provide a comparison with U.S. documentation.

Overall, the purpose of this book is to fill a vacuum in the literature of the Korean War based on research in recently declassified Chinese and Russian archival materials and Chinese oral histories. It not only examines air operations from a Communist perspective, particularly a Chinese one, but it also addresses broader issues regarding the Korean War, China's development of airpower, and the Sino-Soviet relationship. This book thus should significantly modify conventional wisdom about the Korean War.

The conduct of the Chinese air war in Korea was first revealed in the published official history of the PLAAF: *China Today: The Air Force* (1989), and *History of the Air Force* (1989).[13] These two books contain useful details about the organization, equipment, and military conduct of the air force since 1949, but they provide only sketchy information about policy making and Soviet assistance. Perhaps the most regrettable shortcoming is their tendency to idealize the past and ignore the harsh truth about the tragedy of those days. Primary documentation of Chinese involvement in Korea became available with the respective publications of *Mao Zedong's Manuscripts since the Founding of the People's Republic* beginning in the mid-1980s, and *Collections of Mao Zedong's Military Papers* in the early 1990s.[14] In spite of sanitizing some "security sensitive" information, these collections afford unprecedented insight into Chinese leaders' thinking and their subsequent decisions on Chinese intervention.

What makes the systematic analysis of the air war from a Communist perspective possible are the documents from the Archive of the President, Russian Federation (APRF), which became available after the 1990 collapse of the Soviet Union. More than 130 documents were translated by Kathryn Weathersby and Alexander Y. Mansourov and published in the 1996-97 issue of the Cold War International History Project *Bulletin,* while Evgeniy P. Bajanov and Natalia Bajanova incorporated extensive quotations of documents from the presidential archives in their unpublished manuscript, "The Korean Conflict, 1950–1953."[15] Also valuable to this study is a more complete collection of Russian documents on the Korean War from the APRF, which has been translated into Chinese and compiled by the Military History Research Department of the PLA Military Science Academy.[16] Combinations of these new Russian sources render a critical addition to available evidence on the high-level decisions and the Sino-Soviet alliance during the Korean conflict.

It is even more interesting to note that the release of Soviet archival sources on the Korean War prompted Beijing to publicize additional Chinese documents. Many new telegrams and memorandums that had been drafted by Zhou Enlai as instructions for the CCP Central Military Commission (CMC) from October, 1950, to July, 1952, are included in the *Selected Military Works of Zhou Enlai* (1997).[17] *The Chronicle of Zhou Enlai, 1949–1976,* includes ample citations of documents from the CCP Central Archives.[18] Based on these declassified government documents and Russian publications, four chapters analyze the airpower factor on Beijing's decisions about intervention, Soviet assistance, the Chinese air war plan, and Soviet air operations in Korea.

The remainder of this book relies primarily on personal recollections and interviews with retired PLAAF personnel in piecing together an overall view of the air war from a Chinese perspective. Since the early 1990s, a number of reminiscences by those who participated in the air war in Korea have been made available. Especially useful are the volumes produced by the Political Department of the PLAAF for internal use. These offer substantial information about personal experiences and the history of individual units.[19] The sources are generally insightful, and some remain classified and thus cannot be found anywhere else. Presented on a selective basis, the accounts tend to glorify individual experience and contain much bravado and political cant.

In drawing inferences from this source, there is always the danger of overestimating the PLAAF's role in the war, and in accepting the idealized and self-projected invincible image as fact. Efforts have been made, therefore, to compare Chinese materials with Russian and American sources, and to double-check archival material with information from interviews, and vice versa. Instrumental for such an approach is the database of Soviet and American claims and losses in Korea compiled by Stephen L. Sewell of the U.S. Defense Department.[20] Information drawn from the Far East Air Forces' (FEAF) Weekly Intelligence Roundup, archived at the USAF Historical Research Agency at Maxwell Air Force Base, Alabama, is also useful.

Between 1996 and 1999, I traveled twice to China to conduct interviews. Because of a deeply engrained tradition of military secrecy, and a certain suspicion of Westerners, I found that any inquiry by a researcher living in the West still arouses paranoia about the security of military information. To protect my sources, I promised I would not cite their names unless they agreed, and I tried to use published information as much as possible after the accuracy had been verified by an interview with the participant. Despite their hesitation to tell me what they knew, my interview subjects made no discernable effort to hide anything from me. On the contrary, the people with whom I talked were trying to remember some very complicated and confusing events almost fifty years in the past, and did their best to tell the truth about those events. I did come to understand, however, that what they were trying to tell me may not be an honest recollection, but a memory shaped through repeated telling of the same story. I did not take this to mean their stories were unreliable, but I have nonetheless treated them with a certain amount of caution.

Since we do not have full access to the PLAAF's records, validation of Chinese claims appears problematic. Evidence from government-controlled sources is always self-serving, intended to shape history in their favor. Even if all of the archives were accessible, it would still be impossible to fully correlate Chinese and Soviet records with American documentation. For example, the PLAAF's combat reports came mainly from pilot after-action debriefings. Because of tension, fatigue, and the excitement of combat, the memory of the event could be seriously affected by the psychological, physical, and intellectual capability of the participants. The records of a complex event always contain errors and inconsistencies, so persons trying to write an account of it must endeavor to produce a narrative that makes sense based on their own interpretation of it. The combat reports from both sides, therefore, rarely match. This is particularly true in the claims of enemy planes shot down. The kill ratios presented in this book represent the official versions available in Chinese and Russian records, and thus may be not only obnoxious, but also belie the true nature of the air war in Korea.

Moreover, Chinese accounts involve stylistic problems concerning place names and times. In U.S. records, cities, towns, and airfields were known by their Japanese names, whereas Chinese and Korean pilots preferred their own names, which I have used. Chinese accounts used Beijing time, which is an hour later than in Korea and two hours later than in Japan. In addition, the Chinese and Russians used the metric system for altitudes and distance, which may discomfort American readers more familiar with the English measurement system.

The PLAAF was officially established in November, 1949. Since then, the modernization of the Chinese air force has been a major focus of China's national security objectives. The Korean War accelerated its development. The Chinese leadership initially planned to build an air force drawing only upon the existing Nationalist airpower. However, fighting against the most powerful air force in the world in Korea propelled the PLAAF to expand until it became the third largest force by the end of the war. Many of its aircraft were highly advanced. The Korean War experience limited the Chinese air force to an air defense role. Although the PLAAF's modernization process began fifty years ago, it still has not yet reached Western standards despite China's recent efforts. From a historical perspective, the experience of the PLAAF may be useful to identify the effect of airpower on Beijing's security policy and conflict-resolution behavior, analyze its role and capability in supporting China's national security objectives, and reveal aspects of the institution of the Chinese armed forces in general, and the air force in particular.

Unlike Americans who refer to the Korean War as the "Forgotten War," the Chinese regard it as their most memorable war, one symbolizing the restoration of China's pride. For more than a century, China lost every war to the West or Japan, and, as a consequence, paid indemnities and lost territory—a humiliating experience. Despite obvious inferiority in weaponry and economic resources, China emerged from the Korean War with great pride for having fought against the mightiest and wealthiest power in the world. The Chinese victories have since been consistently cited in Chinese literature to animate the powerful current of patriotic tradition. The Korean War, the PLAAF's sole war experience, is widely used to legitimize China's will and capability to use airpower, and thus offers historical reference to our understanding of Chinese airpower as a potent force.

CHAPTER 1

Aviation and the Chinese Revolution

A HISTORICAL PERSPECTIVE

n November 21, 1951, having just returned from a tour of the Far East, Gen. Hoyt S. Vandenberg, chief of staff of the U.S. Air Force, announced that China was a potential air menace to the UN war effort in Korea. He appeared more than a little alarmed when he informed the press that Communist China "has become one of the major air powers of the world," seemingly overnight, and was seriously challenging UN air superiority in Korea. According to air force intelligence, the Communists had fourteen hundred planes in Korea, including seven hundred MiGs.[1] How could this happen "overnight"? Americans knew little about how the Chinese air force had expanded from virtually nothing at the beginning of the Korean War to suddenly become an "air power."

During their earlier encounter between the 1780s and 1890s, China, to some extent, was ignominiously condemned by Western powers as an inherently inferior Oriental nation: the society appeared "static," the military was "inept," the people exhibited "cowardice," and the science and technology seemed "backward."[2] This Western understanding of China, influenced by myth, ignorance, and prejudice, continued in the early twentieth century. Since the invention of the airplane in the early 1900s, the Chinese, like their Western counterparts, had recognized its economic, political, and military benefits. The Chinese Communists proved no exception. Before the founding of the People's Republic, a Communist air force was only a concept. To understand how the idea became reality in the form of the PLAAF, it is necessary to examine the rise of the CCP and its early efforts to develop an air force.

Chinese Ancient Civilization and Aviation

The conquest of the skies had been a preoccupation of Chinese civilization for centuries, and abundant stories exist about China's earliest attempts at flight. Early literature and fascinating folk legends venerate deities who were imagined to have mastered flight. Recorded Chinese participation in the saga of human attempts to conquer the air begins with the story of Lu Ban, a famous carpenter, during the Spring and Autumn periods (770–476 B.C.). According to legend, he constructed a wooden bird that reached the altitude of the jet stream and remained aloft for three days. The first military use of aerial devices came with the Chinese invention of the kite in approximately 200 B.C. Since then, the Chinese have used kites for communication during military operations, and to lift men into the air to spot enemy armies and follow their movements.[3] The invention of gunpowder in China around 800 A.D. made rockets possible, and these were used to bombard the enemy during sieges. This marked the first successful unmanned, powered flight.[4] As in the West, some Chinese attempted to fly by flapping wings furiously or gliding with birdlike wings.[5] Around 1500 A.D., a hapless Chinese died attempting to fly in a rocket-propelled device.[6]

In spite of these failures, Chinese efforts to conquer the skies did not stop. As early as 300 A.D. the principle of flight was noted. At that time, a Daoist and doctor of Chinese traditional medicine discovered that aerodynamics was what enabled birds to fly. Although able to design a popular handcrafted object, the *zoumadeng* (a lantern with paper figures of men and animals made to revolve when the lantern is lit, using a mechanism similar to the modern gas turbine), and a child's toy helicopter device, the *zuqinting* (two pieces of bamboo serve as propellers to lift the toy into the air), capable of powered flight, the Chinese were unable to come up with a powered vehicle capable of carrying a man aloft.[7]

Since the 1800s, however, history has witnessed China's stagnation and decline. While the West used gunpowder to make firearms, the Chinese remained focused on making fireworks and firecrackers primarily for social and religious uses, such as scaring ghosts and expressing their cheerfulness in celebrations.

Despite China's premodern efforts to harness flight, the first airplane did not come from the ancient land of the dragon, but from one of the youngest nations in the world, the United States. The honor belongs to Wilbur and Orville Wright, who designed and built the first powered airplane and flew it at Kitty Hawk, North Carolina, on December 17, 1903. The use of aircraft spread slowly in the West, then seemingly exploded in 1914 with the outbreak of war in Europe. While thousands of airplanes dueled in the skies over Europe, colorful kites continued to be the only manmade craft flying over China. Western scholars have seldom acknowledged any linkage between China's ancient inventions and modern science and technology. Instead, China's past is seen as contributing to its backwardness.[8]

Sun Yat-sen and Military Aviation

China's falling behind the West in the modern period encouraged many Chinese to devote themselves to searching for ways to save their country from further decay or foreign domination in the early twentieth century. Sun Yat-sen, one of the first Chinese with an appreciation for the potential of airpower, advocated the concept of using "aviation as the nation's salvation." During his travels across the Atlantic to raise funds for the Chinese republican cause, he had the opportunity to see air events in America and western Europe. Pondering the failures of the revolution thus far, Sun Yat-sen took notice of the airplane and considered its latent benefits to the Chinese revolution. In 1911, he began to urge members of the Revolutionary Alliance (*Tong Meng Hui*) overseas to study aviation technology and learn how to fly and manufacture airplanes. He was convinced "aviation personnel will bring unexpected advantage" for the party's struggle against the Manchu regime.[9]

Although the airplane had appeared just a few years before, and the aviation age had not yet begun, Sun discerned its significance for warfare and nation building, and prophesied, "the airplane will become a new weapon of war, and will be greatly useful to the nationalist revolution in our country." Sun had come to realize that no other instrument would prove more important in extending effective control over such a vast country as China, or in forging the social cohesion of so many different ethnic peoples. Like latter-day airpower proponents, he adopted the theories of Italian airpower champion Giulio Douhet and American aviation crusader, Brig. Gen. William "Billy" Mitchell, believing that aircraft would play an increasingly decisive role in warfare. Sun concluded that "no air force means no national defense."[10] Since China had no industry, he suggested the Chinese first buy naval, army, and air weaponry from the Western powers to strengthen the armed forces, and then try to copy and manufacture the weapons to meet China's own needs. This became the essence of Sun's theory of saving the nation using aviation. After the formation of a military government in Guangzhou in 1917, to further challenge the warlord regime in Beijing Sun started to build his own air force, establishing an aviation bureau within the Grand Marshal Office, a flying squadron, and an aviation school.[11]

In the aftermath of World War I, Sun foresaw many future issues concerning airpower. In June, 1924, at a ceremony honoring the establishment of the Huangpu (Whampoa) Military Academy, Sun delivered an inspirational directive in which he further elaborated on his own understanding of aviation. He associated the development of airpower with international relationships, and the future direction and emphasis of national defense. When the airplane joined the order of battle, Sun claimed the notion of territorial sovereignty would expand from land and water to airspace, and airpower would dramatically change the manner and nature of combat. He further concluded that the buildup of an air force would be essential for national defense in the modern era.[12] The influence of Sun's views on the development of airpower in China is difficult to gauge accurately, but a number of pioneer Chinese pilots were his acquaintances and served under him.[13] As they enjoyed success in their missions, Sun's vision and contribution would seem to be validated. People's Liberation Army Air Force literature regards Sun as one of the few Chinese able to articulate an understanding of the potential role of airpower, even though his view on the subject was indeed sporadic. It nevertheless argues that his concepts of airpower should be treated equally with those advanced by Western theorists like Douhet, Mitchell, and Air Marshal Hugh Trenchard of Great Britain.[14] Unfortunately, an international arms embargo imposed by the Western powers in an effort to end civil strife in China prevented serious efforts, if any, to develop an air force.[15] The newly founded aviation school had only ten students, two U.S.-made Curtiss trainers, and three German World War I veterans serving as flight instructors. Sun died in early 1925 before he could put his aviation theories into practice.[16]

The Nationalist Course in Aviation

After Sun's death, the Guomindang (GMD) continued to emphasize the importance of aviation to China's growth. Stymied by the international arms embargo, the GMD forged an alliance with Moscow and the CCP, and the Soviets began supplying the GMD with arms and advisers, many of whom were highly skilled veterans like P. A. Pavlov and Vasily K. Blyukher.[17] Zhou Enlai, a Communist leader, was named director of the political department at the Huangpu Academy. During the years 1925–27, several thousand middle-class youths outfitted with modern equipment received rigorous military training based on the Soviet Red Army model. Additional cadets were selected for flight training at the aviation school.[18] As they completed their training, some were sent to the Soviet Union for more advanced aviation studies.[19] Others were assigned to air squadrons attached to the GMD armies, and flew Russian-supplied aircraft during the northern expedition campaign aimed at defeating the warlords in the fall of 1926.[20] Notwithstanding, no viable achievements were made until after the embargo was lifted in 1929.

In the late 1920s, after the breakup of the alliance with the CCP and the Soviet Union, Jiang Jieshi and the GMD emerged as the dominant power in China. However, the Nationalist government established in Nanjing still could not claim effective control over the whole country, so development of the air force took priority over the army and navy. The GMD leadership realized that no military arm offered more potential for unifying China and compelling obedience from officials in isolated provinces, than a well-organized and efficient air force. The plan calling for the promotion of aviation in China was adopted at the National Aviation Conference in Nanjing in April, 1931.[21]

After a brief battle with the Japanese at Shanghai in early 1932, many Chinese realized that the time was near when China would be obliged to fight for its survival. Nationalist strategists knew it would take years, and enormous funds, to build an effective navy, so creation of a modern air service became the focus of China's national defense efforts in the 1930s.[22] One foreign observer noted that the Chinese were air-minded and eager to develop an air force.[23] Beginning in 1932, new aviation training programs were undertaken with the assistance of American and Italian professionals, and a substantial number of military aircraft were imported from those countries. An American aviation group headed by a retired army colonel, John H. Jouett, along with nine nonactive military flying instructors and five mechanics, arrived in China in June, 1932, for a three-year training mission at the newly established Central Aviation School in Hangzhou. Almost a year later, Gen. Roberto Lordi led a group of Italian military officers (forty flying officers and a hundred mechanics) to join this effort in Louyang, where a school was set up to provide initial flight training.[24] The arrival of both Americans and Italians demonstrated the Nationalist leadership's eagerness to build a viable air force with all available sources in a short time. By the end of 1936, the Nationalist Chinese air force had expanded to nine flying squadrons with more than seven hundred pilots and six hundred aircraft of various types. Some progress was also made in the construction of airfields and development of an aircraft industry.[25]

Under the leadership of the GMD government in Nanjing, there was slow but perceptible movement toward unification in China during the first half of the 1930s. Possession of an air force was a startling development, one that, at least in part, served as a means to encourage the peaceful settlement of differences in China.[26] However, after the Nationalist government devoted so much effort and investment in airpower, the air force used to subdue domestic opposition was destroyed within weeks of the outbreak of hostilities between China and Japan on July 7, 1937.[27] Thanks to Soviet assistance in late 1937, followed by U.S. assistance in 1942, China was able to keep an air force in service against the invading Japanese.[28] A number of Chinese pilots were crowned with eternal glory for their heroism and sacrifice in defending China's skies during the war against Japanese aggression.

With assistance from the United States, the inventory of the Nationalist air force expanded to over a thousand aircraft by the end of the war. These figures by themselves are impressive, however, having a monopoly on airpower did not provide a military advantage for the Nationalists in the ensuing civil war with the Chinese Communists. The number of available airworthy aircraft was reduced to fewer than three hundred by mid-1947 as a result of enemy action and poor maintenance.[29] Although Nationalist troops became bogged down in isolated cities and dependent on aerial resupply, combat aircraft did not fly often enough to provide adequate air support, and were, therefore, no great threat to Communist ground forces. When the PLA swept over the continent of China in 1949, airpower did not prevent the GMD from losing control of the mainland, and the bulk of the Nationalist air force fled to Taiwan. The Communists used the planes, airfields, repair shops, and other aviation facilities abandoned by the GMD government to help build their own air force.

The CCP's Initial Quest for Aviation

The Chinese Communists trace their aeronautical origins to 1924. Despite having no armed forces, but accepting the Marxist theory that revolution is a violent process, from the very beginning, the CCP attached importance to building military forces, and accordingly sent party members to Soviet Red Army schools to receive training. During the first unified efforts of the GMD and CCP, a large number of party and youth league members enrolled in the Huangpu Military Academy.[30] After a military flying school was opened at Guangzhou in 1924 with Russian assistance, two classes totaling fifty-two people received twelve months of aviation training. Eighteen of the students, including nine Communists arranged for by the Third Communist International (Comintern), were sent to the Soviet Union in 1925 and 1926 for advanced flight training. When the GMD and CCP split in 1927, the Communist leadership twice, in 1927 and 1935, chose nineteen people who had already studied in Moscow to enroll in the Soviet air force schools for additional flight training and courses in aviation engineering. Among them, four individuals, Chang Qiankun, Wang Bi, Liu Feng, and Wang Lian, (a Korean national whose name will later be referred to in Korean pronunciation as Wang Yong), are regarded as pioneers in the CCP's quest for airpower. After graduation, Chang and Wang Bi served in the Soviet air force, then returned to China in 1938 and 1940, respectively, to work in the CCP's military headquarters at Yan'an, where they were responsible for aviation affairs.[31] When the PLAAF was established in 1949, Chang and Wang were appointed deputy commander and deputy political commissar, respectively. After China intervened in the Korean conflict in October, 1950, Chang was sent to Andong as deputy commander of the Chinese air force in Korea. After returning to Korea in 1946, Wang Lian served as commander of the North Korean air force, and later deputy commander of the Chinese-Korean joint air force.[32]

While CCP leaders who were close to the Comintern were keen on seeking Moscow's assistance, Mao Zedong and Zhu De inaugurated armed struggles against the Nationalist government, and in 1929 established a new regime, the Jiangxi Soviet. Cut off from the outside world and any military aid, Mao and his Red Army survived by depending on capturing arms and equipment and by following a strategy of guerilla warfare. It was during this period that the Red Army obtained its first combat aircraft, a Nationalist Vought Corsair V-65 light bomber. In February, 1930, it became lost on a reconnaissance and communication mission and was forced to land in Communist-controlled territory in Hubei. Red Army leaders persuaded the pilot to join the Red Army and the Vought was renamed the *Lenin*. For the next two years, the *Lenin* was used on communications and reconnaissance missions. On September 8, 1931, it dropped leaflets over the city of Wuhan, and two months later supported the Red Army's attack on Nationalist garrisons at Huangan, dropping two mortar shells that severely shook the enemy's morale. The Nationalist defense line collapsed and the Red Army seized the town in three days.[33] In July, 1932, Jiang Jieshi launched a new extermination campaign against the Communists. The Red Army had no choice but to dismantle the airplane and hide it in a remote mountain area. Local people unearthed the plane in 1951 and turned it over to the government.[34]

The second Red Army aircraft also belonged to the Nationalists, a Douglas "Moth" general-purpose plane that was captured at Zhangzhou airfield on April 20, 1932. During a battle ten days earlier, a Red Army machine gunner wounded the pilot, who later died. After repairs, the plane flew over the recently captured city during the May Day rally and dropped propaganda leaflets. The Moth was later transferred to Ruijing, capital of the Jiangxi Soviet. The GMD's increasing military pressure on the Jiangxi Soviet, coupled with a lack of gasoline and spare parts, meant the Red Army could not use the aircraft, so it was abandoned. Political and military restraints, as well as technical ones, kept the Communists from acquiring any more airplanes, but their efforts did symbolize the beginning of the Chinese Communists' quest to develop their own air force.[35]

The CCP's Xinjiang Aviation Unit

The onset of the Sino-Japanese War in 1937 gave birth to a new alliance between the Soviet Union and the Republic of China. Once again, CCP leaders began to ponder the possibility of creating an air force. As Soviet arms and supplies flowed steadily into the Nationalist government's arsenal, Moscow expanded its influence in Xinjiang, the main overland route for Soviet aid. Party leaders saw an opportunity to use the strong Soviet presence in Xinjiang to further Communist military strength in China, particularly with access to Soviet weapons, advisers, and supplies. In May, 1937, the

CCP opened a small military academy named New Camp at Dihua, capital of Xinjiang, and some four hundred Red Army soldiers enrolled to study artillery, motor vehicle operation and repair, logistics, armor, medicine, radio, infantry operations, and foreign languages with Soviet instructors, and using Soviet equipment.[36] In the meantime, Chen Yun, a Politburo member and CCP representative in Xinjiang, suggested the central leadership at Yan'an take advantage of a united front with the local military warlord, Sheng Shicai, who also received Soviet support and supplies, to initiate an aviation training program at New Camp.[37]

In 1937, Sheng Shicai, with Soviet assistance, created a small air force consisting of six trainers and nine bombers. He believed that starting a training program for the Communists would help him secure additional Soviet aid.[38] Ever since the founding of the Red Army, Communist soldiers had endured bombardment by enemy aircraft, and several CCP leaders were wounded during the raids. Chen believed Soviet patronage and uniting with Sheng Shicai would allow the Communists to train their pilots and ground crews in Xinjiang. With trained aviation personnel of their own, Chen reasoned, the Communists could build an air force once they secured access to aircraft. Leaders at Yan'an promptly endorsed his proposal.[39] Chen initially recommended selecting aviation trainees from the ranks of Red Army soldiers studying at New Camp in Xinjiang, but they used to belong to the units once commanded by the contestants for the party's central leadership. Considering the need for maintaining a balance of power for internal politics, party leaders thought it more appropriate to include candidates from Yan'an, particularly those from the central Red Army.[40] Chen Yun, who by then was in charge of CCP organizational work, personally engaged in the selection process. The primary criterion was party membership. Because few Communist candidates had been educated beyond the elementary level, the CCP representative in Xinjiang had to negotiate with local authorities to waive the requirement for a literacy test. Since his own Soviet instructors already sided with the CCP, Sheng granted this request. In the end, forty-three Red Army officers (twenty-five from New Camp and eighteen from Yan'an) were selected to join Sheng Shicai's air force for aviation training.[41] The sons of peasants, these Communist soldiers obviously were excited about the prospect of becoming pilots. Party leaders, anticipating that they would become the core of a red air force, exhorted them to stand up to any ordeals they might encounter during their aviation careers. They subsequently formed the first CCP aviation unit, often referred to as the Xinjiang Aviation Unit in CCP history, and several later served in the Korean War as air force division commanders.[42]

Classes began in March, 1938, with twenty-five cadets in flight training and eighteen studying ground support. Great effort was taken to camouflage their Communist identity. They wore Nationalist uniforms, used pseudonyms, and their records were purged of previous unit affiliations, but the unit remained under the direct control of the party. The ground training proceeded with basic aviation courses, including aviation history, aircraft engine structure, aircraft structure, flying theory and principles, navigation, air combat tactics, and aviation meteorology. Because of their limited education, the Communist students encountered difficulty with the study of aviation theory, but all passed the final examinations, including preflight instruction, and started flying U-2 biplane trainers in early April.[43] After six to eight hours of takeoff and landing drills, all but one soloed. Beginning in October, they received more than a year's training in the Russian-built R-5 reconnaissance bomber learning basic flying and combat techniques. In 1940, the Communist pilots' flight training program was suspended when Moscow failed to satisfy Sheng Shicai's demands for more arms and military equipment. The Xinjiang Aviation Unit did not resume flight training until early 1941, when the Russians gave Sheng six I-15 biplane and two I-16 monoplane fighters recently dumped by the Soviet air force.[44] By April, 1942, the Communist pilots had accumulated an average of three hundred flying hours each, and were capable of flying I-16 fighters in combat.[45]

The Xinjiang aviation training program allowed a handful of Communists to earn their wings. In the summer of 1942, Sheng Shicai reached a political arrangement with the Nationalist government at Chongqing and abandoned his alliance with the Soviet Union, which was busy enough with its own war with Germany. Meanwhile, the CCP was experiencing the pressure of the GMD's anti-Communist campaign. In September, Sheng began to clamp down on Communist activities in Xinjiang, and his police rounded up 160 CCP personnel, including the pilots and ground crews of the Xinjiang Aviation Unit. This purge of the Communists in Xinjiang ended the CCP's endeavors to build its first aviation unit. Nevertheless, the Xinjiang experience laid the groundwork for the Chinese Communists to associate themselves with the Soviet aviation training system. According to Lü Liping, a former member of the Xinjiang Aviation Unit, although the abusive attitude of Russian instructors toward Chinese cadets was resented, Soviet training techniques, which were slow but thorough, were more suitable to Communist peasant soldiers.[46] Perhaps even more important, the PLAAF, when it was finally established, was receptive to Soviet doctrine and ready to use Soviet equipment. Personnel of the Xinjiang Aviation Unit became, as Chen Yun once predicted, "the first group of red pilots and the initial core members of a red air force."[47]

The Yan'an Years

The chronology of the CCP history calls the years between 1937 and 1947 the "Yan'an era," symbolizing a remarkable reversal in the fortunes of the Communist movement in China. During this period, the Chinese Communists consolidated their power over the broad stretch of northern China, and gained initial experience in government organization dealing with military affairs, economic production, propaganda and organization, labor, women, and the like. The CCP leadership also laid the groundwork for the eventual establishment of the PLAAF during this period.

In October, 1940, shortly after their return from Moscow to Yan'an, Wang Bi and Chang Qiankun recommended that the party leadership establish an aviation school for training their own air force personnel. Their proposal caught Mao's attention, one of the occasions documented in CCP historical records showing his interest in aviation. The chairman appeared cautious, however, believing the time for such action was not yet proper. Many CCP members, especially those who had been in the Soviet Union, thought that if Moscow could supply the GMD with arms and airplanes, the CCP should also be able to ask for Soviet assistance. Mao doubted, however, that Moscow would bypass the GMD, and was afraid the CCP could not pay for such help. He appreciated the aviators' enthusiasm, but urged them to be patient.[48]

Nevertheless, in 1941, acting on Chang and Wang's recommendation, the CCP Central Military Commission (CMC) decided to establish an avaiation engineering school to teach basic aviation theory and aviation armament. Despite having neither aircraft nor airfields, more than a hundred individuals were selected. The criteria included party membership, at least three years military experience, an elementary education, and good health. The first class began in April with courses in mathematics, physics, and Russian language, to prepare the poorly educated peasant soldiers for the study of aviation theory. However, during the years 1941 and 1942, Yan'an faced a severe crisis. The GMD and Japanese blockades cut off nearly all trade between other parts of China and the Communist controlled territories. Inflation was rampant, and the regime had to pull back for survival. Bad weather during the period also created food shortages. The Communists needed to produce their own food, as well as consumer goods like cotton cloth. According to Liu Yüti, who later became a PLAAF ace in the Korean War, he and many of his classmates initially thought they would go to the Soviet Union or Xinjiang for flight training, but they soon found that hope growing dim. Instead, they had to terminate their studies and cultivate the land or work in shops. The aviation school was finally suspended in early 1943, and only Liu went on to become a pilot.[49]

In the spring of 1944, the Americans received permission from GMD leaders to send a military observer section, later known as the Dixie Mission, to visit Yan'an. Their responsibility was to collect intelligence on the position and movement of Japanese forces in northern China and on the Communists' political, military, and economic situation. This allowed the CCP leaders to make their case for foreign assistance directly to the Americans. Despite the good rapport that developed between the Americans and Chinese in wartime Yan'an, the Dixie Mission produced no direct U.S. assistance to the CCP.[50]

In response to the arrival of the American observer mission, the CMC established an aviation office in the 18th Group's Army General Staff Department, to handle all aviation matters, including building an airfield in Yan'an, providing security and maintenance service for it, and controlling air traffic. Wang Bi and Chang Qiankun were appointed director and deputy director, respectively. Mao, and many other CCP leaders, participated in the airfield construction work. A year later, on August 28, 1945, the chairman, flying for the first time in his life, went from this airfield to Chongqing to negotiate with the Nationalists. In the meantime, the airfield served as the only physical link between the CCP headquarters and Soviet-occupied Manchuria. With Soviet assistance, a number of key CCP leaders flew to Manchuria and established a strong Communist presence to offset any Nationalist influence there.[51]

The end of the war in September, 1945, prompted a new challenge to the General Staff aviation section. The Communists controlled a larger area than ever before, and foreseeing an inevitable civil war between the Communists and Nationalists, the CMC decided to send the entire staff of the aviation section to Manchuria. Their mission was to gather aircraft and aviation equipment surrendered or abandoned by Japanese forces and begin flight training. By October, 1945, the aviation section was abolished, and the Chinese Communists began anew their quest for an air force.

Another major source supporting the formation of a Communist air force at the time was Yan'an's appeal to defecting aviation personnel from the opposition forces. The first group of defectors included four pilots and two

Liu Yuti of the 3d Aviation Division poses here. Liu claimed he shot down four UN aircraft in a single day.

mechanics who flew a small Japanese-made transport from Nanjing to Yan'an on August 20, 1945, but the most important figure was an American-trained pilot, Liu Shanben, who flew a Nationalist Consolidated B-24 Liberator bomber to Yan'an on June 26, 1946. The bomber itself had very little military significance in the unfolding civil war between the CCP and the GMD, and was destroyed in a Nationalist air raid two months later. Liu's defection, however, had great political and psychological impact on the Nationalist air force, and served as an example to encourage air force personnel dissatisfied with the GMD government's corruption and incompetence to defect. The continuing transfusion of trained men reduced the effectiveness of the retreating Nationalist air forces and strengthened the Communists. By June, 1949, defectors had flown twenty Nationalist air force planes carrying a total of fifty-four pilots and aviation personnel to the Communist side. Most of the defectors became mainstays in the PLAAF. Liu Shanben, for example,

became commander of the PLAAF 10th Aviation Division, and led his pilots in bombing raids on the South Korean intelligence posts on Taehwa-do
Island on the evening of November 30, 1951.[52]

The Cradle of the PLA's Pilots: The Northeast Aviation School

At the end of World War II, the CCP leadership became more keenly aware
of the potential significance of airpower in the forthcoming Communist-
Nationalist struggle. As both Communist and Nationalist forces raced for
control of Manchuria during the months following the Japanese surrender,
aviation became the particular concern of CCP leaders, who eagerly pursued the quest to build an air force. Manchuria had been the home base of
the Japanese Kwantung Army's 2d Air Army, housing some one thousand
aircraft, and training facilities.[53] According to Liu Shaoqi, acting chairman
of the CCP, the Communist forces needed to make use of the base to advance their aviation goals.[54] In October, 1945, the CCP decided to send a
small group of its own aviation personnel from Yan'an to Manchuria to
establish an aviation school there, while instructing the party and military
authorities in Manchuria to seize aircraft and aviation equipment from the
defeated Japanese.[55] Although there would be insurmountable difficulties in
inaugurating an air force at that time, this farsighted move facilitated the
growth of Communist military aviation.

By December, 1945, 120 older aircraft had been collected in Manchuria,
and about forty of these machines were made operational after recondition-
ing.[56] Because of the lack of aviation personnel, the CCP military leadership
in Manchuria turned to captured Japanese pilots and ground-support crews
from the 26th Training Group of the Second Air Army under Maj. Hayasi
Yuichiro. Probably because of uncertainties at home, they were persuaded
to stay and help the Chinese Communists. Many did not return to Japan
until 1956.[57]

After several months' preparation, on March 1, 1946, the Northeast Aviation School was founded in Tonghua, Jilin Province, with 660 personnel
and some forty Japanese aircraft. It was the PLA's first true flying school.
Everything had to be built from scratch. The biggest problem, initially, was
the lack of instructor personnel, and thus, the first class was an instructor-
training program. Ten men who had learned to fly at either the Soviet or
Nationalist aviation schools or served in the Nanjing government's puppet
air force during the war began flight training in May, while newly selected

cadets undertook theoretical and ground training. There were two flying classes and one maintenance class. Because the Nationalist forces were waging an offensive operation in Manchuria during the spring of 1946, the school had to move to Mudanjiang in northern Manchuria, and then to Dongan near the Soviet border. Therefore, continuous and systematic training courses could not be initiated until March, 1947.[58]

In addition to the Nationalists' ground and air military threat, the Northeast Aviation School experienced many unique problems. The lack of basic trainers forced new pilots to begin flight training with Japanese Tachikawa Ki.55 type 99 advanced trainers that had been scraped together by maintenance crews and were barely airworthy. The poor performance of these aircraft limited pilots to basic flight training and prevented acrobatic flight. With no radio equipment on the aircraft, they had to depend upon visual signals such as semaphores for ground-to-air communications and waggling wings for air-to-air communications. When gasoline became scarce, highly purified alcohol was substituted. Due to the scarcity of basic supplies, the daily diet at the school was cornbread and pickles. Lacking winter flying jackets and shoes, cadets wore regular winter coats, holding them together with ropes while in flight. Despite the difficulties, by July, 1949, the school had trained 560 people, including 126 pilots, 322 mechanics, twenty-four navigators, and eighty-eight additional ground staff. A few were able to complete combat flight training in Japanese-made Nakajima Ki.43 type 1 Hayabusa fighters.[59]

The Northeast Aviation School had several legacies. The selection of candidates for aviation training became a political rather than a technical matter because of suspicions concerning the loyalty of civilian conscripts. Before the end of the Korean War, most pilot-officer candidates came from the rank and file of the Communist ground forces. They were machine gunners, explosives carriers, and infantry soldiers. Because most men had only limited education, the school stressed hands-on training. Although they received their wings and later displayed immense courage in Korea against a far more powerful adversary, their limited reading and writing skills appear to have prevented them from mastering modern technology. Several Korean War pilots later said they would have performed much better in Korea if they had been better educated.[60]

The basis for the future training and doctrine of the Communist air force was laid down in 1947 after a serious debate at the Northeast Aviation School. The school opened with Japanese instructors, defectors from the Nationalist air force, and others who had received flight training in the United States, along with personnel who received training in the Soviet Union. Great confusion existed as to whose training system was best. In early 1947, the remaining members of the Xinjiang Aviation Unit arrived at the school. They argued that their air force should follow the Soviet model, and that the training program use Soviet techniques. The CCP party and military authorities in the northeast supported this position. Those who had been trained by the Soviets soon became dominant at the school, and Soviet teaching materials and techniques were adopted. By the time a new relationship between the CCP and USSR was forged in late 1949, the Chinese were ready for Soviet aviation assistance and receptive to Soviet doctrine.[61]

Perhaps the most significant consequence of this early training center, however, was that the Northeast Aviation School became the cradle of the PLA's pilots. The pilot candidates demonstrated a spirit of fierce determination; no matter what happened, they intended to build their own air force and earn their wings. This spirit allegedly affected the Japanese instructors, who had been nurtured in the "way of the warrior" and had initially questioned the ability of the Communists to survive under such harsh conditions. Many of them chose to stay with the aviation school and devoted themselves to sharing their aviation knowledge with the Chinese Communists. Hayasi Yuichiro later said he would never forget his days at the Northeast Aviation School, and felt gratified for contributing to the development of the PLAAF in its initial stage.[62] The school turned out the first generation of Chinese Communist pilots, who averaged eighty to one hundred hours of flight training in Japanese aircraft. When the CCP decided to establish an air force, these pioneers became the backbone of the PLAAF, and, after successfully learning to fly Soviet aircraft, became the pilots of the PLAAF's first combat units in May, 1950. Beginning in early 1951, they started flying MiG-15s over the Yalu River, and fought U.S. pilots for two and one-half years. A few became aces in Korea.[63]

A Historical Perspective on CCP Leaders and Aviation

Mao Zedong founded the PLA when he created the Fourth Red Army in August, 1928, pulling together the survivors of the Autumn Harvest Rising and the Nanchang Uprising. As a CCP military strategist, he presented the original concept of "people's war" in the 1930s, a scheme derived from the Communists' military experiences and the constraints under which they had to operate. Under the guidance of the people's war strategy and doctrine, which placed special emphasis on defensive strategy and manpower over weapons, the CCP survived Japan's occupation of China, defeated the Nationalists, and then seized power in 1949. Chinese military scholars agree that Mao's military ideology, which embraced both a set of principles and a flexible view of how those ideas could be implemented, worked for the CCP in guerrilla and conventional warfare.[64]

Despite a recent study highlighting the romantic characteristics of Mao's military strategy, the Chinese leader demonstrated his pragmatism during his military career by adapting his strategy and ideas to suit reality.[65] Unlike Sun Yat-sen, who stressed the importance of an air force even before he actually possessed a military force, Mao did not give the establishment of Communist airpower serious consideration until late 1947, when the CCP's victory was on the horizon. Although constrained by the military conditions the CCP faced, Mao recognized that military technology and new weapons systems would play critical roles in warfare. From 1927 to 1935, the Red Army remained small and poorly equipped, but engaged in guerrilla warfare against the superior GMD forces. Mao, speaking at the Second Jiangxi Soviet Congress in January, 1934, encouraged Red Army soldiers to "know and improve [their] new military techniques."[66] Four years later, in his famous essay on military affairs, "On Protracted War," he conceded that military modernization would be a prerequisite for driving the Japanese aggressors out of China. According to Mao, armed with new weapons, Communist forces would experience a revolutionary change, become "highly centralized and organized with less guerrilla characteristics," and be transformed into "a world class" military power.[67]

Although he longed to turn his Communist guerrillas into a modern, "world class" force, reality led Mao to believe a weak army could prevail in a war against a strong enemy. That, however, could only be done by stressing the concept that men could beat weapons. In June, 1950, while discussing the air force issue with other Chinese leaders, an emotional Mao remarked that the Communist way to deal with enemy airpower was to "not fear death, but be brave, and dare to sacrifice lives."[68] The hardships Mao experienced during his revolutionary career unquestionably contributed to his determination to build a strong air force when the time came. However, his experiences also influenced him to maintain the view that the human factor could overcome the machine.

As a pragmatist, Mao's concern about Chinese Communist aviation was often expressed in a less obvious way.[69] He supported Chen Yun's proposal to send Red Army soldiers for flight training in Xinjiang, and approved the local party leadership's use of membership dues to subsidize the living expenses of the Xinjiang Aviation Unit.[70] On February 10, 1943, Mao instructed the CCP representatives at Chongqing to negotiate with Nationalist leaders for the release of Xinjiang Aviation Unit personnel, along with other Communists jailed by local "reactionary" authorities. When the members of the Xinjiang Aviation Unit eventually returned to Yan'an in the summer of 1946, Mao and other CCP leaders personally received them and ordered them to take three months' rest with special medical treatment and food supplies, despite the poor living conditions in Yan'an.[71] By showing parental concern for a handful of aviation personnel, Mao demonstrated his support for a CCP air force at a time when the reality of it loomed far in the future.

The year following the Japanese surrender, Mao appeared increasingly confident that the Communists would soon defeat the Nationalists. His forces expanded from nine hundred thousand in mid-1945 to 1,270,000 in mid-1946, organized into twenty-seven infantry columns (each roughly equivalent to a reduced-strength corps) and forty-five independent divisions. Although these troops were not well armed by contemporary calculations, Communist political control in their northern base areas permitted the Communists to mobilize their forces and support their war effort against the Nationalists.[72] Mao's early claim that "political power grows out of the barrel of a gun" was working.[73] There was no doubt in the minds of CCP leaders that they should continue to depend upon "rifles plus millets" for their ultimate victory. They nevertheless began to consider the buildup of an air force. Upon his return to Yan'an in June, 1946, Lü Liping learned that the central leadership was air-minded and had already decided to make preparations for the construction of an air force without delay, regardless of the difficulties and pressing situations of the war.[74] People had already been sent to establish the PLA's first aviation school in northeast China, and when the civil war turned in favor of the CCP in late 1947, Mao urged Communist authorities in Manchuria to make the establishment of an air force a priority.[75]

For the CCP leadership, the long contest with the Nationalists came to a turning point in late 1948. Mao began to predict Communist victory and pondered how to take over cities and consolidate control. He believed the most difficult tasks remaining were the crossing of the Yangzi River and the seizure of large cities like Nanjing and Shanghai. Mao also felt that taking Tibet and Taiwan would be a great challenge for the PLA.[76] Perhaps more important was his recognition that the new Communist nation would need to be defended. As had been the case with Sun Yat-sen and the Nationalist leaders, the notion of a mystical connection between aviation and the

Communist revolution began to grow. Aviation appeared to be the single effective tool that could annihilate distance, weld the infant Communist society together, and help it develop economically to provide a standard of living beyond the imagination of a people shattered by foreign invasion and civil war.[77] In consideration of a new China continuously surrounded by enemies, both foreign and domestic, Chinese leaders could not defer a long-term national defense program to modernize the armed forces. A powerful air force, acting as a deterrent with the threat of massive retaliation, symbolized modernization for the PLA. Drafting a document for the CCP's task in 1949, Mao remarked, "we must be devoted to the construction of an air force so that [we will be able to] use it [in our military struggle] in 1949 and 1950."[78]

The desire for the creation of an air force was both a military and a political necessity. At the time, China had no industry, and its economy was bedeviled with political squabbles and military conflicts. The CCP's leaders faced a situation that was not conducive to developing an air force, except for their determination and resolve to do so. Moscow's attitude toward the Chinese revolution remained ambiguous, and the CCP's own ability to pay for assistance was limited. It was against this confused and often uncertain background, that the People's Liberation Army Air Force finally came into being.

CHAPTER 2

Fledgling Years

THE EMERGENCE OF
THE PEOPLE'S LIBERATION
ARMY AIR FORCE

eightened CCP interest in the buildup of an air force coincided with the establishment of new relations with Moscow. After almost four years of effort, the Northeast Aviation School had achieved little success, and was still experiencing insurmountable difficulties in training a core of aviation personnel. This situation would be soon altered. From January 31 to February 7, 1949, Anastas Mikoyan, a Soviet Politburo member, secretly visited the CCP headquarters at Xibaipo. His mission was to make initial contact with the CCP leaders, and proved to be a crucial step toward the formation of the Sino-Soviet strategic alliance. In June, the CCP's leaders decided to adopt a leaning-to-one-side policy as the cornerstone of foreign relations for the soon-to-be created People's Republic. Moscow quickly responded to this goodwill gesture by extending a helping hand, thus precipitating the establishment of the People's Liberation Army Air Force. The PLAAF that emerged proved very different from the Western air forces of the time, and even the Soviet air force. Although Soviet assistance and doctrine would be crucial to the PLAAF, the indigenous efforts of Chinese political and military leaders kept the development of the air force within a Chinese political, cultural, and military context. This chapter examines the CCP's initial experience in building the air force before the Korean War, and its ramifications for the PLAAF's development as a modern air force.

The CCP Decides to Create an Air Force

While the level of Soviet assistance remained unsettled, the CCP continued its own efforts to construct an air force. On March 17, 1949, the CMC decided to transfer aviation personnel from the Northeast Aviation School to form the Aviation Bureau in charge of the CCP's aviation adventure, with Chang Qiankun as director and Wang Bi as political commissar. Both were Soviet-trained aviation engineers. Its mission was to take over Nationalist aviation facilities, equipment, and personnel in areas liberated by Communist forces. Seven months later, in October, 113 aircraft, 1,278 engines, more than four thousand tons of equipment, and 2,267 aviation technicians had been "accepted" from the Nationalist forces.[1] Following Nationalist B-24 bomber attacks on Beijing on May 4, 1949, the Aviation Bureau responded in July by establishing the CCP's first combat squadron, equipped with six U.S.-made P-51s, to defend the capital against air attack. Nevertheless, the CCP's urgent desire for the creation of an air force derived primarily from Mao's plan for the invasion of Taiwan.[2]

By early summer, 1949, the CCP's operations in the civil war had developed rapidly. The Yangzi River barrier was overcome with little difficulty, Nanjing and Shanghai were captured with only modest efforts, and CCP forces advancing farther south met little resistance. On May 26, the Nationalist government fled to Taiwan. It then used Taiwan and other offshore islands still under its control as a springboard for harassing the mainland. On June 21, for instance, the Nationalist government announced a naval blockade against CCP-controlled territory, and sent its aircraft to attack coastal cities. It was in the context of these circumstances that Mao proposed his Taiwan campaign plan.

The liberation of Taiwan would be the greatest challenge yet for CCP forces. Realizing the potential value of an air force for an amphibious assault on the island, Mao turned to the Soviet Union for help. During a mid-June meeting with Stalin's proconsul, Ivan V. Kovalev, the Soviet economic adviser to the CCP, Mao raised the issue of the "liberation of Taiwan," and asked for Soviet air and naval support.[3] While waiting for the Soviet response, Zhu De, commander in chief of the PLA, in early July urged Mao to send Chinese pilots to the Soviet Union for immediate training so they could learn how to fly in six months.[4] Concurring with Zhu's idea, Mao wrote to Zhou Enlai on July 10 stressing that "it is impossible for our air force to overwhelm the enemy in the short run (such as a year); but we may need to consider to send three to four hundred of our people to study in the Soviet Union for six to eight months, and at the same time to buy about one hundred planes." He concluded, "Together with the air force we have now, they will form an offensive unit to support the cross-strait campaign and prepare to seize Taiwan next summer."[5]

The next day, Zhou summoned Liu Yalou, the 14th Army Group commander, and charged him with organizing the air force and making specific requests for Soviet assistance. Based on Zhou's instructions, Liu consulted with the leaders and staff of the CMC Aviation Bureau and came up with a number of proposals. First, he proposed the transfer of all staff and personnel of the 14th Army Group headquarters to form the core of the PLAAF's headquarters. Second, he recommended building new aviation schools and selecting candidates for flight and ground-support training from the PLA's ranks. Third, he sought authority to go to Moscow to negotiate for Soviet assistance in organizing the air force. The CCP leadership approved Liu's recommendations. On July 26, 1949, the CMC cabled the Fourth Field Army, noting that the current priority was construction of the air force so that it would be ready for use in combat within a year. It further ordered the 14th Army Group headquarters to incorporate with the Aviation Bureau and form the proposed air force command.[6]

By that time, Liu Shaoqi was in Moscow negotiating with Soviet leaders. On July 26, the CCP Central Secretariat cabled Liu with instructions to make the following requests: (1) to supply the Chinese with one hundred to two hundred Yak fighters and forty to eighty heavy bombers along with Japanese and German bombs; (2) to help the Chinese by training twelve hundred pilots and five hundred mechanics in Soviet aviation schools; and (3) to send three to five high-ranking air force officers to work with China's air force in September.[7] Should the Soviet leaders agree to the first two requests, the directive continued, Liu Yalou (the future air force commander) would be dispatched to the Soviet Union to negotiate the details. Liu Shaoqi discussed these requests with Stalin and other Soviet leaders the next day, and their response was positive. According to Liu Shaoqi, Stalin felt that the CCP should have asked for Soviet assistance a year earlier. He agreed to provide China with planes, but suggested establishing aviation schools in China rather than training the Chinese at Soviet schools.[8]

In Beijing, Liu Yalou and his associates reevaluated the proposal for Soviet assistance to China's air force and noticed that there were several faults. According to their intelligence estimate, the Nationalist air force still possessed 150 to two hundred fighters and forty to fifty bombers with forty thousand men. The central leadership's request for two hundred Soviet fighters would not give the Communists air superiority over the Nationalists. On the other hand, it was unrealistic to set up a 2:1 training ratio of pilots to support personnel. Furthermore, it was impossible to train combat pilots within six to eight months. On July 29, Liu developed a new proposal asking the Soviets to provide three hundred to 350 fighters and train 350 to four hundred pilots so that China could create an air force with fighters and bombers within a year. Mao approved the new proposal two days later and urged Liu to travel to Moscow immediately, but exhorted him to be thrifty when negotiating for the air force. The chairman said the Chinese Communists faced enormous economic difficulties in rebuilding their nation, and the Soviet Union would not render assistance gratis.[9]

Negotiating for Soviet Assistance

Liu Yalou, accompanied by Wang Bi and Lü Liping, a Soviet trained pilot, departed Beijing on August 1, 1949, and arrived in the Soviet capital about a week later. They remained there until early October. The first meeting was held at the Ministry of Armed Forces on August 13, with Marshal Aleksandr M. Vasiliyevskiy, defense minister; Marshal K. A. Vershinin, commander in chief of the air force; and two other Soviet air force generals. Liu Shaoqi, Wang Jiaxiang, a future ambassador to the Soviet Union, and Liu Yalou, accompanied by his air force associates, also attended. The Chinese started the dialogue with a detailed description of China's tentative plan for an air force. According to Liu Yalou, China had fewer than a hundred pilots, half of whom were capable of flying U.S.- and Japanese-made fighters, plus eighty foreign-made combat aircraft, but only a third were fit for action. In order to establish an air force superior to that of the Nationalists within a year, the CCP asked the Soviet Union to provide three hundred to 350 combat planes at a ratio of 2.5:1 between fighters and bombers, and train Chinese pilots to fly them. Because Stalin had already agreed to help China develop an air force, Marshal Vershinin promised to work out a preliminary plan within the next few days.

Marshal Vershinin met with the Chinese on August 18 at the Soviet air force headquarters and informed them the Soviet air force could train 350 to four hundred pilots within a year, but it would need to establish six aviation schools, four for fighter training and two for bomber training. An accelerated educational program would be used to give Chinese pilots 150 to 180 flying hours in trainers. Chinese-trained pilots would follow a six-month aircraft conversion program to train them to employ Russian-made planes and combat techniques, so China could organize a mixed division consisting of two fighter regiments and one bomber regiment ready to assume combat tasks. A year later, with the graduates of the aviation schools, China would be able to create two fighter divisions and one bomber division with a total of 350 to 400 aircraft. The Soviet Union would supply China with 434 aircraft, including 120 La-9 fighters, 40 Tu-2 bombers, 270 trainers (90 Yak-18, 90 Yak-11, and 90 La-9UT and La-2UT), and 4 Il-12 transports. The combat aircraft, according to Marshal Vershinin, could be used to equip the mixed division, and additional aircraft for the other three divisions could be negotiated in 1950. In order to train the Chinese, the Soviet air force would dispatch a total of 878 personnel to staff the Chinese aviation schools: 100 for each fighter school, 120 for each bomber school, and a small number of Soviet advisers to work at air force headquarters. The Soviets would also furnish all necessary equipment and supplies to guarantee the training program's success.[10]

Apparently, the Soviets could accommodate all that the Chinese had requested. The Chinese immediately voiced their concerns, however, about the prospects of the La-9s in combat with the Nationalist P-51s. The La-9 was capable of climbing quicker, and was more maneuverable and had more powerful weapons, but the Mustang was faster in a dive and had a longer range with more payload.[11] While suspecting that the Soviets may have held something back from them, the Chinese had no doubt that massive Soviet training and material support were essential to the success of China's plans for an air force, so they agreed to accept the Russian offer. Still, the Chinese would soon complain that the Soviets took unreasonable advantage of China's need for their aid by charging new aircraft and equipment prices for old machinery. Ten years later, when the Sino-Soviet relationship was declining, the Chinese remembered how the Soviets had treated them, and criticized the sincerity of the Soviet aid.[12]

At present, there is still little information about high-level Soviet planning for air force assistance to the PRC. Moscow had historical precedents for assisting foreign countries with such development extending back to the 1920s with Weimar Germany and the Chinese Nationalist revolution, the Spanish Civil War, and the Japanese invasion of China. The scale of the Soviet military commitment to the PRC, however, was much greater, and grew as the Cold War extended into Asia. A preliminary agreement calling for Soviet assistance to China's air force was signed on August 18, 1949. Although Stalin did not approve it until October 5, the Soviet air force moved forward immediately. Major General D. Prutkov was appointed to serve as the chief adviser to the Chinese Air Force. The first group of Soviet air force advisers, including twenty-three commanding officers who would take charge of the Chinese aviation schools, gathered in Moscow in early October and arrived in Beijing two weeks later. Due to a shortage of instructor personnel, the aviation experts were also selected from combat units. Many of them were Soviet Communist Party members and had air combat experience in the Great Patriotic War. The Soviet advisers and material assistance brought substantial benefits to the PLAAF, which emerged as one of the largest air services in the world within only a few years.[13]

Liu Yalou and Establishment of the Top-Level Command Apparatus

On October 25, with Soviet assistance assured, the CMC appointed Liu Yalou as air force commander and Xiao Hua as political commissar of the air force, with Chang Qiankun and Wang Bi as their respective deputies. After transferring 2,515 members of Liu Yalou's army unit from Wuhan to Beijing, the PLAAF formally established its headquarters on November 11, 1949. Mao personally designated this new military arm of the CCP as the "Chinese People's Liberation Army Air Force" and announced that its position in the chain of command was equal to that of an army group.[14] To meet the air force's needs at the time, the administrative structure at PLAAF headquarters was composed of six major departments: headquarters, political, training, engineering, logistics, and personnel. Without any operational forces available during the first year, the PLAAF was to devote itself primarily to matters of organization. Its headquarters was merely the central agency for all matters pertaining to aviation.

Meanwhile, regional air force offices were established in six Military Regions: Northeast, North China, East China, South-central China, South-

Military Regions of the PRC, 1949–50

west, and Northwest. These air offices represented a transitional solution, an improvised organizational measure designed to bridge the gap until the PLAAF achieved a tangible level when it would have a sufficient number of commanders, officers, and troops at its disposal. The first military regional air force headquarters was established in Shenyang in August, 1950, and the last was formed in Lanzhou in December, 1951. Each was headed by a general with the rank and authority of an army commander. A CMC mandate of March 29, 1952, placed the regional air forces under the dual leadership of the PLAAF and Military Region headquarters. The former was responsible for administration, personnel, training, and logistics, while the regional air forces were subordinate to the latter for operational use and control.[15]

Following the Soviet model and experience, in September, 1950, and concerned that the war in Korea was expanding, the CMC decided to create the PLA Air Defense Headquarters to provide air defense for key cities like Beijing, Shanghai, and Shenyang. Three months later, a new force brought together antiaircraft artillery (AAA) and air observation units, radar warning facilities, and communications networks under a single banner. In the meantime, the existing district air defense headquarters in east, northeast, and northern China were reorganized and expanded, while a new regional command was established in south central China. After the Chinese air force entered the conflict in Korea, two additional air defense headquarters were set up at Andong and Shuifeng (Supung), respectively. The Soviet Air Defense Forces (PVO) consisted of interceptor units. Despite their dramatic expansion throughout the war, the Chinese air defense forces possessed no air units. Instead, the air defense forces were brought into the air force a few years later to simplify command and control.[16]

Three factors were instrumental in the development of the PLAAF's top-level command structure in its fledgling years. First, and most decisive, was the personality of its commander. Liu Yalou had long since outgrown the guerrilla military persona to which he had become accustomed as a senior Communist army commander. Moreover, his tendency to view policies strictly in their political dimensions rendered him incapable of logical military thinking. The second factor of importance was the newness of the organization and its conspicuous lack of personnel familiar with what an air force did and knowledgeable of its requirements. Copying the Soviet system blindly or mechanically was inevitable. The third factor was the influence exerted by the Soviet air force, whose doctrine stressed air superiority, air defense, and ground-support missions, and never embraced the concept of independent air operations to the exclusion of combined arms operations.[17] From the PLAAF's earliest years, Chinese military leaders perceived the air force as a support unit of the PLA, and considered airpower essential not in a strategic sense but with respect to the tactical support it could provide to the ground forces during operations. No consideration was given to making the air force a service independent of the army.

Despite these failings, there were few high-ranking PLA officers at the time as qualified as Liu Yalou to be the air force commander. Born April 8, 1910, Liu joined the Red Army at the age of nineteen.[18] He participated in the Long March, became a Red Army division political commissar in October, 1933, and became a division commander in July, 1935. A year later, he was selected to study at the Red Army University. Liu then worked at the university until early 1938, and became one of the few Red Army officers to enjoy a close relationship with Mao.[19] As a result, when he was sent to the Soviet Union to study in April, 1938, Mao entrusted him with the task of taking some of his writings to Stalin. Liu was also charged with explaining how the mistakes of the "Left" had harmed the CCP in the past, and the party's current anti-Japanese policy to the Comintern.[20] In January, 1939, Liu became a student at the Frunze Military Academy, and remained in the Soviet Union throughout World War II. In the summer of 1945, when the Soviets entered the war with Japan, he returned to China with an officer rank in the Soviet Red Army. When the civil war in China broke out in 1947, Liu became chief of staff of the Fourth Field Army, and, concurrently, commandant of the Northeast Aviation School.[21] In early 1949, he was appointed commander of the 14th Army Group. When the CCP leadership decided to establish the air force, Mao selected Liu to be in charge of the PLAAF partly because of Liu's reputation as a competent commander in the civil war and partly because of his Soviet connections.[22]

It must also be remembered that Liu was one of the few Red Army leaders possessing the necessary energy and will to develop an entirely new service branch out of virtually nothing in defiance of formidable obstacles. His personality often served as an inspiration to the PLAAF and urged it onward to greater achievements. Yet, raised in Chinese traditions and knowledgeable of the CCP's highly doctrinaire and centralized institutional system, Liu followed orders almost blindly. He would not, for example, support an autonomous aviation force that would challenge the CCP's existing military establishment. After he became air force commander, his goal for the PLAAF was to continue the CCP's military tradition and build an air force based on his experience in the ground force's organization. In an August, 1951 article, Liu warned that the special character of the air force did not warrant any effort to disassociate it from the PLA. Instead, Liu argued that building the air force depended on future airmen's success in embracing the experiences of the ground forces and transferring ground force traditions to the air force. This theme subsequently became the principle used to guarantee that the air force would continue as a component of the CCP's armed forces. Furthermore, any operational or strategic concepts developed by the PLAAF would also follow the lines of the PLA's traditions. Taking this tack, Liu could reassure senior party leaders of the PLAAF's political reliability.[23] In return, Liu's special relationship with the party leaders allowed him to bring his requests on behalf of the PLAAF to Mao's personal attention and be confident of their immediate approval. Money was, therefore, no real obstacle for Liu—nor was his PLAAF to be found wanting in the allocation of human and material resources.[24]

However, Liu's limited knowledge of the air force's day-to-day workings may have restricted the PLAAF's healthy development in the long run. The first operational mission assigned to the PLAAF in 1949 was support of the projected Taiwan campaign. Liu believed the Communists needed an air force linked to the PLA's ground operations, and he tended to discount military aviation as a potentially decisive element in warfare. Nevertheless, he agreed that an air force closely coordinated with the army's movements could dominate China's skies. In that same article, he declared that the air force should perform a supporting role for ground forces, and take their victories as its own.[25] Chinese Communist Party politics and culture also affected Liu's thinking about the air force's roles and missions. Obsessed with Mao's personality cult, he used the chairman's message of encouragement to the air force, "creating a powerful air force to eliminate the remnant enemy and consolidate national defense," to define the PLAAF's contemporary and future roles.[26] Thereafter, no serious efforts were ever made to further explore the different means of employing airpower within the framework of China's defense strategy. Aside from this, the pressing matter of the moment for Liu was to establish aviation schools and train Chinese pilots and technicians to man and maintain Soviet aircraft.

"Devote All of Your Efforts to Making Aviation Schools Successful"

In 1949, the PLAAF's leaders were faced with the unique task of creating an air force that would be operational within a year, ready to overwhelm the Nationalist air superiority. After the Soviet Union agreed to assist, PLAAF leaders immediately undertook large-scale planning of training programs. This included the establishment of aviation schools and the conscription of trainees. On October 30, the CMC approved setting up two bomber aviation schools at Harbin and Changchun (1st and 2d) and four fighter aviation schools at Jinzhou, Shenyang, Jinan, and Beijing (3d, 4th, 5th, and 6th). Two weeks later, the 7th Aviation School was added for transport training at Mudanjiang.[27] The CCP leadership set September and October, 1950, for the graduation of the first class of trained crews from the schools. Liu Yalou instructed that all aviation schools must open within a month, and that air force personnel must "devote all of your efforts to making the aviation schools successful."[28]

The CMC attached great importance to the selection of cadets for the aviation schools. Orders were issued on August 3, 1949, to all field armies and military regions to select candidates for pilot training from ground units and local military-political academies. According to the CMC's requirements, all candidates must be party and youth league members known to be politically reliable, be platoon or company officers with combat experience, be elementary school graduates, be physically fit, and be between age eighteen and twenty-four. From a Communist perspective, peasant and worker origins and infantry experience were essential for instilling the qualities of bravery, adaptability, and toughness required of an airman. Within two months, 1,672 men had been selected, and the air force accepted 930 for pilot training along with another 1,980 for ground crew training. The men were divided into two classes and expected to graduate in late 1950 and early 1951, respectively.[29]

Because of the urgent need for air and ground crews, the training program expanded beyond the original plan. During the months of April and August, 1950, an additional 2,548 trainees enrolled into the program, including 884 selected for pilot training. Because of a shortage of commanding officers who could fly, the air force also selected ninety-seven army officers with the rank of battalion or regimental commander for pilot training. In September, Premier Zhou Enlai urged the air force to double the total number of trainees at the schools, with each fighter school to train an additional 126 pilots and another 112 for each bomber school. In order to give the PLAAF technological superiority over the GMD air force, the 4th Aviation School began in September to specialize in training jet pilots. Three additional schools were founded in 1951, separating ground crew training from the existing schools. For four years, from 1949 to 1952, a total of thirteen thousand soldiers and officers were selected from ground units to undergo flight training. By the end of 1953, these institutions had trained 5,945 pilots, twenty-four thousand ground personnel, and 1,396 other personnel, which assured the activation of combat units for the PLAAF's involvement in Korea.[30]

After completion of an extensive construction program, including runway repairs, depots, billets, and administration and teaching buildings, all of the aviation schools opened in early December with theoretical training. Insurmountable difficulties resulted, however, because of the insufficient educational level of the cadets and language barriers between Chinese students and their Russian instructors. Translators and former GMD aviation personnel were brought in to assist with lectures, and the students, the first generation of peasant, proletarian pilots, remained highly motivated and dedicated as ever to the revolutionary cause. Nevertheless, the standards of instruction were apparently lowered, and the course of theoretical studies abbreviated.[31] Beginning in January, 1950, the eighty-nine pilots previously trained by the Chinese started flight training on Yak-18s. Because of their earlier flying experience and aptitude for pilot training, by May most of them had finished the training program, including aerobatics, formation flying, cruise flying, and air-to-air and air-to-ground firing, with an average of thirty-three flying hours for fighter pilots and 23.5 flying hours for bomber pilots.[32]

Shortly after the CCP leadership decided to intervene in the Korean conflict, the PLAAF faced mounting pressure to produce pilots for forming combat units. In October, 1950, the six aviation schools graduated their first class earlier than the training schedule required, even though these pilots had flown only the Yak-18 and Yak-11, with an average of about sixty-three flying hours, while the standard training time for student pilots was 150 to two hundred flying hours. Although the pilots graduated from the aviation schools in 1950 no doubt made significant contributions to the initial buildup of air units and actions in Korea, the PLAAF's accelerated and shortened training program, in retrospect, resulted in serious defects for which the pilots' enthusiasm and dedication could not wholly overcome their inadequacies. The result was that accidents were frequent. While statistics for crashes at the schools are not available, the PLAAF's acknowledgement of many serious aircraft accidents is instructive: the rate was 3.35 per ten thousand sorties in 1950. According to the former PLAAF chief of staff, the air force continued to experience high accident rates in flight training with more than a hundred fatal crashes during the first half of 1951.[33] The PLAAF authorities later conceded that had Chinese pilots flown more hours at the aviation schools, there would have been fewer crashes and losses, and probably more victories for them in the Korean War.[34]

PLAAF and Russian Mentors

Building an air force for the CCP from the ground up was a remarkable achievement to which Soviet personnel contributed under extremely difficult conditions. Many of these Soviet airmen had fought in World War II, and in 1945 had just reunited with their families after a long period of separation. With the descent of the "Iron Curtain" between the East and West, they were again mobilized and sent to a remote and unfamiliar country to help build a bulwark for defending Soviet interests in Asia. Unfortunately, none of the available archival sources depict the work of Soviet advisers and their involvement in the PLAAF. However, it is also impossible to exclude them from this study. Based on fragmentary Chinese reminiscences, we may at least sketch the role of Soviet advisers in the development of the Chinese air force at this early and critical stage.[35]

Soviet personnel sent to help the Chinese air force included commanding officers, aviation instructors, mechanical technicians, and other ground crew specialists. For secrecy, they wore civilian clothes.[36] All Soviet advisers served under the direct command of the chief adviser to the Chinese air force in Beijing. Major General Prutkov initially commanded Soviet advisers sent to China. He was replaced by General Korotkov in October, 1950. According to the agreement signed by the Chinese and Soviet air forces in October, 1949, Soviet advisers would serve a one-year tour in China, and the Chinese would pay for their living expenses and supplies.[37]

Soviet advisers lived under much better conditions than their Chinese comrades, as China had yet to experience a full economic recovery after the ruinous war.[38] Their task, however, was arduous. On one hand, many Soviet advisers drawn from combat units had little teaching experience. On the other hand, their students or trainees had little education and no knowledge of the Russian language, so lectures had to be given through interpreters who did not know aviation terminology. This often created awkward classroom situations, and classes soon fell behind schedule. This situation did not improve until the PLAAF recruited Chinese university graduates to assist the Soviet advisers with teaching.[39] Nevertheless, the language barrier continued to be a practical problem in flight instruction.

Another difficulty experienced by Soviet advisers was caused by China's eagerness to create an air force. As the training program proceeded, the number of Chinese aviation trainees steadily increased until it reached a level far beyond the number projected in the agreement. In due course, each Russian lecturer was responsible for teaching four to five classes a day, while each flight instructor was assigned to train five to six Chinese student pilots, often flying four to five hours a day. This heavy workload coupled with a rigorous disciplinary system that severely restricted their social activities in China made many Russian advisers homesick and anxious to get their training job done so they could return home earlier. The Chinese complained this was a contributing factor to low training quality and the high accident rate.[40] In the meantime, attempts to make social contact with Chinese civilians, particularly women, often resulted in embarrassing and disgraceful episodes for Soviet military personnel in China, and the Chinese civilians' resentment toward their presence mounted.[41]

Despite China's dependence on Soviet assistance in building an air force, from the beginning the Chinese made it clear that Soviet advisers would be limited to training Chinese pilots and offering mechanical services. By the same token, the Chinese would not interfere in the Soviet advisory group's internal affairs.[42] The same rules applied to Soviet personnel training pilots in combat air units. For the first half-year, however, Soviet advisers were in control of almost every aspect of the program because Chinese commanders had no experience with managing an air force.[43]

As the PLAAF's officers gradually became familiar with the requirements of their new military profession, unpleasant relationships emerged. Lü Liping later recalled that the proper handling of an accident was often an irritant.[44] The Chinese believed that every incident should be fully reported to the air force headquarters in Beijing. The Soviets, however, probably fearing that too many accident reports would damage their prestige, thought there was no need to make a fuss over less serious incidents.[45] Another sensitive issue was the rigorous Soviet aviation standards, which often meant that a Chinese pilot was deemed unfit for flying and eliminated from training. Chinese commanders found that Soviet advisers sometimes made rash judgments, disqualifying Chinese student pilots that the Chinese air force desperately needed and who Chinese leaders thought still had potential.[46] Such differences almost certainly resulted in ill feelings between Russian advisers and their Chinese counterparts.[47] However, air force leaders in Beijing urged their subordinates to exercise forbearance because Soviet assistance to China's air force was so crucial. Liu Yalou once told his subordinates that he had to make strict demands on his own comrades to maintain a good relationship with their Soviet advisers in order to speed up the development of the Chinese air force.[48]

In 1951, the focus of Soviet involvement in flight training began to change. Most Soviet advisers sent to Chinese aviation schools departed by July, and the Chinese began training their own student pilots.[49] In the meantime, the Soviets shifted their efforts to training the PLAAF's combat units. There is almost no material available describing the training system Russian combat pilots employed. No Kum-Sok, a North Korean MiG-15 pilot who defected to the United States in 1953, later recalled that Russian combat pilots, unlike the advisers, appeared more disciplined and humorous, and rarely did things that "offended my pride as a Korean."[50] By the time the Chinese air force entered the war in Korea, Soviet advisers remaining in the headquarters of the Chinese People's Volunteers (CPV) and the CPV's air force played a negligible role in war operations. The Chinese air force, while dependent upon Soviet technology and supplies, mainly operated independently from Soviet control. Despite the fact that the operation of an air force depends upon knowledge and experience, PLAAF personnel often resisted the advice of Soviet advisers, although the latter made recommendations that were based on their well-founded knowledge and rich experiences. This situation later drew sharp criticism from the PLA's leadership.[51]

The Buildup of Air Units

Another characteristic of this stage of development in 1950 was that although the training program was still accorded top priority, the task of activating combat units and equipping them gradually began to increase in importance.[52] In response to the CCP's Taiwan campaign plan, the PLAAF initially projected establishing two fighter regiments and one bomber regiment in six months (with forty aircraft for each). China's vulnerability to air attack by the GMD magnified the importance of forming more units. Despite the CCP's control of the mainland, the Nationalist air force actually owned the airspace over China, and increasingly raided Shanghai and other major coastal cities in early 1950. The new plan thus called for establishing seven fighter regiments for air defense and four bomber regiments to support the scheduled Taiwan campaign during the first year of the PRC's existence.[53] Due to its lack of experience, the PLAAF decided to organize aviation regiments with fewer aircraft (thirty for each fighter regiment and twenty for each bomber regiment) than originally planned.[54] When war erupted in Korea, the CCP leadership adopted an aggressive development plan for the years 1950–53. The PLAAF expected to train 25,400 aviation personnel, establish 97 aviation regiments (23 in 1950 and 1951, 45 in 1952, and 29 in 1953), repair and construct over a hundred airfields, and set up eleven aircraft repair shops. By the end of 1953, the PLAAF's strength would reach 290,000 troops and 4,507 aircraft, including 2,640 combat planes.[55]

In early 1950, the PLAAF's goal for the activation of combat units clearly could not be achieved solely through a training program, well organized though it might be, that relied on Soviet aid. Liu Yalou needed a numerically adequate and highly qualified officer corps for the PLAAF, and that was a much more complicated task to accomplish than the procurement of enlisted personnel. With the graduation of the first two classes of air and ground crews from the aviation schools, the air force would be able to organize six to seven divisions, totaling fifteen aviation regiments, but the cadre of experienced officers in the PLAAF was extremely limited. Liu thus had no alternative but to borrow personnel from PLA regimental and division headquarters.

On April 10, 1950, the CMC approved Liu's recommendation, and twelve army division headquarters and forty-nine regimental headquarters staffs were transferred to the air force in 1950–51.[56] The transferred ground troops included several crack units with victorious combat records in the civil war and many highly competent army commanders like Liu Zhen, Nie Fengzhi, Duan Suquan, and Zeng Kelin whose military credentials and long devotion to the Communist revolution warranted their playing a unique role in the PLAAF. Liu Zhen and Nie Fengzhi subsequently directed the PLAAF's activities in Korea, and Duan Suquan and Zeng Kelin, who commanded army-level air force units, were among the few who possessed flight credentials.[57]

As the need for an air force increased in urgency, the transfer of ground personnel to the PLAAF, though proved expedient, represented the Chinese leaders' intention to maintain the air force as a branch of the PLA.[58] Before the activation of combat units could commence, however, PLAAF leaders had to address the question of how many and what kinds of units were needed to meet the needs of China's security.

Little in the people's war doctrine addressed the uses of airpower, but its defensive doctrine's nature did exert an influence on Chinese thinking about the air force. Liu Yalou and his staff preferred to build an air force similar to that of the Soviet Union, one possessing more fighters than bombers. Lü Liping, one of General Liu's aides during the negotiations for Soviet assistance in Moscow, estimated that bombers composed only a third of the Soviet air strength, although they also maintained attack aircraft for ground support. The role of fighters fit well with the defensive nature of Chinese thinking. Bombers attacked enemy countries or territories, an aggressive act, he further noted, but fighters were defensive in nature. It followed that success in fending off attacks would lead to air superiority.[59] The PLAAF's immediate mission, therefore, was to attain air superiority over the Nationalists, provide support for the planned amphibious assault on Taiwan, and then develop a force capable of defending China's air space and waters. This thinking gave priority to the development of fighter units.[60]

In June, 1950, the PLAAF established its first aviation unit in Nanjing. It was a combined brigade, consisting of two fighter regiments, one bomber regiment, and one attack regiment, and was equipped with 155 aircraft (including 38 MiG-15s, 39 La-11s, 39 Tu-2s, 25 Il-10s, and 14 trainers). Imitating Mao Zedong, who during his days in the Jinggang Mountains named the first Red Army unit the Fourth Army, Liu called this first air force unit the 4th Mixed Aviation Brigade, reminding his subordinates to continue the

A fleet of Chinese La-11 aircraft.

Red Army's tradition. This unit was directly subordinate to the East China
Military Region, and had the mission of supporting the army and navy
effort to conquer the Nationalist-controlled offshore islands. After complet-
ing a three-month aircraft conversion program with the assistance of the
Soviets, it assumed air defense duty in Shanghai on October 19. The real
value of this first unit was to help the PLAAF and its top-level leaders become familiar with air force training and operations. For example, regional
air force commander Nie Fengzhi, who also commanded the brigade, began
a training program for air force commanders that enabled him to fulfill his
future assignment in Korea. In the fall of 1950, the bomber regiment participated in the first joint counteramphibious attack training exercise with ground
forces. Although the air force units were far from being operational, this
drill demonstrated how anxious CCP military leaders were to see the air
force in action.[61]

The Korean War provided the impetus for rapid expansion of the air
force, both in aviation personnel and in equipment. When the first graduates of the aviation schools were available for assignment in October the 4th
Brigade was divided and became the backbone of some of the first air divisions.[62] Shortly after the Korean War began, a great influx of Soviet assistance enabled a major enhancement of the PLAAF's capabilities in both quan-
titative and qualitative terms. By the end of 1950, the PLAAF had established

A formation of Chinese Tu-2s.

another 3 fighter divisions, 2 bomber divisions, and 1 attack division. Between January and May, 1951, the PLAAF organized 8 new air divisions (6 fighter, 1 attack, and 1 transport).[63] It continued to expand rapidly, so that by war's end the air force had deployed a full complement of fighters, bombers, attack aircraft, and transport planes in a total of 28 air divisions and sixty air regiments. Unfortunately, Chinese air doctrine stressed air defense strategy, so the PLAAF emerged with only a small portion of the overall bomber force structure needed for offensive operations.

Development of the PLAAF Ground Support System

Despite the rapid expansion of air units, the PLAAF faced enormous difficulties in developing an effective support system. At the time of the founding of the People's Republic, the Communists inherited 542 airfields from the GMD. Unfortunately, most of them were dirt runways, and many had already been reclaimed for agricultural use. Moreover, the PLA had no existing radar or communication troops for use in support of air force operations. The PLAAF history divides the development of its ground support system into four categories: airfield repair and construction, formation of operational support units, establishment of aircraft maintenance services, and improvement of logistic supplies.[64]

AIRFIELD REPAIR AND CONSTRUCTION

Worried that military expenses would keep rising in the poverty-stricken country, the CCP leadership took a prudent approach to the issue of airfield repair and construction. Top priority was given to airfields used by the aviation schools, whose piston-engine trainers did not need improved runways and could be made serviceable with minimum repairs. Next came airfields used for the defense of large cities. These required expansion to accommodate jet fighters. Third in line were the new airfields needed to support the planned Taiwan campaign and Korean War operations. By the end of 1950, a total of 68 airfields had been repaired and renovated, including 22 for the aviation schools, 17 for the air defense of Shanghai and the campaigns against the GMD-controlled islands; and 21 for the air defense of northeast China and operations in Korea. In addition, 13 temporary airstrips were constructed in 1951–53 to support operations in Korea.[65] In order to assure the quality of airfields and to save costs, five regiment-sized units were created in 1950 for airfield repair and construction, and a sixth group was added two years later.[66]

FORMATION OF OPERATIONAL SUPPORT UNITS

The PLAAF's operational support troops consisted of communications, radar, and meteorological services. In early 1950, the PLAAF had a communications force of about forty-seven hundred people whose primary role was to provide communications and navigation aids. The first radar battalion was established in April, 1950, in Nanjing, with ten sets of Japanese- and American-made radars, and then transferred to Shanghai, where it was equipped with Soviet equipment as part of the Shanghai Air Defense Headquarters. After UN forces entered the conflict in Korea, the unit was transferred to Shenyang to enhance air defense forces in northeast China. The PLAAF's meteorological services were created in November, 1949. By the end of 1953, there were 1,931 meteorological personnel working at various stations across the nation.[67]

Despite these early efforts, the lack of well-trained technicians and obsolete equipment limited the capability of the PLAAF's operational support units. For example, the air force's Soviet-built P-3 and P-3A radars had a range of only two hundred kilometers, which handicapped air operations conducted far from home bases.[68] Another major problem at the time was the failure to establish an integrated network of radars, antiaircraft guns, and fighters. Radar units were divided into two types after the formation of the PLA Air Defense Force, which consisted only of antiaircraft artillery units, in December, 1950. Those assigned to the Air Defense Force were responsible for early warning, while those assigned to the PLAAF directly supported aviation units. Consequently, air defense coordination was still inadequate in the early 1950s despite the rapid growth of the PLAAF.[69]

AIRCRAFT MAINTENANCE SERVICES

From the founding of the PLAAF, aeronautical engineering was one of the major departments at PLAAF headquarters. According to a PLAAF decree issued December 15, 1951, this administrative structure was established at division and regiment level. However, ground engineering support personnel were incorporated with aircrews at group and squadron levels at a 5:1 ratio. The lack of skilled ground crews meant the PLAAF had to depend upon Soviet specialists for exacting technical work and repair activity during its first two years. Although organized along Soviet lines, the PLAAF devised its own system and regulations for aircraft maintenance. For example, encouragement of hard work and collective wisdom was used to compensate for the insufficiency of individual knowledge and competency.[70] Ground crews were expected to acquire an "attitude of wholehearted service to aircraft and flight," which in turn was expected to have positive effects on the quality of aircraft maintenance. Based on incomplete PLAAF statistics, there was a steady improvement in aircraft serviceability from 79.8 percent in 1952 to 83.5 percent in 1953, while accidents caused by mechanical malfunctions were reduced from 0.59 per thousand sorties in 1952 to 0.35 in 1953.[71]

LOGISTICAL IMPROVEMENTS

The PLAAF established the Department of Logistics in January, 1950, with responsibility for airfield repairs, budgeting, equipment, and fuel supply. Each military region continued to be responsible for other logistical functions for air force units assigned permanently or temporarily to its operational area. After the first aviation units were established, a supply group was assigned to each aviation regiment to take charge of supply operations. By the end of 1950, there were a total of seventeen supply groups. Recognizing that an overlap existed between the supply group and the field station, the PLAAF amalgamated the two in early 1951, and these units then became an independent logistics support unit under the regional air force command. Meanwhile, the PLAAF maintained six mobile supply regiments for providing continuous combined service support for operations. In November, 1951, five were sent to Korea in preparation for the deployment of Chinese aviation units there.[72]

Because the PLAAF depended on Soviet equipment and supplies, one immediate task for the air force logistics services was the transshipping of Soviet aircraft and supplies from the ports to aviation schools, where Soviet specialists would assemble them. In an effort to keep expenditures on Soviet supplies to a minimum, the PLAAF also adapted fourteen thousand captured Japanese and American bombs so that the PLAAF's Soviet-made aircraft could use them for training and combat. Because China's own oil production was negligible, petroleum supplies required for air units had to be imported almost entirely from the Soviet Union.[73] This in turn required the availability of adequate storage and transport capacity. Unfortunately, the PLAAF had a storage capacity of less than twelve thousand tons, and the majority of the aviation schools had no fuel storage facilities whatsoever. An endeavor was made to repair eight fuel depots (seven in the northeast and one in Nanjing) to enlarge the PLAAF's fuel storage capacity to seventy thousand tons, a figure adequate to meet current needs.[74]

Financing the Air Force

Enthusiasm alone would not accomplish the CCP's ambitious plan to establish airpower within a short time frame. Financial resources were also needed. A struggling economy, faced at every turn with demands from a war-torn populace, and driven by China's own plans for the construction of a Communist society, required massive capital investment. Thanks to a recent Sino-Soviet treaty, the Soviet Union granted China a $300 million loan at an annual interest of just 1 percent. On paper, the Soviet loan would be used only for civilian purposes, but in secret, the Chinese won Moscow's consent to devote the funds to the purchase of Soviet military equipment.[75] Mao immediately decided to commit a third of the 1950 installment ($20 million) to equip his air force and navy.[76]

In early 1950, four separate orders were placed.[77] The PLAAF initially requested 586 aircraft, including 280 La-9 fighters, 198 Tu-2 bombers, and 108 trainers and other planes. On February 15, 1950, just a day after signing the Soviet loan agreement, Mao wrote to Stalin asking the Soviet Union to sell China 628 planes.[78] In March and April, Beijing placed two additional orders for Soviet equipment and advisers.[79] After China intervened in the Korean War in October, Beijing placed an order for 2,470 aircraft of all types. The Soviets filled most of the Chinese orders by transferring aircraft and equipment directly from Soviet air force troops in China to the PLAAF.[80]

Students from the First Elementary School in the city of Xi'an donate their pocket money for the purchase of an aircraft designated as *Chinese Children* in 1951. *Courtesy* China Pictorial Agency

At home, the CCP leadership also assigned priorities to finance its aviation program. Faced with unexpected monetary demands from the air force, on February 27, 1950, Liu Shaoqi instructed the CMC and the Ministry of Finance to use the state war budget to cover all air force and navy expenditures without restraint. For 1950 alone, the PLAAF made four budget requests amounting to 369.1 million *renminbi* (excluding the expenditures covered by the military regions), which was 13 percent of the total defense budget and 5.39 percent of the total state budget.[81] In early 1952, the CCP leadership transferred most of the $1.5 million Soviet loan to the air force for the purchase of aircraft at the expense of the navy.[82]

Nevertheless, the central government would have found the task of financing the air force increasingly onerous had it not been for the Federation of Chinese People to Resist the United States and Aid Korea. In June, 1951, the CCP leadership called for a nationwide campaign of "making patriotic pledges and donations for weapons" to support the war effort in Korea. Federation members then proceeded to conduct a massive fund-raising campaign throughout the country. Although donations were supposed to be voluntary, they became a contractual obligation in a society based on conformity. Many thousands of workers, peasants, intellectuals, and even elementary school students from throughout China were cajoled or coerced into "donating" some or all of their allowances or income in return for the honor of having a weapon or an airplane named after their factory or village. When the fund drive ended in June, 1952, the Federation had collected 556.5 million *renminbi,* enough to purchase 3,710 fighters.[83] Although it is impossible to determine exactly how the funds were allocated, the air force appeared to be the chief beneficiary, and the places appeared to be built with less strain on the government and its economy.

Even with the central government's full support, the PLAAF's leadership, keenly aware of the state of the nation's economy, was cautious not to overspend. From the very beginning, Liu Yalou laid down principles for strict budgetary accountability for the air force's expenditures. According to the air force commander, air force budget planners must always keep in mind the nation's economic difficulties and prioritize their budgetary requests by urgency and necessity. Although recognizing that the air force deserved special treatment for food, living conditions, and other supplies, Liu warned that it should not act as a "prodigal." All air force personnel were to be mindful of the current material conditions facing the army so they would not demand more than they needed. He required that all expenditures (including hosting a dinner party or seeing an opera) be subject to approval by PLAAF leaders. In early 1950, Liu criticized a budgetary plan for a dairy farm located at an aviation school, using it as an example to reiterate his belief that the best way to build up the air force was through thrift and hard work.[84]

The emergence of the PLAAF as a modern air force was almost entirely the product of China's own military doctrines and concepts. There was no preexisting PLA air arm. With the exception of a few trained aviation personnel who were either technically savvy graduates of the PLA's old aviation school or defectors from the GMD air force, the air force, including most of its senior leaders, was composed almost entirely of personnel shifted from the ground forces. The basis for the thinking of PLAAF leaders with respect to the employment of the Chinese air force in the early 1950s was laid down in the CCP's Taiwan campaign plan. Despite their best efforts, China's poor economic and industrial condition left Chinese leaders no choice but to depend on the Soviet Union to modernize their armed forces. Soviet contributions were vital to the PLAAF. Nevertheless, the outbreak of the Korean

War caught the CCP's leaders off guard. Soviet assistance had just begun, and the PLA remained poorly equipped and ill prepared for combat. When the CCP's leaders pondered how they should respond to the crisis in Korea, they soon found that the airpower issue was an influential factor in their decision-making process.

CHAPTER 3

Promise, Decision, and the Airpower Factor

The first three weeks of October, 1950, were crucial moments in the history of the PRC as China's leaders debated whether or not to intervene militarily in Korea, and, if so, when. One major issue that caused Chinese leaders to vacillate was the lack of air support. This concern was aggravated when the Soviet Union seemingly reneged on its commitment to provide air support for the Chinese People's Volunteers. However, recent studies of Soviet involvement in the Korean conflict based on Russian archival materials suggest Moscow delivered on its promise to furnish China with air support if Chinese leaders sent troops to Korea.[1] Russian pilots began to engage the Americans over the Yalu within just a few days of China's intervention. However, the controversy continues as other scholars have used Joseph Stalin's decision to withhold air support to analyze Chinese and Soviet intentions and motivations, as well as their respective perceived national interests in the Korean Peninsula at this critical juncture of the war.[2]

Did Stalin renege on his promise of air support? Based on Chinese sources available since the late 1980s, along with the recently declassified Soviet archives, it is possible to develop a comprehensive account of the relationship between Beijing and Moscow over the issue of air support to Chinese ground operations in Korea. This chapter will specifically address a series of interrelated questions such as what commitments had been made by Beijing and Moscow, why and how they were reached, how the Soviet Union carried out its commitments, and to what extent they affected Beijing's decision to enter the war and subsequent military operations in Korea.

The Outbreak of the Korean War and Stalin's Promise

Stalin's initial promise of air support for Chinese troops came on July 5, 1950, ten days after Kim Il Sung's army invaded the Republic of Korea (ROK). In a coded telegram to Zhou Enlai, the PRC foreign minister, the Soviet leader urged Beijing immediately to deploy "nine divisions on the Chinese-Korean border for volunteer actions in North Korea" should the enemy cross the 38th Parallel. In order to persuade the Chinese leader that such a move was imperative, Stalin offered to supply air cover for the deployment.[3] Why was the Soviet leader so anxious for Chinese involvement in the Korean conflict? An answer can be found in the earlier discussions between Pyongyang, Moscow, and Beijing of Kim's plan for invading South Korea.

During Kim Il Sung's secret visit to Moscow in April, 1950, the North Korean leader tried to win Soviet support for his war plan. Stalin, however, appeared reluctant to endorse Kim's proposals for the conquest of South Korea. He was preoccupied with the situation in the West, and feared that such an attack would provoke U.S. intervention in Northeast Asia. While agreeing to continue providing North Korea with military supplies and equipment, the Soviet leader insisted that Kim discuss his plans with Beijing. Stalin believed Mao Zedong had a better understanding of the situation in Asia, and that the North Koreans needed assurance the Chinese would help should the tide turn against them. Recent scholarship suggests that a Chinese commitment to North Korea would not only serve Soviet security interests in the Far East, it would also excuse the Soviets from "the onus for the attack, whether successful or not and regardless of the U.S. reaction."[4]

As early as February, 1950, when Mao was visiting Moscow, the Chinese and Soviet leaders had talked about Kim's military scheme to unify the Korean Peninsula. However, Stalin found Mao's attitude ambiguous. The Chinese leader did not believe the United States would intervene in a civil war waged on the Korean Peninsula, nor was he enthusiastic about Kim's

Mao Zedong meets with Kim Il Sung in June, 1951, prior to the latter's visit to Moscow.

proposed action.[5] The Chinese were pursuing their own national unification with a plan to seize Taiwan during 1950. The CCP's dependence upon Soviet assistance became imperative, particularly after the PLA's defeat on Jinmen Island in October, 1949.[6] The chairman did not want China's Taiwan campaign to become hostage to Kim's invasion of South Korea, which also would need Soviet support. In the meantime, he did not think he was in a position to oppose the Koreans' efforts to achieve the same goal.[7] In response to a request from Kim, Beijing agreed to return several thousand Korean soldiers serving in the PLA to the North Korean People's Army (NKPA) in April.[8] However, the Chinese paid no special attention to events in Korea, and did not make any military preparations for a conflict on the Korean Peninsula. By the time Kim's army invaded the ROK on June 25, 1950, the bulk of the PLA's forces were concentrated in southern China, where sixteen armies were preparing to invade Taiwan. There was only one army (the Forty-second) in northeast China, and it was involved in agricultural production in Qiqihar, several hundred miles from the Chinese-Korean border.[9]

Beijing's poor preparation for the Korean situation was probably due in part to the Chinese leadership downplaying the danger of American intervention in East Asian affairs, and also because Kim did not believe he needed any assistance from the Chinese Communists.[10] Since Pyongyang had already secured the Soviets' blessing, the North Koreans did not inform the Chinese of their specific plan and timing of the assault.[11] According to Mao's Russian-language interpreter, Shi Zhe, Kim "arrogantly" turned down Mao's offer to transfer three Chinese armies to the Chinese-Korean border.[12] What the North Korean leader had successfully secured from Beijing, according to Russian records based on a report from Pak Hon Yong, a high-ranking North Korean official, was China's promise to support North Korea with troops if the United States intervened.[13] Access to documents for the period remains restricted in Beijing. It is obvious, according to Russian documents, however, that Stalin's design impelled Beijing not only to endorse North Korea's action, but also to put the Chinese in the position of responsibility for its consequences.[14] One Chinese source suggests that Stalin was the first to voice the notion that the Chinese should deploy several divisions along the Korean border. Mao replied that if the Soviet Union would equip them, he would like to help the North Koreans with his own troops.[15] Unfortunately, no Russian documents concerning the exchange between Beijing and Moscow during the month preceding the war are available. When the war erupted on June 25, Chinese leaders soon felt distressed and probably even offended by the fact that the North Koreans had not further consulted with them.[16]

Beijing Moves at Moscow's Request

Stalin's telegram sent on July 5 is typical of the dialogue between Chinese and Soviet leaders during the weeks immediately after Pyongyang's invasion of the South. Soviet documents released thus far indicate that Stalin's anxiety about possible U.S. intervention was growing as Washington had responded swiftly and firmly to the Korean crisis.[17] The Soviet leader feared that a disaster in Korea might draw Soviet troops into combat against the Americans, and the only way to keep that from happening was to get Beijing to commit. However, Beijing's movement at the time was slow and reluctant.

Beijing took no action to mobilize Chinese military forces during the first week of the conflict in Korea; instead, on June 30, the Central Demobilization Commission was created to carry out Mao's plan to reduce the PLA's strength by 1.5 million in 1950.[18] The only immediate impact of the Korean conflict on Beijing appears to be the Chinese leaders' decision to postpone their Taiwan campaign when Washington dispatched the U.S. Seventh Fleet to the Taiwan Straits.[19] American intervention in Korea and Taiwan evidently presented a new security issue for the Beijing leadership to digest. With no direct communication between Beijing and Pyongyang at the time, Chinese leaders were handicapped by a lack of information about the military situation in Korea.[20] Meanwhile, two other factors may also have contributed to Beijing's slow response. First, Chinese leaders were impressed by the rapid progress North Korean troops made during the first days of the conflict.[21] After the U.S. Eighth Army entered the conflict in early July, Chinese leaders were still confident that the Americans were unable to reverse the course of the war and would only delay South Korea's defeat.[22] Second, while believing the recently concluded Sino-Soviet alliance would be enough to deter the United States from expanding the conflict beyond South Korea, they were increasingly uncertain what military actions the United States would take there and felt that China needed to prepare.[23] Therefore, Chinese leaders wanted to know what Stalin was thinking, and the kind of support they could expect from the Soviet Union if they decided to intervene in Korea. On July 2, before Beijing deployed any troops to the Korean border, Premier Zhou Enlai asked the Soviet ambassador if the Russians would provide air cover for three Chinese armies that "had already been concentrated" there.[24]

Apparently, Beijing's leadership did not begin to take steps toward intervention until after receiving Stalin's telegram on July 5. Two days later, Zhou, who also served as vice chairman of the CMC, called a meeting of that organization to discuss China's military preparations for the Korean conflict. The participants included the leading members of the CMC and senior officers from the PLA's headquarters in Beijing, and regional headquarters in Shenyang and Wuhan.[25] At the meeting, the decision was made to establish the Northeast Border Defense Army (NBDA), and transfer all nine divisions of the 13th Army Group (consisting of the Thirty-eighth, Thirty-ninth, and Fortieth Armies, which had served as the PLA's strategic reserve since late 1949) from central China to the northeast, near the Korean border, by the end of July. They, along with the Forty-second Army and three artillery divisions, would be placed under the new command, whose mission was "to defend the borders of the Northeast, and prepare to support the war operations of the Korean People's Army if necessary." At midnight that same day, Mao approved the resolution and directed its immediate execution.[26] However, the CMC did not issue the implementing orders until July 13.[27] Recently released Chinese documents do not explain why Beijing took almost another week to draft and finalize the orders.[28]

While Beijing carefully considered its own moves in regard to the Korean situation, Stalin dispatched another telegram to the Chinese leaders on July 13 asking if they had decided to deploy nine divisions along the Korean border. The Soviet leader had not heard anything from Beijing for more than ten days, and his anxiety was obvious since the Americans had already entered the fight. Stalin reiterated his earlier promise, noting that if the Chinese "have made such a decision," he was ready to dispatch a MiG division of 124 planes "for covering these troops." However, he did not specify how this Soviet air unit would coordinate with the Chinese ground forces, and left his promise of air support in vague terms. The Soviet leader did imply that Russian pilots would stay in China for two to three months, during which time they would train Chinese pilots to fly jets and then turn over all planes to the Chinese.[29]

More than a week later, on July 22, Mao accepted the Soviet offer to provide air cover. There currently are no other archival materials available that offer any details of how the Chinese leader interpreted the meaning of the Soviet promise of air support. However, this telegram reveals that Mao seemed greatly concerned with the length of the Soviet pilots' scheduled stay—a period that seemed too short to retrain Chinese pilots. He noted that the retraining program could not be completed until March or April, 1951. Only then would China have sufficient pilots to take over the planes from the Soviets.[30] This retraining schedule invites speculation that China would not have an operational air force until the spring of 1951. If Stalin's strategy was guided by his determination to avoid committing Soviet troops to fight the Americans in Korea but instead to encourage the Chinese to assume the burden, he could not hesitate to agree with Mao's request to build his own air force so the Chinese could defend themselves in the air. Thus, on July 25, Stalin approved the proposed training schedule.[31] For the time being, it was clear in both Beijing and Moscow that China would depend on the Soviets for air support. Nevertheless, the Soviet air support remained a cryptic promise.

The Arrival of Soviet Air Units and China's Preparation for Intervention

On July 21, the Soviet 151st Guards Fighter Aviation Division (GIAD), commanded by Maj. Gen. Ivan M. Belov, was ordered to fly to northeastern China to provide air cover for the Chinese 13th Army Group.[32] It was not the first air unit assigned to a tour in China, however. Another air division, under the command of Lt. Gen. Pavel F. Batitskiy, had been stationed in the Shanghai area, assisting Chinese air defenses there since March. Nevertheless, by the time the Chinese troops had completed their transfer and settled into their positions on the Korean border in early August, the 151st was in place at Shenyang, Liaoyang, and Anshan and ready to fly. To Chinese soldiers, the arrival of Soviet air units was a great blessing. Since the founding of the Red Army, Communist soldiers had received no air protection, and had often been victims of air attack. To overcome their troops' fear of fighting the Americans, one indispensable prescription used by ranking officers was to convince their soldiers that they should not be fearful of enemy planes, because this time they would have air cover.[33]

Although the arrival of Soviet air units was an inspiration for Chinese soldiers, difficulties emerged soon after the military leaders of the 13th Army Group started to consider their missions in Korea. Their most conspicuous problems were lack of transportation and antitank artillery, shortage of medical personnel, and the problem of how to establish communications between the ground troops and the air force.[34] The 13th Army Group requested additional time to get ready for combat, and for the CMC to help solve these problems.[35] Mao agreed to extend the deadline for completion of preparation for entering the Korean War until the end of September, and also assured his generals in the northeast that the problems plaguing the NBDA "can be resolved."[36]

In order to establish effective communications between Chinese ground forces and the Soviet air units, Beijing asked Moscow to send sixty-four Soviet military advisers to the East China and Northeast Military Regions to assist with air defense and air force (VVS) matters. On August 27, Stalin replied that the Soviet side would immediately dispatch thirty-eight advisers to China, of which ten were PVO specialists, and twenty-eight were in the VVS. According to Stalin, these Soviet specialists would be sufficient to advise on PVO operations and intelligence, as well as the VVS operations in the two military districts.[37]

While the Chinese were seeking Soviet assistance, the air defense situation in the northeast became increasingly urgent. Throughout the month of

August, the U.S. Air Force intensified bombing operations deep into North Korea after having annihilated most of the small North Korean air force. Day and night, U.S. bombers pounded industrial and strategic targets around Pyongyang and other cities until almost all were destroyed. Despite Washington's claims that U.S. pilots had refrained from violating China's airspace, on August 27, American planes bombed the railroad station and strafed the airfield at Andong, a border city on the Chinese side of the Yalu where the 13th Army Group headquarters was located. The Chinese government lodged a strong protest against Washington and informed Moscow of the incident, at the same time increasing pressure for more air protection.[38]

Meanwhile, General Belov, commander of the Soviet 151st GIAD in Shenyang, sought permission to fly PVO missions to defend the 13th Army Group.[39] It is unclear whether Belov himself initiated this entreaty or if the Chinese approached him for action. Whatever the case, his request demonstrates that the 151st GIAD did not have clear orders on how it should act in terms of protecting Chinese troops. More important, Soviet military authorities in Moscow expressed serious doubts about whether the 151st should concentrate on defending Chinese troops or training Chinese pilots. In a report to N. A. Bulganin, deputy chairman of the Council of Ministers, A. M. Vasiliyevskiy, minister of defense, and his deputy, German Malandin, did not think it "advisable" for the 151st to "fly missions" in defense of the 13th Army Group. What concerned them most was that Belov's units had not yet started the retraining program for Chinese pilots. Subsequently, a directive went to Belov specifying that the 151st should first focus on retraining Chinese pilots and then begin to "organize" the air defense of the 13th Army Group in coordination with the antiaircraft artillery troops. The directive stressed, however, that Soviet pilots were not to fly missions beyond the Yalu River.[40] In other words, the Chinese troops preparing to intervene in Korea would not receive the air cover from Belov's air division that they were counting on.

Recent scholarship suggests Stalin's strategy was to "avoid committing Soviet troops to fighting the Americans," while "prod[ding] the Chinese to move toward entering the war."[41] Thus, on September 4, 1950, when the U.S. Navy shot down one of three Russian aircraft flying a reconnaissance mission over Korea Bay and killed all of the crewmen on board, Moscow muted the incident.[42] Following the UN landing at Inchon on September 15, Stalin became restless with anxiety. He instructed Kim to withdraw his troops from the Pusan front to set up a defensive line near Seoul, and ordered the Soviet Ministry of Defense to develop an emergency plan for sending two air regiments and other air defense forces to defend Pyongyang. It must have been a confusing moment for Stalin since he gave an order apparently contrary to his goal of avoiding a direct confrontation between the Soviet Union and the United States. Marshal Vasiliyevskiy, while reporting the air force's preparations for this deployment, reminded his Kremlin boss that since the pilots would be speaking Russian on the radio, the Americans would discover the Soviet involvement as soon as the two forces engaged in air combat. His warning apparently worked. When North Korea requested direct Soviet intervention after UN forces crossed the 38th Parallel, Stalin sent neither ground forces nor the air force to defend Pyongyang. The best Stalin could do at that point was to keep his word about protecting Chinese forces north of the Yalu.[43]

The presence of Belov's MiG units was of little comfort to Chinese military leaders in Andong. After only a few days in that border city, they had already gotten a feel for the threat the enemy posed from the air. After carefully studying the situation in Korea, which had reached a stalemate by late August, the 13th Army Group command grew increasingly worried that an enemy amphibious assault would be devastating to the North Koreans. In a report to the CMC dated August 31, military leaders of the 13th Army Group noted that if the situation turned against North Korea and the Chinese had to intervene, it would be greatly advantageous "for Chinese troops to fight a short war and win it quickly." To assure the success of Chinese intervention, they concluded that three things were required: (1) air support; (2) superior numbers of troops with proper artillery and tank support; and (3) ample supplies. The key measure, they stressed, was to "organize an air force with a substantial number of [aircraft] to enter the war." Recognizing that China had no air force, they recommended that Beijing make every effort to secure more Soviet air support and equipment before Chinese troops went into combat. If air support by the Soviets could not be guaranteed, they proposed that China delay sending troops into Korea.[44]

In Beijing, the military planners also sensed the danger of the possible reversal of the Korean War. The Chinese General Staff predicted that UN forces would launch a counteroffensive by sea at Inchon. To speed up China's military preparations, the CMC held several meetings in late August, deciding to move two additional army groups (the 9th and 19th) and the Fiftieth Army to the NBDA (for a total of eleven armies, including the four in the 13th Army Group), and to further strengthen the NBDA's artillery units with additional seven artillery divisions and twenty-six antiaircraft artillery regiments. Following an estimation that there would be heavy casualties during the first year of the war, the CMC ordered that hundreds of additional field hospitals be set up and it established three branches under the Logistics Department of the Northeast Military Region in order to guarantee supplies were delivered to combat troops. Nevertheless, an examination of the status of the air force, airborne troops, and tank units found that none of them were in a position to assist the NBDA's planned Korea operations. In order to assure adequate artillery supplies and to deploy four air regiments, nine tank regiments, and eighteen antiaircraft artillery regiments to Korea by the end of 1950, the conference concluded more Soviet assistance was needed.[45]

The paucity of documentation offers little enlightenment on the Chinese approach to the Soviet Union for military assistance and air support. Chinese leaders communicated with Stalin primarily through his diplomatic representative, Ambassador N. V. Roshchin, and his chief military adviser to Beijing, Lt. Gen. P. Kotov-Legon'kov. According to one Chinese Korean War researcher, there were several exchanges of views between Beijing and Moscow about China's military deployment in the northeast in mid-September. Nevertheless, this source cannot confirm whether the Chinese also tried to work out details of the air support issue with the Soviets.[46] Moreover, none of the available records indicate China asked the Soviets for military supplies. Chen Jian notes that not until early October, when Beijing came to the point of making a final decision about intervening in Korea, did the Chinese leadership appeal for Soviet assistance and confirmation that Moscow would provide air support.[47]

China's Decision after the Inchon Landing

September represented a turning point in the Korean conflict. On September 15, U.S./UN forces commanded by Gen. Douglas MacArthur launched an amphibious counterattack on Inchon. The surprise attack, and the preponderant firepower and manpower of the U.S.-led forces destroyed North Korean resistance within less than two weeks. By the end of the month, UN forces were ready to cross the 38th Parallel. However, Beijing remained inactive, even though Chinese leaders had been inclined to send troops to Korea in late August. They had many reasons to lend a helping hand to their North Korean comrades, but the leaders in Beijing were constrained in their decision-making process by the issue of Soviet assistance.

After the Inchon landing, Moscow became more actively involved in managing the Korean situation. While admonishing North Korean leaders

Chinese leaders discuss plans for intervening in Korea in October, 1950.

to make all efforts to organize their resistance, Moscow planned to send air force units, along with other equipment, to help defend Pyongyang. In the meantime, Soviet supplies overloaded Chinese railroads bound for North Korea.[48] It is clear that the Soviets made significant attempts to rescue Kim and his regime from a catastrophic defeat; however, by the end of the month, the situation in Korea appeared hopeless. Seoul fell on September 29, and it did not look like U.S./UN forces would stop at the 38th Parallel. The North Koreans appeared to be on the verge of a total collapse. On October 1, Stalin hastened a telegram to Beijing asking the Chinese to "immediately dispatch at least five to six divisions toward the 38th Parallel," so that the North Koreans would be able to organize their combat reserves under the protection of Chinese troops. The Soviet leader further suggested that the Chinese troops be designated as "volunteers" under the command of the Chinese.[49] However, Stalin failed to mention if the Soviet Union intended to provide military supplies and air support to the Chinese.

Considering the evidence presented above, an important condition for Chinese intervention was that China's troops would receive substantial military support, especially air cover, from the Soviet Union. On October 2, upon receipt of Stalin's telegram, Mao immediately drafted a reply noting that China had decided to send troops to Korea, but stressing that the Chinese troops were at a decided disadvantage: "A U.S. army consisting of two infantry divisions and one mechanized division is armed, according to Chinese intelligence, with 1,500 guns of 70-mm to 240-mm caliber, including tank cannons and antiaircraft guns, while in comparison, each Chinese army (consisting of three divisions) has only 36 such guns." Mao also expressed concern that the enemy would control the air while China's air force, which had just started its training, "will not be able to enter the war with some 300 planes until February 1951." Mao was confident, however, that U.S. technological and air superiority could be met by Chinese troops if properly equipped by the Soviet Union and supported by its air force. Thus, in the initial stage, Mao decided the strategy for Chinese troops was merely "to engage in defensive warfare" against the small enemy units in areas north of the 38th Parallel while "ascertaining the enemy's situation" and "waiting for the delivery of Soviet weapons."[50]

The opening of Russian archives in recent years reveals that Stalin received a different message from Mao via Ambassador Roshchin that day. This document indicates that the Chinese leader had made no final decision on Moscow's request, and that Beijing preferred to refrain from sending troops to Korea, at least for the time being, based on the following considerations: First, the Chinese military was poorly equipped, poorly prepared, and had "no confidence" it could defeat American troops; second, Chinese entry into the Korean conflict would lead to open war with the United States, which in turn, would drag the Soviet Union into the war; finally, Chinese intervention might result in widespread negative reaction to the newly established Communist regime after many years of civil war.[51]

A recent Chinese explanation indicates the discrepancy between the Chinese and Russian sources occurred because no consensus had been reached among top Chinese leaders in early October as to whether or not China should get involved in Korea.[52] Mao was in favor of Chinese intervention, but he was stymied by comrades who opposed or had strong reservations about sending troops to Korea. Moreover, in the absence of definite assurances from Stalin about military assistance and air support for his troops, Mao probably "sensed the need to put more pressure" on the Soviets. He therefore included all of his concerns in his response to Stalin, but the Chinese document had a different tone. This was because the chairman hoped "to reconcile his own determination to enter the war with the disagreements still existing among other CCP leaders, while at the same time keeping the door for further communication (and bargaining) with Stalin open."[53]

Mao's response disturbed Stalin, who was not quite sure whether the Chinese leader "had given his final word or was simply bargaining for better terms for China's participation in the war."[54] Avoiding a military confrontation with the United States was the Soviet leader's primary concern. He had to continue extracting an unequivocal commitment from Beijing to enter the war without at the same time mentioning what price he was willing to pay. On October 5, Stalin sent a cable to the Chinese leaders outlining all of the important reasons why sending Chinese troops to Korea served China's national interests. The foremost arguments Stalin enumerated were that the United States was not ready for a major war, and that China's inaction in Korea would prompt the Americans to occupy Taiwan for future military use, thus making it more difficult for China to regain control of Taiwan. In order to wring consent from Beijing, the Soviet leader reminded the Chinese leaders of the Mutual Assistance Pact that bound the two countries to act in concert if the United States waged a major war in Korea.[55]

Beijing Hesitantly Moves toward Intervention

While Stalin was still perplexed about China's decision regarding Korea, Mao and his colleagues seemed already to have made up their minds. Following a two-day debate at the CCP Politburo meeting in Zhongnanhai (the CCP's headquarters) on October 4 and 5, Chinese leaders agreed they would have to fight America and assist North Korea. Peng Dehuai, deputy commander of the PLA, was subsequently appointed to command the Chinese People's Volunteers.[56] Chinese policy makers had still not resolved one key question: Whether the Soviet Union would provide military assistance and air support for Chinese troops fighting in Korea. On October 7, Mao wired his reply to Moscow, declaring that he totally shared Stalin's views on the Korean situation outlined in his previous telegram, and that he would, in time, "send nine, not six, divisions," to assist North Korea. He asked Stalin to receive Chinese representatives to work out the details of Soviet military assistance. Again, Mao adopted a very Chinese approach to indirectly remind Stalin that his final decision was dependent upon Soviet assistance. Stalin was dissatisfied with such a response, but he understood the Chinese leader had taken a step closer toward intervention. Stalin therefore lost no time informing the beleaguered North Korean leader of this development and urged him to be patient while he further negotiated with the Chinese.[57]

Several Chinese sources state that in early October Stalin agreed to provide China with air force support and promised to equip a hundred Chinese divisions with Soviet weapons and other war materials should China send troops to Korea.[58] Few of these sources, however, explain just when this agreement was arranged. Nor do they divulge details of such an agreement. According to Shi Zhe, who served as an interpreter between Chinese leaders and Stalin some forty years ago, Stalin later acknowledged to Zhou that providing limited air support for Chinese troops was his tentative idea should China intervene.[59] Indeed, there probably had been no concrete agreement between the two sides on such matters, but rather an assumption by Chinese leadership that the Soviet Union would provide air support for Chinese ground troops.[60] Mao, like many Chinese communists, seems to have viewed the Soviet Union as the big brother of the socialist camp and thus obligated to help other Communist nations. With the Soviet air force and China's ground troops, they were confident that the newly made Sino-Soviet alliance would be able to check American aggression in Asia.[61] Acting on this assumption, Chinese leaders further geared themselves for war.[62]

On the morning of October 8, Peng flew to the Northeast Military Region to take charge of the CPV's operations. A few hours later, Zhou and Lin Biao boarded a Soviet charter plane to Moscow to negotiate with the Soviet leadership about military assistance and air support. The next day, Peng summoned the CPV's army commanders to a conference in Shenyang. The purpose of the conference was to convey the Politburo's decision to enter the war and further familiarize himself with the status of the troops. Peng began with a speech emphasizing the significance of China's Korean intervention, and then ordered his troops to complete preparations for battle within ten days. Then, he learned that his troops had only thirty-six antiaircraft artillery pieces (Japanese-made 76-mm guns). Moreover, no orders had been issued for coordination between ground and air forces. His army commanders again expressed strong concern about whether their troops could count on air protection, and wondered how the air force would coordinate with the ground forces.[63] Unable to answer their questions, Peng hastily sent a cable to Mao in the middle of the session, inquiring: "How many bombers and fighters can the CMC send to Korea after our troops are engaged in operations there? When will [the air force] be dispatched and who will be in charge?"[64]

Peng Dehuai upon his appointment as CPV commander on October 5, 1950.

Evidently influenced by his subordinates' anxieties about air support, Peng dispatched another cable to Mao the next day explaining how his troops feared the enemy's tanks and air force, in particular. "Without air cover and antiaircraft weapons," Peng again stressed, "artillery units will be in even greater danger under such operating conditions." He urged Mao to send one or two antiaircraft artillery regiments from other military districts to the Northeast Military Region as soon as possible. Also, because no antiaircraft weapons protected the bridges at Andong and Ji'an, Peng requested authority to amass all of his troops (four armies and three artillery divisions) south of the Yalu instead of sending in only two armies and two artillery divisions as originally planned.[65]

The situation was complicated for Mao. He undoubtedly shared such worries, but he could do little to satisfy Peng's queries. His air force had just started training and was not yet operational. He had only a dozen more antiaircraft artillery regiments and those were stretched thin to defend key cities throughout China.[66] What Mao could best hope for was a definite Soviet commitment to provide assistance, but he remained unsure as to whether or not it would be coming. In a cable to Peng on October 11, Mao started to give his approval to Peng's request for an alternate deployment plan and informed him that he had ordered the immediate transfer of one antiaircraft artillery regiment from eastern China to the Northeast Military Region. He concluded with the observation that "the air force cannot set off for the time being."[67] Mao, as well as Peng and others in Andong, understood that Chinese troops would have to rely on the Soviets for air support. However, the chairman had yet to hear anything from Zhou regarding his negotiations with Soviet leaders on this matter.[68]

Zhou's Negotiations with Stalin

Zhou and his party arrived in Moscow on October 10 and, accompanied by Bulganin, flew to southern Russia to meet Stalin at his Black Sea villa.[69] In the afternoon, Zhou and Stalin, joined by other Soviet leaders, held a meeting to discuss the Korean situation. Unfortunately, neither China nor Russia has hitherto released documents related to this conference. Scholarship is based primarily on personal recollections, which suggest Stalin shied away from his promise.[70] To understand whether or not Stalin reneged on his promise, it is necessary to review these sources.

Shi Zhe, Zhou's interpreter, remembered that following a Chinese non-intervention argument, Stalin commented that the Soviets "have considered how to help [our] Korean comrade," that is, China "can send a certain number of troops" to Korea, while the Soviet Union supplies weapons and equipment, as well as "a certain number of aircraft to offer cover" for Chinese operations there. Stalin made it clear, however, that Soviet pilots "can only be used in rear and frontline positions but not behind the enemy's line," so that they would not be "shot down and captured by the enemy." He then enumerated details about the types and quantities of weapons and equipment the Soviet Union could supply the Chinese if they entered the war. Although both sides were unable to agree on whether, or under what conditions, China would enter the war, Shi Zhe noted that after the meeting Zhou and Stalin sent a joint telegram to Mao about their talks.[71]

Kang Yimin, Zhou's confidential secretary, offered a different version of the story. According to his recollection, after declaring China's decision to send troops to assist the North Koreans, Zhou asked Stalin to "provide

China with military support and send air forces to the Northeast and such coastal cities as Beijing, Tianjin, and Shanghai." Stalin agreed. Shortly after Zhou flew back to Moscow, however, Kang said Vyacheslav M. Molotov informed the Chinese that the Soviets had changed their mind and would not provide the Chinese with military equipment. Zhou argued angrily with Molotov, and then sent a telegram to Mao noting that the Soviet leader had reneged.[72]

The discrepancy between these accounts by Zhou's aides resulted largely because they were trying to recollect an event forty years later. Their stories not only lack consistency, but they may also be inaccurate. A recent article by Alexander Mansourov challenges the Chinese accounts, arguing that Stalin never welched on his promise to Mao to provide Chinese troops in Korea with Soviet air cover. Instead, Mansourov speculates it was Zhou who "invented a 'respectable' excuse" to prevent China from entering the Korean War, thus, shifting the entire burden of saving Communist Korea to Stalin's shoulders. One may question whether Zhou was a Machiavellian Chinese statesman or if he dared risk his own career by coming between the two Communist giants, putting them "at each other's throat," despite his disagreement with Mao on the issue of whether China should intervene in Korea. However, Mansourov's account, based on an interview with Stalin's interpreter, Nikolay T. Fedorenko, who attended the talks between Stalin and Zhou, is not supported by recently declassified Russian archival documents.[73] It is therefore necessary to turn to other Chinese sources for more information on Chinese allegations about Stalin's reneging.

Regrettably, Chinese scholars studying the Korean conflict have failed to locate the telegram Shi Zhe claimed was signed jointly by Zhou and Stalin.[74] Zhang Xi, a PLA military historian, used his special access to the CCP history and military archives to offer a more likely version of what the Soviet leaders promised to Zhou during their October talks.[75] Based on Mao's telegram of October 13, responding to the one Zhou and Stalin jointly sent him two days before, Zhang asserts that after explaining China's difficulties in assisting the North Koreans and fighting against the Americans, the Chinese premier asked Moscow to supply weapons and equipment for at least forty CPV divisions, and Soviet air support for their ground operations in Korea. Stalin responded, "the Soviet Union will fully satisfy China's need for the supply of aircraft, artillery, tanks, and other military equipment," and agreed to outfit twenty Chinese divisions immediately. Stalin also consented to commit air force units as Soviet volunteers to support CPV operations in Korea, but he made it clear that they "will need two to two and one-half months to get ready for action."[76] He then directed Molotov and Bulganin to take charge of the details involving Soviet military support to the Chinese.[77]

The evidence presented in this document indicates Stalin would keep his promise to commit his air force to support the Chinese in Korea, but what surprised Mao was the timing of its involvement. Since July, Stalin had pushed Beijing to prepare to intervene in Korea with the promise of Soviet air support. Then, when Chinese leaders finally agreed to send ground troops to Korea, they became aware that the Soviet air support commitment fell short of what had been promised. As a result, Beijing was plagued by oscillation, reservations, and doubts. Should China send troops to Korea without Soviet air protection? Could the poorly equipped Chinese troops hold back an enemy supported by planes, tanks, and artillery? How would the Chinese counter the enemy if the war expanded across the Yalu into their own territory? On the evening of October 12, Mao ordered his troops to halt their movements, and summoned the Politburo to an emergency meeting to reevaluate the decision to send Chinese troops into Korea.[78]

Convinced that China's physical security was threatened when U.S./ UN forces crossed the 38th Parallel and began marching toward the Yalu River, Mao had already made up his mind in favor of intervention and subsequently yielded to no one at the Politburo meeting on October 13. Nevertheless, he still felt it necessary to continue bargaining with the Soviets. While notifying the Soviet leadership of the CCP Politburo's resolution via Zhou that evening, Mao once again registered Chinese uncertainties about the Soviet air support promise, stating: "If the Soviet Union could send volunteer pilots to support our military operations in Korea in two or two and one-half months, as well as dispatch an air force to Beijing, Tianjin, Shenyang, Shanghai, Nanjing, and Qingdao, we will not fear the [American] air attack. We will, however, endure losses if the American air attack occurred during the coming two to two and one-half months."[79] The chairman further instructed Zhou to ask Stalin whether the Soviet air force could "continue to send bombers to Korea to support the operations of the Chinese troops after the dispatch of the sixteen jet plane regiments," and whether it could "send more air units to station in big cities in China's coastal area besides sending volunteer pilots to join operations in Korea."[80] In this telegram, Mao apparently accepted Moscow's decision to postpone committing Soviet air force units to the war, but he also made clear the kind of Soviet air support Beijing expected: "to support our military operations in Korea" meant direct Soviet air support for Chinese ground operations.

No records are available of Zhou's negotiation of these requests with the Soviet leaders. It is alleged that after receiving Mao's October 13 telegram, and Stalin's October 14 telegram, Zhou forwarded Beijing's decision and questions to Stalin through Molotov.[81] In a conversation with Kim Il Sung in 1970, Zhou recalled that Molotov initially agreed to send the Soviet air force to support Chinese troops, but then, "Stalin telephoned us saying that their air forces could not go beyond the Yalu River."[82] None of the documentary evidence made available thus far confirms Zhou's recollections. Nevertheless, based on Mao's October 13 telegram to Zhou, and Zhou's 1970 statements to Kim, Chinese scholars believe Zhou later received a disappointing reply from Stalin via Molotov that the Soviet air force could not support Chinese ground operations within the requested time frame, and hence concluded the Soviet leader had reneged.[83]

Recent revelations from the Soviet archives demonstrate Stalin did not have "any last-minute change in heart" about what kind of air support he was willing to grant to the PRC. Rather, he never intended to offer the support the Chinese expected. On October 14, Stalin, through the Council of Ministers, ordered Vasiliyevskiy to deploy four MiG-9 IADs (a total of 208 jet fighters) along with three Il-10 attack regiments of thirty planes each to China. The MiG units were scheduled to leave for China within two weeks. Perhaps in response to China's request for bombers to support ground operations in Korea, on October 20, while arranging the transfer of the second echelon of air units to China, the Soviet leadership included a Tu-2 bomber division along with eight MiG regiments. These units would arrive in China in a month. However, the Soviet leadership sternly decreed that Soviet pilots were "strictly forbidden" to fly at the front, and were only "to cover [Chinese] troops and targets near the Chinese-Korean border." According to these orders, their primary mission would be to train Chinese pilots and provide air defense for China's industrial cities. Upon completion of the training mission, they would transfer all their planes and equipment to the Chinese and return to the Soviet Union.[84] All along, the Soviet leader reiterated his willingness to provide the CPV with air cover if Beijing sent troops to Korea. However, these documents are evidence that Stalin did not intend to deliver on his earlier promise, at least in October.

This shows Stalin's cleverness. The Soviet leader had been pledging Soviet air force support for Chinese troops while never defining exactly what *kind* of air support he would provide. Once he secured Beijing's decision to send troops to Korea, he postponed the date when the Soviet air force would enter the war and limited the scope of the air support to China proper.

Stalin thus cannot be said to have reneged since he never withdrew his promise. This was unfortunate for the Chinese leaders, who retained their high hopes for Soviet air support at least until October 13, and only on the eve of intervention realized that the support they thought had been promised would not be forthcoming. They thus faced an extremely difficult decision.

The Final Decision

Peng was reportedly agitated when he learned from Mao's cable of October 11 that there would not be an air umbrella for his troops. A few days earlier, Mao had assured him the Soviet Union had committed to sending its air force to support the Chinese fight against the Americans. However, at the critical moment when he and his troops were ready to cross the river into Korea, Peng became aware that "the Soviet air support" was just "wishful thinking" and the Beijing leadership, particularly Mao, was indiscreet to have decided to enter the war before securing a guarantee of Soviet assistance. At the CCP Politburo meeting on October 13, Peng wrathfully threatened to resign as CPV commander. Only after Mao explained to him that the Soviet Union would supply the Chinese troops with arms and munitions as well as defend China's cities from air attack did Peng agree to continue.[85]

Although Mao's determination to go to war prevailed at the meeting, the lack of air support compelled the Chinese leaders to restrict CPV operational goals during the initial stage of their intervention. According to Mao's telegram to Zhou on October 14, the CPV would establish two to three defensive lines in the areas north of Pyongyang and Wonsan, so that "the American and puppet forces will hesitate and cease advancing." In this way, Mao noted, the Chinese troops would not "have to engage in fighting but gain time to become well equipped and trained, and in the meantime wait for the arrival of the Soviet air force" before waging attacks.[86] Despite whatever defensive strategy would be taken, Peng still believed that much depended on whether or not there would be air support for his troops. He promoted the idea that Beijing must get China's own air force into the war as quickly as possible. That urging from Peng subsequently motivated the dispatch of China's air units into action.[87]

Lack of air cover had been a widespread concern among troops preparing to begin operations in Korea. Although Peng was all for the decision to intervene, as the CPV's commander in chief, he still needed to convince his troops of the necessity for sending them to Korea even without air support. On October 16, he chaired a conference attended by CPV division commanders at Andong to explain the reasons behind the decision to enter the Korean War. Peng emphasized that if China did not "dispatch troops to actively support the Korean revolutionary government and people, the reactionaries at home and abroad will be swollen with arrogance and the pro-American people will be more active." Also, Peng warned, the occupation of the Korean Peninsula by the Americans would "present a direct threat to our country, causing an unfavorable situation for our national defense and frontier defense." Given the real threat to China's security, Peng concluded, "to support Korea is also to consolidate our own national defense." Understanding his subordinates' concern about the lack of air cover, Peng stressed that, although the U.S. dominated the air, the air force could not "decide the outcome of the war," nor was it "as fearsome as people think." To keep the commanders' hopes for air cover alive, Peng also noted, "We will have eight air regiments by next month and sixteen air regiments by the month after that."[88] Because the PRC had no operational air force units at the time, what Peng referred to could only mean the Soviet air force. It is unclear to what extent Peng still believed Soviet air support would come in the next two months. Clearly, he had not given up hope.

Peng's mobilization speech did not achieve the desired results, however, and the news that there would be no Soviet air support cast a pall over the minds of senior officers. According to the memoirs of Jiang Yonghui, deputy commander of the Thirty-eighth Army, as early as mid-July they received the promise from the Northeast Military Region headquarters that their operations in Korea would be supported by the air force.[89] Since then, Chinese troops had been making preparations with the understanding they would have Soviet air support. Whenever soldiers inquired about air cover, officers always responded that thanks to the brotherly Soviet Union they would receive "as many cannons and planes as they wanted."[90] The temporary withdrawal of Soviet air support thus created tremendous pressures for commanding officers in the 13th Army Group.

An Army Group Party Committee meeting was held to discuss this new development. The participants' consensus was that if the Soviets were not ready for action, they should be urged to speed up their preparation, and the Chinese should postpone their entry into the war.[91] Deng Hua and other senior commanders in the 13th Army Group sent a telegram to Peng and Gao Gang, commander of the Northeast Military Region, in Shenyang on October 17, expressing serious reservations. Realizing that they would "have

very few antiaircraft artillery pieces and no air support," Deng and his colleagues reported, "the troops are in an extremely anxious state of mind,"
and the opinion of the majority was that China should postpone intervening until the end of the winter, "when there will be a guarantee for new
equipment, particularly the air force support."[92] There were very good reasons for the 13th Army Group commanders to make such a suggestion. Many
of them had had the bitter experience of fighting in the cold northeast during the civil war. They knew it would be difficult to construct defensive
works in the much more frigid conditions of North Korea. If the enemy
started an all-out offensive with the support of planes, tanks, and artillery, it
would be almost impossible to prepare an adequate defense, and as a result,
they would likely suffer heavy casualties.[93]

Peng understood their worries about the consequences of no Soviet air
support in Korea and reported these misgivings immediately to Mao. In
Mao's mind, the question of whether or not there would be Soviet air support was no longer a factor influencing his determination to send Chinese
troops to Korea. The chairman could not tolerate the presence of U.S. forces
on the banks of the Yalu River inasmuch as they posed a serious threat to
northeast China. If Chinese troops failed to hold out against the enemy and
were pushed back, Mao believed China could still launch a counterattack.
"Otherwise," he said, it would be hard for China "to find other excuses to
fight against the U.S. even though we feel it necessary in the future."[94] On
October 18, Mao issued the final order to his field commanders, and the 13th
Army Group began crossing the Yalu River according to the original plan.[95]

Chinese ground troops moved secretly into Korea on October 19. Without air support, they planned to entrench north of Pyongyang and Wonsan
and not attack U.S./UN troops until they had been equipped with Soviet
arms, received adequate training, and were assured of air support.[96] With
the fall of Pyongyang on the same day they crossed the Yalu, however, Chinese leaders realized the CPV would be forced to engage the enemy earlier
than planned. American airpower became an overwhelming concern. On
October 23, Mao cabled Peng inquiring about the extent to which enemy
planes threatened Chinese personnel and military action. Mao pointed out
that if the threat were serious, Chinese troops would be in an extremely
difficult situation for six months to a year, because of the shortage of air
cover.[97]

Despite Chinese leaders' concerns about U.S. air superiority, Chinese
ground operations progressed smoothly. Following an unexpected encounter with South Korean troops in the Unsan area on October 25, the CPV

launched its first-phase offensive campaign in Korea. In less than two weeks, the CPV impelled South Korean troops back from the Yalu to the Chongchon River, allegedly inflicting fifteen thousand casualties on the enemy in the process. Despite this initial victory, CPV leaders remained sober-minded. In view of General MacArthur's aggressiveness and the CPV's shortage of air cover and firepower, they adopted a strategy of luring UN forces deep into an area so their poorly equipped troops could slam into the enemy with overwhelming manpower. On November 16, Peng ordered all CPV troops to withdraw northward. He also released about a hundred prisoners of war (POWs) in hopes of creating the false impression that the Chinese could no longer withstand the superior U.S./UN forces.

His deception tactic seemed to work. The UN command dismissed all the warning signs of possible Chinese assaults and pushed its troops northward with the promise that the war would be over within a few weeks. On the evening of November 25, a day after General MacArthur ordered the "home by Christmas" offensive by the UN forces, Chinese troops launched a powerful counteroffensive. Massive "human wave" attacks soon turned the tables on the U.S./UN forces, which fled southward in a desperate retreat. By the end of the year, CPV and NKPA troops had recovered much of the lost territory in the north, and Seoul again fell to the Communists on January 4, 1951. Soviet leaders, apparently encouraged by these military successes, started to commit air support, but on a limited scale.

CHAPTER 4

From Defending China to Intervention in Korea

O n November 1, 1950, UN pilots and their planes faced a surprise attack by swept-wing jet aircraft over the Yalu River. In contrast to official American accounts, Russian pilots, not Chinese, flew them.[1] This encounter opened a new chapter in the annals of air warfare in Korea. Since the beginning of the Korean conflict, U.S./UN forces had dominated the sky. However, the appearance of Soviet-built MiG-15s, which made every other aircraft in Korea obsolescent with their speed and performance, presented a potential threat to UN air superiority. More importantly, they signified the Soviet air force's official entry into the conflict. How could Stalin refuse to provide Chinese troops with air cover a few days earlier, then suddenly allow Soviet pilots to engage the Americans over Korea? Recent revelations from Russian archives identify Soviet high-level planning for their air intervention and the nature of Soviet involvement in Korea. The contribution of the Soviet air force to the war effort on the Communist side was significant, but always appeared too little and too late. Fearing a direct confrontation with the United States, the Soviet leader limited the air force's involvement, especially in comparison to the role Chinese ground forces played. However, without Soviet assistance, it was impossible for China to fight an almost independent war in Korea. Moscow's contributions to the development of the Chinese air force and the latter's role in the Korean conflict were crucial. The story of Soviet pilots engaging Americans over the Yalu began in February, 1950, several months before the crisis erupted on the Korean Peninsula, when the former went to China to help with the air defense against the Nationalist air invasion.

Seeking Soviet Assistance in China's Air Defense

In early 1950, the GMD ruled the skies over China, and its air force put many Chinese cities under siege. For example, between October, 1949, and February, 1950, Shanghai sustained twenty-six air raids. The most serious attack was on February 6, when fourteen B-24 and B-25 aircraft bombed the city, inflicting heavy damage on the power plant and shipyard and killing more than fourteen hundred people. What was more serious was the psychological impact on Shanghai residents, who felt insecure living and working under Communist rule. Chen Yi, Shanghai's mayor, had to acknowledge that the city was only partly governed by the Communists if they could not control its skies.[2] The local party authorities repeatedly appealed to the central government for help in stopping GMD air bombardment.[3] Without an air force, the CMC could only transfer two antiaircraft artillery regiments from Beijing to Shanghai, a force that was inadequate to defend the city. On February 8 and 9, Nie Rongzhen, acting PLA chief of staff, sent two cables to Mao, who was visiting Moscow, suggesting an immediate negotiation for Soviet assistance with the air defense of Shanghai and other coastal cities. He told Mao that Shanghai was in panic and the local government was preparing to evacuate factories. Sharing the concern of his people, Mao made a formal request to Soviet leaders asking them to dispatch air units to defend China.[4]

There are only a handful of sources showing how Mao negotiated with Soviet leaders on the issue of their direct involvement in defending China. As early as July, 1949, the Chinese leader had asked Stalin to provide military assistance for the invasion of Taiwan. Despite the bold suggestions Stalin made during his earlier conversation with Liu Shaoqi about sending forty fighters to help the PLA liberate China's western regions, Stalin rejected the idea of involving Soviet forces in the CCP's Taiwan campaign. Fearing direct confrontation with the U.S. Navy and Air Force, he told the Chinese that the Soviet Union had suffered countless losses in World War II, and the Russian people would not support a decision that would risk the country becoming involved in another war. Liu had to drop his request at the time.[5] When Mao personally raised the same issue during his conversations with Stalin in December, 1949, the Soviet leader again appeared equivocal, although he did not rule out Soviet assistance.[6] In February, 1950, relations between China and the Soviet Union were redefined by a new alliance treaty that included a Soviet military commitment to defending China. Furthermore, the new Chinese solicitation made no direct reference to Taiwan. After a careful study by Stalin and the Soviet high command, the Soviet leader accepted China's entreaty. Realizing his people at home were anxiously awaiting the Soviet response and only a few hours before his departure from Moscow on February 17, 1950, Mao cabled Liu Shaoqi about the decision and asked him to pass along the good news to Shanghai. He also asked his comrades at home to keep it a secret so that the Soviet air force could surprise the Nationalists with a fatal blow.[7]

On the evening of February 13, 1950, the Ministry of Defense sent orders to the Moscow Military District and the Maritime Military District to prepare troops for China. The forces mobilized included the 106th Fighter Aviation Division (IAD), 52d Antiaircraft Artillery Division, 1st Guards Searchlight Regiment, 64th Radar Battalion, and other small units. Lieutenant General Pavel F. Batitskiy was appointed to command the newly formed air defense corps in China, with Lt. Gen. Sidor V. Slyusarev as his deputy, and Col. B. Vysotskiy as his chief of staff.[8] Their mission was to protect Shanghai from the enemy's air bombardment and prevent the enemy's navy from blockading the mouth of the Yangzi River. It is interesting to note that during the negotiations, Mao specifically requested that MiG-15s, Russia's best fighters at the time, be deployed to China. The Soviets, apparently equally eager to see how their newly developed jet interceptors would perform under combat conditions, agreed to include a MiG-15 fighter unit in the China mission. However, to prevent an incident that might involve Soviet forces in China's Taiwan campaign, the Soviets restricted their pilots from flying beyond the coastline and attacking Nationalist air bases.[9]

Since pilots in the 106th Fighter Aviation Division had not yet flown MiG-15s, the Moscow Military District Air Force decided to reorganize it by transferring its own three regiments [147th Guards and 415th and 726th Fighter Aviation Regiments (IAP)] to a newly formed division (133d IAD).[10] Meanwhile, Lt. Gen. Vasiliy I. Stalin, commander of the Moscow Military

District Air Force, assigned the 29th Guards Fighter Aviation Regiment (GIAP) from the 324th IAD, together with the 351st IAP and 829th Mixed Aviation Regiment from the Maritime Military District at Dalian (Port Arthur), to form the bulk of the 106th IAD.[11] The Soviet "volunteers" (including forty-four MiG-15 pilots) gathered in Moscow for three days to study their orders and exchange their clothes for Chinese-type uniforms. Their identifications and party documents were also removed. They left their aircraft and equipment behind because they were to receive forty new MiG-15s from Novosibirsk, and set off for the Far East by train on February 15.[12] Almost simultaneously, the 351st IAP (forty-one pilots with forty La-11s and one La-9UT) and the 829th Mixed Aviation Regiment (ninety-two aircrews with twenty-six Il-10s, and ten Tu-2s) completed reorganization at their respective bases on the Liaodong Peninsula. The special military train carried the 29th Guards across the Chinese border on the same day Mao's private train returned to China. It has been alleged that Mao was dissatisfied with his first trip to Moscow, but he should have been pleased with his success in bringing back to China Soviet assurances of friendship and support, particularly a Soviet air umbrella that China desperately needed.

Soviet Air Operations over Shanghai

Moscow's involvement in the air defense of Shanghai in early 1950, the first real action by the Soviet air force since the end of World War II, has not been thoroughly analyzed in a broader historical context. Although operations over Shanghai constituted a petty war, they marked the beginning of air combat in the jet age. The West paid little attention to the MiG-15's appearance over Shanghai, and was surprised to encounter it a few months later in Korea. Shanghai provided the Soviets a laboratory in which to test their aircraft and try out air tactics under actual combat conditions. Moreover, it began the trend of using Soviet pilots in combat beyond the borders of the USSR as part of Moscow's foreign policy commitments in the forty-year Cold War confrontation between East and West, although it had been a tradition of the Soviet Union before World War II.[13]

The Soviet air defense of Shanghai began with a preparation phase from late February through March, during which the Shanghai government mobilized more than 223,000 people to repair and construct four airfields and other facilities for the Soviet air units. Despite the Nationalist air bombardment, by the end of March, all four airfields were ready for use. On March 10,

Lieutenant General Batitskiy flew to Nanjing, then, accompanied by Su Yu, deputy commander of the Third Field Army, traveled to Shanghai by train.[14] The next day, a joint meeting was convened. Batitskiy conveyed to Chen Yi, commander of the Third Field Army and mayor of Shanghai, Stalin's order that subordinated the Soviet troops to his command for assisting with the air defense of the city and training Chinese air defense forces.[15] He also urged the Chinese to speed up the transshipment of equipment and supplies for his forces so they could assume air defense duties in Shanghai by the end of the month.[16] Several days earlier, the 351st IAP under Lt. Col. V. Makarov had already flown to its staging base in Xuzhou, where their La-11s provided an air umbrella while the crews of Col. A. V. Pashkevich's 29th GIAP assembled their MiGs. On March 13 and 14, the Soviets recorded their first kill when La-11 pilots V. D. Sidorov and P. D. Dushin claimed to have shot down a Nationalist B-25 Mitchell over Xuzhou. A Taiwan source acknowledged the loss of only an F-10 on the fourteenth.[17] Following a Nationalist attack on Longhua Airfield on March 14, Batitskiy transferred a group of La-11s from Xuzhou to Shanghai. Suffering from poor ground and air coordination, as well as a run of bad weather, the Russian propeller pilots failed to have a major impact until the arrival of their MiG-15 unit in Shanghai.

Beginning in April, Soviet air operations entered a new stage. The Nationalist air force deployed ten B-25 Mitchells and thirty P-51 Mustangs on Zhoushan and Daishan Islands to wage an air war against Shanghai and its surrounding area. The 29th GIAP joined the 351st IAP, and began to assume full responsibility for defending Shanghai. In response to a projected GMD attack involving all the aircraft from the islands, the Soviet generals decided to employ the main force of MiG-15s to intercept the enemy bombers while engaging the enemy fighters with La-11s. In case the GMD troops blockaded the Shanghai coast and launched an amphibious assault on the city, the Soviets would counterattack enemy naval vessels and landing craft with Tu-2 bombers and Il-10 attack aircraft. The presence of the Soviet MiG-15s, coupled with the Nationalist pilots' inexperience, deterred the enemy from carrying out any substantial attacks on Shanghai. The MiG-15s finally made their combat debut on the afternoon of April 28, claiming a P-38 Lightning, and Maj. Yu. Ya. Kelenichkov became the first MiG-15 pilot to shoot down an enemy aircraft in combat.[18] Afterward, the GMD minimized its daytime intrusions, but increased the number of evening attacks, resulting in the first MiG-15 night kills on May 11. Captain I. I. Shinarenko and his wingman successfully intercepted a B-24 Liberator with the assistance of searchlight units in the area. Within less than a week, the GMD withdrew all of its troops from the two neighboring islands, and its air threat to Shanghai diminished. By the end of June, the Soviet air force units had completed their combat mission over Shanghai.[19]

Although most of the Soviet pilots were anxious to return home, on June 20, 1950, the 106th IAD was ordered to conduct a training program for the PLAAF's 4th Mixed Aviation Brigade. Stalin believed it was in the best interests of the Soviet Union to help the Chinese assume the burden of opposing the United States in East Asia. The creation of a modern Chinese air force in a very short time thus became a priority mission. Since late 1949, Soviet advisers had been actively involved in training Chinese pilots. The presence of the Soviet air force units set a precedent for transferring the technology of modern warfare to the Chinese Communist forces on a large scale, but in a short period.

From mid-July to mid-October, Batitskiy's units embarked on training their Chinese counterparts. Batitskiy and his pilots were confronted with such problems as the language barrier and the lack of training equipment. There was an urgent need to teach the Chinese all they needed to know about employing an air force and enabling them to control the advanced war machines that the Soviet Union had supplied. According to Soviet standards, it took five to six months to upgrade an air force unit from propeller-driven aircraft to jets. However, Batitskiy and his units completed the training program in three months. By the time the Soviet units left Shanghai in October, the Chinese air defense troops were able to defend the sky over Shanghai themselves with the Soviet equipment.[20]

During their Shanghai tour, Soviet pilots flew 238 combat sorties (including fifty sorties by MiG-15s) and claimed eight GMD aircraft between March and October.[21] Although there were some snafus and mistakes, the Russian airmen looked effective in the operation against the Chinese Nationalists. They gained valuable combat experience with jet aircraft, and tested their aircraft and equipment under combat conditions.[22] Before Shanghai, Soviet pilots generally believed that jet fighters could only make one attack—from head on—and that the speed of the MiG would not allow the pilots to continue to engage their opponents. The experience at Shanghai taught them that if proper formations and tactics were used, the MiG-15s could conduct consecutive attacks on enemy aircraft without depending on ground control intercept (GCI) operators for coordination. In reality, the Shanghai operations were limited in terms of time and geographical extent, and the Soviet air force was faced with a weak foe incapable of conducting effective or intensive offensive operations. The pilots of the 29th GIAP came from the "Parade" Aviation Division, the first unit to fly MiG-15s, and took part in air parades over Red Square and at the Tushino air show.[23] They were alleged to have better training and more flying time. However, when they flew combat missions over the Yalu River during late 1950 and early 1951, they exposed their weaknesses in terms of strength, technical equipment, and standard of training. Nonetheless, they were victors during their operations over Shanghai. Unexpectedly, their superiors in Moscow were mulling over a journey home through Korea. There, the Soviet airmen would confront a much more powerful foe: the U.S. Air Force. Their experience in Shanghai was only the prelude to a major contest in the Cold War.[24]

Soviet Air Insurance, November and December, 1950

When Shanghai appeared safe from the Nationalist air menace, Beijing's focus shifted to the northeast after Chinese ground forces began infiltrating into North Korea in late October. Chinese leaders worried the United States might expand the war through air bombardment against China's cities and industrial centers. Rumors spread about possible U.S. attacks and generated increasing fear in the cities. However, mass evacuations would create chaos and shake public confidence in the newly established Communist rule. At the national air defense meeting chaired by Zhou Enlai on October 31, leaders decided to keep a low profile on the entire issue and order no immediate evacuations of industry or people from cities, but instead made preparations for protecting themselves during air raids and treating bombing victims.[25] Indeed, the best defense against U.S. air attacks was the Soviet air force troops Moscow was sending to China.

Soviet leaders apparently had similar concerns, and began to devote their time and resources to constructing air defense systems in China immediately following their promise to Chinese leaders. The first order, calling for the transfer of four MiG-9 fighter divisions (a total of 248 MiG-9s) to China in ten days, was issued on October 14. A week later, another four MiG-9 divisions were ordered to China as the second echelon of the Soviet deployment. These air divisions were reorganized with two regiments each and only thirty-two planes per regiment.[26] Due to a shortage of MiG-9 units, the Ministry of Defense recommended including two divisions of the much more advanced MiG-15, without aircrews. These aircraft could be used to reequip the pilots of Belov's division, which was scheduled to turn over its machines to the PLAAF by the time the aircraft arrived in China. In addition to these jet fighters, the Soviets also included an La-9 fighter division, an Il-10 attack aircraft division, a Tu-2 bomber division, and ten tank regiments in the deployment to China. Measures again were taken to conceal the transfer of the Soviet air force units to China. According to Jon Halliday, the "double whammy of *simultaneous* entry by hundreds of thousands of Chinese Communist ground troops," and the Soviet air force "would have been too much for the U.S. administration to take."[27] Strict instructions were issued not only to remove Soviet markings from aircraft and equipment, but also to mandate that all personnel wear Chinese uniforms.[28]

Beginning in mid-November 1950, Soviet air defense forces swarmed into China, destined for Chinese cities and industrial centers. Besides the air divisions, eleven antiaircraft artillery regiments (1,186 AAA pieces and 648 AA machine guns) and several searchlight and radar battalions were also rushed to China. By the end of December, a Russian air umbrella was in place. Beijing, for example, was defended by two MiG-9 regiments, five antiaircraft artillery regiments (117 guns), and a searchlight regiment, while Shanghai was covered by two MiG-9 regiments and two antiaircraft artillery regiments along with several searchlight batteries. As a staging area for Chinese operations in Korea, northeast China was extremely vulnerable to UN air attacks. The bulk of the Soviet air defense troops in the region were concentrated in an area radiating out from Shenyang to Andong, and included four MiG-9 regiments and four MiG-15 regiments, as well as a number of antiaircraft artillery regiments.[29] For an effective air defense, Moscow's military authority integrated Soviet and Chinese command and control into a single system covering the area from Beijing to Harbin and then along the Korean border and the seacoast down to Shanghai.[30] This integration included the Soviet 39th Group Army, the 83d and 55th Fighter Aviation Corps (IAK; consisting of three fighter divisions, a reconnaissance group, and a radar regiment), and the Red Navy Pacific Fleet units (including a torpedo-bomber division) garrisoned in the Lüshun-Dalian area.[31]

Between November and December, 1950, eleven Soviet air divisions arrived in China, including six MiG-9 divisions, two MiG-15 divisions, an La-9 division, an Il-10 attack division, and a Tu-2 bomber division (see Appendix B).[32] All the Soviet air force units were then grouped under the 67th Aviation Corps, commanded by Col. Gen. Stepan A. Krasovskiy, commander of Soviet air force units in the Far East.[33] Their main responsibility was to help China with air defense, but they were also charged with training Chinese air and ground crews. The deterioration of the situation in Korea left the Soviets with the unpalatable options of either building up Chinese air capabilities or preparing their own intervention, and they chose the first alternative. All of the orders associated with this deployment underscored the primary mission of quickly training Chinese crews and then handing their aircraft and equipment over to the Chinese. Following the example of Batitskiy's units, the large-scale transference of Soviet airpower to the PLA was undertaken in late 1950 and early 1951. All Soviet units turned their aircraft and equipment over to the PLAAF at the end of their mission. In the short span of six months, the PLAAF would expand dramatically to sixteen air divisions, and appear to be almost ready for action in Korea.[34]

The establishment of the PLAAF in this brief period was no doubt fully ascribable to Soviet assistance. However, some problems concerning the nature of Soviet aid to China at the time deserve further analysis. Supplying China with such a large number of MiG-9s had raised Chinese suspicions about the Soviets' sincerity. The MiG-9, powered by two engines copied from the Germans, was the first jet fighter to enter service in the Soviet air force in 1946, and had a very short range (eight hundred kilometers with a full payload), and poor maneuverability. With its own air force being upgraded with the advanced MiG-15bis, the Soviet Union appeared to seize the opportunity to dump its retired MiG-9s on China.[35] Although two MiG-15 divisions were also transferred to China at the same time, their deployment was made because no additional MiG-9 units were available.[36] When Chinese leaders later began planning to send their air force troops to Korea, they were disturbed to discover the PLAAF had more MiG-9s than MiG-15s. They subsequently lodged complaints with the Soviets that those obsolete jets were not frontline aircraft. Russian advisers appeared resentful about this negative view of the quality of Soviet planes. Stalin himself intervened, and ordered the delivery of additional MiG-15s to the Chinese without charge.[37] However, this delay prevented the early entry of the Chinese air force into the war.

The deployment of Russian-manned Tu-2 bombers, Il-10 attack planes, and tank units to northeastern China in November, 1950, raised American fears about their entrance into the conflict. Such involvement would drastically change not only the military balance on the Korean Peninsula, but also the political context.[38] It was difficult for the Americans to tell who was operating the new weapons, and to know whether the units were there to protect China or possibly to intervene in Korea. Chinese sources suggest that Moscow never endorsed the earlier Chinese request for bombers to support ground operations in Korea.[39] Recently available Russian documents indicate that their primary role was defensive and that the use of the

Soviet troops "at the front and to cover troops and targets near the Chinese-Korean border is categorically forbidden." The flight personnel from Russian bomber units were the training cadres.[40] The tank regiments were assigned on "a purely training mission," and organic infantry and artillery units had already been stripped before their departure for China. Obviously, the Soviet move was calculated to avoid a direct Soviet-American conflict. If any bombing mission would be carried out in Korea, it would be the responsibility of the Russians' Chinese and Korean comrades.

Initial Soviet Actions over the Yalu

On the afternoon of November 1, 1950, the pilots of Belov's units engaged U.S./UN planes for the first time over the Yalu, claiming they shot down two F-80s with no friendly losses.[41] On the UN side, no losses were reported from this enemy encounter. Nevertheless, the engagement marked the beginning of a two and one-half year air war fought by the Soviet air force in Korea.[42] This has also raised an intriguing question. Why did Stalin refuse to provide Chinese troops with air cover, then turn around a few weeks later and allow his air combat units in China to engage the Americans over Korea? A careful analysis of Soviet records may provide insight into high-level Soviet planning for their air intervention in 1950.

While the massive transfer of troops and equipment from the Soviet Union to China was under way, vital elements of the Soviet air defense system would not be in place until at least late December. In early November, Belov's 151st GIAD (consisting of the 28th, 139th IAPs, and 72d GIAP) was the sole Soviet unit available to act over northeast China. On November 3, Moscow ordered the 151st GIAD to reorganize into the same two-regiment configuration as other units destined for China. A new division, the 28th IAD, commanded by Col. A. V. Aleyukhin, was formed with 67th and 139th IAPs from the 151st GIAD. Colonel A Ya. Sapozhnikov took command of the 151st, which retained the 28th IAP and 72d GIAP. Each division was equipped with sixty-two MiG-15s. Their missions remained unchanged. They would train Chinese pilots and then turn their planes and equipment over to the PLAAF.[43] There was no mention what corresponding actions the divisions should take as Chinese ground forces began crossing the Yalu, but their air defense mission in China still seemed valid. The pilots of the 151st GIAD had already flown in the air war over the Yalu River for two days. It is worthwhile to note that although Stalin did not immediately commit his air force to the Korean conflict, USAF attacks on Andong Airfield and the bridge across the Yalu might have prompted Belov to follow the existing mission order by sending his pilots into action. Meanwhile, their action could also serve the purpose of showing Chinese leaders that the boss of the Kremlin was respecting his word to support their moves in Korea and defend China with his forces if necessary. The presence of MiGs flown by Soviet pilots inside China was, therefore, destined to trigger the first jet-age dogfights between American and Communist jet aircraft.

The USAF official history regards November 8, 1950, as the first day of jet-to-jet combat in aviation history, and credits Lt. Russell Brown of the 51st Fighter-Interceptor Wing with shooting down the first MiG of the war that day.[44] However, a recent Russian study disputes these records, arguing that the first jet engagement may actually have taken place on November 1, and that Lt. Semyen F. Khomich of the 72d GIAP was the first pilot to score a jet kill.[45] The Far East Air Forces (FEAF) did acknowledge an encounter between Mustangs and MiGs that day, but denied any friendly loss. It made no mention of an engagement between the MiGs and Shooting Stars, although it did admit the loss of an F-80 to "intense, accurate" antiaircraft fire from the China side of the Yalu in the morning.[46] Did the FEAF lose another F-80 in the afternoon, or did the Soviets wrongly claim their victory? The Russians do not believe an affirmative answer to either question would be of help to Lieutenant Brown's claim, because Soviets records show no MiG losses on November 8.[47] What could prompt the UN pilot to mistakenly believe that he had actually shot down a MiG? Russian scholars speculate that the jettisoning of external fuel tanks by Senior Lieutenant Kharitonov of the 72d GIAP and his method of escaping from the Shooting Stars might have suggested to U.S. pilots that their prey was hit and falling. The Soviet records do agree, however, with the claim by U.S. Navy aviator William Amen that he blasted Sr. Lt. Mikhail F. Grachev's MiG with his 20-mm cannons on November 9, causing it to crash into a North Korean hillside and explode. The Soviets believed that their pilots also shot down an F-80, but U.S. records do not support such a claim. Therefore, the first jet-to-jet kill in history should probably be awarded to the U.S. Navy.[48]

As the air war intensified over the Yalu, Colonel General Krasovskiy arrived in Shenyang in early November and met with Liu Yalou, commander of the PLAAF, to discuss Soviet assistance with the air defense of northeast China. On November 8, accompanied by Lieutenant General Belov, Krasovskiy went to Andong and two days later personally witnessed a large air battle over the Yalu.[49] Soviet air units reached their monthly operational peak, flying fifty-eight sorties against more than a hundred UN aircraft that attacked Sinuiju, which faces the Chinese city of Andong across the Yalu.[50] As air engagements intensified over the Yalu, Stalin, on November 15, ordered the creation of the 64th IAK to control the MiG-15 divisions on "special assignment" in China. Belov was promoted to lieutenant general and given command of the newly formed air corps in Shenyang.[51]

In early November, the FEAF began an air campaign to destroy "every means of communication and every installation, factory, city, and village" up to the Manchurian border. The Truman administration had instructed the UN commander not to bomb objectives within five miles of the Korean border for fear that such attacks might involve China. General Douglas MacArthur, however, won the Joint Chiefs of Staff's support by arguing that any indecision "will be paid for dearly in American and other United Nations blood," and that the destruction of the border targets "would greatly demoralize and retard Chinese Communist troops entering the Korean conflict." On November 6, the Pentagon authorized the FEAF to use all means necessary against the Yalu bridges on the Manchurian frontier.[52] Two days later, the FEAF Bomber Command executed maximum strength strikes against Sinuiju with seventy B-29s firebombing the city and nine others pounding the two international bridges. The attack leveled the entire city, killed more than two thousand civilians, and sent a chilling message to the Chinese that U.S./UN forces would likely extend their air raids across the Yalu.[53]

Soviet air force generals in China were also apparently caught by surprise while traveling from Shenyang to Andong that day. The 151st GIAD and 28th IAD managed to launch fifty sorties, the highest number yet in the war, against UN fighter-bombers over the Yalu, claiming two enemy aircraft shot down. However, they failed to intercept any of the Superfortresses that hit Sinuiju and the bridges. One American scholar infers that the Soviet air force units might have reached their full capacity for combat by flying from their bases at Shenyang and Anshan, which were almost two hundred and three hundred kilometers from the border, respectively. It was, therefore, impossible for them to refuel and have adequate time to return to defend Sinuiju.[54] Nevertheless, the latest raid on Sinuiju signaled a possible expansion of the conflict, and the Soviet air force in China needed to prepare for any contingency.

We do not know how Colonel General Krasovskiy and his associates evaluated the situation when the FEAF began an all-out effort against the bridges across the Yalu after November 8. Their apprehensions about UN air pressure were unquestionably rising. For three days in a row, Belov's pilots flew maximum strength missions for a total of 160 sorties (50 on November 8, 51 on November 9, and 58 on November 10).[55] Although they claimed some victories over UN forces, Belov's units experienced significant limitations in operations as GCI operators proved unreliable in directing the MiGs close enough to visually locate UN aircraft. The shortage of drop tanks allowed each mission just over an hour of flying time. Probably even more serious was the fact that the reorganization created unexpected strains for Soviet pilots flying combat missions. Because of the aforementioned reorganization, many had new wingmen, and they were not yet proficient at working together.[56] Given such drawbacks, the 64th IAK could, at best, mount only limited operations, and the MiGs demonstrated no superiority over the enemy's propeller aircraft and slower jets. In the meantime, the Soviet duty to train Chinese pilots required a significant amount of their time, fuel, and manpower.

Moscow's position had become extremely delicate, and any action or inaction was fraught with potential disaster. Soviet leaders remained uncertain how the United States would react to the internationalization of the war on the Communist side. A security line was already drawn along the Yalu River. "Should China's Northeast region be bombed," Russian diplomats informed their British counterparts in Beijing, "the Soviet Air Force will respond with a large-scale counterattack."[57] On the other hand, the Soviet generals probably also realized that a lack of resolute action would bring the Soviet commitment to China's security into question, as well as the reputation of the Soviet air force. Moscow therefore concluded that only its best units should be sent to fight the Americans. The Soviets released both the 151st GIAD and 28th IAD from combat duty so they could concentrate on their training mission and allow the replacement of Soviet aircrews at the front by Chinese pilots. Kathryn Weathersby points out that this was the only way for the Soviets "to minimize the damage to Soviet interests that might ensue from the presence of Soviet pilots in Korea."[58] On November 15, Stalin told Chinese leaders that he would send an additional 120 MiG-15s to reinforce Belov's forces. Chinese leaders welcomed this proposal, and assured Stalin that they would work closely on China's air defense with Col. Gen. Semyon E. Zakharov, Stalin's personal military envoy to Beijing. They also agreed to construct an additional airdrome near the Korean border besides those airfields already being used by the Soviets at Shenyang, Liaoyang, Anshan, and Andong to facilitate Soviet operations.[59]

The First Trial of Strength: MiGs versus Sabres, December, 1950

The 50th IAD was the reinforcement Stalin had in mind for Korea. Located at the Soviet's Sanshilibao Air Base on the Liaodong Peninsula, the 50th IAD had recently been formed with two of the best MiG-15 regiments of the Soviet air force: the 29th GIAP and the 177th IAP. The former had just returned from the Shanghai mission and the latter had been part of the 303d IAD commanded by Maj. Gen. Georgiy A. Lobov. Both were among the first units to fly MiG-15s in early 1950, and had just completed training with the MiG-15bis (which had a more powerful engine—the VK-1—that increased its speed to 1,075 kilometers per hour) in October. On November 15, the Soviet Ministry of Defense directed Col. Aleksey V. Pashkevich, a hero of the Great Patriotic War and commander of the 50th IAD, and his units to prepare for immediate movement.[60] He was ordered to leave some junior pilots behind and allowed to retain only thirty-two pilots and thirty MiG-15s for each regiment, instead of the normal forty. Five days later, they were airborne to Anshan. Their tasks were (1) to defend the bridges across the Yalu at Andong that were crucial for transporting the CPV's supplies; (2) to prevent enemy planes from attacking the hydroelectric stations on the Yalu; (3) to respond to enemy air raids within its own flying radius; and (4) to provide cover for the cities of Andong and Sinuiju.[61] Unlike other Soviet units sent to China at the time, the 50th IAD was the first to assume a mission directly associated with the Korean conflict, and had no responsibility for training Chinese pilots. It was also evident that Stalin was continuing to be prudent, drawing a line to limit the involvement of the Soviet air force in the conflict. The introduction of the upgraded MiG-15bis displayed the Soviet leader's interest in testing the best weapon system in the Soviet air defense arsenal, one crucial to his own country's air defense in the nuclear age.

The expansion of Soviet air commitment, however, was paralleled by a CPV counteroffensive: the second phase campaign, which began on November 25 and ended on December 24, 1950. Although he possessed no airpower and had a limited amount of artillery, Peng Dehuai, the CPV commander, decided to concentrate his nine armies, totaling thirty infantry divisions, to conduct a major offensive against the U.S./UN forces inaugurating General MacArthur's "home-by-Christmas" campaign. On the evening of November 25, Peng sprang his trap. The CPV's 13th Army Group, along with the Fiftieth and Sixty-sixth Armies, launched strong attacks against the U.S. I and IX Corps and the ROK II Corps. Within a day, the CPV's Thirty-eighth and Forty-second Armies crushed the two South Korean divisions, successfully ensuring the encirclement of the main forces of the U.S. 1st Cavalry and 2d and 25th Infantry Divisions. Chairman Mao congratulated the CPV command on November 28, and urged Peng to finish off the Americans in twenty days. On December 1, supported by the air force, the U.S. Eighth Army began retreating from positions north of the Chongchon River, abandoning many of its vehicles and much of its heavy equipment. The CPV's assault on the western front halted the next day.[62]

On November 27, the CPV's 9th Army Group struck along both sides of the Chosin Reservoir in eastern North Korea, cutting off the U.S. 1st Marine and 7th Infantry Divisions, which had been marching toward Kanggye, the provisional capital of North Korea. Despite a shortage of supplies, and battling in subzero temperatures, CPV soldiers mounted a full-scale assault on the UN forces. On November 30 and December 1, the Twenty-seventh Army inflicted heavy casualties on the U.S. 7th Infantry Division. Thanks to airpower and airdrops, the 1st Marine Division and the remnants of the 7th Infantry Division escaped the encirclement after thirteen days of isolation.[63] While UN ground forces engaged in battle in late November and early December, the FEAF increasingly concerned itself with the strength of Communist airpower. According to an air force intelligence report, the Communist air forces appeared to be capable of diverting the UN air effort from the direct support of ground action, hindering the UN airlift in Korea, striking UN vessels and installations in Korea, and affording effective support to enemy ground action.[64] Despite the FEAF's concerns, none of these scenarios ever happened. Instead, hammered by U.S./UN aircraft, Peng Dehuai urgently sought air cover for his own troops, and urged Beijing to take action.[65]

Before the 50th IAD's deployment, Belov's units were constrained by the availability of planes and pilots. During the month of November, the Soviet air force command in China managed to fly only 384 sorties in response to 2,525 detected enemy sorties.[66] During the last ten days of the month, Soviet pilots were kept mostly inactive and no air combat was reported. Furthermore, the Soviets made no effort to coordinate their activities with the CPV ground offensive. However, the arrival of the 50th IAD expanded the strength of the 64th IAK to three fighter divisions, totaling 170 MiG-15s. In early December, the 29th GIAP, led by Colonel Pashkevich, the division commander, moved to the airfield at Andong and intensively engaged the Americans over the Yalu.[67]

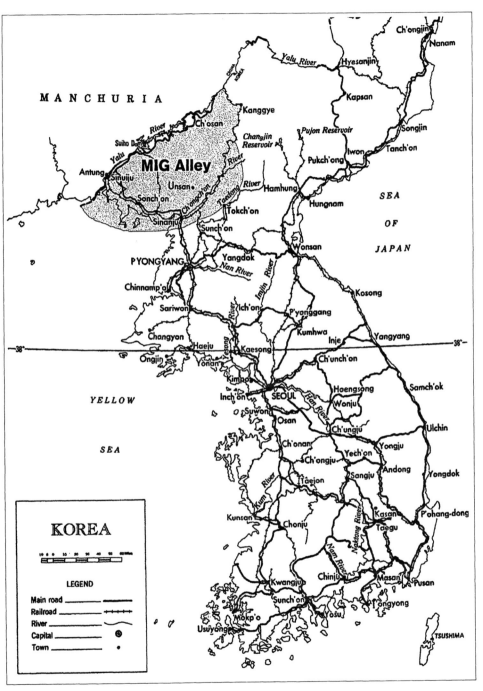

Mig Alley, Korea

F-86s of the 4th Fighter-Interceptor Wing, USAF, the chief opponents of Soviet and Chinese MiGs in Korea. *Courtesy* John R. Bruning, Jr.

The FEAF, employing reconnaissance flights and monitoring enemy radio transmissions, learned of the Soviet involvement and feared that it might be the prelude to an all-out Soviet air assault.[68] In late 1950, the FEAF estimated there were a minimum of 650 combat aircraft in China, of which about 250 operated by the Soviets were available for an all-out air campaign in Korea. Another 400 to 500 aircraft in Soviet units in the Dalian area on the Liaodong Peninsula might be called upon to support such an effort.[69] Thus, the UN Command was rightly concerned about the potential employment of such an air force by the Communists, which, as a U.S. air force historian remarked, would have turned "the United Nations retreat into a virtual holocaust."[70]

Although the Soviets did not make maximum use of their forces, the FEAF Bomber Command began to feel the pain of B-29 and RB-29 losses. Its straight-wing F-80 fighters were no match for the swept-wing MiGs, which were clearly superior to the old Shooting Stars. General MacArthur appealed to Washington for help, arguing that the appearance of the MiGs was demoralizing both his air and ground troops. On November 8, the U.S. Air Force ordered the 4th Fighter-Interceptor Wing, which was flying the best fighter in the UN arsenal, the F-86, to Korea. It was given the task of establishing and maintaining air superiority. A detachment from the 4th Wing established itself at Kimpo Airfield near Seoul, and it flew its first combat mission over the Yalu on December 17, initiating a two-and-one-half-year-long duel between Sabres and MiGs in Korea. During the engagement, the F-86 pilots claimed their first MiG-15 victim.[71]

Probably concerned about combat losses, or about the employment of a new type of fighter by the FEAF, the 50th IAD stepped up the contest for air superiority.[72] The day following the first encounter of MiGs and Sabres, ten MiGs from the 177th IAP were shifted from Anshan to join the 29th's MiGs at Andong. The Soviet air strategy was to send its best pilots to engage Sabres while using other pilots to attack enemy fighter-bomber formations. Accordingly, Pashkevich assigned the 177th's Andong-based 1st Flying Group to engage the enemy's combat air patrol (CAP) and the 2d Flying Group to attack the enemy fighter-bombers, while keeping the 3d Flying Group in reserve at Anshan. On December 23, the MiGs and Sabres fought the largest jet battle of the war to date. The 50th IAD scrambled 20 MiG-15s (10 from the 29th and 10 from the 177th) from Andong, and 16 MiG-15s (from 177th) from Anshan, to intercept U.S./UN aircraft some thirty-seven miles south of the Yalu. The 177th's 1st Flying Group surprised a flight of F-86s from below, and Sr. Lt. N. Ye. Vorob'yev, the deputy group leader, claimed the first of many F-86s destroyed by MiG-15s during the war. However, the 177th ran out of luck in the afternoon when eight MiGs of the 2d Flying Group went canopy to canopy with two flights of F-86s. Passing too close to get off a shot, the MiG flights eluded the Sabres, which eventually outmaneuvered the MiGs and caught them in a tight turn. The squadron leader, Sr. Lt. S. A. Barsyegyan, was killed, and Capt. A. A. Zub ejected from his damaged plane. Zub, who broke his leg when he hit the ground, never flew again. In return, the 2d Flying Group claimed three F-86s destroyed for the day, although the FEAF records indicate otherwise.[73]

The U.S. pilots reported that they had "definitely destroyed" six MiGs and damaged another one in the afternoon engagement, but with no losses. Robert Futrell concludes that this "bloodletting" was good enough to force the MiGs to avoid combat for several days.[74] Mark O'Neill offers a rebuttal, however, noting that the 50th IAD's pilots had never "eschewed" engagement with U.S./UN fliers. Instead, they continued to fly combat sorties with the same intensity, claiming the destruction of eight enemy planes during the rest of December. Without being burdened by training tasks, the 50th spared no effort in its air defense mission, almost doubling the total number of sorties flown in November, including sixty sorties in a single day on December 22. Forty-one victories were credited to Pashkevich's units, which suffered only six losses for the month.[75] American pilots disputed this record, but agreed that their opponents' performance was particularly "aggressive" and "capable" in the air. This left the FEAF wondering if the Communists had thrown their "first team" into action.[76]

When Did Soviet Air Intervention Begin in the Korean Conflict?

Despite the heroic actions by Soviet flyers over the Yalu in late 1950, one question remains: Was the deployment of Soviet planes and pilots to Andong and their engagement with the UN air forces the manifestation of a formal Soviet air intervention in Korea? Western studies generally regard the November 1 air engagement over the Yalu between Soviet MiGs and U.S./UN aircraft as the beginning of Moscow's air intervention in the Korean conflict. Mark O'Neill suggests that Stalin had promised only limited air support and sent Soviet pilots to fly over "the area of Andong-Sinuiju to cover ground troops and the railroad bridge across the Yalu River at Andong."[77] However, Chinese sources all point out that not until January 10, 1951, did Moscow agree to commit the Soviet air force to the Korean conflict by providing limited air support for the Chinese.[78] How can we reconcile this discrepancy between Russian and Chinese sources?

China's decision to intervene during the first half of October, 1950, was considerably influenced by the Soviet promise of air support for Chinese troops fighting in Korea. Yet no matter how hard Chinese leaders bargained with Stalin for air support for their ground operations in Korea, the best they could obtain from Moscow was the assurance of a Soviet air umbrella over China. When UN air operations moved closer and closer to the Chinese border, particularly the B-29 raid on the international bridge and the city of Sinuiju on November 8, Soviet air force units in northeast China could no longer remain idle. The U.S./UN bombardment posed a serious menace to the safety of Andong and other important industrial installations on the Yalu, and the Soviet air force units were responsible for their defense. It is probably reasonable to argue that Soviet air operations during this period ought to be comprehended as an extension of the air defense of northeast China. In the meantime, the ensuing engagements with U.S./UN aircraft over the Yalu enabled the Soviets to study the air war while allowing their leaders to gauge Chinese ground offensives and then determine how deep the Soviet air involvement should be in the Korean theater.

There is no doubt the deployment of the 50th IAD at Andong greatly hampered UN air attacks along the Yalu. However, recently released records of the Soviet air force's order of battle in Korea categorize this division as supporting the actions of the 64th IAK in Korea between November, 1950, and March, 1951 (see Appendix B). Moreover, Soviet air involvement had little effect on Chinese ground operations, as Soviet pilots were mainly limited to engaging the Americans within a radius of thirty miles of their home base at Andong. Moreover, there is no evidence whatsoever that Soviet pilots flew their combat sorties in coordination with CPV ground operations. Therefore, Soviet air operations over the Yalu seem irrelevant to the CPV's early success in its counteroffensives. On the UN side, the FEAF, by intensifying its efforts to interdict Communist supply lines and provide firepower in support of ground troops, actually saved U.S./UN forces from further disasters.

The CPV's cry for air support continued. On December 8, while questioning Mao's decision to mount another offensive immediately following the end of the second phase offensive, Peng complained that his troops were suffering from food and ammunition shortages. Rail transportation lines were repeatedly interrupted by enemy bombings because there was no air cover. The chairman, however, determined to have the CPV make a nonstop advance to cross the 38th Parallel so the Americans would not be able to gain a respite. He comforted Peng with the observation that the possibility of increased Soviet air support looked very promising.[79] We still do not know the details of how the Chinese negotiated for Soviet air support in December, 1950. However, Chinese leaders appeared to be very much aware of the Soviets' reservations and concerns. On December 23, Peng suggested that Beijing persuade the Soviets to commit their air force to shield only the area between the Yalu and Taedong Rivers, and that the Chinese and North Korean air forces assume responsibility for supply lines south of Pyongyang and Wonsan after the badly damaged airfields there were repaired.[80] According to Chinese records, Soviets did not agree to provide air cover for the railroad lines between Ji'an and Kanggye and Andong and Anju until January 10, 1951.[81]

After two months of Chinese intervention, Moscow apparently realized that the United States was unlikely to enlarge the confrontation in Korea, and therefore became less concerned with increasing its own air commitment there. The first documentary evidence of Soviet air intervention from Russian sources is a directive dated January 17, 1951, from Col. Gen. Sergey M. Shtemenko, the first deputy of the chief of staff, instructing Soviet air force units in China to play an active defense role against the UN.[82] However, at the time there were only two regiments from the 50th IAD available. How could they be expected to fight the entire UN air force? The CPV ground offensives eventually shoved the F-86s out of bases in South Korea, thus allowing Soviet pilots to reign over "MiG Alley" between the Chongchon and Yalu Rivers in early 1951. Without adequate air protection from its own fighter-interceptor wings, the FEAF Bomber Command had to keep its bombers out of northwestern Korea and away from the hazardous MiGs.[83]

The CPV did not feel any relief from UN air pressure, though, and when the CPV's third phase offensive ended in early January, the Chinese supply lines stretched farther south to the 37th Parallel. The FEAF was then able to concentrate its interdiction attacks outside "MiG Alley," and continue to inflict heavy losses on the CPV's logistics operations. In February and March, Chinese leaders made another attempt to secure Soviet air support in advance of another ground offensive scheduled for April. Probably encouraged by the early Chinese victory, or perhaps because he felt he could no longer renege, Stalin agreed to increase the Soviet air commitment in Korea.[84] The subsequent deployment of the 324th and 303d IADs, the most elite units in the Soviet air force, signified the beginning of a new stage of Soviet air involvement in Korea.

CHAPTER 5

Months of Frustration

PLANS AND PREPARATIONS

Beijing's decision to intervene in Korea with ground forces raised new and urgent problems for the Chinese air force that had just been created, and which remained far from operational. On October 18, 1950, Mao convened another high-level military meeting concerning China's intervention in Korea. When the chairman decided to send Chinese troops to Korea, even without Soviet air cover, the Chinese air force came under increasing pressure to get into the action. At the meeting, Peng expressed the hope that Liu Yalou would dispatch PLAAF units to support his ground forces. Liu responded with a promise that whether or not the Soviets provided air support, he would overcome all obstacles and get Chinese pilots into the war as soon as possible.[1] Chinese military leaders were combat-tested veterans, but all of their experience was on the ground, and they knew little about organizing an air force and air warfare. At that moment, they discerned the importance of airpower in their upcoming ground operations in Korea, but they probably did not realize the complexities and difficulties involved in constructing an air force from scratch. For almost a year after China's military intervention—from November, 1950, to August, 1951—the PLAAF and its leadership experienced frustrations and failures in the effort to get China's own air force into the war.

Beijing Establishes Its Air War Strategy

By the time the Chinese entered the Korean conflict, the leaders in Beijing were fully aware of the strength and superiority of the U.S. Air Force in the Korean theater. It had fourteen wings, including two fighter-interceptor wings, three fighter-bomber wings, two light bomber wings, three medium bomber wings, one Marine aviation wing, and three navy carrier groups, amounting to some 1,100 combat aircraft. Most of the American pilots were World War II veterans with more than a thousand flying hours.[2] In contrast, the PLAAF consisted of only two fighter divisions, a bomber regiment, and an attack regiment, totaling about two hundred combat aircraft. Chinese pilots had less than a hundred hours of flying time, and most of the MiG pilots had just began to solo.[3] More crucial for the PLAAF at that moment was the fact that no Chinese, either pilots or commanders, had air combat experience.[4] Although Liu promised Peng he would rush Chinese air units into the war, he understood well the consequences of such a small and weak force facing the Americans' superior airpower.

The PLAAF convened a meeting on October 30 to discuss when and how the air force should enter the war. Participants agreed that Chinese ground forces were at a decided disadvantage in Korea since the United States had air superiority. Chinese pilots needed additional training, but some argued that the Chinese airmen could learn what they needed to know about aerial warfare through hands-on training under combat conditions. The PLAAF's leaders understood that they could not compare with the U.S. Air Force in either the number of aircraft available or in terms of technology. Based on their confidence in the CCP's leadership, their countrymen's support, and their own ground combat experience, they were nevertheless certain that the PLAAF could hold its own against the USAF, and that ultimate victory would depend upon ground operations. The air force, the participants concluded, would play only a supporting role. Chinese officers thus devised a strategy calling for the newly established air force to avoid engaging in a war of attrition that would work to America's advantage. Their method was to train fliers for the one hundred to 150 aircraft that they could mobilize. Those planes then would be concentrated for timely attacks on the Americans.[5]

An ambitious but cautious air plan for Korea emerged. The PLAAF would commit four air regiments (120 MiGs) to provide protection for transportation in January and February, 1951, if the two Soviet air regiments would coordinate the operation. By mid-April, there would be six fighter regiments (five MiG and one La-11), two attack aircraft regiments, and four bomber regiments—360 planes in all—available to take part in the war. However, the PLAAF's involvement would largely depend upon whether there would be sufficient airfields for them in Korea. By the end of 1951, according to the plan, the PLAAF would grow to twenty-eight fighter regiments (twenty-five MiG and four La-9 and La-11 regiments), four attack aircraft regiments, seven bomber regiments, and four transport regiments, amounting to thirteen hundred aircraft.[6]

Recent Chinese sources reveal that the PLAAF's leadership considered two options for employing the air force in the Korean conflict. One was to move the Chinese air force's fighters, bombers, and attack aircraft into North Korea to provide direct support for CPV ground operations. The other called for basing air force units inside China and engaging the Americans over Korea. Chinese air force leaders realized the first option would provide greater support for the ground troops, but it would also involve greater risk for the air force. Such a lesson could be drawn easily from the North Koreans' experience during the first month of the war.[7] However, CPV leaders, particularly Peng Dehuai, demanded a maximum effort from the PLAAF. In early December, the PLAAF's leaders drew up an air plan that called for the Chinese air force to coordinate with the ground offensives while placing emphasis on concentrating strength for a timely attack.[8] Mao was inclined to take a prudent approach, but the chairman could not evade pressure from CPV leaders pleading for close air support. He approved a plan calling for the PLAAF to give priority to direct ground support on December 4.[9]

The CPV Air Force Command Takes Shape

Following China's shocking ground offensive in the winter of 1950–51, the PLAAF's leaders decided to establish a CPV Air Force headquarters. Because they had no air combat experience, the task naturally fell on the shoulders of those who were combat-tested PLA veterans. On November 4, Liu Zhen, the recently appointed commander of air force units in the South-Central China Military Region, was ordered to take the same job in the Northeast Military Region, and assume responsibility for organizing the CPV Air Force.

Because of his lack of experience with air operations, he appeared reluctant to take the position. Only after learning that his appointment had been recommended by Peng and Gao Gang, commander of the Northeast Military Region, and already approved by Mao, did Liu agree to go to northeast China.[10] Indeed, it was difficult to find anyone to command the CPV Air Force as all of the PLA generals at Liu's level lacked aviation experience. He seemed to be the ideal candidate for the position, having served as deputy commander of the 13th Army Group before joining the PLAAF. Liu was also historically connected to the current CPV leadership, an important advantage in the Chinese bureaucracy. Liu might be able to win understanding and support from his former colleagues if any divergence over air strategy occurred between PLAAF and CPV leaders in the future.[11]

In early 1951, the PLAAF transferred most of its own staff officers, including those who were in charge of operations, signal, command and control, and aviation navigation in Beijing's headquarters, along with personnel from the various regional headquarters, to form the core of the CPV Air Force headquarters in the Northeast Military Region.[12] Given the fact that the air force had few aviation professionals, and that the skills of those it did have did not measure up to Western standards, on February 12, Zhou Enlai asked the Soviets to dispatch fifteen advisers to assist the Chinese with aviation planning and organization.[13] Stalin agreed, and recommended Maj. Gen. D. Golunov, a member of the Soviet military advisory group led by Gen. M. V. Zakharov, to the PLA general staff as the best choice for the top position.[14]

In spite of the obvious need for a joint command to coordinate the Communist air forces' efforts in Korea, the Soviets persisted in acting alone. On January 7, Zhou suggested to Kim Il Sung that a joint command be set up for the Chinese–North Korean air army based on the principles that applied to the CPV-NKPA joint command.[15] On March 15, the CPV's air force headquarters was formally established at Andong. It consisted of four departments: headquarters, political, engineering, and logistics. Chang Qiankun, deputy commander of the PLAAF, and Gen. Wang Yong, commander of the North Korean air force, were appointed deputy commanders of the CPV-NKPA joint air force.[16] Shen Qixian was made chief of staff. The CPV Air Force headquarters officially assumed command on April 25. Initially, five Chinese air divisions were put under its authority, but they would not be ready for operation until the fall.[17]

The CPV Air Force was placed under the dual leadership of the CPV's headquarters in Korea and the PLAAF's headquarters in Beijing. However, the actual decisions about when the air battle should be carried out, how many aircraft should take off, which units would be involved, and how the battle should be conducted, were reserved for the CPV Air Force's headquarters. The Chinese did not seem to have any authority over North Korean air force units, which were a part of this joint force. Plans for using them had to be negotiated between Beijing and Pyongyang. North Korean officers allegedly rarely showed up in their offices at the joint air force headquarters at Andong.[18]

In early 1951, PLAAF and CPV leaders gave serious consideration to using the air force in a direct ground support role. In February, the air force ordered Chang Qiankun to establish a forward command post in Pyongyang that would be solely responsible for constructing airfields and supplying air force units stationed in Korea.[19] The CPV Air Force's Bomber Command and Attack Aircraft Command were set up in July. Nie Fengzhi, commander of the East China Military Region Air Force, headed the Bomber Command at Dongfeng in Jilin Province, while Xu Dechao, air force commander in the North China Military Region, was in charge of the Attack Aircraft Command at Kaiyuan in Liaoning Province. However, the PLAAF disbanded the bomber and attack aircraft commands in December, when the CPV Air Force's direct ground support mission was dropped from Beijing's air war plan.[20] The significance of this change was that the command and control structure of the CPV Air Force was confined to carrying out the air defense mission. The air force and CPV headquarters never collocated, so further organizational separation between the two services became inevitable.

The Air Force's Baptism by Fire

The PLAAF leadership believed that the establishment of a Chinese air force must result in three verifiable outcomes. First, the Chinese would run aviation schools by themselves and educate their own aviation personnel; second, the Chinese would train their own aviation troops and flying warriors; and third, Chinese pilots would fight in the air. The greatest uncertainty for PLAAF leaders was whether young Chinese pilots could persevere against experienced American fliers. To gain hands-on combat experience thus became crucial before China officially entered the air war. Chinese air force leaders decided to rotate small units to Andong for "real combat practice" under the protection of Soviet pilots. On December 4, 1950, the PLAAF ordered the 28th Flying Group of the 10th Aviation Regiment from the 4th

Fang Ziyi, commander of the 4th Aviation Division *(second from left)* and Li Han, flying group leader *(third from right)*, pose with pilots from the division's 28th Flying Group, 10th Regiment, on December 21, 1950.

Aviation Division to prepare to go to Andong as soon as the Russian unit at Anshang transferred there.[21]

In late October, 1950, the 4th Aviation Division had moved from Shanghai to Liaoyang. After receiving MiGs and other equipment from Belov's division, it reorganized with two regiments (the 10th and 12th), each having three flight groups and thirty aircraft. The 4th Aviation Division then engaged in intensified training in group formations and combat. By early December, the pilots of the 10th Aviation Regiment had accumulated some twenty flying hours in MiG-15s. Cognizant of the reality that both Chinese commanders and pilots knew nothing about air combat, the PLAAF's directive included five specific requirements for Fang Ziyi, the 4th Aviation Division commander. First, he was limited to using only one four-plane flight on each mission, and he had to await further instructions before sending two flights into combat. Second, he must be decisive and vigilant, and avoid being foolhardy if the weather and enemy activities were too disadvantageous. Third, he should keep on good terms with the Soviet units there, so that the Russians would devote themselves to providing cover and guidance for the Chinese pilots. Fourth, he must submit a report to PLAAF headquarters immediately after each mission. Finally, he should work out a plan of action with the Russians and submit it for approval.

Two weeks later, Fang consulted with Colonel Pashkevich, commander of the Soviet 50th IAD, and came up with a two-stage course of action for his pilots. They would initially spend three days studying enemy air tactics and practice their own combat techniques on the ground. Then, in the absence of enemy activity, they would spend three or four days flying over Korea and becoming acquainted with combat conditions. Later, they would fly combat missions with Soviet cover when the enemy's forces were weak. In order to facilitate close coordination between the two sides, Fang and Pashkevich also agreed to set up a joint command post. Liu Yalou approved this plan on December 15.[22]

On December 21, the 28th Flying Group—consisting of ten pilots flying MiG-15s under Fang Ziyi's command—shifted to Langtou Airfield at

Li Han of the 4th Aviation Division poses here. Li was the first Chinese pilot credited with shooting down a U.S. aircraft in the Korean War.

Andong. A week later, the Chinese pilots flew their first combat mission with the Soviets. At noon on December 28, a Chinese flight led by group leader Li Han took off with two Russian flights, and headed toward the Anju area. However, the Chinese pilots, who were not proficient in combat flying, became confused as they flew into the combat zone. When Russian pilots suddenly broke off and dove in search of targets, they left their disconcerted Chinese comrades behind. After failing to spot any enemy aircraft, the Chinese were ordered to return to base. For the next few days, the Chinese pilots experienced similar problems. Anxieties grew because the Chinese believed the Russians were not interested in showing them how to engage the enemy. From the Russians' point of view, communicating with their Chinese comrades in the middle of a battle was difficult because they did not speak a common language. Although Pashkevich repeatedly promised to improve his pilots' coordination with the Chinese, nothing changed.[23]

In early 1951, the withdrawal of U.S. Air Force units from Kimpo and Suwon significantly reduced U.S./UN air activity north of the Chongchon River. Believing that this would give Chinese pilots a better opportunity to gain combat experience against fewer enemy aircraft, the PLAAF leadership ordered the 29th and 30th Flying Groups of the 10th Aviation Regiment to join the 28th Flying Group at Andong on January 17. In about a month of combat, the pilots of the 28th Flying Group flew seven combat missions, but encountered no enemy planes. However, their luck changed on January 21 when six Chinese and eight Russians MiGs were vectored to intercept UN fighter-bombers over Anju. The Chinese flight caught four F-84s dive-bombing the Chongchon River bridge. Group leader Li Han damaged a Thunderjet, and Russian pilots confirmed his claim.[24] The PLAAF's leaders congratulated the 28th Flying Group pilots for proving that the young CPV Air Force was "capable of air battle with considerable effectiveness."[25] A week later, the Chinese claimed their first kill when Li Han shot down an F-84 off the North Korean coast. The FEAF's records concede the loss of an F-80C that day, and the Soviets made no claims.[26] Although Li misidentified his claim as a Thunderjet—a common mistake made by Soviet pilots, too—the victory left the Chinese feeling that air war was no longer a mystery to them. More important, the event had a morale-building effect because it proved that Chinese pilots could defeat the Americans in the air, just as their army had done on the ground.[27]

Buoyed by such encouragement, on February 2 the PLAAF's leaders ordered the 12th Aviation Regiment to replace the 10th Aviation Regiment at

Andong, hoping to allow more Chinese pilots to gain combat experience. The pilots of the 12th Aviation Regiment had only fifteen flying hours in MiGs, and had just concluded their basic training courses for combat.[28] Their inexperience proved fatal shortly after they arrived at Andong, along with Russian pilots from the 151st GIAD commanded by Col. A. Ye. Sapozhnikov. On the morning of February 10, Russian radar operators wrongly identified a returning Chinese flight as enemy planes. There was confusion on the Chinese side when eight Russian MiGs scrambled into the air. Two MiGs from the 12th Aviation Regiment collided on takeoff, and a third crashed in an attempt to land after its fuel ran out. Without firing a shot, the 12th Aviation Regiment lost an entire squadron within a few days of being stationed at Langtou Airfield.[29] Although PLAAF leaders wanted Chinese pilots to continue to stay at the front and gain hands-on combat experience, they were disappointed by the level of competence displayed by their pilots. Fang Ziyi claims that bad weather and reduced UN air activity were the major factors limiting Chinese combat opportunities. Regardless, the 12th Aviation Regiment was ordered to return to its home base at Liaoyang in early March.[30]

Meanwhile, the pilots of the 151st GIAD racked up several kills and appeared much more successful than the Chinese. Although Soviet records for the period February 10 to March 1 are incomplete, Soviet pilots reported the destruction of six F-80s and F-84s and six B-29s.[31] In contrast to their Russian comrades, in a little over two months the pilots of the 4th Aviation Division flew 145 combat sorties, but encountered enemy planes on only twenty-four of them. In exchange for downing one U.S. plane, and damaging two others, the Chinese lost two MiGs and one airman. Although the PLAAF's leaders at first believed their pilots would benefit from "real combat practice" in Korea, the harsh reality of the air war forced them to be more realistic: Chinese pilots needed additional training. For the next six months, the responsibility for air operations in MiG Alley fell solely on the shoulders of Soviet pilots.

Organizing and Training an Air Force for the Korean Conflict

In early 1951, an urgent issue facing the PLAAF was how to organize its combat units. Immediately after the Chinese ground intervention in Korea, the 4th Mixed Brigade was reorganized into three fighter divisions (the 2d, 3d, and 4th), with hastily graduated student pilots in late October, 1950. The arrival of large numbers of Soviet air force troops further triggered a

Chinese MiGs wait for the order to take off. During the earlier stages of the war, the front part of each plane's fuselage was painted red and bore North Korean insignia.

boom in Chinese airpower. In December, three fighter divisions (the 6th, 7th, and 9th), the 8th Bomber Aviation Division, and the 5th Attack Aviation Division were added to the PLAAF's order of battle. During the first half of 1951, ten more air divisions were formed: the 10th Bomber, 11th Attack, and 13th Transport Aviation Divisions, and the 12th, 14th, 15th, 16th, 17th, and 18th Fighter Aviation Divisions. In an effort to be consistent with the Soviet system, the Chinese fighter divisions each contained two regiments, but each was equipped with only twenty to twenty-five MiGs.[32]

Because these units were created within such a short period, their quality was uneven. The majority had not received any combat training, and were ill-prepared to go to war.[33] Nevertheless, time was pressing: The CPV's leaders had scheduled another offensive for the spring of 1951 in an attempt to drive the UN forces out of Korea.[34] Twelve air force regiments were scheduled to participate in the operation.[35] On January 16, the PLAAF decided to require these units to reach operational standards within two and one-half months by undergoing rigorous training.[36] Between mid-January and early April, Chinese fighter units conducted a series of intensive training programs, emphasizing aerobatics, formation flying, cruise, and operational unit training; bomber crews concentrated on regimental formation flying and bombing training, while attack squadrons were trained to fly in various formations and to make ground attacks.

On April 8, at a division commanders' meeting, the PLAAF's leaders assessed the battlefield conditions in Korea. They analyzed the number of aircraft and their missions, and then decided on which air force units would enter the war so they could focus their training on tactical movement and coordination, including swift takeoffs and assembling, disassembling, landing, and combat formations. In the meantime, the pilots of the 28th Flying Group made a tour of the CPV Air Force units giving lectures about their combat experience. One particular demonstration they made was how to properly use gun sights, because selecting the correct lead angle was so difficult.[37] From April 25 to April 28, the CPV Air Force organized an exercise on "air army's operational movement in an offensive campaign" on the outskirts of Shenyang to test air-ground combat coordination. The outcome was disappointing. Chinese air force leaders scheduled a second larger drill to coordinate fighter, bomber, and ground-attack aircraft from Andong, Liaoyang, and Shenyang from May 28 to June 16. A total of 180 planes from the 3d and 4th Fighter Aviation Divisions, the 5th Attack Aviation Division, and the 8th Bomber Aviation Division took part in this large-scale aerial maneuver, practicing surprise attacks on enemy airfields, interception of enemy bomber fleets, and direct support for ground assaults. The exercise provided the pilots, ground crews, and the ground and air commanders with insights into how the air force would operate in combat. Although the PLAAF units demonstrated considerable improvement this time, they still exhibited deficiencies in ground command and air combat communication, as well as the pilots' gunnery and bombing techniques.[38] The combat experience of the 4th Aviation Division earlier in the year and other problems forced the PLAAF to further postpone sending the air force into combat in Korea until September.[39]

Airfield Construction Given Top Priority

One of the greatest challenges in preparation for the PLAAF's deployment to Korea was constructing enough airfields. As the CPV recovered most of North Korea's lost territory by mid-December, 1950, military leaders in Beijing began seeking sites for airfield construction and locating airfields that could be repaired so the CPV Air Force could commence a full-scale air offensive against UN forces. China's air war plan called for the deployment of twelve air regiments, about 350 planes, to Korea by April, 1951. However, implementation of such a plan required building airfields in North Korea that could handle jet aircraft.[40] Construction of airfields was given a priority schedule. On December 13, 1950, Zhou Enlai invited Kim Il Sung to send representatives to Beijing to discuss the matter. In the meantime, a survey team from the PLAAF set out for Korea to study the situation there.[41]

When the conflict started, North Korea had only four airfields in Pyongyong and other places, along with several advanced strips near the 38th Parallel.[42] They were not only primitive but also badly damaged by the war by late 1950. Recognizing China's own difficulties involving materials, manpower, equipment, and transportation, the air force survey team recommended only repairing the existing airfields by filling bomb craters, pressing the runways, and building oil depots and bunkers.[43] However, UN air superiority, coupled with the freezing weather, presented a formidable barrier. After several months of effort, the Chinese by early 1951 had been unable to establish an operational airfield in North Korea. Beijing's frustration was expressed in Mao's telegram to Stalin on March 1. "We plan to send ten air regiments to the war in April and May," the Chinese leader complained, "but so far we are unable to find a single operational airfield inside Korean territory." In addition to the natural problem of frozen ground, he said the fundamental difficulty was that "the Chinese will be unable to construct any airfield in the days to come because they do not have a reliable air force to provide cover." Urged by his field commander, Peng Dehuai, Mao appealed to the Russian leader to take steps to improve the situation.[44] Stalin quickly responded to China's entreaty. He agreed to send Soviet air force units to North Korea, and to supply the Chinese with enough pierced-steel planking for two airfields. The Soviets would also send along antiaircraft guns and ammunition for airfield defense. He asked that in return, the Chinese build four additional airfields with concrete runways for use by Soviet MiG units.[45]

Having received such a positive reply from Stalin, Zhou met with the chief Soviet military adviser in Beijing, and then directed Liu Yalou and his Russian adviser, Major General Golunov, to go to Shenyang and consult with their Korean colleagues about where airfields sould be constructed and how their air forces would operate from them.[46] From the PLAAF's point of view, it would be better to take a step-by-step approach. Zhou explained to Peng that the Chinese would first build two airfields with pierced-steel-plank runways for a Soviet air division to use, and then construct two more airfields in the Pyongyang area for a Chinese MiG division. After that, Zhou continued, two other airfields would be built for another Soviet MiG division, and three advanced airfields at Anak, Pyonggang, and Sinmak could be constructed under the protection of Soviet air units. Beijing believed that the burden of manpower, materiel, and transportation would be relatively lessened in this way, but it also acknowledged that the air force's entry into the war would be delayed.[47]

The Russians argued that a single Soviet MiG division would not be able to hold its ground and insisted the Chinese build the four Soviet airfields simultaneously, while North Koreans construct the four airfields the Chinese needed.[48] The Soviet proposal put the Chinese in a predicament. The PLAAF had few engineering units able to undertake the task. With little engineering equipment available, progress would depend on how much manpower could be mobilized. The Chinese leaders originally planned to employ two or three newly recruited NKPA divisions for airfield construction, and have Chinese air force engineering units assist in hopes that the first airfield could be completed by the end of March. Although Kim Il Sung had agreed to cooperate, no North Korean soldiers were ever sent.[49] The Soviets compounded the problem by insisting the four airfields be built at the same time. That meant Beijing would have to employ combat troops, something Peng was reluctant to accept.

The CPV had just suffered a serious battlefield setback. The CPV forces that had entered the war in October were severely weakened and badly in need of rest and reinforcement. Peng did not want any of his three crack armies (the Thirty-eighth, Thirty-ninth, and Forty-second) that had just been pulled back from the front and were resting in the Wonsan-Hamhung area, to assume the airfield construction mission. He also disagreed with the idea of using one of the newly arrived armies. The agreement worked out between Beijing and Pyongyang required the Chinese to construct two airfields with concrete runways at Sunan and Sunchon, and two airfields with pierced-steel-plank runways at Yongyu and Namyongni for the Soviets. During the same period, the North Koreans would build two airfields in Pyongyang for the Chinese.[50] Zhou advised Peng that constructing an airfield for jet aircraft in China required twenty-four thousand man-days. Considering the difficult conditions in North Korea, he believed the construction of the four Soviet airfields would require ninety-six thousand man-days. North Korea could not supply that amount of manpower. Concluding that this task could only be handled by combat troops, Zhou urged Peng to accept the proposed arrangement, reminding him that if the Soviet air force units did not move into Korea, the Chinese air force would never be able to operate from advanced airfields there.[51]

In late March, the CMC assigned the Forty-seventh Army (three divisions and two engineer regiments), three air force engineer regiments, and more than a thousand civilian engineers to perform airfield construction work. Later, additional troops (including four newly recruited regiments from the Thirty-eighth Army, plus two divisions and the headquarters from the Fiftieth Army) were mobilized for construction when it became evident that progress was too slow.[52] In view of the Soviet request for an equal number of Chinese air force units to move into Korea along with theirs, Zhou on April 1 implored Moscow to furnish China with an additional set of pierced-steel planking for a third airfield in the Pyongyang area.[53] China eventually employed some two million man-days, and shipped thirty thousand tons of cement, thirty-six thousand pieces of pierced-steel planking, and other supplies and equipment constructing the airfields. The Chinese troops worked day and night, and completed the airfields at Sunan, Yongyu, Namyongni, and Pyongyang by the end of May.[54]

The airfield rehabilitation program in North Korea had been an alarming concern to UN military authorities. During the months of April and May, the FEAF Bomber Command conducted a campaign intended to make sure all of these airfields were "unserviceable."[55] China deployed eleven CPV antiaircraft regiments and eight Soviet regiments to protect these airfields, while leaving many important targets along the supply lines inadequately shielded.[56] They failed, however, to prevent U.S./UN aircraft from hitting their targets. Chinese records show that U.S./UN planes attacked these air facilities seventy-two times. A third of their ordnance (6,826 bombs) hit runways, taxiways, or surrounding facilities. When the last airfield, at Sunchon, was finished in late July, the Chinese realized that the Soviets could not use any

Engineers work on an airfield in North Korea being built with pierced-steel-plank runways.

of the recently built airfields because they were too far away to be supported from airfields inside China.[57]

In Beijing, Premier Zhou Enlai, Marshal Nie Rongzhen, Gen. Liu Yalou, and Gen. Liu Zhen, together with North Korea's Gen. Wang Yong and the Soviet's Colonel General Krasovskiy, had to reevaluate the Communist air war plan on August 4 and 5. A general view prevailed that the Soviet air units alone could not handle UN air pressure unless a considerably large number of aircraft could be involved on the Communist side. According to their estimate, seven air divisions from the Soviet Union, China, and North Korea were needed to take control of the skies over North Korea, which would require the construction of three more airfields south of the Yalu and north of Anju. Only after having achieved air parity would the PLAAF be able to provide direct support for ground operations. They therefore proposed to postpone the air force's entry into the war until November. With this change, the CPV had to cancel a planned new offensive in Korea scheduled for September, and an uneasy relationship emerged between Peng and the PLAAF.[58]

Peng Dehuai and PLAAF's Air War Plan

Fearing U.S. military superiority, Chinese leaders initially adopted a defensive strategy along the line between Pyongyang and Wonsan. They soon found hope, however, that the CPV could beat the U.S./UN forces. Realizing that MacArthur had underestimated Chinese strength, they became confident that the Chinese troops would prevail in mobile warfare. Despite China's lack of firepower and air support, leaders in Beijing, under the illusion that Chinese forces could win a swift, decisive victory in Korea, ordered the CPV to conduct four consecutive offensive campaigns against the U.S./UN forces during the first four months after China's military intervention. By mid-February, 1951, it became obvious to the CPV's commanders that the poorly supplied Chinese soldiers could not outmaneuver the motorized enemy forces while under constant U.S. air bombardment in the biting cold. Moreover, their morale was rapidly declining. In particular, lack of air cover became a widespread concern among CPV soldiers, who consistently griped that they had been promised air cover and had yet to see a single plane of their own.[59] On February 20, in the middle of the fourth phase offensive, Peng rushed back to Beijing to review China's war strategy with Mao and other Chinese leaders.[60]

Since he had halted all offensive actions at the front that were contrary to Mao's earlier orders, Peng went to see the chairman immediately after he arrived on the afternoon of February 21. It is unfortunate that no official records are available for the Mao-Peng talks. Recent Chinese as well as Russian sources suggest that Peng came straight to the point with Mao about the serious conditions plaguing CPV forces. He complained that the fighting capability of his troops had been severely weakened due to mounting casualties and inadequate supplies during the past few months of offensive operations. For Peng, the principal reason was that the CPV had no air cover and lacked adequate antiaircraft artillery to protect its lines of communication, resulting in only 60–70 percent of the needed supplies reaching the CPV's frontline troops. He concluded that if the situation could not be reversed soon, his men would not be able to fight much longer. After a moment of pondering, Mao finally acceded to a protracted war strategy and authorized the CPV to take two months to reorganize before waging another offensive.[61]

Although he felt satisfied after his meeting with Mao, Peng realized that his problems could not be so easily resolved. The biggest problem he had was whether his troops would have adequate air cover. On February 24, he made a direct appeal to Col. Gen. Semyon Zakharov, the chief Soviet military adviser in Beijing, suggesting that the two Soviet air divisions cover the CPV's supply lines all the way down to the 38th Parallel. The Soviet adviser was less than enthusiastic about this proposal.[62] In a follow-up conference with other military leaders on February 25, many participants complained that the supporting system at home was too incomplete to satisfy the CPV's needs at the front. It is unclear whether Liu Yalou mentioned the difficulties that kept him from committing China's own air force at the time. Peng reportedly became very upset, pounding the table and uttering aloud, "This is a problem, and that is a problem. You act like the only one who is patriotic, but not the CPV. You need to go to the front to see what the soldiers are eating and wearing. There are so many casualties. Who do they die for? At present, we have no planes, very few [antiaircraft] artillery guns, and the transportation at the rear has no protection. Many soldiers have died of hunger and frost because the food and clothes could not reach them. Can people at home overcome the problems?" The meeting broke up in discord.[63] Peng disagreed that China could not afford to risk expending the PLAAF's limited resources, as Liu had argued at the meeting. He also did not understand why the Soviet Union was not supplying air support for Chinese military operations.

On February 26 and 28, Peng twice went to see Mao, urging the chairman to make another effort to persuade Moscow to provide air support for his ground operations.[64] While informing Stalin of China's new war strategy on March 1, 1951, Mao specifically noted Peng's keen desire for the Soviet air force to extend air cover to the area north of the Pyongyang–Wonsan line, and to move units to air bases in Korea. The chairman then explained that if the Soviets did not do so, the Chinese could not complete the construction of the airfields inside Korea, and not committing the Chinese air force to the war would make ground maneuver more difficult. Mao apparently did not want to force the issue, however, and tactfully reminded Stalin that his final decision should be based on consideration of the entire international environment.[65] The modest tones here certainly reflected Mao's respect for the Soviet leader, and probably also demonstrated he had reservations about the effect of the enemy's airpower in Korea. Zhu Guang, commander of the 2d Artillery Division, later recalled that when he returned to Bejing several months later, Mao invited him to his office and asked for Zhu's opinion about how serious a threat UN airpower was to ground operations, and how many casualties were actually inflicted upon Chinese forces by aircraft. The chairman appeared displeased with those he thought exaggerated the role of enemy airpower.[66]

On March 3, Stalin announced his decision to move Belov's 151st and 324th IADs into Korean territory to provide protection for the CPV and NKPA supply lines. However, he said air defense in the Andong area would have to be shouldered by the two Chinese air divisions.[67] On March 15, Stalin further informed Mao that it would be better to send two Chinese air divisions to the front to support the upcoming offensive, at which time the Soviet Union would dispatch an additional large fighter division (three regiments and ninety MiG-15s) to Andong. Stalin did not indicate his reason for this change, other than to argue that the Chinese needed "a large number of aviation both at the front and in the rear."[68] He evidently was still concerned about the military and political danger of basing Soviet air force units in Korea. As mentioned before, the Soviets had no confidence that the current strength of their air force in China was equal to the UN's. To avoid the danger presented by such an imbalance, Stalin believed the Chinese must rely on PLAAF air support at the front.

Stalin's decision to strengthen the Soviet air presence along the Yalu was welcomed by Chinese leaders, but they were far from being satisfied. On March 7, U.S./UN forces launched an attack in central Korea. The FEAF mounted hundreds of sorties in support of the advancing ground forces and also attacked the CPV's supply lines. Short on both reinforcements and supplies, the CPV was suffering its first serious reversal on the battlefield since China's intervention. On March 11, a worried Peng again complained to Beijing that without air protection for his supply lines, his troops would continue to suffer a food shortage, a problem that would definitely affect the CPV's ability to resume offensive operations.[69]

While CPV leaders and soldiers anxiously yearned for their own air force to be put into action, Russian air units were having little success defending the crossings over the Yalu. In late March, U.S./UN aircraft repeatedly knocked out the rail bridges at Ji'an (Manpojin) and Changdianhekou (Chongsongjin), as well as a pontoon bridge at Andong. Chinese leaders became desperate and turned to the North Koreans for help, asking them to use their propeller-driven fighters to supplement the Soviet jets in providing cover for the supply lines.[70] More critical to leaders in Beijing was the fact that there appeared to be no way to secure a full air commitment from the Soviet air force. Hong Xuezhi, deputy commander of the CPV, recalled telling Zhou Enlai in April that Chinese soldiers at the front longed to see their planes in action. He said Zhou replied: "China has planes, so do many countries which have great friendship with our nation. However, it is not yet time for sending planes into the war."[71] Zhou offered no further explanation. Recently available archival records and other sources reveal that the Chinese leaders were in an awkward position. The Soviets had agreed to satisfy the Chinese request for more air support in Korea, but the Chinese were responsible for meeting the Soviet demand for airfields from which Soviet air force would operate. Without effective Soviet air cover, the Chinese found themselves unable to complete the construction on time. On the other hand, both Chinese and North Korean leaders did not want to risk their own air forces. Zhou Enlai once argued with Col. Gen. Semyon Zakharov, the Soviet military representative to Beijing, that China would "have no problem enduring the loss of 500 thousand to a million soldiers, but we will not sacrifice our newly built air force" in Korea. According to the premier, China's air force remained small and it would be difficult to develop a larger one if its strength was severely sapped by the war.[72]

On April 22, the CPV launched the fifth-phase offensive campaign to push U.S./UN forces farther back from the 38th Parallel.[73] The Chinese ground forces had been promised air support for their offensive, but the PLAAF was unable to assist as planned. Continuing to operate on the ground without air cover, the Chinese troops failed to recover much territory or destroy a large concentration of enemy troops. Instead, they suffered heavy casualties and material losses.[74] The CPV's leaders became increasingly anxious for air support. In 1959, Peng recalled that the fifth offensive campaign was one of the few military mistakes he made during his revolutionary career.[75] "Had the Chinese controlled the skies during the early offensive campaigns," he often muttered to his colleagues and subordinates, "the American and British invaders would have already been eliminated from Korea."[76] One Chinese military historian points out that the CPV's defeat in May, 1951, demonstrated the Communist forces' inability to overwhelm the enemy without air cover to guarantee the delivery of supplies.[77] Although the PLAAF had already established an air inventory of MiGs and other combat planes, the question remained: Could inexperienced Chinese pilots challenge U.S./UN pilots for control of the air if the Soviets continued to limit their support and involvement? The PLAAF's leaders did not doubt that Chinese pilots needed additional training before they were exposed to combat, but this attitude is inconsistent with their early rhetoric that Chinese pilots should be trained under actual combat conditions. Liu Yalou, however, had to play safe, and revised China's air war plan in June.[78]

Stalin Urges the Chinese Air Force into Action

While the Chinese were frustrated by the limited Soviet air involvement, leaders in Moscow were also becoming uneasy about the situation in Korea. At the start of the Korean War, Stalin and other Soviet leaders reportedly were convinced that the combination of Chinese troops and Soviet weapons would be unbeatable.[79] However, by mid-1951, the news from the battlefront indicated that the Soviet-supported Communist troops were unable to destroy any significant number of U.S./UN forces. According to Peng's report to Mao, which was forwarded to Stalin by Colonel General Krasovskiy from Beijing on June 4, U.S./UN troops possessed not only a great quantity of aircraft, tanks, and strong artillery, but also had relatively high morale. Incapable of operating in the daytime, the Chinese had yet to find an effective way to negate the enemy's effective strength.[80] Peng did not express any grievances in this report, but it is unlikely that Stalin did not feel China's pressure for more Soviet assistance.

As Stalin read the secret Chinese reports, he became increasingly dissatisfied with the progress of the Chinese air force, which was apparently more critical to the Communist war effort in Korea than anticipated. In the meantime, a dispute erupted between PLAAF negotiators in Moscow and the

Soviet Ministry of Defense. The Chinese protested that the MiG-9s the Soviets insisted on selling them could not compete with F-86s. Marshal Vasiliyevskiy replied that the problem was not with the aircraft, but the Chinese pilots who flew them.[81] Stalin finally intervened, promising that the Soviet Union would send 372 MiG-15s to the Chinese to replace the antiquated jets within two months. According to Stalin's telegrams to Mao on May 22 and 26, the Russians had sought to equip the Chinese air force with MiG-9s because they thought the aircraft was superior to the best British-American jets. However, the air war over North Korea had proven them wrong, and in order to enhance China's national defense, he had to take measures to improve it. Stalin particularly excused the Soviet failure to satisfy China's demands in the past, and made a gratuitous offer to compensate the Chinese.[82]

The Chinese welcomed this decision.[83] The question is, was the Soviet leader being generous? A recent Russian study shows that by early 1950, the Soviet Union had already introduced the MiG-15bis, which performed better than the basic MiG-15.[84] By the end of that year, thirteen hundred of the new MiGs had rolled off the assembly lines and production of the old model had already halted. In other words, the Soviet air force was upgrading its own units as fast as the new MiGs could be produced.[85] If the Soviets were not trying to dump obsolescent aircraft on China, the question should be to what extent they had a hard time assessing the characteristics of the enemy's aircraft, which their pilots had been encountering in Korea for several months. The MiG-9 and F-80 were among the first operational jet fighters in aviation history, and the former was inferior to the latter.[86] In Korea, the Shooting Star, when flown by skillful American pilots, appeared to be more maneuverable than the MiG-15bis. Nevertheless, in one of the aforementioned telegrams Stalin reminded the Chinese that although the MiG-9 was not as good as the best U.S. and British jet fighters, it could still be used to engage bombers and less advanced fighters.[87] Regardless of what explanations Stalin offered to the Chinese, it soon became clear that what he actually had in mind was for the Chinese to be dependent on only their own air force at the front.

On June 13, Stalin wrote to Mao stating in no uncertain terms that he considered it "absolutely necessary now to start forming at least eight fighter aviation divisions from the sixteen Chinese divisions." In addition to creating two or three new MiG-15 divisions, the Soviet leader asserted that the Chinese "could take to the front from central and southern China five or six MiG-9 divisions, which can operate effectively against bombers." He also appeared highly critical and impatient about the Chinese leaders' hesitation, noting that Chinese pilots should have been able to participate in combat after receiving seven to eight months of training. Otherwise, they would be only "paper pilots."[88] Stalin also sent a telegram to Colonel General Krasovskiy in Beijing, criticizing him and General Belov for training "the Koreans very slowly and in a slipshod manner," while intending to "make professors rather than battle pilots out of the Chinese." He could not understand how Russian pilots could be trained in five or six months, while Chinese pilots were unable to complete their training in seven to eight months. He urged his generals to throw away their "harmful overcautiousness" and devote themselves to creating "more quickly a group of eight Chinese fighter divisions and send them to the front." Concluding his directive, Stalin instructed Belov to free up two airfields for the deployment of Chinese fighter divisions, emphasizing that the Chinese must be made to rely on only their own aviation at the front.[89]

Stalin's pressure made the Chinese leader feel ill at ease. Mao did not believe that airpower should play a determining role in the war, but he also did not want to see the young Chinese pilots become "paper pilots," as Stalin insinuated. After he received Stalin's cable, Mao ordered the PLA General Staff to draw up a plan for sending eight Chinese fighter divisions into battle.[90] He then summoned Liu Yalou and urged the PLAAF commander to use every opportunity to help his troops gain combat experience. To dispel Liu's misgivings, the chairman pointed out that it was impossible for the air force, as a newly created arm of the service, to get everything ready for the war. No one, Mao continued, expected the air force "to amaze the world with a single brilliant feat," but they did expect it to get into the fight.[91]

By mid-June, 1951, the PLAAF had six fighter divisions (three MiG-9, two MiG-15, and one with a regiment of MiG-15s and a regiment of La-11s) ready for combat, while five other fighter divisions (four MiG-15 and one La-9) were in the process of retraining.[92] On June 23, Liu Yalou reported to Mao that the PLAAF would deploy eleven air divisions (fifteen fighter regiments, four attack aircraft regiments, and three bomber regiments) with a total of six hundred aircraft to Korea in September. While urging the North Koreans to complete the construction of six airfields for jet aircraft as soon as possible, and to build two additional airfields south of Pyongyang, the air force commander disagreed about sending their MiG-9 divisions to the front. He and other air force leaders did not believe that obsolete MiG-9s would be a match for U.S. F-84s.[93] They insisted that it would be better to spend another one and a half to two months retraining the pilots of three MiG-9 divisions (6th, 16th, and 14th) on MiG-15s, and then send them to the front. Stalin apparently disagreed. He said it took only ten days to train MiG-9 pilots to fly MiG-15s in Russia, and wondered why the Chinese needed a course of two months to do so.[94] Nevertheless, on June 26, Stalin instructed Soviet air units (17th Guards, 144th, and 328th IADs) in China to start retraining the Chinese pilots in three air divisions on MiG-15s immediately, so that they could participate in the forthcoming operations in Korea.[95]

In the meantime, following Mao's directive, the PLAAF stepped up its preparations by moving three regiments from the 3d and 4th Divisions to Langtou Airfield in early July, hoping that the Chinese pilots would gain more combat experience before they deployed to Korea. Again, the result was disappointing. During the first day of combat flying, a MiG-15 piloted by a regimental commander was downed by four B-29s. This loss, along with the bad weather throughout the month of July, frustrated the Chinese attempt to engage the Americans in the air in the summer of 1951.[96] Perhaps even more significant, this failure proved correct an earlier assessment by air force leaders that employing a large number of Chinese air force units in Korea might surprise the enemy, but it also could result in huge losses on their own side.[97] The PLAAF's inexperience and cautiousness, together with the airfield problem, again forced Beijing to postpone implementing the newly revised air war plan.

Peng once again was disappointed. Since late June, the CPV had been planning an offensive campaign to retake UN possessions north of the 38th Parallel in September in order to give the Communists a better position at the bargaining table. Perhaps Peng had been feeling more positive because this time his troops were better equipped with Soviet weapons, had adequate supplies and more firepower, and would at last have air support.[98] On August 8, he reported to Mao about the offensive plan and asked that the CPV's joint air command move to Pyongyang in two weeks. He further requested the deployment of ten air force regiments to airfields at Pyongyang within a month so he could launch the offensive on September 10.[99] After meeting with Nie Rongzhen, Liu Yalou, and others on the evening of August 10, Zhou Enlai informed Mao that because the air force was not ready for deployment to Korea, supplies could not be guaranteed for the front and the CPV should not conduct its all-out counterattack for at least the next few months.[100] Left with no choice, Peng Dehuai canceled the planned new offensive on August 21. This was understandable in view of the CPV leader's discontent with Moscow's lack of support for China's war effort in Korea and the PLAAF's inability to offer air cover for ground operations.[101]

The Chinese air force's failure to take part in the war also presented a dilemma to Moscow, which appeared unable to do anything but approve the proposed delay.[102] Still, it is interesting to note that Stalin's personal attention to the air force issue probably reflects the difficulties encountered by the Soviet leader. On one hand, it was imperative that he continue to minimize the damage to Soviet interests that might ensue if Soviet pilots were based in Korea. On the other, he had to avoid losing credibility when his Communist allies were sacrificing their lives against a common enemy. In doing so, he also felt the severity of the burden placed on Soviet production capacity, which had not yet fully recovered from the devastation of World War II.

In the early summer of 1951, the ground war developed into a stalemate along the 38th Parallel. Chinese leaders had begun to reorganize for a protracted conflict, and decided to adopt a new strategy for waging the war. The eighteen armies would be divided into two groups and rotated through the front line every two to three months. The PLAAF would move MiG divisions into the bases at Andong first, then to newly built airfields north of Pyongyang in November, and later would move bomber units to Andong, and propeller-driven fighters, together with ground-attack planes, to the airfields south of Pyongyang. Chinese pilots would be rotated by divisions.[103] However, faced with limited Soviet assistance and U.S. air superiority, the PLAAF's leaders soon discovered that the price would be too high to implement such an air war plan. They thus were forced to drop the close air support mission completely from their air strategy during the months to come.

CHAPTER 6

Soviet Air Operations in Korea

U ntil the collapse of the Berlin Wall in 1989, the story of air operations over Korea was dominated by Western literature, which highlighted the overwhelming success of U.S./UN fliers, while belittling their Communist adversaries. American records, for example, claim about 950 enemy aircraft destroyed in the air, including more than 850 MiGs, while admitting only 147 air-to-air losses in FEAF, Marine, and UN units.[1] The account gains credibility if one accepts that inexperienced Chinese and North Korean pilots were no match for competent and experienced veteran U.S./ UN flyers. However, recent revelations of Soviet involvement in Korea offer a contrary picture: It was the Soviet air force, not the PLAAF, that went head-to-head with UN air forces from the beginning of the Chinese military intervention. The Soviets claimed the destruction of more than a thousand UN aircraft against only some three hundred losses of their own.[2] It is impossible to reconcile the discrepancy between the UN and Soviet records. Still, one cannot understand the history of the Korean War without reference to air operations from a Soviet perspective. This chapter attempts to recapitulate those air battles of fifty years ago as they were perceived by the Soviets, including new information, disputes, and unresolved conflicts of evidence.

The Hesitation Ends

Soviet sources divide the Soviet air operations in Korea into three phases. During the first phase, from November, 1950, to March, 1951, Soviet air units fought limited actions against UN forces over the Yalu. Despite the MiG-15's technical superiority, they seemed barely able to hold their own against the FEAF's F-80s, F-84s, and F-51s. The second phase began with the deployment of the 324th IAD in April and the 303d IAD in May, and continued into early 1952, when those units were rotated out of Korea. Because many of the pilots in those two divisions were World War II veterans and had amassed many hours flying MiG-15s, they claimed to have reversed the UN domination of the skies over Korea, and achieved an overwhelming victory. The third phase began in early 1952 and lasted until the end of the conflict. During that period, the Soviet Union deployed thirteen fighter regiments to Korea. However, the replacement of the veteran units with less-experienced pilots resulted in higher MiG losses and fewer enemy kills. Despite flaws in their air operations, the MiG forces continued to attempt to prevent U.S./UN forces from regaining the supremacy they had enjoyed in the initial phase of the air war.[3]

On the evening of December 31, 1950, the CPV and NKPA forces began the third phase offensive campaign. Following incessant artillery fire, Chinese ground forces poured southward in great strength against the UN defense line along the 38th Parallel. The ferocity of the Communist ground attack, coupled with the sudden collapse of ROK army defenses, alarmed the new U.S. Eighth Army commander, Lt. Gen. Matthew B. Ridgway, who had just replaced Lt. Gen. Walton Walker, killed two days earlier in a vehicle accident. Ridgway considered an overall withdrawal from Seoul. The day after the new year began, the U.S. Air Force 4th Fighter Wing's Sabres retreated from Kimpo back to Japan, and on January 4, 1951, the 51st Wing's Shooting Stars flew to Kyushu just a few hours before Communist forces recaptured the South Korean capital. The most surprising aspect of this retreat, the official FEAF history notes, was the inactivity of the Communist air forces, which surprisingly "made no effort to support the ground offensive," and scaled down their MiG operations.[4]

Peng Dehuai ordered a halt to the offensive on January 8, a decision that allegedly drew furious criticism from V. N. Razuvayev, Soviet ambassador to North Korea, who said the CPV should not stop advancing "on the crest of the victory," but should continue to push the enemy out of Korea. Peng stood firm, however, arguing that "without rest, air support, and supplies, it would be impossible for my soldiers to catch the enemy on foot and even to annihilate them." What he mostly worried about was not repeating the mistakes the North Koreans had made the summer before when they overstretched their lines of communication and became vulnerable to UN attacks. Interestingly, Chinese sources report that Stalin agreed with China's conduct of the war, and reassured the Chinese leadership that no one should interfere with Peng's military authority.[5]

We do not know exactly how the Soviet leader viewed the military situation in Korea. However, Peng's argument seemingly touched on the Soviets' failure to give adequate support to the CPV. Despite a number of engagements between Soviet MiGs and UN aircraft over the Yalu after November, 1950, the Soviets contributed little to the Communist victory in early 1951. While supporting Peng's decision, Moscow promised to speed up the delivery of trucks and other supplies for the front. On January 17, 1951, the Soviet General Staff directed the 64th IAK to undertake an "active defense against enemy aircraft on land and in the air, as well as protecting important strategic objectives, railways, highways, communications junctions, and troop formations in rear areas."[6] This directive marked the beginning of Soviet air operations from China that would directly relate to Communist war efforts in Korea.

Following a relatively quiet first part of January, air activity resumed over northwestern Korea as the FEAF Bomber Command and Fifth Air Force intensified their campaigns against the railroad bridges and marshaling yards in MiG Alley between January 19 and 31. The pilots of the 50th IAD responded by engaging in furious battles with enemy fighters and fighter-bombers during the same period. After-action reports from both sides reveal that pilots on both sides made unusual efforts to gain control of the sky over the Yalu. On January 21, Soviet pilots flew farther south than they had previously and operated in a more aggressive manner against U.S./UN attackers over Anju and Sunchon, the sites of key railroad junctions in North Korea. After all MiGs had returned safely to base in China, the 50th IAD posted a claim of eight F-84s destroyed.[7]

Allied pilots surprised the Communists early in the morning on January 23 with a strafing pass across the airfield at Andong. The 29th GIAP managed to scramble fourteen MiGs, and eight others from a Chinese regiment rose to engage the enemy aircraft. When the roar of jet planes and the smoke of gunfire disappeared from the sky over the Yalu, the Soviets claimed to have shot down six F-84s against the loss of one of their own. The FEAF, on the other hand, claimed one MiG destroyed and another damaged, while admitting to the loss of one Shooting Star destroyed and one Thunderjet damaged on January 21. Claims for the attack two days later included four MiG kills confirmed, three more as probables, and another four damaged, with no Thunderjet losses reported. The Soviet and FEAF reports are difficult to cross-reference, but they give a good indication of how far apart their records could be. Both sides obviously overestimated their victory tallies, but the Soviets seemed to have done the worse job. The U.S. Air Force history concedes that the margin of UN air superiority was steadily reduced over northwestern Korea and that its pilots had to avoid air combat with MiGs.[8]

Despite the initial edge the Soviet MiGs had in northwestern Korea, some technical defects, such as problems with the elevators, soon became conspicuous. For example, in two cases the elevators failed completely, resulting in the loss of two MiGs and the death of two 50th IAD pilots. Although factory engineers soon corrected the poor design of the elevators, Soviet pilots were still afraid to make sharp high-speed maneuvers that would result in high force loads on the elevators. The other major problem was the ASP gun sight, which was incapable of selecting the correct lead angle to the target at speeds of over eight hundred kilometers per hour. After only two months of action, Soviet pilots had come up with a number of requests for modifications by the aircraft designers. Although many of their requests were not satisfied until 1952 or 1953, the improvements sought by the 64th IAK ensured Soviet pilots flew aircraft that were on a par with their opponents throughout the air war in Korea.[9]

On February 3, the 50th IAD finished its two-month tour in Korea during which it established a staggering record: the destruction of sixty enemy planes against only seven friendly losses. Air combat duty reverted to Belov's original units, and the 28th GIAP began to fly combat patrol on February 8. Its pilots continued to prove their competence in skirmishes with U.S. Air Force F-80s, F-84s, and F-51s. Due to the lack of enemy activity and poor weather conditions over northwestern Korea during the winter months, no major battles took place until March 1, when Soviet pilots claimed four kills: one F-84 and three B-29s. With the return of Sabres to action a few days later, the tempo of the air war soon picked up, and the limited experience and skills of the Soviet pilots was exposed. Within a week during mid-March there were two mid-air collisions. The first involved two MiGs from the 28th GIAP, and the second a MiG of the 72d GIAP and an enemy F-80. The Soviet pilots, recalled Evgeniy Pepelyaev many years later, "began evading and breaking off combat," and the situation at the Yalu River turned into "one of flight and panic."[10]

Recently available Soviet archival sources reveal that Stalin initially planned to escalate Soviet involvement in Korea by sending two fighter divisions from the 64th IAK (the 151st and 324th) to Pyongyang, so that Soviet pilots would be able to challenge UN air superiority. The UN's sustained air campaign against the Communist airfield projects in the area between Anju and Pyongyang forced the Communists to abort their plan, but they continued to stage operations from China. The replacement of the 151st GIAD with a new group of pilots who were better trained and more experienced symbolized a new effort by the Soviets to try to regain air superiority in northwestern Korea.[11]

Soviet Air Involvement Escalates

The second phase of Soviet air operations in Korea involved two of the air force's best fighter divisions. The first was the 324th IAD, commanded by Col. Ivan N. Kozhedub, one of the Soviets' top World War II aces and three-time recipient of the Hero of the Soviet Union award. It was an elite unit consisting of the 196th IAP and 176th GIAP, whose pilots often took part in air parades over Red Square and at Tushino on Aviation Day. Many of the 324th's pilots were World War II veterans who had accumulated many hours in jet aircraft, particularly MiG-15s. Kozhedub and his units left their home base at Kubinka near Moscow for China in late December, 1950, and were first assigned to train Chinese pilots at Dongfeng Airfield in Jilin Province, about 180 miles from the Korean border. Having learned that U.S. fighters "were up to the mark," and that the proficiency of their pilots "was of high standard," the 324th's pilots began preparing for future actions, engaging in an intensive combat training program between December, 1950, and March, 1951. When the 324th was ordered to Korea, Lt. Col. Evgeniy Pepelyaev, commander of the 196th IAP, claimed pilots in the division "were adequately trained" and that his pilots had "the best training of all of them."[12]

While mulling over the deployment of Soviet air units to North Korea, Stalin expressed concerns about the security of the railway bridges and hydroelectric plant on the Yalu River, and hence decided to reinforce the air defenses there with another large fighter division from the Soviet\Union. This task fell on the shoulders of the 303d IAD, which had a complement of three regiments (the 17th and 523d IAP and 18th GIAP), each with thirty MiG-15s.[13] It was among the first Soviet air force units to convert to MiG-15s in early 1950, and then transferred to the Far East from the Moscow

Military District shortly after the Korean War started. Major General Georgiy A. Lobov was given command of this division, which crossed the border to China in late March, 1951. However, the 303d did not move into Korea until June because of the shortage of airfields near the Yalu.[14]

Following the deployment of these two air divisions, Moscow also assigned the 87th and 92d Antiaircraft Artillery Divisions, 10th Searchlight Air Regiment, and 18th Aviation Technical Division to the 64th IAK at Shenyang. Each antiaircraft artillery division consisted of five regiments with four batteries of six 37-mm guns and four batteries of eight 85-mm guns each. Target-acquisition and director-type radars and computers assisted them. Their primary responsibility was to provide air defense for the four Soviet airfields under construction inside North Korea, as well as the airfield and bridges at Andong. Fearing an enemy attack at night, the Soviets transferred the 351st IAP, a night fighter regiment, from its Liaodong Peninsula base to Anshan. Between April, 1951, and January, 1952, the Soviet air force not only expanded its commitment to the fighting in Korea, but claimed more MiG victories than during any other period of the war.[15]

Kozhedub's units replaced the first batch of Soviet pilots at Andong on April 2, 1951, and flew their first combat sorties the next day. It was, however, an inauspicious day for the Soviet pilots. American pilots reported that they had engaged the most aggressive MiG pilots they had seen to date, but claimed four of them without a friendly loss. Pepelyaev, commander of the 196th IAP, attributed the poor showing to the "poor combat instruction" the 176th GIAP—the other regiment in Kozhedub's division—received during its training. Colonel Boris S. Abakumov, a former element leader in the 196th, recalled that they were ordered to intercept fighter-bombers bent on attacking the bridge over the Yalu, but forgot the enemy fighters, which attacked them through the cloud cover and outnumbered them at least three to one. Nevertheless, Soviet sources record the loss of only one MiG, and list three others as damaged in action that day. The 324th's pilots soon took their revenge on the Sabres, however. On April 6, Abakumov claimed he scored hits on two different F-86s, one of which was forced to crash-land near Pyongyang and the pilot was taken prisoner.[16]

One dominant concern for Moscow at the time was the threat posed by long-range, nuclear-weapon-carrying bombers. The memories of German air attacks in World War II remained fresh and prompted the Soviets to spend vast amounts of money on air defense. Korea provided an opportunity to test the Soviet air defense system. Countering the American B-29 bombers was a primary mission of Soviet air force units in Korea. Although

A B-29 formation approaches its target in North Korea. *Courtesy* John R. Bruning, Jr.

MiGs had been shooting down Superfortresses since the earliest days of their participation in the air war, the B-29s continued to raid important targets in North Korea. It was not until April 12, 1951, that Soviet pilots struck the UN Bomber Command a heavy blow. On that day, Kozhedub's 324th IAD launched thirty-six MiG-15s to intercept forty B-29s heading for targets along the Yalu. Ignoring the enemy fighter escort, the MiGs dove through the Superfortress formations from above and behind, pouring automatic-cannon fire into the lumbering enemy aircraft. Many of the B-29s were burning, falling, and turning away toward the sea after jettisoning their bombs prematurely. When the sky finally cleared, the Soviets claimed ten Superfortresses against no losses for the day. The U.S. Air Force history records a toll of three B-29s lost and seven more damaged, but, as one American scholar observed, made the "absurd claims" of four MiGs destroyed and six damaged by the F-86s, plus ten more by B-29 gunners.[17] Soviet pilots might have inflated their scores, but several of the damaged B-29s crash-landed either at Okinawa or at fighter bases in Korea and were scrapped.

The FEAF could not accept the prohibitive loss of bombers, and Gen. George E. Stratemeyer suspended B-29 operations in the Sinuiju area until a way could be found to provide effective escort for them.[18]

The FEAF Bomber Command suffered its worst losses of the Korean War in October, and was forced to employ B-29s on night missions after that.[19] Soviet military authorities had concluded that it was a great mistake to use the old B-29s in a World War II–type bombing role when jet fighters reigned in the sky. For Soviet pilots, the defeat of the B-29s also called into question the risk and efficacy of the use of even jet bombers on daylight missions. When recalling their combat actions with B-29s in Korea, Soviet pilots thought it preposterous for Superfort gunners to claim they destroyed MiG-15s with their machine guns. Lobov, former commander of the 64th IAK, wrote: "our cannons had a much greater capacity to damage than the B-29's .50-caliber machine guns. Besides, B-29s demonstrated poor survivability. The computing devices and gun mounts themselves did not provide for aiming at, and effectively firing on, fighters attacking at a high closing rate." Other Soviet Korean War veterans added that they usually broke off their attacks before coming in range of the B-29s' machine guns. Although some MiGs were nicked by the bombers' machine guns, they all returned safely to their bases and flew again after repairs were made.[20]

Another dispute Soviet pilots bring up regarding their counterparts during this period of the fighting concerns who became the first jet ace. American records show that Capt. James Jabara of the 4th Fighter Wing established himself as the first jet ace in aviation history on May 20, 1951. One Soviet study argues that this claim is questionable. Jabara had been credited with shooting down four MiG-15s during the month of April, 1951. In order to set the record, he was allowed to stay in Korea after the rest of his squadron returned to Japan on May 7. Two weeks later, on May 20, Captain Jabara reached his goal when he claimed the destruction of another two MiGs. However, even if all the MiG losses recorded in Soviet documents were credited to him, he would remain one victory short of the title he was awarded.[21] On the Soviet side, Sr. Lt. Fedor Shebanov of the 196th IAP was credited with four F-86s and one B-29 downed by May 8, 1951, and needed one more fighter victory to make him history's first "jet" ace. It is an interesting coincidence that he claimed the destruction of his fifth jet on May 20. The FEAF denied losing any F-86s that day, but gun-camera film and pilot reports indicate that the Soviets should be credited with four kills that day. With only one enemy wreck recovered on the ground, whether Senior Lieutenant Shebanov should be credited with becoming the first jet ace could not be positively determined. The Russian study concludes, "the first verifiable jet ace in Korea could not be identified until the late summer or early fall of 1951."[22]

While air operations in Korea steadily intensified, Russian leaders also became increasingly worried about U.S. attempts to acquire Soviet jet technology. Although the Communists operated under strict orders to prevent aircraft from falling into enemy hands, the UN side managed to recover a downed MiG-15 that crashed in shallow water on North Korea's west coast in July. Moscow appeared to be disturbed by this news, and reproaching cables were sent to the Soviet air force headquarters in Shenyang, inquiring why U.S. navy ships were allowed to carry out a salvage operation to recover the MiG's wreckage under the very noses of their pilots as well as the North Korean and Chinese forces. The commander of the 64th IAK was also enjoined to ensure such an incident did not occur in the future.[23] The USAF did not have access to a complete MiG-15 until two years later, when a North Korean defected in September, 1953. The Soviets, on the other hand, were guilty of trying to capture American weapons. Their first success came in October, 1951, when an F-86 made a forced landing on the coast of the Yellow Sea after an air battle. It was later shipped to Moscow via China.[24]

From mid-August, 1951, onward, the U.S./UN air forces waged an interdiction war against rail communications between Pyongyang and the China border code-named Operation Strangle. Attacks on railroads were conducted sometimes twice a day by "group gaggles" of thirty-two to sixty-four fighter-bombers under cover of a fighter screen. In response to U.S./UN interdiction attacks, the Soviets, joined by the Chinese, escalated their efforts against FEAF fighter-bombers. The recent completion of the airfield at Dadonggou (Russian sources called it Manpo) enabled Lobov's division to fly combat missions with units of the 324th IAD at Andong. The UN pilots reported that "as many as 90 MiGs now entered North Korea at one time," and "employed practically any formation they desired."[25] Soviet information on their operations in Korea during this stage remains fragmentary. Lobov, who had replaced Belov as the commander of the 64th IAK, recalled sending eighty MiG-15s into the fight on September 12, and they intercepted up to 150 F-80s attacking various targets between Anju and Pyongyang. The MiGs came down directly on the Shooting Stars, and claimed the destruction of fifteen enemy fighter-bombers within a few minutes. Although this claim does not correspond to the number of aircraft reported lost in U.S. records for that day, the intensified Soviet air activity prompted the FEAF commander, Lt. Gen. Otto P. Weyland, to ask Washington to send additional

Sabre jets to Korea. Weyland's superiors were unable to satisfy his request, so the FEAF had to pull its fighter-bombers' out of MiG Alley and confine attacks to railway lines in the area between Pyongyang and the Chongchon River.[26]

Because of their superior numbers, the Communist air forces continued to maintain their counterattacks at a high level over North Korea throughout the remaining months of 1951. The air war reached its peak during the last week of October with one bloody battle after another. October 23 went down in the history of the Korean War as "Black Tuesday" for the U.S. Air Force.[27] Soviet pilots estimated that they had intercepted twenty-one B-29s and more than two hundred fighters over Namsi, and claimed the destruction of twelve B-29s and four F-84s while reporting no losses. In fact, the FEAF had sent up only nine bombers (one turned back earlier because of a mechanical problem) with an escort of some fifty-five F-84s, and thirty-four F-86s streaked toward the Yalu in an effort to intercept any MiGs going after the B-29s. The Americans reported the loss of only three bombers and one Thunderjet, but four out of five severely damaged B-29s crash-landed, and two had to be written off. The U.S. pilots countered with claims of nine MiGs destroyed and a dozen more damaged.[28]

John Bruning's *Crimson Sky* contains an anecdotal account of this mission from the American perspective with reference to Russian materials such as Lobov's recollections in Yefim Gordon and Vladimir Rigmant's *MiG-15*. It seems unthinkable for the author to cast doubt on the credibility of the reports given by either Soviet or, particularly, American pilots. Since the Soviets suffered no losses that day, his rationalization of the discrepancies is that "kills scored by the Americans . . . must have come at the expense of the North Korean and Chinese MiG pilots."[29] However, recently released Communist records indicate that no North Korean MiG units joined in air operations before 1952, and although one Chinese unit (the 4th Division) had been operational since early September, it had been sent to Shenyang for rest and reorganization on October 20, three days before the Namsi raid.[30] The confusion of high-speed jet combat and inconclusive gun-camera footage most likely accounts for the discrepancies in the claims by both sides. Individual honor and unit pride, along with the incentives of promotion and decorations, afforded strong motivation for claiming victory. Another overlooked factor is that the MiGs had a high survivability rate when hit by F-86 machine-gun bullets. A reasonable conclusion is that while the Americans scored many hits with their .50-caliber weapons and might even have inflicted heavy damage on some of the MiGs, all returned safely to their bases.

The battle over Namsi doomed the FEAF's daylight bombing campaign and changed the course of the air war. The next day, Bomber Command was able to muster eight B-29s for an attack on a railway bridge at Sunchon escorted by F-86s, F-84s, and Royal Australian Air Force F-8 Meteors. Soviet pilots from the 303d IAD's 18th GIAP and 523d IAP were sent to rendezvous with the enemy aircraft. While the pilots of the 523d were breaking through the UN escort formation with their swept-wing jets, the 18th GIAP's MiGs pounded the bombers with their powerful 37-mm and 23-mm cannons. After a furious dogfight with the UN escorts, the 523d's pilots claimed four F-86s and three Meteors destroyed with only one friendly loss. Their comrades in the 18th GIAP simultaneously chased the lumbering Superforts almost all the way to Wonsan, claiming one B-29 and one Meteor destroyed.[31] The FEAF conceded the loss of one B-29, but listed the Meteor as only damaged. Meanwhile, the FEAF after-action summary of the action over the Sinanju area that Wednesday afternoon recorded three F-86s destroyed, the highest reported loss by Sabre squadrons in Korea. Based on evidence gathered from pilot debriefings, gun-camera footage, and the interrogation of two captured American pilots, the 64th IAK later credited only two Sabre kills to the 523d IAP. The third one most likely made it to the Gulf of Korea, where the pilot bailed out and was quickly rescued. The USAF official history is mute on this "day of infamy," calling its losses that day "operational" rather than combat losses.[32] Whatever actually happened over Sinanju on October 24, several days later, the Americans suspended daylight B-29 operations.

America's allies made only a token commitment to the air war in Korea. The Royal Australian Air Force's No. 77 Squadron, flying F-8 Meteors, was one of the few UN units to take part in air operations over MiG Alley. The Soviets, however, showed little respect for the British-made twin-engine jet fighters. After their appearance in North Korea in late August, 1951, the slow, straight-wing Meteors quickly fell prey to MiGs. In an effort to drive a wedge between the Americans and their allies by "stoking disaffection" among the latter, the Soviets, recalled Lobov, purposely picked on the Australians. On December 1, 1951, a group of twenty-four MiGs from the 176th GIAP led by Lt. Col. S. Vishnyakov were patrolling over Anju at an altitude of ten thousand meters, according to a premeditated mission plan. Their targets were the Australian Meteors. After letting the fighter-bomber and F-86 formations pass, the MiGs dove down on sixteen Meteors flying behind the Americans. In the course of the battle, seven Soviet pilots each claimed to have shot down a Meteor, and Capt. S. M. Kramarenko, a group leader, was credited with two. Although UN sources acknowledged the loss of three Australian aircraft and three others damaged, such a thrashing by MiGs convinced the FEAF's leaders to reassign the Meteors to ground-attack missions outside of MiG Alley.[33]

The second stage of Soviet involvement in Korea ended in early 1952. Russian sources claim that by then the domination of American airpower in Korea had been "reversed" by the MiGs, which had regained superiority over the Yalu River area during the latter part of 1951.[34] The 303d and 324th IADs reported a "kill" ratio of about 10:1. Kozhedub's division destroyed 215 enemy aircraft, including 107 downed by the 176th GIAP and 108 by the 196th IAP by February, 1952. The 303d's three regiments, operating between June, 1951, and January, 1952, claimed the destruction of 302 UN aircraft. In exchange, the Russians reported the loss of twenty-seven pilots and some fifty MiG-15s. Although the UN air forces certainly would not agree with the 10:1 ratio in favor of the MiGs, they did concede the defeat of some U.S./UN air efforts during this period. Robert Futrell, for example, described the battle on October 23, 1951, as a "holocaust," a "blood bath" for the UN forces. After returning to Washington from the Far East in November, 1951, Gen. Hoyt Vandenberg exclaimed that "Communist China has become one of the major air powers of the world" almost overnight. Interestingly, USAF leaders at the time knew that the Communist air victories over UN bomber forces in late 1951 should be attributed to Soviet participation in the war. They nevertheless credited the MiG resistance to the Chinese air force in order to avoid stirring up public sentiment for a war with Russia.[35]

Soviet Pilots Try to Regain Their Glory

For Soviet pilots, the period between February, 1952, and the signing of the armistice agreement in July, 1953, was the most arduous time of the war. In early 1952, the UN command hoped to use its air superiority to influence the Communists at the peace negotiations in Panmunjom, which started in July, 1951, but had made no progress at all since then. The Americans thus took steps to strengthen their airpower in Korea. New, improved F-86Es were slated to equip FEAF's fighter-interceptor wings. Veteran pilots had their combat tours extended when the FEAF decided to no longer rotate Sabre pilots as soon as they completed a hundred missions but to instead wait for available replacements. Following an evaluation of the interdiction campaign, the FEAF called a halt to Operation Strangle and commenced

Operation Saturate, which involved sustained day and night attacks on short segments of railway lines in the vicinity of Sinanju and Pyongyang. In the meantime, FEAF strategists initiated an air campaign aimed at knocking out North Korea's hydroelectric power facilities.[36]

While the U.S./UN forces conducted powerful raids on North Korean communication systems, Moscow replaced older air divisions with new ones. In February, the 97th and 190th IADs moved to air bases at Andong. From Moscow's point of view, the complete replacement of an entire division would significantly raise the combat capabilities of the Soviet forces in Korea. Although the new group of pilots had flown only some fifty hours in MiG-15s and knew little about operational tactics and combat practices in Korea, they had received the best training marks from the supreme military authorities and were deemed ready for combat. This soon proved false. According to fragmentary Russian accounts, the pilots in both divisions scored fewer enemy kills while sustaining higher losses. Within just three months, the 256th and 494th IAPs of the 190th IAD, for example, lost sixteen and twenty MiG-15s, respectively, eleven of which belonged to the latter's 3d Flying Group. By July, Soviet pilots in this group were near the breaking point and had begun to evade combat duty.[37] Colonel Boris Abakumov recalled that many of the 97th's pilots were hospitalized for treatment of physical problems caused by exhaustion.[38] The main reason, according to one recent Russian study, was that the Soviet pilots were still wearing World War II flying gear: leather jackets, leather helmets, and goggles, but no "G-suit" to mitigate the strains of jet combat. As a result, they often suffered from stomach and internal organ problems resulting from the physical stress of executing high-speed maneuvers.[39]

When Lieutenant General Lobov, commander of the 64th IAK, complained to Moscow about the quality of the new pilots, an inspection team was sent to study the problem. It is not known what conclusion the inspectors drew in "this ticklish situation." One former pilot from the 324th recalled that they decided to "delay conferring decorations upon pilots" in his unit so that "the relative performance" of old and new pilots would not be "so strikingly in contrast."[40]

No matter what grievances Kozhedub's pilots might have had, Soviet leaders appeared unable to ignore the alarming allegations from Beijing that the United States was engaging in bacteriological warfare in Korea. When Chinese leaders asked the Soviets to dispatch an additional all-weather jet division to protect China from U.S. aircraft carrying germs, which they claimed were sneaking into the northeast, Stalin agreed to reinforce Soviet air units involved in the war.[41] Simultaneously, Soviet air force leaders decided to regain air superiority in Korea by transferring new fighter divisions to replace those already in China. These were the 32d, 216th, and 133d IADs, which did not organize into the two-regiment configuration assumed by earlier units deployed to China, but maintained their regular three regiments. An additional naval aviation regiment was attached to the 133d IAD. While serving as the second echelon forces of the 64th IAK, they engaged in practice combat flights in Korea and studied operational tactics. Shortly after a surprise attack by U.S./UN air forces on the Supung hydroelectric power plant on June 23, 1952, the fresh forces of the 64th IAK were deployed to the frontline air bases at Andong in early July and allegedly turned the tide of battle. However, they were unable to achieve the same glory in Korea as their predecessors.[42]

Despite numerical advantages, Communist air strength continued to be offset by the UN's technological superiority. For example, beginning in August, the FEAF phased out the troublesome Thunderjets and replaced them with F-84Gs while bringing three fighter-bomber wings up to full strength. The conversion of two other fighter-bomber wings with modified F-86Es further increased the UN attack forces' ability to conduct air strikes as well as engage in dogfights. Pilots flying F-86Fs in the fighter-interceptor wings quickly discovered they had an airplane that negated many of the advantages previously enjoyed by the MiGs. For example, the increased engine power and new wing, with less thickness-to-chord ratio and no slats, improved the Sabre's high-altitude maneuverability and gave it a rate of climb equal to that of the MiG-15bis.[43] Perhaps a more crucial element was that the Soviet pilots assuming frontline duties had little combat experience. According to Russian sources, only 20 percent of their pilots at the time had World War II combat experience, and none had flown in Korea. As a result, pilots in the fresh Soviet units would first pay with their own blood before claiming any victories against the U.S./UN forces.[44]

In June, the pilots of the 133d IAD were relocated to forward airfields at Andong and Dabao. They engaged in their first large battle with Sabres on August 1. When twenty-four MiGs were scrambled to intercept enemy aircraft, they were jumped by Sabres from the 334th Fighter Squadron. Because they lacked combat experience, the Soviet pilots were in near panic. Captain Nikolay I. Ivanov, a deputy group leader, reported that he relied on his own flying skill, eluding the enemy's initial attack with a spiral dive, and then fiercely pulling up behind his attacker and firing his first shots in Korea. He later reported that he saw hits on the enemy plane, but he did not see it go down because he was attacked by another Sabre. With a series of acrobatic moves, Ivanov managed to get behind the second Sabre and furiously pound it with cannon fire. This time he saw his target burst into flame and fall from the sky. After safely returning to Andong, he claimed both F-86s as destroyed. Still, it was a sad day for the 133d, which lost three MiGs and their pilots, including Ivanov's wingman. Interestingly, the U.S. 4th Fighter Wing's records seem to agree with the Soviet account. They show one F-86 was lost and four others were damaged, against claims of three MiGs destroyed and two others damaged. Wreckage recovered on the ground showed that Ivanov had bested an American jet ace: Maj. Felix Asla Jr., who had been credited with five MiGs destroyed and four damaged before he went down that day.[45]

Soviet adversities during this period of the war can also be attributed to the end of the so-called Manchurian sanctuary. Since the beginning of the war, Washington had repeatedly declared that UN pilots were prohibited from infringing on Chinese air space unless in hot pursuit. However, U.S. airmen have since acknowledged that they had been attacking MiGs across the Yalu on a frequent basis from quite early on.[46] The situation intensified in early 1952 as Russian MiG pilots found themselves subjected to attacks during takeoff and landing. On August 18, 1952, the 64th IAK reported the loss of twenty-six MiGs in this manner during the first six months of the year.[47] Later, some Soviet pilots remembered that conditions turned even worse in September. A flight of two F-86s would often circle at high altitude over the mouth of the Yalu, on the lookout for Communist air forces. When they saw dust swirling on airfields on the other side of the river, they knew the MiGs were taking off. The Sabres would then swoop down on the MiGs as they lifted off from runway. No pilots, one Russian pilot recalled, survived such attacks. He claimed that almost half of the Soviet losses that month occurred over their own airfields. In order to avoid unnecessary casualties, the Soviets simply kept their MiGs on the ground when Sabres were reported to be bearing down on the airfields.[48]

In 1952, the FEAF Bomber Command permitted its vulnerable old B-29s to fly only nocturnal missions in an effort to avoid the Communist MiGs. Attempts to thwart the UN night attacks became a primary focus of Soviet air force units in Korea. In June, 1951, the Soviets deployed the 351st IAP's thirty La-11s from Lüda (Port Arthur) to Anshan, where its mission was to protect the bridges and airfields at Andong from night attacks. However, the 351st's pilots rarely succeeded in intercepting any bombers because the La-11s lacked the speed needed to catch the B-29s. On December 4, 1951, for example, Maj. Anatoliy M. Karelin, the regiment's deputy commander, failed to bring down a Superfort that had been detected by searchlights. The result was that the 64th IAK's leaders decided to employ the MiG-15bis in night operations. In February, 1952, one 351st IAP flying group converted to jets while the others retained their propeller-driven fighters. However, the MiG-15s did not have airborne-intercept radar. The pilots depended on the GCI controller for guidance to the combat area, where they then tried to make visual contact with the enemy aircraft. The MiGs did not become lethal until late May, 1952, when Major Karelin, with the help of searchlights, sent a lone Superfort down in flames. It was the first night MiG "kill" in Korea, an inspiring victory. When pilots in the 133d IAD who had night experience were organized into an additional flying group, the Soviets began to take a toll of B-29s at night. On the evening of June 10, the FEAF Bomber Command reported that two bombers were blown out of the sky and one was severely damaged. Soviet sources claim that Karelin shot down two and Sr. Lt. Zhakhamaniy Ikhosangaliyev destroyed another Superfort that night.[49]

The B-29 losses forced the FEAF to employ night fighters with airborne-intercept radar to counter the MiGs. In early November, the 351st lost two MiGs to U.S. Marine Corps F3D-2 Skyknight all-weather jets. However, the Soviets also claimed to have brought down one F-94B Starfire on November 7. Even with no radar, GCI controllers were able to guide Lt. I. P. Kovalev's MiG-15 so precisely that he was able to ram a Starfire and both aircraft burst into flames. The Soviet pilot ejected safely and later received the Order of the Red Banner for his kamikaze-like act. It was also recorded as the first Soviet jet-versus-jet night kill.[50] What might be more important, however, is that the commitment of night fighters did not prevent Soviet MiGs from shooting down enemy bombers. In response to increasing UN night attacks, two flying groups from the 32d IAD were also assigned to night operations in late 1952. According to Soviet records, during the first two months of 1953, their pilots destroyed nine B-29s, and Major Karelin scored his fifth Superfort kill at night. Although the B-29's gunners hit Karelin's MiG, the Soviet pilot succeeded in landing his crippled plane at Andong with 117 holes in it, including nine in the cockpit. On February 18, 1953, the 298th IAP replaced the 351st, which returned to the Soviet Union. By the end of the war, Soviet night fighters claimed the destruction of eighteen B-29s, six B-26s, one RB-50, two F-84s, and four F-94s over Korea.[51]

During the last few months of the war, American pilots detected a difference in their Communist opponents: they appeared more inexperienced, and some Western analysts suggested that "Project Moolah," an offer to encourage Communist pilots to defect, "scared the Russian out of the skies." Other American sources speculate that the Soviets withdrew their pilots from Korea in an effort to wind down the war. The Soviets did not leave Korea, however, and pilots of the 64th IAK continued battling against U.S./ UN air forces until the truce went into effect.[52] On April 12, 1953, the 32d IAD scrambled all three of its regiments' MiGs to counter a large force of UN fighter-bombers that was pounding targets along the Yalu. They scrapped with the enemy aircraft for about an hour and claimed four F-86s against the loss of four of their own (two Soviets and two Chinese). For many Russian pilots, it was one but of many battles fought in MiG Alley. However, it was an unforgettable day for Maj. Semyon A. Fedorets, a group leader in the 913th IAP, who got his fifth and sixth Sabres. One of them was flown by one of the leading USAF aces in Korea, Capt. Joseph McConnell, who was rescued and immediately flew again. The Soviet pilot was injured in the engagement and had to stay in the hospital for a month before he was back in action. On July 19, Fedorets and his group were ordered to intercept a group of F-86s attacking their airfield at Dabao. After scrambling off the runway, he destroyed the leader of enemy flight with a long burst of fire from below.[53] It was the last Sabre downed by a Soviet pilot in Korea. Fedorets, who claimed seven Sabre kills, was recognized as one of the few pilots who enjoyed most of their success during the last stage of the war.[54]

Peculiarities of Soviet Operations in Korea

When the armistice was signed on July 27, 1953, Moscow had rotated twelve fighter air divisions (twenty-nine fighter air regiments), ranging from 150 to three hundred fighter planes, throughout Korea. More than forty thousand Soviet troops (including four antiaircraft artillery divisions and other support units), served in Korea, with a peak figure of twenty-six thousand from July, 1952, to August, 1953.[55] The Communist air forces flew more than ninety thousand sorties, of which more than two-thirds were made by the Soviets, and the rest were by Chinese and North Korean pilots. The 64th IAK claimed that its fighter units were responsible for 1,106 enemy planes destroyed, and antiaircraft artillery units were credited with 212 planes downed. In return, it acknowledged the loss of 335 MiGs and 120 pilots, plus sixty-eight antiaircraft gunners killed in action.[56] Apparently, one historian recently noted, fighting between Communist and UN aircraft over Korea "was on a much larger scale than has hitherto been suggested by either side."[57]

It is difficult to reconstruct a true picture of the Soviet-American air war in Korea. Despite the recent unveiling of the Soviets' secret involvement in Korea, the accounts of Russians and Americans conflict in almost every aspect—including the place, time, type, and number of aircraft involved. These discrepancies should not belie the true nature of the Soviet involvement in the Korean air war. Beginning in late 1950, the Soviet Union committed several hundred combat planes to Korea, but political considerations circumscribed Soviet air operations there. Fearing the conflict might escalate into a full-blown war between the Soviet Union and the United States, Moscow placed security restrictions on Soviet pilots in an effort to conceal their participation in the Korean conflict. Soviet planes were disguised with North Korean markings, and Soviet pilots were required to wear Chinese uniforms when they arrived in China. Every Russian pilot had a Chinese pseudonym, and they were expected to speak Chinese on the radio in combat, although few pilots ever did.[58] Moreover, they were prohibited from flying over enemy-held territory or the sea. In the event of capture, they were to say that they were Eurasian Chinese of Soviet extraction.[59] Fortunately, not a single Soviet pilot was taken prisoner by UN forces during the war.

Political restrictions alone did not make the air war in Korea "highly asymmetrical." Based on the experience of World War II, and the traditional doctrine of the Soviet military, the Soviet air force was regarded as a supporting arm of its large land army, which was primarily responsible for defeating the enemy's troops in the field and capturing territory. In Korea, Soviet air force troops supplemented the Chinese and North Korean ground forces.[60] The air force deployment was intended only to provide air defense for the rear areas in Korea. Moscow actually committed more resources to a vigorous program equipping sixty Chinese army divisions, so that they could play a decisive role in the battlefield.[61] Soviet pilots were given the mission of protecting the bridges over the Yalu and the main supply lines running from China into North Korea. Their goal was to try to shoot down as many enemy bombers and fighter-bombers as possible. The aircraft of the 64th IAK were armed with no offensive weapons like bombs, rockets, or napalm tanks, and Soviet pilots were never allowed to engage in ground support activities by attacking U.S./UN forces, ships, or their bases behind the front lines or in Japan. The Russian pilots' air operations were purely defensive, and the Americans held the initiative, choosing the time for every engagement. According to Lobov, Soviet pilots had to sit in their cockpits for hours every day awaiting takeoff, an act that was very demoralizing.[62]

The Soviet manning system also contributed to the peculiarities of air operations in Korea. Soviet generals thought it better to deploy smaller, less bulky troop organizations because of the small area of operations and many inherent restrictions. Aviation divisions and regiments were dispatched to Korea with only half of their normal strength. Division had two regiments, and each regiment had some thirty pilots. During one ten-month stretch there were only "two regiments against all of imperialism," according to Kozhedub—a mistake for which the system would pay in pain, blood, and lives as Soviet pilots carried out their combat duties.[63] Not until the second half of 1951 did the Soviet leadership realize that the shortage of pilots prevented air force units from reacting quickly and effectively to combat situations. Exhausted by the tension of combat flying, many Soviet pilots reached the point when they could no longer take to the air. Losses of pilots and aircraft, as well as injuries and wounds, soon rendered Soviet air force units unable to meet the demands that the war placed on them. By the fall of 1951, the Soviet General Staff had revamped the organization of air regiments, increasing the number of pilots to between sixty and seventy each. At least a third of the additional pilots were reserves, used to replace those who needed rest.[64]

Still, unlike the Americans, Moscow abandoned the practice of rotating individual pilots, a plan that had proven effective in World War II. Instead, the Soviets rotated entire divisions in and out of combat. Because the Soviets conducted operations in Korea behind a cloak of secrecy, newly arrived units often had little knowledge of jet combat tactics. Moreover, many pilots had not been trained to high combat standards, and the highly uneven performance of Communist pilots proved enigmatic for their American foes. Each time a unit was replaced, the Americans found themselves facing rookie Soviet pilots. Nothing so characterized this situation as the mischief done to Col. A. Shevtsov's 97th IAD, which replaced Kozhedub's veteran units at Andong in early 1952. Within four months, his division was almost decimated. Despite repeated requests from the Soviet field commander that pilots be better trained before sending them to the front, nothing was ever changed.[65] The commander of the 64th IAK believes this was largely due to the opposition of air force and air defense leaders, and to a bureaucracy that found it easier to move divisions around in Korea than individual pilots.[66]

By the second half of 1951, the North Korean skies were crowded with Communist aircraft piloted by Soviets, Chinese, and North Koreans. However, there was no single air command system on the Communist side. From the very beginning, Soviet air operations were under highly centralized control. The commander of the 64th IAK could do nothing but "take orders directly from Moscow." The Chinese and North Koreans formed a joint air command in April, 1951, and invited the Soviets to join and to lead it, but the Soviets refused, continuing to operate alone throughout the war.[67] According to the Soviet air force commander in Korea, it was a good idea to have a single joint command from a military standpoint, but for political reasons, the Soviets could not accept such an offer. Nevertheless, both sides assigned liaison officers to each other's headquarters for close coordination. Chinese military leaders even required the air force to make reports of its own accord to the Soviet air force command for instructions and solutions.[68] The lack of a single command system and poor coordination between Soviet air units and Sino-Korean forces caused confusion. On occasion, Chinese and North Korean antiaircraft batteries blasted away at Soviet MiGs, and Russian pilots shot down Chinese MiGs mistaken as enemy Sabres.[69]

Stalin and other Soviet leaders reportedly expected the presence of battle-tested Soviet troops to have an overwhelming effect on the enemy in Korea.[70] Unfortunately, such was not the case. Moscow failed to realize there were substantial differences between air operations in the jet age and World War II. The MiGs and Sabres were about equal technologically, and the edge went to the side with the most experienced pilots. The U.S./UN forces outnumbered the Russians by nearly ten to one (although there were more MiGs than Sabres), however, and many of their aircraft were capable of combat day and night, and in adverse weather. American pilots, moreover, were highly qualified and professionally trained in comparison to their adversaries. They made the best use of the circumstances created by the Soviet restrictions, frequently waging aerial battles near the coastline. If they found themselves in an unfavorable situation, they could quickly head for sea and return to the battle later.[71] Despite American claims that they were forbidden from crossing the Yalu, beginning in early 1952, MiG pilots found themselves subject to attack during takeoff and landing from their airfields in China. Many Soviet pilots died before they had a real opportunity to engage their opponents. One Korean air war historian pointed out that U.S. attacks on bases in China "put the Soviet-American 'kill' ratio in air-to-air combat in a somewhat different light."[72]

Not surprisingly, given the increasing losses, exhaustion from constant combat, and the danger involved in dueling with Sabres, the aviators' morale suffered significantly.[73] Many pilots were hospitalized with combat fatigue brought on by their lack of proper equipment and clothing. Although the Soviets serving in Korea were called volunteers, few were there by choice. Pilots are usually young and vainglorious by nature, and it was common knowledge among Soviet pilots at the time that those who had been trained to fly jets would fight in Korea. Nevertheless, not everyone was enthusiastic about a tour of duty against the Americans. Only five years earlier, they had been allies and embraced each other at the Elbe River. Accordingly, some pilots found excuses to avoid flying jets. When Soviet pilots became aware that a truce would materialize in 1953, combat-weariness gripped many Soviet pilots. No one wanted to be the last to be killed in action, and they tended to be evasive during their encounters with enemy planes to avoid casualties, recalled one veteran pilot.[74] Soviet commanders had to devote much of their time to trying to improve the morale of their pilots. Organized tours to North Korean cities scorched by B-29s were used to convince Soviet pilots that they were fighting to save the North Korean people and to check American aggression. Awards like the Order of the Red Banner, the Order of Lenin, Hero of the Soviet Union, and even small cash prizes, were used as incentives to encourage pilots to shoot down American aircraft.[75] According to one unofficial Soviet source, thirty-two Soviet pilots became jet aces in Korea. Captain N. V. Sutyagin emerged as the top Soviet ace with twenty-one kills. The runner-up was Evgeniy Pepelyaev with twenty kills. Only twenty-two pilots were awarded the distinction of being Heroes of the Soviet Union.[76]

During the Korean conflict, the Soviets expended immense resources and manpower defending the Communist supply lines. On reflection, Soviet air operations were crucial in sustaining Chinese and North Korean ground forces undergoing intensive bombing by UN aircraft. Nevertheless, the contribution of Soviet pilots and antiaircraft artillery gunners was quite small in comparison to the role played by the Chinese volunteers. Although Soviet pilots engaged in every major air battle from late 1950 on and inflicted heavy casualties on U.S./UN air units, they made little attempt to coordinate their efforts with ground operations. The limited role the Russians could play in Korea probably prompted Moscow to believe that a strong Chinese air force, capable of fighting an independent air war, would better serve Soviet interests in the Far East. The Soviet leaders thus authorized and supported increasing Chinese involvement in air operations. On September 3, 1952, Stalin told Zhou Enlai, who was visiting Moscow, that China should maintain an air force of two hundred air regiments instead of 150, as the Chinese had projected. He promised that if they did so, the Soviets would supply the aircraft they needed.[77] In retrospect, the most productive Soviet contribution to the air war in Korea involved the creation of the Chinese air force, which not only became the world's third largest air force but also shared in the experience of the first jet warfare in the crimson sky of Korea.

CHAPTER 7

China Enters
the Air War

n the summer of 1951, the war in Korea entered a new stage as the front became stalemated along the 38th Parallel and armistice delegates from both sides began to meet at Kaesong seeking a political end to hostilities. Believing that airpower would continue to play a decisive role in either destroying the Communist fighting machine, or forcing them to accept peace terms in favor of the UN, on July 13, Lieutenant General Ridgway ordered the air force to "exploit full capabilities" during the period of negotiations. Beginning on August 18, the U.S./ UN air forces launched Operation Strangle against the CPV's supply lines and other strategic targets in North Korea.[1] The Communist leaders, on the other hand, realized the conflict would be protracted despite armistice talks and transformed their military strategy from large-scale offensives to "piecemeal" warfare beginning in mid-June. Their hope was that by employing an active defense they would gradually cripple U.S. military strength. In order to halt the U.S./UN air interdiction campaign, the CPV Air Force's troops were urged to seize any opportunity to enter the war so they could gain combat experience.

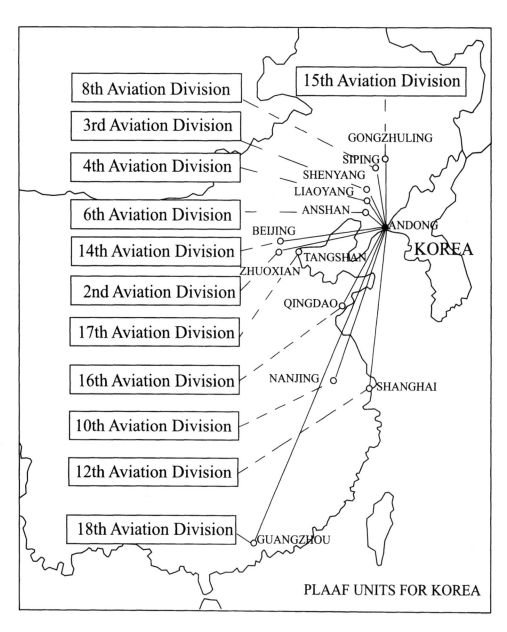

8th Aviation Division

3rd Aviation Division

4th Aviation Division

6th Aviation Division

14th Aviation Division

2nd Aviation Division

17th Aviation Division

16th Aviation Division

10th Aviation Division

12th Aviation Division

18th Aviation Division

15th Aviation Division

GONGZHULING

SIPING

SHENYANG

LIAOYANG

ANSHAN

ANDONG

KOREA

BEIJING

TANGSHAN

ZHUOXIAN

QINGDAO

NANJING

SHANGHAI

GUANGZHOU

PLAAF UNITS FOR KOREA

Home Base

To Front Base

The PLAAF history conventionally divides air operations in Korea into two phases. The first—from September, 1951, to May, 1952—was a learning period for Chinese pilots. However, the Soviets limited their involvement to air defense of the rear areas. The MiG-15 had a short range, and no airfields in North Korea were serviceable. The PLAAF thus could only engage in air defense operations alongside the Russians. The second phase lasted from July, 1952, until the armistice was signed on July 27, 1953. During that period, the Chinese conducted increasingly independent operations and eventually emerged as an experienced fighting force. Given that the PLAAF failed to provide direct support for ground troops, not only its involvement but also its experience remained limited. In spite of these shortcomings, Chinese air operations against U.S./UN forces helped establish basic principles of strategy and tactics for future employment of the Chinese air force. The following two chapters attempt to describe those air battles of fifty years ago as the Chinese involved viewed them. It seems imperative to caution, however, that difficulties in assessing Chinese accounts, along with the lack of access to complete PLAAF records, present obvious limitations to providing a full, systematic view of the air war in Korea from the Chinese perspective.

The 4th Aviation Division Begins Air Operations in Korea

In September, 1951, the CMC ascertained that the recently intensified U.S./UN air campaign against rail supply lines in North Korea was creating further difficulties for Communist war efforts, and exerting pressure on the truce negotiations at Kaesong. In order to counter the UN air bombardment, the Chinese General Staff made four decisions. First, China would furnish more manpower to enhance the repair capability of the Railway Engineering Corps; second, Beijing decided to transfer large quantities of bridge materials to Korea, and ordered more from the Soviet Union; third, transportation units were instructed to use all available ferries to get shipments across the rivers; and fourth, additional antiaircraft artillery units would be deployed to protect railroads and bridges, and the air force would begin operations in Korea.[2]

As early as August 26, the PLAAF was ordered to prepare aviation troops to join Soviet air units protecting the line of communications and constructing airfields in North Korea. Still, no consensus was reached about how the air force should be used. The ground forces yearned to see the air force play a strong supporting role, but air force leaders insisted that ground support would require stationing Chinese planes on Korean airfields, and that would expose the fledgling air units to attacks by superior U.S./UN forces. On September 22, Liu Zhen went to the CPV's headquarters near Pyongyang to explain the PLAAF's concerns to Peng. During the meeting, Liu promised to move Chinese planes from bases inside China to repaired airfields in North Korea as soon as Chinese pilots became more experienced and proficient. Peng had little choice but to agree.[3]

On September 12, the 4th Aviation Division (fifty-five MiG-15s and fifty-six aircrews) moved to Langtou Airfield. Unlike previous deployments at Andong, this time it would be under the control of the 64th IAK commander, Lieutenant General Lobov, and would fly independent combat missions. Because the Chinese pilots were inexperienced, the Soviet commander assigned them the mission of attacking UN fighter-bomber and bomber formations. At a mobilization meeting, Liu Zhen encouraged the 4th Division's pilots to actively engage large enemy formations, so they could improve their combat effectiveness. Still concerned about the callowness of their pilots and lower-level commanders, the CPV Air Force commander insisted that he should personally control every detail of air operations from planning to engagement. After a week of orientation flights over Korea, the 4th Division began to fly combat missions, and Chinese pilots were soon embroiled in their first large air battle.[4]

On the afternoon of September 25, the Andong GCI controller picked up a formation of twenty F-86s flying air cover for thirteen F-80s against targets in the Sinanju area. Sixteen MiG-15s of the 12th Regiment, led by the deputy regiment commander, Li Wenmo, lifted from Langtou together with Soviet pilots to defend the bridge on the Chongchon River, an important link in the CPV's transportation network. It was the third time that day Chinese pilots were sent to combat. However, they encountered no enemy aircraft during the morning missions because of their inexperience. After assembling over the Yalu, the three flights stayed together in a tight formation and headed south with Li Yongtai, leader of the 1st Flying Group, and his six-plane flight bringing up the rear at an altitude of six thousand meters. Over Anju, Li first saw several Soviet flights headed northward on their way home and then spotted eight F-80s underneath them. It was the first time he had seen any enemy planes. He was excited, but also nervous. After informing his regimental leader, Li ordered his pilots to drop their external tanks, then led his flight in a sharp left turn and began descending on the Shooting Stars. His MiG came arcing down in an excessively wide curve that left him out of position for a proper attack. His wingman and the accompanying pair of MiGs followed, firing wildly, causing the enemy fighter-bombers to disperse. At that moment, he discovered four F-86s on each side, bouncing him from behind. Before pulling up, Li felt his plane shudder and realized it had been hit. Fortunately, it was still controllable. He knew that to survive he had to climb as high as possible. Although the enemy's .50-caliber machine guns scored a second time as he ascended, Li succeeded in breaking off the Sabre's pursuit at twelve thousand meters. When he finally landed at Langtou, there were more than thirty bullet holes in his MiG's fuselage, wings, landing gear, and cockpit canopy.[5]

While Li Yongtai struggled to survive, the third pair of MiGs in his flight, which had been assigned to provide cover for the other two attacking pairs, engaged in a fierce dogfight against superior numbers. Stormed by six F-86s, the wingman became separated from his leader and opened fire with his 37-mm and 23-mm cannons as the Sabres swarmed around him. Machine-gun fire ripped through the MiG and the pilot tried to bail out of the stricken aircraft. Unfortunately, he was too low and died in the attempt. It had been another bad day for the 12th Regiment, which suffered its third defeat in Korea since early 1951, losing one MiG and suffering damage to another one. Li's number six pilot was credited with the destruction of a Sabre—the first Chinese F-86 kill in Korea. The FEAF records report that only one F-86 was hit during the engagement, suffering 23-mm hits in its wing root. Furthermore, it is unclear whether the Russians made any claims or how the Chinese actually confirmed the kill. On September 26, the PLAAF sent a telegram commending Li and his pilots as "inexperienced pilots who bravely engaged with more than a hundred of the enemy planes and won the battle." A week later, Mao Zedong also cited the 4th Division pilots for their "courage and spirit" in confronting superior U.S./UN air forces.[6]

In the Chinese Communist military system, such compliments could be inspiring. On September 26 and 27, the 4th Division's pilots fought two consecutive large-scale battles. Because of their poor performance, however, the division lost several MiGs. Nevertheless, the Chinese pilots found a way to redeem their pride in October. On the morning of October 5, forty-two MiGs were launched to provide cover for ground troops crossing the Chongchon River. Shortly before noon, the pilots of the 10th Regiment caught a group of F-80s (FEAF records indicate they were F-84s) that had just completed a bombing run and were climbing away southeast of

Sinanju. This time the Chinese avoided their earlier mistakes and swarmed around the enemy planes like moths around a porch light. Flying in a tight formation of leaders and wingmen, they claimed three F-80s destroyed and two others damaged against the loss of only one MiG.[7]

October, 1951, also saw the emergence of the first PLAAF pilot to score multiple air-to-air kills in Korea. On the tenth, Hua Longyi and his 2d Flying Group of the 12th Regiment took off at 3:30 P.M. to help pilots from the 10th Regiment who were boxed in by an overwhelming number of enemy planes over Anju. Heading south, Hua's flight saw four F-84s flying below them headed toward the Yellow Sea. He started to attack, unleashing a torrent of cannon fire from seven hundred meters behind the enemy leader, who responded with a banking dive that foiled the attack. The Chinese leader persisted in pursuit, caught up, and fired again. The Thunderjet, Hua's wingman reported later, streamed smoke on the way down, while Hua chased the enemy wingman to an altitude of nine hundred meters. He blasted away with his cannons until smoke erupted from his adversary's fuselage, and then broke away in a 180-degree climb to eighty-five hundred meters after he saw the enemy plane plunging toward the ground. Hua was credited with two kills for the day, but he did not become a Chinese ace. Although he scored his third kill a week later, a single long machine-gun burst exploded through his canopy. His right arm was badly broken and he did not return to action.[8]

Between September 12 and October 19, the 4th Division flew 508 sorties and participated in ten engagements. Eight times, Chinese pilots engaged in air battles involving more than two hundred aircraft. They claimed twenty kills and ten enemy planes damaged, while losing fourteen of their own planes. There is no way to determine if Chinese pilots padded their scores. However, many of their claims appear questionable, not only because they misidentified the type of enemy aircraft they engaged, but also because the FEAF records indicate no friendly losses or damage whatsoever during these engagements.[9] Air forces tend to be accurate when reporting their own losses in official reports, and the PLAAF records reveal the fact that the 4th Division paid a heavy price, losing two MiGs during each engagement. By mid-October, its pilots were exhausted. Following Mao's instruction that the air force should "lose no time in getting more air units to gain live combat experience" in Korea, the PLAAF ordered the 3d Aviation Division (fifty MiGs and fifty pilots) to Andong to replace the 4th, which returned to Shenyang for rest and reorganization on October 20.[10]

The 3d Aviation Division Takes Its Turn in Korea

In November, 1950, the 3d Division became one of the few Chinese air force units to fly the MiG-15. The division included many pilots who had trained at the Northeast Aviation School. After the Soviets graduated the 3d Division's pilots in late January, 1950, the division carried out its own intense training program that included flying in tight formations, navigation, aerobatics, and simulated dogfights every day. Its pilots participated in four war exercises organized by the PLAAF to test ground command and air combat coordination, as well as the pilots' combat skills. By the time of their deployment to Korea, the 3d Division's pilots had accumulated an average of seventy flying hours in MiG-15s, and were better prepared for combat operations. During its first combat tour in Korea between October 21, 1951, and January 14, 1952, the 3d Division had more success than any other PLAAF unit.

Apparently drawing lessons from their predecessors, the leaders of the 3d Division approached initial air operations in Korea with caution. Pilots from the 4th Division and Soviet units were invited to give lectures on American fighter tactics and how to resist them. It was crucial that young Chinese pilots build their confidence early. The 3d Division drew up an operation plan that called for avoiding confrontations with F-86s and engaging only small flights of enemy fighter-bombers. If this tactic proved effective, Chinese pilots could gain combat experience and turn small successes into victory. On November 2, the 3d Division made an orientation flight over MiG Alley, marking its entry into combat.[11] During the first eight days, its pilots had five engagements with single aircraft and small enemy formations. They claimed five UN aircraft destroyed and three damaged, against no losses of their own. Perhaps more important, this early success produced the first generation of Chinese top guns. Their stories added glory to the annals of the PLAAF and are often cited in its literature.[12]

Among them was Zhao Baotong, China's first Korean War ace. He joined the PLAAF in late 1949 as an aviation cadet and received his wings in October of the following year after flying Yak-18 and Yak-11 trainers. He joined the 3d Aviation Division and, after four months of Soviet instruction, became a MiG-15 pilot. His flying talent and diligence made him an above average pilot in his outfit, and in July, 1951, he was promoted to deputy leader of the 3d Flying Group in the 7th Regiment. Three months later, he claimed the 3d Division's first victory in Korea.[13]

Zhao Baotong, a group leader in the 3rd Aviation Division, poses here. Zhao was China's leading Korean War ace with seven UN aircraft shot down and two others damaged.

On the morning of November 4, twenty-two MiGs from the 7th Air Regiment led by deputy commander Meng Jin flew across the Yalu and headed toward Kaechon, where their mission was to intercept UN F-84 and F-80 fighter-bombers. Zhao flew as the number three in a covering flight, which had an extra element attached, giving it six aircraft. Just after swinging around and heading north over the Chongchon River, the group was informed by a GCI controller that enemy aircraft had been spotted fifty kilometers southeast of Kaechon. The formation commander decided not to pursue, but continued flying northward. Flying far behind, Zhao led his flight southward at seven thousand meters rather than follow the rest of the regiment when its formation made a left turn to the north.

Near Sunchon, they spotted two dozen F-84s below them at about four thousand meters, streaming in a southeasterly direction in two layers. The group leader immediately ordered six of his MiGs to bounce the enemy formation—four-to-one odds. The MiGs following the group leader dropped down behind the Thunderjets and blasted through their formations, scattering the enemy, who were panicked by the surprise attack, in every direction. The scene turned chaotic. Zhao rolled his MiG behind a Thunderjet in a tight turn and almost blacked out. As he lined up the target in his gun sight, however, he realized his wingman was no longer behind him and that several enemy planes were on him. He squeezed off two short bursts of cannon fire and then broke as hard as he could before the enemy pilots opened up on him with their .50-caliber machine guns. The violent maneuver sent the MiG into a spin. Not panicking, Zhao recovered from the spin and saw the results of his attack: an F-84 falling with a cloud of thick black smoke trailing behind it.

Exhilarated, Zhao ignored the fact that he was alone and continued to press his attack. A pair of enemy planes dropped in front of him, and he streaked directly toward them, holding the trigger down. As cannon shells slashed through the wingman's Thunderjet, the radio crackled with a call for him to return. He made a final circle over the battle zone and saw one plane with its nose plunged deep into the mud on the shoreline, and another one burning on a hillside. At Andong, the MiG pilots were full of excitement. When the debriefing showed that two F-84s had been shot down and another had been damaged, the self-confidence of the pilots of the 3d Division surged. Although U.S. records do not corroborate this Chinese account, Zhao Baotong was the PLAAF's hero of the day. He not only scored the 3d Aviation Division's first kills, he became China's first jet ace and wound up with a total of seven UN aircraft destroyed.[14] However, he very nearly did not complete his tour in Korea. He was shot down in an air battle

Wang Hai *(first from left)*, leader of the 1st Flying Group, 9th Regiment, 3d
Fighter Aviation Division, poses with several of his pilots. *Courtesy* PLA Daily

on December 2, 1951, in which he claimed to have blasted two F-86s out of
the skies, but survived after successfully bailing out of his flaming MiG.

The 3d Division's most famous pilot was Wang Hai. Although he did not
qualify as an ace—he scored only four kills (and another five damaged)—his
leadership and commitment to teamwork resulted in his flying group achieving
a superior victory rate of fifteen to none (including three damaged) against
U.S./UN forces during their first tour of duty in Korea.[15] His group's first
success came on November 9, 1951, when he and his flight of four MiGs ran
into a lone F-8 Meteor south of Pyongyang. According to a PLAAF account,
they pounced upon their prey like a hungry tiger, opening fire from maximum range. It was an undisciplined attack, and the flight ended up totally
dispersed. None of the pilots knew if they had hit the enemy fighter-bomber
until the number-four man reported that a huge explosion of smoke and
flames had erupted from the plane. All four pilots received credit for destroying the Meteor. In doing so, Wang Hai and his pilots learned the lesson that
personal glory and individual success should come second to staying together
and protecting each other during air combat. Thereafter, teamwork became
the hallmark of Wang Hai's flying group, and he and his fellow pilots were
soon rewarded by their dedication to each other.[16]

Nine days later, on November 18, Wang Hai and his group engaged in a furious dogfight in which they downed five Thunderjets. While patrolling with six of his MiGs over Sunchon around 2:30 in the afternoon, Wang sighted a group of F-84s about fifteen hundred meters below them headed toward the Chongchon River bridge. Wang immediately ordered his pilots to attack, and as the MiGs swung behind the enemy fighter-bombers, the F-84s went into a Lufberry circle, a World War I tactic that allowed pilots to cover each other's tail while seeking opportunities to strike back. The Thunderjets were more maneuverable than the MiGs in low-level flight, but the latter enjoyed an edge when climbing. Wang ordered his pilots to climb and then come back down, making diving runs through the enemy circle, repeatedly if necessary. Wang himself managed to get behind two F-84s and blast them out of the sky. His wingman also destroyed two Thunderjets, and an element leader another one. That was enough for one day. After ordering his pilots to disengage, Wang and his group headed home. Because of their devotion to teamwork and collective success, Wang Hai was later awarded the first-degree Medal of Combat Hero, and his group was proclaimed a "Hero Flying Group."[17]

Scoring four jet kills in a single day was a rare feat in any of the air forces involved in the Korean War. One Korean War historian recently noted that jet-to-jet air battles were "so quick, intense, and violent that most pilots did not get a chance to line up on four separate targets, let alone shoot down them."[18] Liu Yüti, a group leader in the 3d Division, not only scored four kills in a day, he did it in one mission on November 23, 1951. Liu recalled that he was leading two flights from his flying group, together with four other MiG flights, to stop UN fighter-bombers from striking transportation lines in the Yongyu area. Over north Sunchon, Liu spotted two flights of F-84s that had just completed their bombing run on a North Korean village and were heading toward the sea. He dove toward the last pair of Thunderjets, and as he lined up on the enemy's wingman and was about to fire, six F-84s in the front broke off in 360-degree turns and maneuvered behind him. His targets, meanwhile, dove straight for the sea. Liu checked behind and saw his own wingman. Safely protected, he decided to chase his quarry down to the deck. When the enemy leader pulled up and to the left to avoid hitting the water, Liu opened fire and sent the plane crashing into the sea. At this point, enemy plane number two was only about 130 meters in front of his nose, making a sharp left turn. Liu did not hesitate, and claimed his second victim with a series of short, disciplined bursts.

Liu Yuti describes how he shot down an enemy aircraft.

As his wingman traded fire with the six other Thunderjets, Liu began to climb to thirty-five hundred meters and headed back toward Yongyu, where he saw seven enemy fighter-bombers striking a railroad line. Now, he was alone and his tail exposed to attack, but Liu ignored convention. He swung down for a stern attack on the trailing enemy plane. The enemy suddenly slowed, hoping to get Liu to overshoot and expose himself to the Thunderjet's machine guns. The MiG pilot had already prepared for this move, however, and slightly nudged the stick, causing him to curve around until he was on his pursuer's tail. Separated from his formation, "the enemy was panicked and tried to dive to escape," Liu wrote in his memoirs. "I steadfastly followed him and unleashed a torrent of cannon fire as soon as I lined up." He then saw the plane crash against the side of a mountain.[19]

Critically short of fuel by now, Liu turned northward for home. However, on the way back he encountered a large group of enemy planes over the mouth of the Chongchon River. Thrilled by his recent kills, Liu quietly dropped down behind the last pair. He subsequently claimed he shot down one of them in a fiery explosion. Available U.S. records do not report the loss of any F-84s that day, but they do record major damage was inflicted on two Thunderjets.[20] Nevertheless, the PLAAF recognized Liu's claims after recovering the wreckage of several F-84s on the ground.[21] In a citation telegram, the air force's party authority congratulated Liu for setting "the best record for destroying and damaging enemy aircraft," and wished him "still greater victories." Liu was also commended for being "a brave and resourceful air force commander."[22]

Encouraged by the early success of the 3d Aviation Division, the PLAAF's leaders urged it to "begin to engage in large-scale air battles." Recognizing that "there will be some losses in combat," air force authorities asserted that the 3d Division should not worry too much about casualties as improvements in command and combat tactics would help avoid losses.[23] In the meantime, the CPV's joint air force command instructed the 3d Division to operate independently of Soviet air units and to seek and challenge large enemy formations and F-86s.[24] It is unclear why the PLAAF's leaders were suddenly so anxious to see Chinese pilots play a more decisive role in the air war, but it was probably in response to the CPV leader's frustration that the air force still could not provide support for ground operations. On November 23, Peng paid a visit to the 3d Division at Andong, and remarked, "if the air force with such wonderful aircraft could control the enemy activities like the ground forces, [we] could defeat the enemy much sooner."[25] The PLAAF apparently tried to do what it could to satisfy Peng's wishes.

Under this mandate, the 3d Division was switched from concentrating on intercepting UN fighter-bombers running interdiction missions to seeking engagements with the Sabres in an effort to gain control of the skies over North Korea. This change of strategy soon proved bloody. By mid-January, 1952, the 3d Division had lost sixteen MiGs and several pilots, including the deputy commander of the 7th regiment. It nevertheless claimed to have had a successful tour during the period. According to its own records, the 3d Division flew 2,319 sorties resulting in twenty-three engagements from October 21, 1951, to January 14, 1952. Fifty-five UN aircraft (including seventeen F-86s) were reported downed and eight others damaged. Mao expressed his gratitude to the division on February 1, 1952: "I wholeheartedly salute to and congratulate the 3d Aviation Division."[26] The PLAAF's leaders, meanwhile, recognized that the 3d Division had successfully undergone its baptism by fire and was ready to play a new role in Korea.

Bloody Ride to Taehwa-do Island

From the beginning of China's intervention in Korea, the PLAAF had planned to employ bombers to support CPV ground operations. When the CPV's joint air force headquarters was established in March, 1951, the 8th and 10th Bomber Divisions were immediately placed under its command. They then engaged in an intensive training program under the Soviets with an emphasis on group and regimental formation flying and bombing exercises. Pilots of the 10th Division were selected to receive training in night flying under an American-trained pilot, Liu Shanben, who defected to the PLA from the Nationalist air force with a B-24 in 1946. In early September, the bomber units were ordered to prepare for action in Korea.[27] Because no airfields in North Korea were serviceable, they first moved to Andong, and from there carried out bombing missions against enemy targets in Korea.[28]

Recognizing the vulnerability of its World War II–vintage propeller-driven bombers in a sky crowded with modern jets, CPV and PLAAF leaders carefully selected the South Korean controlled islands beyond the mouth of the Yalu as their first bombing targets. Taehwa-do Island was one of the most important ROK outposts. The South Koreans had stationed twelve hundred troops there with radar and radio monitoring equipment for collecting Chinese and North Korean intelligence and sending commando forces on sabotage missions along the northwestern Korea coast. Meanwhile, UN delegates at Panmunjom insisted that ROK forces would not be withdrawn from the offshore islands north of the 38th Parallel until the Communists agreed to territorial concessions in the Kaesong area. In late October, 1951, in order to reinforce Communist diplomatic efforts at the negotiating table, CPV headquarters decided to launch amphibious attacks to take over Taehwa-do and the surrounding islands. The Fiftieth Army was assigned the task, and air force units were ordered to provide air support. The air force missions included protecting the landing troops during their assembly, flying reconnaissance missions, and bombing enemy command posts on Taewha-do and enemy warships in the nearby waters.[29]

The air force anticipated a number of problems in carrying out these missions. For one thing, there was little information about enemy fortifications on the islands, or of the activities of enemy ships in the area. Although a number of fighter pilots had flown combat missions, the air force as a whole had no experience conducting joint operations with ground forces. Pilots in both bomber and fighter units had not been trained to fly in bad weather or over water, and were, therefore, virtually incapable of hitting targets at sea. Accordingly, the PLAAF took several measures to overcome these obstacles during its preparation for the air assault. Beginning on October 13, bomber units repeatedly practiced at a bombing range near Siping Airfield. A three-level command structure was established. Combat orders would be issued directly by the commander of the joint air forces. A bomber post was set up at Andong Airfield, and a forward air controller site was established at Chongsa, near the Fiftieth Army command post, to coordinate air and ground operations.[30]

On November 1, four MiG-15s from the 3d Division flew a photo mission over Ka-do, Sohwado, and Taehwa-do Islands in the morning, and a flight of La-11s from the 2d Aviation Division conducted another reconnaissance mission in the afternoon. Both flights gathered a considerable amount of important intelligence information about enemy positions on the islands. Aided by the photo information, ground forces began their first attack on Ka-do Island on the night of November 5. The fight lasted just three hours.[31] Air force bomber units were then called to action in an effort to prevent ROK counterattacks against CPV positions on Ka-do from Taehwa-do.

Throughout the PLA's history, the enemy had been able to bomb Communist soldiers unchallenged. This was particularly true in Korea, and Chinese military leaders and soldiers were obsessed with the idea of striking back at the enemy with their own airpower. When the 8th Division received the order to attack, morale ran high at Yuhongtun Airfield near Shenyang. Every pilot promised to show courage and strength in the Taehwa-do strike. At 2:35 P.M. on November 6, nine Tu-2s took off from Yuhongtun led by their group leader, Han Mingyang, and headed south in a wedge formation. They rendezvoused with their escort, sixteen La-11 fighters from the 2d Aviation Division, around 3:16 P.M., and the latter spread out by flights behind and to the sides of the Tu-2 formations. At 3:38 P.M., twenty-four 3d Division MiG-15s began patrolling the area between Sonchon and Sinmi-do Island at seven thousand meters, ready to intercept any UN aircraft coming up from the south.

When the bombers were three minutes away from their targets, enemy antiaircraft fire burst around them, rocking the aircraft with the turbulence from the explosions. While bomber gunners returned fire at enemy flak units, the group leader ordered all planes to maintain their tight formation. At 3:38 P.M. they dropped eighty-one bombs, including nine incendiaries, destroying the command posts, food, and ammo storage on the island. No UN fighters came up to intercept them, and the bombers returned to Andong flushed with success forty minutes later. The mission was accomplished as planned, which encouraged the Chinese to employ the same tactics in future attacks. This proved to be a fatal mistake.[32]

The air war in Korea had already demonstrated that piston-engine bombers were easy targets for swept-wing jet fighters. Just two weeks earlier, on October 23, Soviet MiGs had inflicted heavy damage on American B-29s over Namsi (see chapter 6). When the 8th Division prepared for the second raid on Taehwa-do, no one seemed to remember this lesson—or the brutal reality that there would be a good chance of getting shot down if they ran into Sabres. More catastrophically, the preparations were carried out with much publicity several days before the mission, and the operation plan (including the number of planes, flight route, and takeoff time) was exactly the same as for the November 6 raid.[33]

Meanwhile, the Americans were waiting for a chance to avenge the Namsi disaster. The FEAF appears to have carefully analyzed the November 6 raid on Taehwa-do and prepared countermeasures in the event there were any further attacks. On the morning of November 30, U.S. Army intelligence informed the 4th Fighter Wing at Kimpo that another assault was expected shortly after Communist bombers hit Taehwa-do again at midnight. Sabre pilots were ordered to patrol over the island and protect the ROK units stationed there.[34] According to historian John Bruning, this assignment "enthralled" the F-86 pilots, who had been hoping to run into a formation of prop-driven bombers and cut them out of the sky. The 4th Wing called on every available pilot for this special afternoon mission.[35]

Not knowing what lay ahead, Gao Yueming, the formation leader, felt uncertain as he sat in his cockpit waiting for the takeoff order from the control tower. He had been flying since 1946, but his crews had flown for less than a year, and the youngest pilot was only nineteen. Although they all had sworn to sacrifice their lives if necessary, a traditional PLA way to mobilize its warriors before going to combat, he wondered how many of them would survive. His uncertainty soon turned into anxiety. He and his group lifted off from Shenyang at 2:19 P.M., a minute earlier than scheduled. After gathering his nine Tu-2s in a "vee-of-vees" formation with three bombers in each flight, the squadron leader made an unexpected early 180-degree turn to the southeast. These tiny mistakes brought the bombers to the rendezvous point five minutes ahead of schedule. Gao's formation thus picked up an escort of just sixteen prop-driven La-11s, while the MiGs were still taking off from Andong, right on schedule. In modern air combat, five minutes is a lifetime. The bombers continued toward the target area, unaware no MiGs were in position to protect them from the enemy Sabres moving down the

Gao Yueming *(first from right)* and his crew pose beside a Tu-2. Gao led nine Tu-2 bombers on a mission over Taehwa-do Island on November 30, 1951.

Yalu to intercept their formation. The La-11s were the Tu-2s' only hope of avoiding a massacre. But, even more mistakes were made at this juncture. According to Chinese calculations, the enemy's MiG Alley patrol usually ended at 3 P.M. Thus, when the Chinese pilots saw a jet formation streaking toward them, they believed it was friendly MiGs heading for home.[36]

In reality, it was three squadrons from the 4th Fighter Wing, totaling thirty-one F-86s, on a special bomber-busting mission led by Col. Ben Preston. Preston later said he sighted the Chinese bomber formation at 4:07 P.M. (Seoul time, one hour ahead of Beijing time, which was used by the Chinese) and launched an immediate attack. The F-86 leader claimed he shot down a Chinese La-11 two minutes later. Chinese records show their pilots did not see the enemy aircraft until 3:12 P.M. (4:12 P.M. Seoul time). Surprised by the Sabre attack, Gao ordered his bombers to fly closer, and they pressed on toward Taehwa-do, a two-minute flight ahead of them. It was too late for Gao's number nine and ten aircraft in the trailing formation, however. They were already in flames and falling behind. One of the bombers exploded, and the other plunged into the water. The sky turned chaotic with "F-86s darting in and out of the lumbering Tu-2s like sharks excited by the scent of blood in the water."[37] Meanwhile, the leader of the trailing formation was himself under heavy fire from the F-86s. His rudder

Zhang Jihui poses in the cockpit of his MiG-15bis. Zhang was credited with shooting down U.S. fighter ace George Davis of the 4th Fighter Interceptor Wing on February 10, 1952.

According to USAF records, Davis led his squadron of eighteen Sabres north to shield a fighter-bomber attack near Kunu-ri on the morning of February 10. When they reached their patrol station, Davis spotted a large formation of MiGs over Manchuria, heading in their direction. He and his wingman left the rest of the Sabres and sped toward the Yalu in an attempt to keep the MiGs from bouncing the allied fighter-bombers. The attack leader, Wang Tianbao, was particularly successful. He lined up on an F-86 and fired a long burst that sent his target spinning out of control toward the sea. He thus became the first PLAAF pilot to down an enemy jet with a Soviet-built propeller-driven fighter. The Americans reported no losses that day, but Wang's story was not a total fabrication. An F-86 from the 335th Squadron was severely damaged, taking hits in the left wing and the back of the fuselage from a La-11. A 23mm cannon shell exploded through the canopy and hit the pilot's headrest, knocking him out and sending his plane into a spin. He regained consciousness, however, recovered from the spin just before hitting the water; and then nursed the badly damaged plane back to base.[38]

The valor and sacrifices of the escort pilots did not stop the ensuing slaughter, however. The six remaining bombers held their course despite the Sabre attacks, and all but one took hits either during the enemy's initial pass or within the next few minutes. Flames poured out from both engines of the number six aircraft as the Tu-2 staggered along with the formation for three minutes before exploding. The right wingman in the lead fight was singled out by four Sabres, who detonated his fuel tank with machine-gun fire. Gao Yueming ordered the crew to bail out of the fire-engulfed plane immediately, but his wingman chose to stick with the aircraft as it tumbled toward the beach below. The shattered remains of the Tu-2 formation reached the island at 3:21 P.M., and Gao salvoed his bombs before turning left toward the coast. The rest of the Tu-2s in the formation dropped their bombs a few

Surviving crewmen of the 1st Flying Group, 24th Regiment, 8th Bomber Aviation Division, pose with maintenance personnel in front of a Tu-2 after the bloody mission of November 30, 1951.

seconds later. They were still short of their target—the enemy's forward positions and command post—and their bombs landed harmlessly on the beach, doing nothing but churn up sand.[39]

For nine minutes, Gao's bomber group and its prop escorts fought the battle despite a great disparity in strength. Twenty-four MiG-15s from the 3d Division took off at 3:04 P.M., but it was too late for them to get into position ahead of or above the bombers. Only one flight, led by the leader of the 3d Flying Group, bounced the Sabres at the tail end of the American attack. According to U.S. sources, they almost destroyed one F-86, which managed to escape with "a good-sized hole out of his right wing," from a MiG cannon shell. His survival came at the expense of a Chinese MiG.[40] The Chinese later acknowledged that the flight leader died in the action over Taehwa-do while trying to rescue his bomber comrades.[41]

The November 30 mission was a complete disaster for the Chinese air force, which lost four Tu-2s, three La-11s, and one MiG-15. Only one navigator survived, although wounded after he bailed out from his flaming bomber, while the other fifteen bomber crews and four escort pilots shed their last drop of blood over Taewho-do Island. The Chinese claimed three F-86s were shot down during the raid, but that number was surely inaccurate.[42] On the other hand, the American pilots were not immune to the inflation of their victory scores. According to USAF records, they intercepted twelve Tu-2s and made an initial claim of six, but they added two more destroyed after examining gun camera evidence from the mission.[43] Gao and the rest of his group landed at Langtou at 3:30 P.M. and flew back to Shenyang the next day.

The Taehwa-do disaster demonstrated the PLAAF's inexperience. During a 1999 interview, Gao appeared very regretful when recalling how they might have avoided the defeat. He said he believed that would have been possible had the attack been conducted much later in the day. However, since none of his pilots had any night training, such a tactic was not an option for PLAAF leaders at the time. Indeed, Gao did not know the tragedy was accidental. Had his bomber formation not taken off early and reached the rendezvous point five minutes ahead of schedule, it would not have encountered the enemy F-86s that had already reached their patrol limit. Gao, because of his heroism, received the second-degree Medal of Combat Hero, and his group was awarded with the first class merit citation. Meanwhile, the PLAAF assimilated the lessons from the Taehwa-do disaster and became less interested in the offensive air war plan they had adopted in late 1950. No further attempts were made to use bombers in daylight raids, and the PLAAF increasingly relied on its fighter units in the Korean air war.

A group of F-86 pilots is pictured here at Kimpo Air Base, Korea, 1951. Winton W. Marshall *(second from left)*, George A. Davis *(third from left)*, and Ben Preston *(center)*. *Courtesy* Alfred W. Dymock, Jr.

The PLAAF Seeks Revenge

Could the PLAAF find a way to avenge the disaster of the third Taehwa-do mission? Shooting down the Americans' top ace, Maj. George Davis, on February 10, 1952, certainly would qualify. Major Davis was one of the first Americans to become an ace in both World War II and Korea. He was also the only U.S. pilot to score four kills in a single day, a feat he accomplished twice in two weeks. Over Taehwa-do Island, his marksmanship allowed him to shoot down three Tu-2s and one MiG. Thirteen days later, on December 13, 1951, he ended up with "four MiG scalps" after two furious battles. With twelve kills, Davis became the leading ace on the UN side at the time.[44]

When the Chinese learned Davis had been shot down over North Korea, they were eager to find out whether they could claim the credit. Pilot reports and evidence retrieved on the ground led the Chinese to award Zhang Jihui, a group leader in the 4th Division, with the kill.[45] Recent revelations of Soviet involvement in the air war assert that Sr. Lt. Mikhail Averin and his wingman from the 97th IAD were responsible for shooting Davis down.[46]

Zhang Jihui poses in the cockpit of his MiG-15bis. Zhang was credited with shooting down U.S. fighter ace George Davis of the 4th Fighter Interceptor Wing on February 10, 1952.

According to USAF records, Davis led his squadron of eighteen Sabres north to shield a fighter-bomber attack near Kunu-ri on the morning of February 10. When they reached their patrol station, Davis spotted a large formation of MiGs over Manchuria, heading in their direction. He and his wingman left the rest of the Sabres and sped toward the Yalu in an attempt to keep the MiGs from bouncing the allied fighter-bombers. The attack surprised the Chinese pilots, and Davis shot down two MiGs in one vigorous maneuver. As he tried for a third victory, another MiG fired a deadly blast at him from behind, sending his Sabre down. Major Davis died a hero after achieving his thirteenth and fourteenth MiG kills. However, this account does not explain why a squadron leader would abandon his command in the air and take independent action when there was no emergency. Even if Davis thought it necessary to "nip the hostile threat in the bud," it stands to reason that he should have taken some, if not all, of his Sabre force with him to intercept the enemy MiGs over the Yalu. It was a tactic consistently used by Sabre pilots throughout the war. What happened to Davis that day thus remains unclear.[47]

A recent book on the Korean air war points out that Davis's action that day was "highly unorthodox," especially for a squadron leader.[48] Davis's irresponsible decision is attributed to his individualistic style of fighting, an attitude that might have made him reckless. He seems to have become bored with the routine patrol, and took only his wingman when he headed toward the Yalu to look for action. Whether this was true or not, a pair of F-86s had no chance of survival in a confrontation with a large MiG formation. In due course, the American leading ace fell from the skies of MiG Ally, as the same publication concluded, because enemy MiGs were able to overwhelm him. According to the debriefing of his wingman, Lt. William W. Littlefield, they bounced a flight of ten MiGs about eight thousand feet below them, and Davis shot down two as the F-86s flashed through the formation. When Davis was about to score his third victory, a MiG that appeared to come from nowhere dropped behind the Sabre leader. Before Littlefield could respond, a burst of cannon fire ripped into Davis's fuselage and canopy, sending the American ace plunging from the sky over MiG Alley.[49] The tragedy may have been caused by Davis's "overzealousness" and "brashness," as well as his increasing contempt for Communist pilots and obsession with his own MiG tally.[50]

However, the Americans initially reported no allied losses that day, but claimed one MiG was destroyed and three more were probably destroyed, pending a review of gun-camera footage. The USAF did not publicly acknowledge Davis's loss until February 12, at which time it revised its victory tally for that day to two destroyed and one probably destroyed. Davis, however, was credited with shooting down both MiGs even though no photographic evidence supported the claim.[51] This means that the claims submitted by other pilots that day were probably discredited due to the lack of photographic evidence. Facing with a congressional inquiry and Davis's wife's demand for a thorough investigation of the incident, USAF authorities made no mention of how the squadron leader made an undisciplined move that resulted in his death. Since the Sabre pilots received a great deal of public attention, the USAF believed that what happened over MiG Alley that day was irrelevant. They wanted Davis to die a national hero, and he was posthumously awarded the Medal of Honor for his actions that day, becoming the only Sabre pilot to achieve that distinction.

The publicity of Davis's death also caught Chinese attention. On February 15, Liu Yalou, commander of the PLAAF, sent a telegram to the joint air command and the 4th Aviation Division instructing them "to use all methods quickly to find out whether Davis was shot down by the pilots of the 4th, or the Soviet units, or antiaircraft artillery units."[52] After more than a week of investigation, the Chinese concluded that Zhang Jihui, a group leader in the 4th Division that day, should receive the credit. According to Fang Ziyi, former commander of the 4th, his division launched thirty-six MiG-15s in two groups at 7:30 on the morning of February 10 to intercept enemy fighter-bombers over Kunu-ri. In the meantime, four Soviet air regiments scrambled their MiGs to counter a UN air attack over an area between Songchon and Kusong. The Chinese pilots tangled with a large formation of F-86s in two battles. One occurred over Taegwan-dong, forty-five miles southeast Sinuiju, with no losses on either side. During another encounter over Taechon, Chinese pilots claimed two Sabres destroyed, but lost three of their own aircraft. Zhang Jihui was credited with both kills.[53] It is interesting to note that Zhang and his wingman were also Sabre victims that day, and the latter was killed in action. Without gun-camera evidence, the Chinese account of Davis's death hinges upon Zhang's own report. Zhang said he led six MiGs from his flying group in front of the entire Chinese formation that morning. Soon after crossing the Yalu, Zhang spotted a large number of black dots far over the sea headed northwest. After making a report to the formation leader, he ordered his wingman to climb with him up to ten thousand meters. He lost sight of the enemy planes during the maneuver, and was separated from his regiment's formation. They then sped southward trying to catch up with the main formation.[54]

Flying over an area between Taechon and Chongye at 7:40 A.M., Zhang saw eight F-86s to the east coming on fast in an effort to get behind them. Zhang and his wingman made a right turn, jettisoning their external tanks as they climbed, then swung down in a 180-degree arc onto the tail of two Sabres. The Sabre leader responded with a sharp dive, and then pulled up toward the sun in an attempt to lose Zhang. As the Sabres made another dive, Zhang closed quickly and fired, but missed his target. After calming himself, Zhang aimed steadily and fired again from a range of six hundred meters. This time he observed strikes along the enemy's fuselage, and a thick stream of black smoke poured from the diving Sabre. His wingman cheered his victory from behind. At that moment, Zhang had no intention of disengaging but went in for another kill. He rolled in on enemy number two as the plane began climbing. When Zhang squeezed the trigger at four hundred meters from the fleeing fighter, his cannon shells caused a massive explosion. With two kills in minutes, Zhang decided to head for home. As he leveled off, however, enemy reinforcements caught him and severely damaged his aircraft with machine-gun fire. He had no choice but to eject.[55]

Zhang was rescued by CPV ground troops and made a complete report of his engagement when he returned to Andong. To determine whether Zhang had shot down Davis, the 4th Division sent two search teams into North Korea on February 16 and 18, respectively. They located the wreckage of an F-86E, together with Davis's body and other belongings on a hillside about a kilometer north of Sambong-ri—five hundred meters from the spot where Zhang landed. A number of soldiers from the Fiftieth Army's 149th Division who saw the crash offered a letter that supported Zhang's account. The CPV's joint air command confirmed that the only pilots operating near the Chongchon River that morning were from Zhang's 12th Regiment. On February 23, Liu reported the air force's findings to Mao, specifically mentioning that Davis was responsible for shooting down eleven MiGs and three Tu-2s, and credited Zhang Jihui with killing the USAF's top ace.[56]

Soviet pilots apparently resented China taking credit for shooting down Davis.[57] After more than forty years of silence about their involvement in Korea, a Russian study states that pilots of the 148th GIAP of the 97th IAD fought a successful air battle on February 10, 1952, in which they claimed to have shot down three Sabres without loss. Mikhail Averin was credited with bringing down the noted American ace jet pilot. Despite their access to the 64th IAK's summary reports, the authors of the study depended upon the recollections of a Soviet pilot who was there, as he was probably the only witness still living who could offer an account of how the Russians shot Davis down. According to Leonid I. Savichev, who had been a group leader in the 148th, they launched a regimental sortie with twenty-two MiGs that day, patrolling over the Supung hydroelectric power station in a "stagger" formation. Suddenly a pair of Sabres popped through the clouds and moved to attack the first group, which was flying below. Leading his group, Savichev managed to get behind the lead Sabre at a range of about eight hundred meters, and saw one of his pilots, Senior Lieutenant Averin, firing from above. "The fire was dead on," he recalled, "a cloud of smoke poured out of the tail of the Sabre and it flipped over into a dive, where it soon struck the ground."[58] In view of the fact that the wreckage of Davis's F-86 was found far south of where the Russians actually patrolled, this description certainly gives no conclusive evidence to prove the Soviet claim.

However, one can conjecture, based on the U.S. and Russian accounts, that Davis first shot down Zhang and his wingman, and the Russian pilot in turn got Davis. Because the wreckage of Davis's F-86 was in an area where the Sabres were patrolling, it is possible that Zhang shot down Davis, and then was hit by another U.S. pilot. Because both the U.S. and Chinese accounts could not be supported by gun-camera footage, and the Russian records not only overexaggerated the victory claims but also misidentified the location of incident, all of their credibility is uncertain.[59] None of that was important to the PLAAF. For several months, particularly after the major setback at Taehwa-do Island and on several other occasions, the PLAAF had been seeking a way to encourage and inspire young Chinese pilots and give the people of China something substantial to cheer about. The downing of a top U.S. ace by a young Chinese pilot certainly served that purpose. Zhang subsequently received the first degree Medal of Combat Hero and became almost a household name in China.

Throwing More MiGs into Air Battles

Several months before Davis was shot down, the PLAAF began planning to beef up its efforts in Korea. In mid-November, 1951, shortly after the Chinese began conducting air operations, PLAAF leaders assessed the military situation in Korea. Since there were increasing prospects for a truce, they felt an urgent need to get Chinese pilots and troops trained and tested in the conflict.[60] It is not clear whether the Chinese asked the Soviets to continue to protect their inexperienced pilots on their first missions and were turned down. This time the air force leaders decided to assign their own "experienced" units, the 3d and 4th Divisions, to cover new air force troops in aerial combat. Because the airfields in the Andong area could serve no more than three to four divisions, the PLAAF decided each Chinese aviation unit would remain for a brief period at the Andong bases and then rotate after engaging in five to seven large-scale air battles.[61]

In November, the 2d Aviation Division (one MiG-15 regiment and one La-11 regiment) and the 14th Division (forty MiG-15s and forty-three pilots) were assigned to the conflict. Because the PLAAF was committed to producing a cadre of experienced pilots, air force leaders devised a procedure that would gradually engage new pilots in combat. Drawing on the experience of the 3d and 4th Divisions, new pilots at first flew into battle areas only when there were no enemy planes present. Later, they flew into increasingly threatening situations, leading up to attacking small flights of fighter-bombers, then small flights of F-86s, and finally large formations of aircraft. Early missions were conducted with the aid of experienced pilots. Later, "experienced" and new units operated together.[62]

The Chinese paid heavily because of the inexperience of their pilots. On the afternoon of December 13, 1951, pilots of the 14th Division flew their first combat mission under the protection of the 3d Division. They sought an engagement with U.S. fighter-bombers, which seemed less difficult for the young Chinese pilots, unexpectedly ran into a large formation of F-86s over Pakchon. The Sabres came in behind them before the MiGs could even drop their wing tanks. The encounter became a turkey shoot for the "aggressive and disciplined" F-86 pilots. Within about six minutes, seven MiGs went down and two others were damaged. Of seven pilots who bailed out, six were successful. It was one of the worst losses by a single Chinese division to that point in the war. The PLAAF was convinced that it was this kind of bloody lesson that helped the Chinese pilots gain combat experience. Two days later, pilots from the 14th Division flew another mission. This time, they surprised a formation of F-84s and claimed the destruction of seven fighter-bombers and two others damaged with the loss of only one of their own.[63] Once again, their claims do not match the U.S. records, which show one MiG destroyed and six damaged, while admitting the loss of one F-86, with two others damaged.[64]

On February 4, 1952, Mao instructed the PLAAF's leaders to attach more importance to the significance of real combat and seize opportunities to gain such experience, even if Chinese pilots could participate in only a few engagements. In early 1952, four more divisions joined the CPV's order of battle on the Yalu. These were the 15th Division (48 pilots and MiG-15s) at Shenyang, the 12th Division (45 pilots and 49 MiG-15s) at Shanghai, the 17th Division (52 pilots and 42 MiG-15s) at Tangshan, and the 18th Division (39 pilots and 40 MiG-15s) at Guangzhou. At any one time, from November, 1951, to the armistice, the Chinese air force maintained three to four aviation divisions, totaling 150 to 200 MiG-15s at the airfields on China's side of the Yalu.[65]

By the end of May, 1952, a total of nine fighter divisions (seventeen MiG-15 regiments and one La-11 regiment), and two bomber divisions, had been in combat. Some 447 Chinese pilots flew combat missions over Korea. The Chinese air force claimed 123 kills and 43 planes damaged, while admitting 82 losses and 27 planes damaged, for a kill ratio of 1:1.46 in favor of the PLAAF. Since there is faint hope that all of the PLAAF's Korean War records will be made available to scholars from outside of China anytime soon, it will be impossible to validate its claims. Nevertheless, an analysis of the existing PLAAF account remains necessary, and the memoirs of those who fought the war are helpful.

Despite their claims to a marginal "victory" over U.S./UN pilots, Chinese air operations encountered many problems during this period. Inexperience and a lack of proficiency were the most formidable handicaps facing the PLAAF in Korea. Chinese pilots made 11,100 sorties, but just 15 percent (1,602 sorties) actually involved aerial combat. Of the nine fighter divisions in the PLAAF, only the 3d and 4th Divisions engaged American aircraft with fairly well executed tactics. They scored two-thirds of the Chinese victories, while other units flew more sorties but scored fewer victories. For example, the pilots of the 12th and 17th Divisions took off twenty-nine times in the months of April and May, but fought only one battle.[66] To USAF scholars, such a low percentage of air combat engagements perhaps means most Communist pilots did not want to engage, even though their formations usually outnumbered those of their U.S./UN counterparts. Chinese military historian Xu Yan contends that a jet pilot was required to log at least three hundred hours of flight training to be declared proficient for combat. China's urgent needs resulted in Chinese pilots sent to the war in Korea with an average of only fifty to sixty hours of flight training.[67] According to the recollections of Chinese Korean war veterans, inexperience and incompetence, including inability to locate enemy planes even at a close range, was the major cause of their failure to engage. If there is any tactic used by the Chinese during the earlier stages of their involvement that corresponds to U.S. observations, it would be their preference for engaging F-80s and F-84s rather than F-86s so the technological superiority of the MiG-15 would compensate for their deficiency. Meanwhile, the aggressiveness of U.S. pilots often complicated the situation. During the middle year of 1952, poor performance by Chinese pilots caused Chinese leaders much concern. On May 13 and 15, 1952, the 3d Division lost five MiG-15s and two pilots due to enemy sneak attacks over their airfields. On June 11, 1952, Mao ordered Liu Yalou to go to Andong and personally take charge of air operations. Chinese pilots suspended flying combat missions for about a month, during which time the pilots summarized the experience of their losses.[68]

The major setback for the PLAAF during this phase of air operations was the abandonment of its plan to provide ground support. Because the U.S. Air Force made sustained attacks on Chinese efforts to construct airfields in North Korea, the Chinese air force was prevented from deploying planes South of the Yalu. According to Chinese statistics, airfields under construction were bombed 119 times. About 13,760 bombs hit the airfields, almost 28 percent of which fell on or near the runways, taxiing areas, and other facilities. In late December, 1951, the PLAAF had to set aside plans for ground support and opted to use only airfields inside China to engage the Americans over Korea.[69] As a result of being unable to use airfields in North Korea, the Chinese, flying the short-ranged MiG-15s, were restricted to an area no more than one hundred miles distant from home base. The lack of air cover continued to influence the morale of the Chinese ground forces throughout the war.[70] Nevertheless, during the period of fighting between September, 1951, and May, 1952, the PLAAF's air and ground crews started to gain experience. Many lessons were learned during these operations, lessons that helped the Chinese continue their air war efforts in Korea.

CHAPTER 8

From MiG Alley to Panmunjom

D uring the spring of 1952, the armistice talks at Panmunjom seemed unlikely to progress since neither side was willing to make concessions on how prisoners of war should be repatriated. In mid-May, the CMC made an appraisal of the war situation in Korea, believing it would continue beyond 1952. It therefore ordered the CPV Air Force to rotate all fighter units through the battle zone to enhance the CPV's fighting power and gain more combat experience for the air force. From June, 1952, to the end of the war, the PLAAF carried out sustained operations involving a large number of air force units for the first time in its history. Although the PLAAF's weaknesses were obvious in combat against a superior enemy, when the armistice was signed in July, 1953, the Chinese air force could look back on the previous months' operations with considerable satisfaction. From the PLAAF's perspective, the Korean War yielded several accomplishments. By the end of the war, it had established a command and logistical system, and acquired a substantial number of modern combat aircraft from the Soviet Union. Its pilots, staff, and support personnel gained critical combat experience. Modern warfare also proved that the PLA's political commissar system guaranteed Chinese victory in the air. To Western observers, these achievements

Chinese Air Operations, September, 1951 – July, 1953

may not have brought the PLAAF to a modern standard of airpower, but one cannot understand the history of Chinese airpower without reference to how the Chinese air force attained those achievements and dealt with operational problems in Korea, as well as their attitude toward the effect of UN airpower on truce negotiations.

The CPV Air Force Command System: Problems and Improvement

After several initial months of operations in Korea, the command structure of the Chinese air force appeared problematic. While PLAAF units at

Andong were designated as the CPV Air Force, its commander remained subordinate to the PLAAF commander, from whom he received all orders, instructions, and directives. At the same time, the CPV Air Force commander enjoyed a relatively high degree of freedom of action. The command structure was highly centralized partly because the Soviets' World War II experience taught that effective defensive operations required central control and direction, and partly because the CCP's hierarchy had always been personalized. Liu Yalou frequently interfered in CPV air operations from Beijing while reporting to and receiving instructions directly from Mao. At CPV Air Force headquarters, the commander controlled every aspect of daily operations from mission planning to directing Chinese pilots to the patrol area. Liu Zhen, the first CPV Air Force commander, recalled that his authority included giving combat orders directly to flying group leaders. Division commanders at each airfield were responsible only for aircraft taking off and landing. The PLAAF's leaders believed this command system gave the senior ground commander better control of the combat situation.[1]

However, reverses suffered by the Chinese air force in Korea showed that centralized planning and control was too rigid and inflexible. Indeed, a more serious problem was that PLAAF leaders lacked air combat experience and thus often made fatal decisions. According to Duan Suquan, the CPV Air Force's deputy commander, the major defeat sustained by the PLAAF on December 13, 1951, was largely attributable to interference from Liu Yalou, who happened to be visiting the CPV Air Force headquarters at Andong. The PLAAF commander ignored the advice of others and wrongly ordered the Chinese pilots to descend lower than a large formation of U.S. F-86s approaching from a thousand meters below. Without the advantage of altitude, the Chinese pilots found themselves in an inferior position as the aggressive and disciplined Sabre pilots attacked them from above. As a result, more MiGs went down that day than in any other mission of the war (see chapter 7).[2]

The CPV Air Force's command and control system was also seriously handicapped by a lack of experienced radio and radar operators. From time to time, communications between the ground and the air were held up in the midst of air operations, and GCI radar was unable to provide accurate information for the ground commander to make decisions. Because there were many low-level gaps in radar coverage, Chinese pilots often failed to intercept approaching enemy bombers and fighter-bombers even when they were very close to each other. In December, 1951, the PLAAF decided to establish frontline auxiliary control posts with GCI radar and communication equipment at Pakchon and Pyongyang.[3] Observation posts were set up in known radar blind zones in North Korea to improve the efficiency of Chinese pilots intercepting enemy aircraft while preventing surprise enemy attacks on MiGs. The forward control posts in Korea were also responsible for conducting rescue missions to recover Chinese pilots whose planes had been downed in combat.[4]

As ground war veterans, the PLAAF's leaders had no knowledge of air war, but they vigorously devoted themselves to improving their pilots' combat effectiveness by trying different tactics and adjusting them as necessary. In the beginning, the CPV Air Force proceeded on the assumption that PLAAF principles of command and employment were valid. These principles included careful planning, concentration of superior forces to overwhelm a weak enemy, and flexible employment. Specifically, the young and inexperienced Chinese pilots were initially employed to engage the slower F-80 and F-84 fighter-bombers using Soviet World War II tactics that called for flying in large combat formations. If the situation appeared favorable, the Chinese pilots would move

Wang Hai discusses his most recent combat experience at a mission debriefing. Liu Yalou (second from left), the PLAAF commander, is among those listening.

in for the attack, otherwise, they would avoid contact. After suffering several losses early in the war, PLAAF leaders came to realize that flying large formations was too rigid and inflexible, and made combat difficult. Also, the enemy could easily splinter such formations, forcing individual Chinese pilots into disadvantageous situations.[5] In November and December, 1951, Gen. Liu Yalou went to the front to study the air war for himself. After examining the records of Chinese pilots, he concluded that flying small, tight, supportive formations would achieve better results. Evaluation of the patterns of U.S./UN air activities also clearly indicated that the Americans employed more effective tactics by flying in pairs or in formations of four to eight aircraft, with different altitudes for supportive interaction. A few months later, Liu devised the tactical principle of flying in one zone, multilayered, four-aircraft formations. This underscored the importance of coordination between pairs and flights and their collective role in air operations. Liu Zhen, former commander of the CPV Air Force, wrote in his memoirs that this tactical principle represented a leap in their understanding of how to conduct air warfare and had a significant influence on the PLAAF's theories of air combat.[6]

In order to make combat experience available to the largest possible number of officers in the air force's early stages of growth, PLAAF leaders decided in June, 1952, to rotate the regional air force headquarters through duty in Korea. They would be rotated at three-month intervals, beginning with the headquarters of the East China Military Region, and followed by those from the North China and South-central China Military Regions. Between July 2 and 10, 558 command post personnel from the East China Military Region moved to Andong. After a two-month learning period, they assumed responsibility for directing Chinese air force operations in Korea. Simultaneously, Nie Fengzhi, the air force commander in the East China Military Region, succeeded Liu Zhen as the joint air force commander, and remained in that post until the end of the war.[7]

After several months, air force leaders recognized that the frequent replacement of CPV Air Force headquarters staffs with inexperienced personnel had an adverse effect on the planning and conduct of effective air operations. As a result, an adjustment was made in early 1953. Personnel from various regional command headquarters would be dispatched to CPV Air Force headquarters to study air operations. The first group, seven hundred men from the North China Military Region air force headquarters, arrived in Andong in May. The armistice was signed before personnel from other regional command headquarters had the opportunity to experience wartime air operations.[8]

The CCP's senior leaders were well aware of the importance of higher commanders gaining adequate combat experience. For them, the Korean War was a great school in which the commanders of divisions and larger organizations could gain more knowledge of modern warfare than they could from military academies. In his response to the General Staff Department's August 16, 1952, report on the dispatch of army and division commanders to Korea, Mao stressed that "all those army and division commanders must attend, only those who are ill can be excused."[9] Following Mao's instruction, the air force developed a plan to send leaders from aviation schools and commanders of air divisions not yet scheduled for action in Korea, to CPV Air Force units to study and gain combat experience. By July, 1953, more than 1,070 officers and enlisted men from various levels of air force headquarters had rotated through Korea. In addition, some three hundred officers from the General Staff Department, naval aviation, and antiaircraft artillery force headquarters were sent to Andong to study air war operations.[10]

The developments and modifications experienced by the PLAAF during its twenty-two month assignment in Korea were many. Progressing from the first stage of initial difficulties and stopgap solutions, all the requirements implicit in continuous development in the fields of tactics, organization, and technology were recognized and provided for as time went on. Some modifications had a long-term effect on basic principles of command and employment. With the disbanding of bomber and attack aircraft commands, the concept of ground-support missions was relegated more and more to the background. Although the experience PLAAF leaders gained in Korea was important, it was limited to air defense. It is open to question whether this experience was really an advantage for the PLAAF in the long run.

Political Mobilization and PLAAF Operations

In the military tradition of the Chinese Communists, CCP military leaders regarded the human factor as one of the most important elements of victory or defeat. Even though the U.S./UN forces had higher-quality equipment and technology, they believed that a weak force like the CPV could discharge its duties in Korea and overwhelm superior enemy forces if its soldiers maintained high morale in combat.[11] Following this military tradition, PLAAF leaders were convinced high morale could make the young, inexperienced Chinese pilots brave, an important factor that would help them improve combat efficiency and cope with other war-related difficulties. Throughout the Korean War, the Chinese air force placed much emphasis on morale and political mobilization to improve combat efficiency.[12]

In the early stages of the PLAAF's entry into the Korean air war, Chinese pilots experienced profound fear and a sense of uncertainty about fighting the U.S./UN air forces. Many Chinese pilots thought engaging F-80s with MiG-15s was no problem, but they were afraid of coming up against the F-86s. A survey by the 4th Aviation Division Political Department demonstrated that 10 percent of pilots were particularly pessimistic during their first tour in Korea.[13] According to the postwar analysis of the MiG-15 and F-86, the two aircraft were "about equal when flown by experienced pilots," and which aircraft would prevail depended upon the "tactics, experience, and personal qualities of pilots."[14] To overcome their pilots' fears, PLAAF leaders used political propaganda to instill patriotism, internationalism, and revolutionary heroism. While accusing the United States of fighting an unjust war, and proclaiming China's obligation to aid Korea because it was a close neighbor, the PLAAF stressed to Chinese pilots that the Korean War was a training field and that they could not improve their combat ability without engaging in real air battles. Because the air force was a new branch of the PLA, the political work focused on exhorting pilots to continue the tradition of the ground troops and contend for the title of hero. On October 29, 1951, the PLAAF Political Department issued a decree to award those who shot down enemy aircraft a merit citation. To honor the pilot who shot down an enemy aircraft and distinguish his plane, the ground crews who supported the pilot were allowed to paint red stars on the front fuselage of the aircraft, each star representing a victory.[15]

Regardless of whether these measures really worked, the PLAAF literature asserts they helped prepare Chinese pilots to fight the Americans. However, the early battle experiences brought new concerns and problems for the PLAAF forces. After suffering losses, some pilots became afraid to fly at the end of a formation because the position was extremely vulnerable to enemy attack. On the day of a mission, they would use sickness as an excuse to avoid combat or they would declare a mechanical problem and return to base before an engagement took place. Others felt the F-86s were better than the MiGs, and that American pilots were not only proficient, but also brave. They complained that ground commanders did not care about their lives and that air commanders did not give adequate consideration to protecting pilots. After the 4th Division's 12th Regiment suffered consecutive losses in September, 1951, the morale of the pilots at Andong was very low.[16]

The CPV Air Force relied on CCP organizations to solve these problems. Party meetings were convened to criticize regimental and squadron leaders who showed no courage in air battles. After identifying pilots who lacked the will to fight and who attempted to evade combat, party officers used one-on-one methods of indoctrination to change their attitudes and held group meetings to condemn their cowardliness. In addition, they closely monitored these pilots' words and actions. The PLAAF's political authorities had to be harsh when faced with misconduct in operations. Zhang Zhongxiang, a wingman, was court-martialed and imprisoned because he broke off an engagement when an enemy plane attacked his element and killed his leader. The severe punishment of deserters, coupled with criticism and self-criticism of undisciplined behavior and cowardice, enabled party authorities to effectively control pilots. In this way, they felt the unity of troops was consolidated and the combat morale of pilots boosted.[17]

Inflated combat morale, while welcomed, also caused anxiety among Chinese pilots, who were eager to redeem themselves with personal glory and individual success. The basic principles of air operations—teamwork, protecting each other, and tactics—were often ignored. According to PLAAF records, five of eight regimental commanders were killed in action over Korea because of their brashness. For example, when many pilots of the 3d Aviation Division claimed victories over the Americans during their first two and one-half months of war in Korea, Meng Jin, commander of the 7th Regiment, who had scored no hits, became increasingly impatient and felt embarrassed. He wrote in his diary that the pilots "of an heroic unit cannot tolerate someone as their commander who has not shot down any enemy aircraft."[18] With that frustrated mind-set, Meng took off on the afternoon of January 11, 1952, leading sixteen MiG-15s. He and his regiment had orders to defend against enemy aircraft attempting sneak attacks on homeward-bound MiGs. They encountered a large formation of F-86s over Taechon, and afterward claimed to have shot down three enemy planes.[19] On their return to Andong, however, they discovered that their formation leader had not come home. Political authorities in the 3d Division regretted losing one of their few precious regimental commanders only two days before they were to rotate out of Korea, and wondered if by reducing his anxieties about success they might have saved his life. Meng was one of a few of those who started to receive flight training at the Northeast Aviation School in 1946, and we probably will never know exactly what happened to him that day.

Inexperience is most likely the sole reason for his death. However, PLAAF leaders concluded from this incident that political work in the air force could be a life-and-death matter.[20]

According to PLAAF literature, constant nervous and physical strain from combat actions also had a serious effect on the health of pilots and troops' morale. Political work was therefore regarded as a guarantee for sustaining the force's strength and preventing the noncombat loss of pilots. Political officers were assigned to keep a close eye on the well-being of their pilots, working together with supply and health authorities to ensure they had the best food, enough time to sleep, and proper medication when needed. A number of PLAAF song-and-dance ensembles were sent to airfields at the front to entertain the troops. Despite continued emphasis on the paramount importance of ideology, showing paternal concern for the pilots' welfare and greater sympathy for their problems was encouraged as a practical and humane approach from superiors toward subordinates. Liu Yalou often urged division commanders to be especially solicitous of their pilots, especially regarding their love affairs and marriages.[21]

To reduce unnecessary pilot casualties, PLA and PLAAF leaders also paid special attention to pilot rescue work. In June, 1951, CPV headquarters issued a directive requiring ground troops to make every effort to help rescue downed pilots. The air force dispatched eight rescue teams to North Korea, each headed by a competent political officer. In recognition of the growing importance of air-sea rescue work, the General Staff transferred ten naval patrol boats to the CPV Air Force. By the end of the war, 147 Chinese pilots had been rescued, and many of them were able to return to combat duty.[22]

Nevertheless, PLAAF leaders understood it was dangerous to assume combat effectiveness could be improved simply by political actions. From the very beginning, air force political authorities also helped pilots develop tactics and in the search for improved technology. Lacking combat experience of their own, the PLAAF relied heavily on the Soviet air force as its model, emulating the combat experience of Russian comrades. Soviet pilots were invited to give lessons on the best ways to engage F-86s,[23] and Chinese pilots were asked to memorize a well-known saying by Soviet hero Kozhedub: "you must check whether there is an enemy aircraft behind you when you are about to make an attack."[24] In the meantime, PLAAF leaders believed it was even more important for the pilots to develop Chinese role models. A routine task for unit political officers was to help pilots summarize their combat experiences and then circulate the information throughout the air force. They used concise, colloquial language to describe tactical principles so that Chinese pilots, who often lacked formal education, could easily memorize and employ them in air combat.

Getting involved in military matters was also a duty of political officers required by PLAAF leaders. Because many of them came from the army with combat experience, their presence at preparation meetings before each mission and after-action debriefings allowed them to help inexperienced pilots gain a better understanding of combat tactics. They also offered political counseling. For example, at mission briefings they discussed all possible tactical conditions that might occur in air operations, and then rehearsed the plans for dealing with every conceivable contingency on the ground. Besides regular debriefings after each mission, there were review meetings at least once a week to evaluate everything, including the formation leader's ability to command, the competence of pilots, and how they observed combat rules and maintained discipline. Because such reviews dealt with individual conduct and attitudes toward the war, the role of political officers appeared crucial to help military leaders and pilots diagnose the causes of losses, and to provide psychological counseling for pilots with problems. Although review and counseling systems were common in other air forces, the involvement of political officers in the process cultivated an institutional culture during the Korean War, leaving control of the entire aviation division to political commissars, a practice designed to ensure pilot loyalty, good discipline, and unit morale.[25]

The PLA's military traditions stressed the importance of amity and the unity of armed forces as basic elements of morale. As China's air operations intensified in Korea, the question of how to maintain a trustful relationship between leaders and wingmen, new pilots and old pilots, and combat experienced units and inexperienced units became critical. Although morale ran high in squadrons, many young Chinese pilots had an unhealthy attitude, believing that a wingman was good for nothing because he had no opportunity to score victories in combat. This situation became salient as combat casualties mounted. Beginning in early 1952, inadequately trained replacement pilots were sent to frontline units. This imposed an unwanted task on the remaining original pilots. They were reluctant to accept them as combat comrades because they thought the new pilots lacked the proficiency needed to provide protection for them, and they did not want to assume the responsibility of training them because the effort would divert their energy and attention from combat. Likewise, sensing their ill treatment, replacement pilots became either resentful or depressed. A comparable situation occurred when older, more experienced units were requested to provide protection for new and inexperienced units in air operations.[26] To solve these problems, the PLAAF again employed ideological exhortation. While persuading wingmen of the importance of protecting the lead pilot, the PLAAF made a rule that the wingman should receive partial credit for the leader's victory claims in order to encourage mutual reliance in combat.[27] Simultaneously, those who sought only personal glory in combat were castigated at party meetings, and resolutions were adopted to underline the magnitude of helping young pilots and inexperienced units gain the combat experience essential to the growth of the Chinese air force. According to the 4th Division's report, the political doctrinal remedies helped eliminate those things that impeded the development of combat efficiency during its second tour of duty at the front from January 16 to May 30, 1952.[28]

Considering that an accurate confirmation of combat victories would affect troop unity, integrity, and morale, the CPV Air Force regarded the review of aerial victory claims as a political matter. During the war, pilots' victory claims were subjected to a careful review process involving regimental and division party committees. The party cadres worked together with the flying officers in charge of gunnery and photograph interpreters in examining gun-camera footage to determine every victory claim. To avoid mistakes, the Chinese also called in the Russians to double check photographic evidence. In the case of a pilot who made a claim but failed to produce any gun-camera evidence because his own plane had been destroyed or because the film image was blurred, he and other pilots were required to submit a written account of the entire engagement. The division party committee would only accept such a claim if ground observation by the forward command post and corroborating evidence such as wreckage obtained by local military and civilian authorities supported it.[29] The PLAAF's political authorities were allegedly serious about preventing fraudulent victory claims. However, as more and more MiGs were lost, the pressure on units and pilots to exact revenge mounted, and the tendency for exaggeration became inevitable.

The PLAAF Plan for Redoubling Its War Efforts

During the first part of 1952, CCP leaders calculated that the war in Korea would be protracted. In May, Zhou Enlai instructed Nie Rongzhen, acting chief of the General Staff, and Su Yu, his deputy, to confer with Peng Dehuai. They all endorsed the central leadership's new policy, which called for fighting the war in Korea while stabilizing the economy and building up the

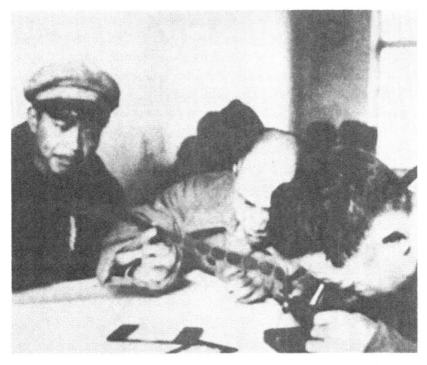

Acting Commander Yuan Bing *(right)* and Political Commissar Gao Houliang *(center)*, of the 3d Aviation Division examine gun-camera footage.

nation at home. Given the protracted nature of the war, they supported the principles of rotation and replacement of CPV troops in Korea. On May 15, the CMC decided to replace weary ground units with fresh troops newly equipped with Soviet weaponry, and specifically required the air force to maintain three fighter divisions at the front to carry out air operations.[30] At command meetings held from June 6–9, CPV leaders agreed that the best way to sustain a protracted war was to conduct "an active positional defense" that would allow their forces to stand fast in their present positions along the CPV's main line of resistance. They considered the loss of positions detrimental because the enemy could use ground victories to boost their military and political positions at the front and at the negotiation table. In order to maintain a superior number of forces in Korea, the CPV commander wanted every available man, and did not, therefore, release any troops until the end of 1953. That meant he would have superior manpower supported by thirteen thousand artillery pieces to counterbalance UN firepower.[31]

In response to the CPV's new strategy, on May 19, 1952, PLAAF leaders announced a plan to redouble the Chinese air force's operational efforts in Korea, placing emphasis on actual combat rather than training. Chinese MiG-15 pilots continued to be too inexperienced to present much of a threat to U.S./UN air forces, but after a three- or four-month rotation, they started to gain proficiency and were capable of conducting independent air operations. This appeared encouraging. The PLAAF decided to employ all nineteen MiG-15 regiments in Korea, first deploying eight to forward airfields at Andong to handle frontline battles, while stationing six others at air fields in Shenyang and Liaoyang as reserves. These regiments were to rotate every three months. Replacement pilots were drawn from the ranks of those who had flown solo in MiG-9 units. In the meantime, the 2d Division's La-11 regiment was ordered to speed up its training for night missions at Andong. In view of the fact that Chinese planes were extremely vulnerable to attacks when landing or taking off from bases along the Yalu, one primary intent at that time was to push the line of battle to the south of the Chongchon River, so the Chinese could avoid air battles over their own bases. Another goal was to send MiGs deep into the Pyongyang and Chinnampo areas, protecting ground troops from enemy fighter-bombers.[32]

While trying to implement this plan, the PLAAF experienced a shortage of planes. Although it could assemble sufficient MiGs for the frontline units, it still needed an additional 154 MiG-15s to maintain the full strength of these regiments. Because the USAF had introduced upgraded F-86s into Korea, the PLAAF asked Moscow to supply the improved MiG-15bis for Chinese units. According to an earlier development program for the Chinese air force, the Soviet Union was expected to supply China with 600 aircraft in 1952, so the PLAAF could equip twenty new air regiments that year. China's solicitation apparently exceeded Russia's production capacity because the Soviet Union was also supplying planes to other Eastern European nations. On April 9, Moscow informed Beijing the Soviet Union would be able to supply only 450 aircraft by the end of 1952, and reminded the Chinese not to waste the 120 MiG-9s that had been kept in PLAAF warehouses. Estimating that each division would lose 10 to 15 aircraft during a three-month tour to Korea, Mao insisted the Soviet Union provide an additional 100 MiG-15s so Chinese air units could be kept at full strength.[33]

We do not know how the Soviet leader responded to the last request. There is no doubt that Soviet supplies allowed the Chinese to conduct intensive air operations in Korea. Beginning in May, the conversion of PLAAF fighter units to the MiG-15bis was well under way, and during the month of August alone, the Chinese air force received 267 of them. By October, most of the frontline air units had converted to the upgraded MiGs, giving Chinese pilots technical equality with the F-86s.[34] Nevertheless, because China had been relying mainly on Soviet military assistance, when the Soviets appeared reluctant to satisfy their demands, the Chinese became suspicious about Moscow's sincerity as an ally.[35] They attributed any inadequate Soviet response to "Stalin's twin fears of fighting a world war with the United States and of China's becoming too strong."[36] This turned out to be a grave problem, one that continued to impair Sino-Soviet alliances throughout the 1950s.

While making efforts to double the quantity of their MiGs available for the air-superiority mission, the PLAAF continued to include the use of bombers for attacks on UN targets south of the 38th Parallel as a strategic option. After suffering heavy losses at Taehwa-do Island in late 1951, the Chinese recognized that their slow speed made conventional light bombers vulnerable. This was especially so in daylight attacks, even with MiGs flying escort. Their night-attack potential, however, kept the Chinese hopeful of striking back, although their objectives seemed poorly defined. When the CPV Air Force planned an attack on Kimpo Airfield, the home base for more than a hundred UN aircraft, on the night of February 8, 1952, Zhou Enlai ordered the mission canceled a few minutes before takeoff.[37] Chinese leaders seemed aware that Washington had restricted bombing targets north of the Yalu River to limit the war. In reciprocal fashion, they sought to confine Chinese air units to defensive operations by not allowing attacks on the U.S. safe haven south of the 38th Parallel.[38] The PLAAF's leaders never abandoned the idea of sending Chinese pilots on those suicidal missions until Peng questioned the wisdom of doing so.

It is necessary to understand that Peng had been begging for air support since the beginning of China's intervention, and appeared to have been frustrated by the repeated delay of the PLAAF's entry into the war. This experience may have given rise to Peng's negative opinion of the PLAAF. When the joint air force command at Andong plotted to launch consecutive night bombing missions against the airfields at Kimpo and Suwon on June 13 and 14, 1952, he believed air force planners were disregarding the consequences. Peng, on medical leave in Beijing, criticized the proposed attacks, arguing that the air force neither intended to "guarantee our [ground] attacks, nor assist ground forces in resisting the enemy attacks." Worried that "if the enemy retaliated by bombing our bases, we would not have enough forces to prevent the enemy's reprisal," he ordered the air force to scrub the mission. Subsequently, all bomber units were released from immediate combat duties in Korea.[39]

There are no Chinese sources available that allow an assessment of why

Yao Changchun of the 10th Aviation Division *(second from left)*. Yao led a night raid on Taehwa-do Island on November 29, 1951, and was later ordered to carry out a bombing mission against Kimpo Air Base in South Korea on the evening of February 8, 1952. Zhou Enlai ordered the latter mission aborted just before takeoff.

air force leaders in Korea were unable to comprehend the political concerns Zhou had raised earlier. Having failed to find a way to strike back since the creation of the CPV Air Force, PLAAF leaders appeared anxious to redeem themselves, even showing no concern whatever for possible political and military fallout. They allegedly were not reluctant to commit their precious pilots to kamikaze-type attacks, demanding that they not bail out or surrender.[40] Peng's objection actually saved PLAAF leaders from a greater humiliation, as recent scholarship demonstrates the U.S. response to such attacks would have been both vigorous and catastrophic.[41]

UN Hydroelectric Attacks and the Communist Response

In June, 1952, U.S. air policy also took a new direction. Ten months of sustained air attacks on North Korea's railroads resulted in only limited disruption of the Chinese logistical system. The USAF's leaders thus adopted a plan designed to "achieve air pressure" by the FEAF "through the selective destruction of items of value" to the Communist countries fighting in Korea. On June 23, 1952, the USAF and navy carrier-based aircraft mounted the biggest air raid to date against the hydroelectric power plant at Lagushao/Supung on the Yalu. Soviet and Chinese air units made no attempt to resist the attack.[42] Historian Robert Futrell notes in the USAF's official history that the Communist air force not only failed to intervene, it removed the bulk of its MiGs from the Andong area while the Americans were attacking the Supung plant. Jon Halliday later tried to explain the Soviet inaction that day by saying the Soviets were not expected to defend the Supung hydroelectric system because a North Korean antiaircraft artillery unit was garrisoned there, and because U.S./UN troops had made no air strikes on North Korea's major power plants during almost two years of war. As a result, he believes the Soviets may have assumed there had been some agreement the Americans would not bomb the hydroelectric system on the Yalu.[43]

Despite such speculation, both Soviet and Chinese sources cite inclement weather as the single most important factor preventing their pilots from taking off and responding to the attack. In late June, North Korea entered the monsoon season and only half of Chinese pilots were able to fly in the adverse weather conditions. According to Lobov, commander of the 64th IAK, on June 23, 1952, the day of the U.S. attack on the hydroelectric plant, a powerful storm front with low cloud cover and heavy rain completely closed the airfields around Andong, as well as alternate airfields. Soviet and Chinese pilots would have had no chance of landing safely had they taken off. Thus, Soviet and Chinese commanders at Andong could not send their MiGs up to repel the massive air strikes. Lobov asserts that Futrell's account of MiGs taking off and heading for interior bases, although cited from a U.S. intelligence report, has no basis in fact.[44]

It is hard to know if Soviet and Chinese commanders muffled their accounts of a rather embarrassing incident, but the U.S. air campaign against the key dams and hydroelectric power stations presented a powerful dilemma to the leadership in Beijing and Pyongyang. From Beijing's perspective, U.S. bombardment would, as Mao wrote to Kim Il Sung, put the Chinese and North Koreans "in a disadvantageous position in political and military relations." The Americans would definitely continue to exploit this Communist weakness to pressure Beijing and Pyongyang to accept U.S. terms for a truce. If the Chinese and North Koreans could not come up with a response to such bombardments, they might lose the war.[45]

Faced with the ravages of the bombardments, the North Korean leader wanted both the Chinese and Soviets to increase their assistance in Korea, and the CPV to conduct aggressive military operations instead of a passive defense. According to Kim, three measures were urgently required: (1) to deploy ten additional antiaircraft artillery regiments to protect key targets in North Korea; (2) to improve the air operational command system so that it would be able to effectively direct air battles in Korea; and (3) to extend air operations to the Pyongyang area rather than limit air defense to the Yalu River area. Kim's most critical demand was that the Chinese reconsider the use of bombers to attack enemy targets in the south at night.[46] He also urged the Soviets to quickly release North Korean pilots being trained on Tu-2s in Russia and equip them with bombers so they could carry out strikes on the enemy's important facilities.[47]

Kim's request did not generate an enthusiastic response from either Beijing or Moscow. By mid-1952, Chinese leaders had already assigned priority to economic reconstruction. Although China's policy was to continue fighting in Korea, it would not support any action escalating the conflict. The Chinese thus turned down North Korea's request for the CPV to launch a new offensive. During further discussions on this issue between Stalin and Zhou Enlai in August, the Soviet leader agreed to dispatch five antiaircraft artillery regiments, and asked the Chinese to contribute another five. Fearing escalation of the conflict, he also warned the Chinese not to send their air force across the 38th Parallel because "the air force belongs to the state," and "Chinese volunteers should not use state planes."[48]

Calculating that a strong Chinese air force would enable China to fight an independent air war in Korea and any future war against Western imperialists in the Far East, the Soviet leader encouraged China to build an air force of two hundred air regiments instead of the 150 they had projected. He promised that the Soviet Union would soon supply them with new fighters capable of speeds of 1,000–1,100 kilometers per hour, presumably MiG-17s. Because the air war in Korea served Soviet interests, Stalin continued to support Beijing's war efforts there with military supplies and limited air involvement, while managing to avoid direct confrontation with the United States.[49]

Immediately following the surprise U.S. attack on the Supung hydroelectric system, the CMC directed the PLAAF commander and the CPV Air Force joint commander to use antiaircraft artillery forces against future U.S. attacks on the most important strategic targets. On July 9, Chinese, Soviet, and North Korean air force commanders met at Andong. They agreed to take several measures to strengthen their air operations to counter the

U.S. bombardment. First, seven Chinese divisions (fourteen regiments) and one North Korean division (two regiments) would join the air forces already on the Yalu front. Second, an additional Chinese MiG division was deployed to Dongfeng Airfield in Jilin to protect the Supung hydroelectric plant. Third, the Soviet Union agreed to send a third MiG division (a total of nine regiments) to join air operations in Korea. Finally, a large air defense force (including three antiaircraft artillery regiments, a scout aviation regiment, and a searchlight battalion) was brought up to cover the Supung hydroelectric plant.[50] In view of the shortage of airfields, the Soviets would deploy only seven regiments to the forward airfields at Andong. They would be responsible for engaging F-86s and conducting night operations and operations in severe weather conditions. Eight Chinese regiments would engage U.S./UN attack and bomber formations so that those sent into combat for the first time could gain experience, and one North Korean flying group would fly "free hunter" missions against the lone flight of enemy aircraft so that inexperienced pilots would feel less threatened and hopefully secure an easy victory.[51]

Because of Moscow's opposition, the PLAAF had to continue to concentrate on the air defense mission. However, as U.S./UN air campaigns were sustained against North Korean industrial facilities throughout the summer and early fall of 1952, the North Koreans began to waver and became increasingly unsteady, and some members of the North Korean leadership began to panic. In early 1953, Kim Il Sung sent Gen. Nam Il, the NKPA chief of staff, to Andong to ask the Chinese to bomb Seoul. Fearing U.S. retaliation against the airfields north of the Yalu, and painfully aware of the PLAAF's inability to defend them, the Chinese refused to take immediate action, but agreed to maintain adequate strike forces to deter a possible U.S./UN attack on North Korea's west coast. The best the CPV's joint air commander, Nie Fengzhi, could do was support North Korean pilots flying biplanes at night to "heckle" the U.S./UN forces. During the remaining months of the war, the little Po-2 biplanes were the only Communist aerial weapons employed against the U.S./UN forces.[52]

The PLAAF Struggles to Attain Air Superiority

During the fall of 1952, Chinese MiGs became more aggressive and often headed south to the Anju area, where they initiated engagements before enemy planes could reach their targets on the Yalu River. The MiG tactics had come to include engaging F-86s. After converting to the upgraded MiG-15bis in October, the 3d and 12th Divisions were assigned to fight the Sabres, while the 17th and 18th Divisions (which continued to fly older model MiG-15s) attacked the fighter-bombers. In an effort to cope better with U.S. air tactics, aviation squadrons made excellent use of the "four-four formation," which featured flights, groups of pairs, and aviation regiments stretching and flying at different altitudes. This gave them the freedom to maneuver as groups, and guaranteed fire support among flights and pairs. In the December air battles, the Chinese lost twelve MiGs but claimed thirty-seven U.S. planes, for a kill ratio of 3.1:1. In seven separate air battles fought early that month, according to PLAAF records, twelve F-86s were supposedly destroyed. Despite a lack of corroboration in U.S. records, fighting the F-86s seemed less daunting for Chinese pilots.[53]

While the PLAAF concentrated its MiGs in battles against F-86s in MiG Alley, it also sent flights of four to eight planes under cloud cover to Chinnampo and even to Sariwon to engage fighter-bombers. This proved to be an effective tactic. Chinese pilots were able to engage fighter-bombers attacking ground targets south of Pyongyang. For four months, between July and October, the MiG-15's superior characteristics enabled Chinese pilots to overwhelm USAF fighter-bombers and conventional navy planes. During that time, the Chinese lost only two MiGs while claiming thirty enemy planes destroyed and six others damaged.[54]

Beginning in September, 1952, the U.S. Navy increasingly focused on industrial targets in northeast Korea and found little opposition in the air.[55] The MiGs were hardly ever sent to the east coast, not even in the northeast part of the country, where there were fewer military targets to be defended anyway. Since the beginning of the war, North Korean pilots had enjoyed few successes, and they remained generally reluctant to engage the Sabres. The joint air force command assigned the North Korean 1st Division to a special mission on the east coast where it would face the U.S. Navy's weaker propeller-driven carrier aircraft. According to Nie Fengzhi's autobiography, during three days in early October North Korean pilots claimed fifteen aircraft destroyed or damaged.[56]

In December, America's newly elected president, Dwight D. Eisenhower, called for stronger measures in the Far East, and Chinese leaders feared a possible U.S./UN amphibious assault on the coast of North Korea. On December 20, Beijing ordered the CPV to prepare for antiamphibious operations. In early 1953, CPV headquarters gathered seven infantry armies (nineteen CPV divisions and one NKPA corps, plus an independent brigade), fourteen artillery regiments, plus nine battalions, two antiaircraft artillery regiments, plus thirteen battalions, and six tank regiments on the western coast. Four infantry armies (seven divisions, and two NKPA corps, plus two independent brigades), two artillery regiments plus three battalions, five antiaircraft artillery battalions, and one tank regiment were deployed on the eastern coast. Fourteen air force divisions (including two bomber and two attack aircraft divisions) were also mobilized. Meanwhile, five fighter divisions were intensively involved in air-to-air battles with the Americans in support of ground troops' preparing to defend against a possible UN invasion.[57]

In the early months of 1953, Chinese pilots flew more sorties than in all the previous months. A large number of MiGs were often sent to counter large formations of enemy planes. For example, on January 13, ninety-six MiGs from five different divisions took off to engage a large formation of F-86s and fighter-bombers attacking the Chongchon River bridge and transportation lines between Yongyu and Chinnampo. The Chinese claimed that the American attackers were repelled with two F-86s destroyed and one damaged. During the first months of 1953, the Chinese recorded that ninety-seven of 123 U.S. bomber formations were prevented from reaching their targets north of the Chongchon River. The 12th and 15th Divisions, along with the 3d and 4th divisions, turned out to be PLAAF's most capable combat units.[58]

Despite persistent Chinese aerial counterattacks, the air war in Korea continued to favor the Americans. In the spring of 1953, the USAF expanded its attacks from transportation interdiction to irrigation dams on the Yalu and in other North Korean areas. The FEAF's strength grew to four F-86 wings with more than 320 planes. At a time when attacks on MiGs during landing and takeoff became more aggressive, the Soviets withdrew 40 percent of their aircraft from the Korean front. Meanwhile, the Chinese prepared for redeployment. The strength of Chinese air units was severely depleted because of combat losses and the mental and physical strain of combat action.[59] Although MiG-9 pilots were sent as replacements, they could not fly combat missions before receiving sufficient training on the MiG-15.[60] In January, 1953, after hearing a report from Liu Yalou about the operations of the CPV Air Force in Korea, Mao instructed the PLAAF leader to preserve the strength of veteran units and to train additional pilots.[61] Subsequently, the 3d Division rotated out of the Andong bases and was replaced by 6th and

16th Aviation Divisions, which had little or no combat experience. On March 31, the 12th Division pulled back from the front and was replaced by the 17th Division.[62] After Nie Fengzhi sent two urgent cables requesting the return of veteran units, the 4th Division was reassigned to Korea for a fifth time.[63]

At the same time, Sabre pilots became more aggressive in crossing the Yalu, hemming in Communist MiGs when they were low on fuel and in their landing pattern over their airfields. The PLAAF history shows the Chinese suffered several losses from such U.S. attacks. On March 27, Wang Hai and his flight were surprised by a bold Sabre attack north of the Yalu. In the swift engagement that followed, Wang's MiG was destroyed by James P. Hagerstrom, a "hot" pilot, and his wingman, John L. Metten, both from the 67th Fighter-Bomber Squadron.[64] Nevertheless, USAF flyers paid a heavy price for their aggressiveness. On April 7, 1953, Capt. Harold E. Fischer Jr., a double ace in the 51st Wing, pursued a Soviet MiG into China.[65] He then caught a Chinese MiG landing at Dabao Airfield and damaged it, but another MiG got behind him and powerful cannon shells ripped into his Sabre between its left wing and the tail, causing the plane to burst into flames.[66] Fischer, a veteran pilot with 170 missions under his belt, ran out of luck. He ejected and was captured.[67] He spent about two years in a Chinese jail, and was the only American ace to become a prisoner of war. Han Dechai, the Chinese pilot who shot Fischer down, was only twenty years old and had flown less than a hundred hours in MiGs. Han was later awarded the Medal of Combat Hero.[68] Although negative accounts about Chinese pilots in Korea abound in Western literature, the shooting down of a U.S. double ace was a glorious moment in the PLAAF's combat history, marred only by the Soviet claim that Fischer was downed by one of their pilots.[69]

With the reopening of the truce talks at Panmunjom in April, 1953, the CPV's leaders believed an armistice was likely, and they hoped to get as many troops combat experience as possible before the cease fire went into effect. The CPV command made plans for a summer offensive that would allow the Communists to consolidate their control on the ground by sending additional troops to the front so that the China–North Korea position could be bolstered at the negotiating table. The CPV's headquarters ordered air force units to actively defend the area north of Pyongyang.[70] Six fighter divisions—including the 4th Division, the best PLAAF unit at the time—with about 350 MiGs were based in the Andong area, supported by three second-line North Korean aviation divisions. Despite its numerical advantage, the PLAAF's combat ability was still hampered by its pilots' inexperience and deficiencies. Most Chinese air units were going into action for the

Lu Min of the 12th Fighter Aviation Division claimed to have shot down five U.S. jet aircraft in December, 1952. He is welcomed by ground crews on his return from a victorious mission. *Courtesy* China Pictorial Agency

first time, while the FEAF was applying maximum pressure on the Communist war efforts in Korea. The PLAAF acknowledged in April that the tide had turned as U.S./UN forces racked up a kill ratio of 1:1.4 in their favor.[71]

The situation turned even worse in May as the air war in Korea entered a white-hot stage. The USAF launched 22,639 sorties for the month, with sixty-one large formations engaging in furious raids on targets deep in North Korea and along the Chinese border. Both Soviet and Chinese air units appeared unable to meet the challenge. For the month of May, the CPV Air Force managed only 1,164 sorties. Although the U.S. admitted the combat loss of just one Sabre that month, the Chinese claimed eighteen F-86s destroyed and three others damaged.[72] Chinese sources reported a kill ratio of 1:1.5 for the month, so it would appear that twenty-seven MiGs were destroyed in air operations. The PLAAF authorities in Beijing were apparently appalled by such unusually high casualties in a single month, and Wang Bingzhang, first deputy commander of the air force, was sent hastily to Andong to rescue the situation.[73] After a number of meetings and interviews, he came up with five reasons for heavy losses. The first three centered on the increasing

Chinese air force ground crews are preparing for takeoff. During the latter part of the war, the front of MiG's fuselage was painted with CPV's air force to distinguish those flown by the Soviets and North Koreans. *Courtesy* China Pictorial Agency

strength of the enemy's F-86s and the American use of massive strike groups. The latter two were the result of China's own problems with the employment of inexperienced units and the failure to maintain two airfields in serviceable condition. He ultimately concluded the fundamental problem was the inexperience and poor proficiency of Chinese pilots in terms of coordination, tactics, intelligence, and marksmanship. Wang made no mention of what measures were taken to deal with the predicament when Chinese military historians later interviewed him, so it is impossible to know what was done without gaining access to the original document.[74]

Nevertheless, the one tiny bright spot for the month in the PLAAF's records was night operations. In response to U.S./UN night bombing activities, the Chinese air force deployed a night-fighter outfit to Andong consisting of experienced pilots from the 2d and 4th Divisions flying eight La-11s and eight MiG-15bis aircraft. At midnight on May 29, 1953, two MiGs were launched on an interception mission. Hou Shujun, deputy commander of the 4th Division's 10th Regiment spotted an F-94 and shot it down over Anju. The recovery of the wreckage the next day was proof of this first, and only, night victory by the CPV Air Force. Furthermore, it signified the air force's improved ability in night operations.[75] Available U.S. records do not record the loss of any F-94 aircraft that day, but a U.S. Marine F3D-2 night fighter was reported lost.[76]

Beginning in June, the dank weather of Korea's monsoon hampered operations. On many days, heavy multilayered clouds hung over northwest Korea, and Chinese pilots had to yield their altitude advantage and fly lower to prey upon the enemy fighter-bombers. Despite the Sabres, which were most lethal below five thousand meters, the Chinese made 994 combat sorties, claiming twenty-five enemy aircraft destroyed and five others damaged in June and July. The PLAAF's records show it was particularly successful in thwarting UN attempts to knock out the Yalu bridge on June 13, 19, and 24. As both sides approached final terms for a cease-fire, on July 8, PLAAF leaders instructed pilots to not relax their efforts, but to continue countering enemy attacks from the air. On July 19, the PLAAF scrambled twenty MiGs to engage UN aircraft headed for the Sinuiju and Uiju airfields south of the Yalu. The Chinese pilots claimed one F-86 destroyed and two others damaged. Although they continued to encounter UN attackers before the cease-fire, that day marked China's final claim of air victory in Korea.[77]

Airpower and the Truce Negotiations

Western studies generally assert that the intensive U.S./UN air campaign conducted during the last few months gave UN negotiators greater diplomatic leverage at Panmunjom. Beginning in May, 1953, the FEAF intensified Sabre operations in MiG Alley. It also offered a financial reward in an effort to induce Communist pilots to defect. During the last few months of the war, American pilots detected a difference in their opponents, and they taunted the MiG pilots with jeers, saying they had "more enthusiasm than know-how." The Americans believed the Soviets had withdrawn their pilots from Korea as the war began to wind down.[78] The scores of Sabre pilots soared as the Americans claimed the destruction of 163 MiGs against the loss of but three of their own during the months of May and June. United Nations bombers and fighter-bombers intensified their attacks on strategic and military targets all over North Korea during the same period, and the destruction of several North Korean irrigation dams by the FEAF Bomber Command in May was regarded as a devastating factor that helped prompt the Communists to accept the UN truce terms.[79]

Recently released Soviet and Chinese documents suggest the extreme burden on Russian industry, which was still rebuilding from the devastation of World War II, played a vital role in Moscow's decision-making. The Soviets feared the escalation of the conflict in Korea would give both Beijing and Pyongyang further excuses for pressing them for more assistance, which had already exceeded Russia's economic limitations.[80] In 1951, Soviet leaders had agreed to outfit sixteen Chinese army divisions with Soviet arms and equipment, but by April, 1952, China had received equipment for only four divisions, of which three would be transferred to the NKPA.[81] In August, 1952, Peng Dehuai asked the Soviets to supply the Chinese air force with new Il-28 light jet bombers to upgrade their Tu-2 fleet. The Soviets found it difficult to fulfill the order, and asked the Chinese first to buy 120 outdated Tu-4s, which were about to be replaced by their latest medium jet bomber, the Tu-16.[82] Political considerations, as well as a strained economy, forced Moscow to strictly limit its assistance. In the meantime, Stalin, believing the war was getting on "America's nerves," took a "hard line" toward the armistice negotiations, insisting the East Asian allies continue fighting despite their heavy losses. Obviously, Stalin's desire to continue the fighting in Korea was a major factor in the prolongation of the war.[83]

On March 5, 1953, Stalin died. If the aged Russian leader was the mastermind of the Korean conflict, his death certainly gave the Communists reason to pause. William Stueck contends that the new Soviet leaders, troubled by continuing uncertainty within the Kremlin, political instability in Eastern Europe, and economic burdens resulting from the Korean War, decided to choose an "approach of dividing the West through a less confrontational foreign policy."[84] According to a Soviet government resolution on March 19, ending the war in Korea became a high priority for the new leaders in Moscow. Although Mao continued to hold a strong position in the truce negotiations, he eventually yielded to the new Soviet leadership's opinion that Moscow could not "augment aid to China for the implementation of its First Five-year Plan" unless the Korean War ended. On March 28, after consulting with the Soviets, Beijing announced China's willingness to accept the UN proposal outlining the process for repatriating prisoners of war (POWs), and the truce talks then reopened at Panmunjom.[85]

In *Mao's Military Romanticism*, Zhang Shu Guang argues that the Chinese should be partially blamed for dragging out the peace negotiations for two years. Overconfident in the CPV's defensive capabilities, they failed to understand "why negotiations on an armistice agreement were not the time" to gain peace settlements on terms favorable to China and North Korea. As a result, Chinese delegates paid more attention to "major issues" like "the withdrawal of foreign troops and the demarcation line" than "minor issues" like "POW repatriation."[86] The timing of the new Communist attitude toward the war, however, suggests it was Stalin's death, rather than U.S. air pressure, that finally brought a breakthrough in the armistice negotiations. A prevailing American view is that U.S./UN air operations not only forced enemy air activities mostly north of the Yalu, but they also tore up Communist ground forces and infrastructure in North Korea, resulting in the Communists' acceptance of the cease-fire agreement.[87]

The final U.S./UN effort to bomb the Communists into submission started in May, 1953, two months after the Soviet leaders resolved to bring the war to an end. The intensive aerial attacks on the Yalu dams represented the growing exhaustion of Washington's patience, which, Conrad Crane observed, might have led to escalation of the war.[88] Overexaggerated F-86 kills may have further inflamed the unrealistically high expectations for the air force and prevented a realistic assessment of its role in Korea. Likewise, President Eisenhower's threats to use nuclear weapons had little influence on the Communist leaders' thinking during the last months of armistice negotiations.[89] Although one of the Fifth Air Force's fighter-bomber squadrons was pulled back to Japan in early 1953 to be equipped and trained for delivering tactical nuclear weapons, there is no evidence Soviet and Chinese leaders had any knowledge of such a threat.[90] Even if they had received secret intelligence of such a move, Mao and other Chinese leaders would probably have continued to regard it as blackmail because they calculated that the Western allies would not support the United States in the use of nuclear weapons.[91]

The U.S. air campaign against irrigation dams in North Korea may have had a demoralizing effect on Kim Il Sung, whose will to continue the war was wearing thinner and thinner as neither the Soviet nor the Chinese air forces appeared able to protect his homeland from wanton bombing by U.S./UN aircraft.[92] The North Korean leader was anxious to see the war end, arguing that "a further dragging out of the existing situation is not in the interest of the DPRK and PRC, or of the entire democratic camp." Every day, three hundred to four hundred North Koreans were being killed, and Kim felt it "hardly advisable to conduct further discussion with the Americans regarding repatriation of a disputed number of prisoners of war."[93]

Chinese military leaders, who did not want to stop fighting in Korea, instead adopted a tit-for-tat strategy in late April, initiating offensive actions along the 38th Parallel to compel the enemy to accept peace. When the truce negotiations at Panmunjom reached a critical stage in the early summer of 1953, the CMC sent instructions to CPV headquarters urging Chinese forces to pay no attention to the talks, but to continue their scheduled military operations.[94] On June 10, CPV ground forces attacked South Korean troops at several points along the front line. The onslaught kept on until Peng Dehuai informed CPV headquarters of the June 15 settlement of a military demarcation line. Syngman Rhee's illegal release of twenty-seven thousand North Korean POWs on June 17 offered the CPV another opportunity to continue to attack ROK positions along the 38th Parallel. On June 20, Peng Dehuai, who was on his way to Panmunjom to sign the armistice agreement, decided to halt his journey in Pyongyang, where he persuaded Kim to agree to put off the truce signing and launch a punitive attack against the ROK forces.[95] On July 13, the CPV resumed attacks on the outposts of the ROK IX Corps near Kumsong, and devastated its adversaries. Concerns about supply difficulties caused by rainy weather forced CPV leaders to halt attacks four days later, however, and the troops were ordered to dig in and defend the newly captured territory.[96]

Chinese sources show that U.S./UN air superiority did not play a significant role in halting CPV ground offensives during the summer of 1953. During the last two and one-half months of the war, UN air forces flew as many as twenty-six hundred sorties per day, but the CPV continued to provide sufficient supplies for the 530,000 Chinese troops in Korea. When the last Communist offensive was launched on the evening of July 13, the CPV concentrated 1,360 artillery pieces along the front, and for thirty minutes fired nineteen hundred tons of shells. It was the first time in Korea the Communists enjoyed a firepower advantage. From July 13–26, during the last thirteen days of fighting, the CPV consumed more than double the ammunition it had used during the first eight months of the war. By July, 1953, the CPV had stored an eight-month food supply, and had greatly improved the combat and living conditions of Chinese soldiers.[97] Moreover, at the time the armistice agreement was signed, Mao appeared even more confident, claiming the war should continue for another year. He believed the CPV could break through the enemy's defenses and gain control of more favorable borders along the Han River.[98]

On the other side of the Yalu, Communist pilots' loyalty and morale were too high to be tempted by Project Moolah's offer, and the Soviets did not leave Korea until the end of the war.[99] Problems replacing Chinese and Soviet units and crews were the main factors placing the Communists at a decided disadvantage in the air war. As Sabre pilots became more aggressive in MiG Alley, the PLAAF rotated three new divisions (the 6th, 16th, and 17th) to the forward airfields, and Chinese pilots suffered heavy losses because of their inexperience.[100] Although Chinese sources give no breakdown of their monthly losses, an estimate based on indirect information such as kill ratios and their claims show that its actual monthly losses were far below the claims made by U.S. pilots.[101] The Russians also experienced similar problems, but they somehow attributed the significant reduction of their combat effectiveness during this period to the entrance of inexperienced Chinese and North Korean pilots, who often "caused a different situation and influence on results of combat operations."[102]

Despite failure to seize control of the sky in North Korea, the Communists did not cease their endeavors to establish airpower on North Korean soil before the armistice took effect. Throughout the war, U.S./UN forces successfully kept the Communists from maintaining an air force inside North Korea, and at war's end expected the armistice agreement to also prohibit the Communists from deploying a strong air force there. When it became evident a cease-fire was imminent, FEAF intensified its airfield neutralization efforts. On the last day of the war, Communist air forces, instead of taking off to meet the enemy's final challenge, raced against time to transfer North Korean air force units south of the Yalu River before the truce went into effect. At Andong, ground crews from three Chinese air divisions were mobilized to dismantle and crate MiGs and Il-10s. At the hour when the cease-fire went into effect, some one hundred crated planes had been loaded onto trains and river barges ready for shipment across the Yalu River.[103] This appeared to be the first evidence of the Communists violating the truce. Ironically, after three years of hard fighting in Korea, the air war came not to a military conclusion, but a political one, and the combatants drew the cease-fire line at almost the spot the war started on June 25, 1950.

The American strategy of using air bombardment achieved few political or military goals despite the initial belief of many in Washington that airpower alone could defeat the enemy in Korea. As the fighting dragged on, inflated expectations led U.S. airmen to frequently complain that they fought the war "with one hand tied behind our backs," because they were not permitted to go after targets beyond the Yalu River. In fact, the failure of the air strategy was much more complicated. The low consumption of supplies by the Communist forces, and the large supply of labor required to maintain communications, made it impossible for American air interdiction efforts to keep the CPV from continuing the fight. Furthermore, restrained by inadequate technology and equipment, as well as the limited number of suitable aircraft for interdiction efforts, the FEAF probably could have done little as it was too occupied in North Korea to attack, even if political restrictions had been lifted. The effect of air interdiction in a limited war remains controversial. Although the FEAF abandoned its interdiction efforts in August, 1952, because it was under the impression an armistice had been achieved in part by UN air pressure, the Americans failed to learn the lesson that air bombardment could not win the war, and made the same mistake in Vietnam a decade later.[104]

CHAPTER 9

Conclusion

ESTIMATIONS, LESSONS,

RETROSPECT, AND

FUTURE PERSPECTIVES

hen the armistice agreement was signed on July 27, 1953, the strength of China's air force had expanded to twenty-seven air divisions (seventy regiments), with more than 3,000 aircraft, many of which at that time were highly advanced. The PLAAF had flown 26,491 sorties over Korea, and engaged in 366 battles, claiming to have shot down 211 F-86s, 72 F-84 and F-80 fighter-bombers, and 47 other types of planes. They also claimed hits on 95 other enemy planes. On the other side of the ledger, they acknowledged the loss of only 224 MiG-15s, 3 La-11s, and 4 Tu-2 bombers (totaling 231) and damage to 151 aircraft. Only 116 airmen were reported lost. In addition, 168 planes were lost due to other causes. As to their overall record for air-to-air kills, the Chinese claimed a victory ratio of 1:1.42. Before entering the air war in Korea, the

question of whether the young Chinese pilots could master air combat and endure the test of modern warfare had puzzled Chinese air force leaders. At the end of the war, ten fighter divisions (twenty-one regiments) and two bomber divisions (three flying groups) with some eight hundred pilots and 59,700 ground personnel were engaged in air operations in Korea, and had gained valuable combat experience (see Appendix D).[1]

The growth of PLAAF activity in the skies over Korea would not have been possible without Soviet assistance and involvement. Since early November, 1950, the Soviet air force had committed thirteen air divisions to defend China and train the Chinese air force, rotating twelve air divisions (thirty fighter regiments) with over forty thousand Soviet servicemen through Korea at one time or another. Soviet pilots flew 63,229 sorties of which 818 were carried out in regimental or greater strength. They fought 1,683 combat missions and claimed the destruction of 1,309 UN aircraft, including 30 at night and 212 shot down by antiaircraft artillery units. They lost 335 MiGs and 120 pilots, of which 319 aircraft and 110 pilots were combat losses. Soviet records show a loss ratio of 7.9:1 from November, 1950, through December, 1951, in their favor. However, Soviet airmen sent to Korea from 1952 until the end of hostilities were not as competent as those who served in the early years, and the loss ratio fell to 2.2:1 in 1952, and then, 1.9:1 in 1953.[2]

We still do not know exactly how many MiGs the North Korean air force lost in the war. The evidence suggests that the North Koreans consistently avoided air combat in order to keep their own air force from being destroyed. According to one Russian source, while the Soviets and the Chinese flew 2,500 and 1,500 sorties monthly respectively, the North Koreans mounted only 12 sorties. The most sorties they flew in a single month during the war was about 370.[3] During interrogation, No Kum-Sok, who defected to the USAF with a MiG-15bis in September, 1953, confessed that during a year in combat his regiment lost a total of nine MiGs. Only three were destroyed in air engagements, however; the others were lost in flying accidents or destroyed on the ground by UN bombers.[4]

Considering that the technical and psychological qualities of the Soviet pilots were an even match for those of their opponents, we now know that UN estimates of their air-to-air victories were overestimated while that of their air-to-air losses might be underestimated. American pilots claimed a clear victory with a kill ratio of about 8:1 or 10:1 in their favor. Official U.S. sources mention only 152 losses in air combat. Although the total UN losses ran as high as thirty-five hundred planes, only about half were credited to "enemy action" or "combat." Jon Halliday suggests that "an insurmountable methodological problem" exists when comparing the Communist and UN accounts of the air war in Korea.[5] One major problem is the way each side determined its victory tallies. Because the Americans were always in action over enemy territory, gun-camera film became the sole means of verifying pilots' claims. American pilots generally were awarded credit for kills as long as their gun cameras showed hits on a MiG, even if no one saw it go down.[6] The Soviets believed that only 75 percent of the aircraft shown being hit in gun-camera footage might be actually destroyed.[7] The number of aerial victories claimed by American pilots thus was apparently exaggerated. In addition, of the sixteen hundred UN aircraft reported lost in combat, most were attributed to either Communist ground fire or unknown causes. Regrettably, none of the USAF records available on their losses in Korea provide even moderately detailed information, such as date, unit, and crew status. Researchers complain that materials sent to the National Archives from various air force repositories are "disorganized" and "generally uncataloged."[8] Nevertheless, realizing the Korean War was not an "alleged walkover," a recent study notes that some American accounts have revised the kill ratio downward to 2:1 for all UN losses.[9]

While not accusing the Pentagon of attempting to cover up U.S. losses, recently released Russian sources insist the Communists used a stricter system to confirm aerial victories: gun-camera film, pilot reports (including those of their comrades), and evidence obtained from ground authorities. Claims generally were disapproved if no confirmation was forthcoming from other sources. The Chinese also would call upon the Russians to double-check photographic evidence. Did the Communists inflate their victory claims? Given tension, fatigue, and inexperience in air combat, the opportunities for deception of the eye, and thus for exaggeration, seem almost limitless. This situation worsened when personal glory and unit success were involved, along with the desire to create a positive image of their own for propaganda purposes. Evgeniy Pepelyaev, who commanded the 196th IAP, observed that "not everything that was scored was actually shot down."[10] Duan Suquan, former deputy commander of the CPV Air Force, was the most vocal in disclosing the inflation of the Chinese MiG kill ratio. He once sent a report to Peng Dehuai claiming it was difficult for Chinese pilots to achieve a 1:1 kill ratio against U.S. Sabres, and warning CPV Air Force leaders not to exaggerate the claims.[11]

However, kill ratios do not explain the tactical or strategic outcome of the Korean air war. Even from a Chinese perspective, the USAF maintained overwhelming air superiority throughout the war. United Nations aircraft outnumbered those of the Chinese and Soviets. At any one time, the United States alone had an average of twelve hundred aircraft in the theater of war. American pilots were also more experienced and skillful than their Communist adversaries. The U.S./UN air forces flew 1.04 million sorties, with an average of about eight hundred and a maximum of twenty-four hundred sorties per day, delivering approximately 690,000 tons of ordnance. Chinese records show that with 47.5 percent of U.S. combat sorties flown against interdiction targets, approximately 190,000 bombs were dropped on railroads—one bomb for every seven meters of rail line. The Chinese admitted that for three years their ground forces were unable to carry out large military activities in the daytime because of such intensive bombing.[12]

Although the Communist air forces were unable to stop the UN bombing campaign, their involvement was crucial to keeping supply lines open and allowing Chinese ground forces to sustain the war effort in Korea. The Chinese faced severe restraints from the beginning. The PLAAF had just been established, and the Chinese Communists did not yet have sufficient experience with air warfare. Only with Russia's help were the Chinese able to commit a suitable air force for service in Korea by September, 1951. The Russians limited their involvement, however, to air defense at the rear. The MiG-15 had a short range, no airfields in North Korea were serviceable, and the PLAAF lacked experienced pilots and ground crews. For three years in Korea, the Chinese air force was forced to fight a war against an enemy numerically superior and more experienced. The Communists had more fighters than FEAF, but they were not able to match the strength of the United States.[13] The PLAAF could average only fifty MiG-15 sorties per day (the Soviets flew the same number of sorties every day), while the USAF averaged nine hundred sorties daily.[14] In the face of sustained U.S./UN air attacks, the Chinese air force was able to respond with only a limited defense, and proved to be incapable of hitting back. Because the UN air forces controlled the initiative and their pilots had superior training and experience, the situation was extremely adverse for the Communist air forces.

Lessons Learned in Korea

Notwithstanding the handicaps the PLAAF faced, the Chinese sought to establish air superiority over northwestern Korea and to extend their air operations to the Pyongyang–Wonsan line. American military analysts believe the Communists sacrificed quality for quantity in Korea in an attempt to attain air superiority. Chinese leaders were very cautious about sending their pilots and planes into the war. Despite the ground forces' desperate need for air support, Beijing was unable to send air force units into battle until September, 1951. Chinese air force leaders initially emphasized direct support for the ground forces, but that proved impractical due to U.S. air superiority. China's air operations in Korea thus were focused on protecting key transportation lines and military and industrial targets, while providing some indirect support for ground units. In contemplating the lessons of the Korean War, it appears that moving bases into North Korea to provide direct air support for ground troops and attempting to contend for air superiority with the Americans would have cost the PLAAF many more planes and lives.[15]

The Korean War marks the first time the CCP's leaders and armed forces conducted military operations with modern technology. This was particularly true for the air force. Believing invaluable lessons could be drawn from Korea for the development of the air force in the future, PLAAF leaders ordered all CPV Air Force units to write summaries of their combat experience. By the end of 1955, the air force had collected 3,653 individual reports. Several months later, 119 of those reports were incorporated in the "Air Force's Combat Experience in the War to Resist U.S. Aggression and Aid Korea" study. The report underscored the importance of the human factor embedded in the PLA's military philosophy, and showed it was equally important for the air force.[16]

While acknowledging that the U.S./UN forces had higher quality, more advanced equipment, the PLAAF still believed in the efficacy of its man-over-weapons doctrine. Young Chinese pilots would be able to defeat the enemy, they argued, because they had come from ground forces accustomed to difficult situations and were willing to sacrifice themselves for China. The PLAAF also recognized that the technical skill of its pilots and ground personnel was the final key to victory. By comparing the kill and aircraft malfunction ratios during the two different phases of the war, the PLAAF tried to demonstrate the improvement of their pilots' techniques and proficiency. From September, 1951, to May, 1952, the PLAAF's kill ratio was approximately 1:1.46 over the USAF, with an average of one flying accident for every 558.8 sorties. After October, 1952, even though PLAAF pilots were engaged primarily by F-86s, the air force's kill ratio improved slightly to 1:1.42, and the average number of flying accidents dropped to one for every 1,003 sorties.[17] Regardless of how contrived the kill ratio may have been, Chinese statistics show they were getting better as fewer planes were lost in combat and flying accidents as the war proceeded.

The lessons of the Korean War also convinced the Chinese of the pivotal importance of equipment. Because of the MiG's edge over the F-80 and F-84 fighter-bombers, the PLAAF claimed a kill ratio of 1:7.8 over the Americans. The situation changed when the Americans committed the more advanced F-86s in Korea. However, the PLAAF's acquisition of the MiG-15bis redressed the balance. In 1952, for example, Chinese pilots engaged in aerial combat eighty-five times with F-86s. In nine of the engagements, they downed at least one enemy aircraft and suffered no losses of their own. Fifteen battles resulted in more kills by the Chinese than the UN forces. The Chinese came up on the short end in twenty-seven engagements, and thirty-four resulted in stalemates. In forty battles against other aircraft, Chinese pilots claimed they won twenty, came out ahead in ten, lost two, and tied the enemy in eight.[18]

Other lessons learned by the PLAAF included awareness of the importance of the political commissar system's emphasis on political work among the troops, and the importance of improving the art of command and leadership. Western analysts do not, however, accept that these learned experiences were either "comprehensive" or "fully candid," but instead demonstrate the difficulty the PLAAF had analyzing the effectiveness of airpower.[19] When the great disparities between Chinese and American military power, as perceived by the Chinese, continued to exist, it is understandable why the PLAAF used the lessons drawn from the Korean conflict to reinforce the CCP's fundamental military thinking: The "human factor still is decisive in determining victory and defeat in modern warfare."[20]

The PLAAF's Korean War Experience in Retrospect

The Korean War demonstrated the necessity and value of a strong and modernized military, and thus pushed China's leaders to transform the PLA from a revolutionary guerrilla force to a modern military organization in a speedy and aggressive manner. When the Korean War started in June, 1950, the PLA was irregularly equipped. It had almost no air or naval weaponry, and ground troops carried a hodgepodge of largely antiquated equipment and had a primitive command structure. Following Beijing's decision to intervene in the Korean conflict in October, the need to modernize the various branches of the PLA became urgent. With almost no industry, and faced with limited resources, Chinese leaders were forced to concentrate their efforts to build a modern military on a few frontiers, and the air force was listed highest on their agenda. Between 1949 and 1953, Mao and other senior Chinese leaders concerned themselves with the air force development program and became personally involved in negotiations with Soviet leaders about aircraft and other related matters. The role of airpower was perceived dialectically. Surrounded by enemies on all sides, domestic and foreign, a powerful air force could act as a deterrent, threatening the remaining Nationalist forces on Taiwan, and defending the new regime from attack by the West. However, there was another distinct aspect of the relationship between the airplane and the Communist revolution in China. Because aviation was the newest and most technical branch of industry, the PLAAF became a symbol of China's strength and progress rather than simply one part of the nation's defensive capability. A large and effective air force thus symbolized the country's ability to use modern technology: If the Communists could make airplanes work, they could make anything work. Providing demonstrable proof of this proposition became the goal of CCP leaders after the founding of the People's Republic.

China's economy had not yet healed from the devastation of the civil war between the Communists and the Nationalists. Moscow and Beijing were allies, though, and the development of an air force within a short period depended on Soviet equipment and Soviet assistance. Moscow, suspicious that Chinese leaders would be like Tito of Yugoslavia, adopted a prudent aid policy for China. However, China's entry into the Korean War eliminated all doubts in Stalin's mind about China's true Communist identity, and a massive influx of Soviet aid began to pour into China. Throughout the Korean War and through the first half of 1954, China received enough Soviet arms and equipment to outfit sixty army divisions and twenty-two air divisions.[21] Much of the equipment was state of the art at the time, and the use of such modern weapons systems helped convert the PLA from a peasant guerrilla force to a combined arms army within a short period.[22]

The air war in Korea served both Soviet and Chinese interests. On one hand, leaders in Moscow kept the war in Korea within strictly limited parameters and let the burden of the war weigh ever more heavily on its East Asian allies. On the other hand, Soviet assistance to China's air defense and the augmentation of China's military and economic capabilities were enough to persuade the Chinese to continue fighting, thus preventing an expanded war beyond the Korean Peninsula. By keeping the United States pinned down in the Far East, Soviet leaders managed to transform the Soviet Union into a superpower in a brief period. In addition, the participation of Soviet pilots in the air war in Korea provided Moscow with an excellent opportunity to test their newly developed MiG fighters as well as tactics for jet air warfare, and to gather data and samples of American weapons systems for use in developing their military technology.

Despite the huge physical losses China suffered during the war, the nation emerged as the only country in the world that dared directly challenge the Western powers, especially the United States. The PLA not only endured the test of modern warfare, by the end of the war it also possessed one of the world's largest air inventories. This can be at least partially attributed to Moscow's calculation that a strong Chinese air force would enable China to fight an independent air war in Korea and or any future war against the Western imperialists in the Far East. The American "sanctuary policy" also allowed the Chinese to build up their air force and use Korea as a training ground for preparing Chinese airmen for future conflicts.

China's partnership with Moscow, however, proved a galling one. Chinese leaders expected the alliance with Moscow to produce unconditional Soviet support. They resented Stalin's withholding of air support they thought the Soviet leader had promised at a crucial time in 1950, leaving China to mount military operations in Korea without adequate air coverage. The Chinese were forced to make repeated requests before the Soviet air force dispatched units to provide limited air cover for supply lines in the rear. The storied Russian air campaigns in Korea could not compare with China's contribution to the war. With their own forces bearing heavy human and material losses, it seemed natural for the Chinese to deem that Soviet involvement and assistance was too little and too late. The fight in Korea against the Americans, though a common enemy to both Mao and Stalin, seemed to become solely China's war. Moreover, during the latter stages of the war, the Soviet Union no longer supplied China with the latest weapons systems, but often sent equipment that had been recently retired by the Soviet armed forces. When the war ended, China owed the Soviet Union three billion *yuan;* it was not able to pay off that debt until 1964.[23] Because Stalin feared direct Soviet-American conflict, the Korean War experience suggested to the Chinese that the Soviet Union was an unreliable ally. In due course, China ended their relationship and emphasized self-reliance as a fundamental principle of Chinese national security.

The Chinese leaders' understanding of airpower gleaned from the Korean conflict was also mixed. While recognizing America's air superiority, they discounted the role airpower played in Korea. Mao was particularly interested in the fact that air bombardment inflicted fewer casualties upon Communist forces than ground fire. Even though his own son was killed during an air raid in Korea, Mao appeared extremely gratified to learn that enemy aircraft had less effect on ground operations than he had previously imagined.[24] During his negotiations with Stalin, Mao confined his efforts to securing only enough Soviet air support to protect transportation lines in the rear. He never asked the Soviet air force to support Chinese ground operations. He may well have shared Stalin's concern for not using air force units at the front in order to avoid a direct Soviet-American confrontation.[25] Given his confidence in the human factor, that men could beat weapons, and his own guerrilla war experience, Mao was convinced that Chinese ground forces could overwhelm stronger opponents and win the war. Throughout the conflict, he refused to allow airpower to affect his strategy.

Nevertheless, Chinese leaders and the PLAAF could not delude themselves about the capabilities and performance of their pilots and aircraft during the war. American air superiority not only prevented the Chinese air force from providing ground support, it also inflicted heavy casualties and materiel losses on the ground. Consequently, the Chinese did not achieve the total victory their leaders had so eagerly sought in Korea. The PLAAF might have been one of the largest air forces in the world at the end of the war, but it was far from being the best. Chinese leaders' interest in building a strong air arm continued to be addressed in the 1953 "First Five-year Plan" for China's military development, which called for expanding the air force to 150 aviation regiments with more than six thousand aircraft, and the construction of 153 new airfields. Although this plan was revised to a more realistic schedule after the war, the air force, along with the army's artillery and tank forces, continued to receive priority funding in the 1950s and 1960s.[26]

The involvement of Chinese air force units in Korea gave air force leaders a clear idea of how to conduct a limited air war within a restricted geographic area. Chinese air and antiaircraft artillery units and signal communications forces possessed a cadre of personnel with firsthand familiarity of tactical and technical expertise. Furthermore, they possessed equipment that had been thoroughly tested under battlefield conditions. Their experience against U.S. forces in Korea also helped the Chinese establish a sound command organization and administrative structure. This, along with the Communist pilots' maturation in combat, brought a new generation of leaders into key positions in air armies and divisions after the war. Many of them became PLAAF leaders in the 1980s and 1990s. Even more significant, the Korean War offered leaders in Beijing an invaluable opportunity to test and define the PLAAF's primary role in Chinese military strategy.

China's People's War doctrine did not envision the need for the strategic projection of airpower, and the Chinese Communists did not develop their first air wing until 1949. The massive transfer of Russian-built equipment and technology to China increased the influence of Soviet military doctrine on the PLA, and the air force was most affected. During the post–World War II years, memories of the 1941 German attack on Russia and the threat of American nuclear-armed bombers drove the Soviets to create a massive air defense program. Soviet doctrine emphasized air defense, followed by air superiority, and then offensive air support.[27] When Beijing asked Moscow to provide air support for China's intervention in Korea, the Soviet Union deployed thirteen air divisions, the bulk of them equipped with MiG-9s and MiG-15s, to defend China against a possible U.S. invasion.[28]

This essentially defensive Soviet air doctrine was subsequently exported to China. There, the Chinese military also obsessed about air defense, a mind-set appreciated in light of the defensive nature of the doctrine of the People's War, and the strong air threat from both the United States and Taiwan since the founding of the People's Republic. The Chinese air force was not designed to be a separate strike force, but rather to act as a subsidiary *junzhong* (armed service) of the PLA. The existing ground force structure was simply grafted onto the air force, and army officers were chosen to command the air force. When the role of the PLAAF in war was discussed, its new leadership made it clear the air force's focus must be on how it would relate to ground operations, or how it could best aid the ground forces.[29] For three years in Korea, the UN's air superiority and the PLAAF's failure to provide air support for ground operations appeared to have little impact on the victory claimed by the Communists. It thus is not surprising that Chinese political leaders and generals sustained their view that future war would be conducted in the context of ground operations with airpower used to supplement the power of the army. The Communist air defense experience thus resulted in the PLAAF continuing to emphasize air defense strategy and the development of fighter planes, radar, and ground antiaircraft systems, while devoting a small portion of the overall force structure to delivering limited air-to-surface ordnance.

Their Korean War experience also taught Chinese leaders that a greater reliance on airpower could have escalated the conflict. The Korean War was the first limited war of the nuclear age, fought within a limited time and space, and with limited means and objectives. Both the Communists and the UN allies restrained themselves, keeping the conflict on the Korean Peninsula. The Americans used conventional weaponry only, and did not seek the total destruction of their Communist opponents. During three years of air war in Korea, the USAF was prohibited from attacking Communist air bases in northeast China. Simultaneously, U.S. leaders kept the American public from knowing about Russian participation in an effort to prevent the war from growing into a more serious conflict with the Soviets.

On the other side of the Yalu, Communist leaders were also obligated by restraints, refusing to allow their air force to conduct any offensive action against the U.S. safe haven south of the 38th Parallel. Neither Moscow nor Beijing wanted to launch air offenses that might escalate the conflict. Apart from making an initial request for Soviet air support for CPV ground operations, Mao apparently came to understand Stalin's concerns, and thereafter made no further solicitations. It is interesting to note that several years after the war Chinese leaders continued to believe the reckless use of the air force would escalate the Cold War standoff to a hot war confrontation with the United States. In 1954, Mao instructed the navy and air force not to engage foreign aircraft or vessels during their patrols and escort missions on the high seas.[30] As the Vietnam War escalated in early 1965, leaders in Beijing further prohibited the Chinese air force from engaging U.S. aircraft, even over China's own airspace, to avoid a direct confrontation with the United States. Chinese pilots were instructed not to fire on intruders unless fired upon. Although this policy was replaced in April by more aggressive rules of engagement that authorized pilots to shoot down any intruding enemy planes, Beijing continued to ignore Hanoi's pleas for volunteer pilots and aircraft to help the North Vietnamese fight against the U.S. air bombardment. As long as Washington limited its involvement in Vietnam, Chinese leaders seemed adamant about avoiding another direct confrontation with the United States. In Chinese strategic thinking, it became evident that airpower was regarded as a defensive, rather than an offensive force, or as a deterrent to threats to China's national security interests during the Cold War.[31]

Despite the repercussions these decisions may have had on Chinese leaders' views about airpower, the actual experience the PLAAF gained in the Korean War was limited. The Chinese air force had just been established when the war erupted. A limited supply of experienced personnel, and the rapid expansion of the PLAAF during the war, forced China to sacrifice quality for quantity. Between 1950 and 1953, it suffered high aircraft and aircrew loss rates, and had to struggle with limited aircraft readiness.[32] Although Chinese pilots experienced real testing throughout the war, their combat proficiency showed no significant improvement. Problems included continuing inefficiency in formation flying skills in groups of two or more planes, poor ability to search and spot enemy aircraft, and an inability to hit targets. Many commanders also proved incapable of providing coherent leadership in combat.[33]

The PLAAF grew into one of the largest air forces in the world, but it remained unable to provide an effective air defense for China after the war. The Nationalist air force continued to control the airspace in Fujian Province and eastern Guangdong Province, and in large areas of the mainland at night until the late 1950s. The PLAAF's Korean War experience also did not help in situations requiring air defense against Nationalist aircraft intrusions. Although many fighter pilots participated in the air war in Korea, many did not improve their flying skills. Accustomed to flying in large formations over Korea, they nevertheless proved incapable of intercepting the enemy's invading aircraft. Because of its poor proficiency, the PLAAF's failure rate for spotting intruding aircraft was as high as 70 percent in 1954 alone.[34] Not until 1958, during the Taiwan Strait crisis, did the PLAAF use its numerical superiority to claim solid control of China's airspace. Korean War veteran Lin Hu recalled that PLAAF officers and pilots gained great confidence during their struggle against the GMD air force over southeast China. Since they believed they had "defeated" the Americans in Korea, they saw the Nationalists as little threat to them.[35]

A Future Perspective

The Korean War not only constituted an important experience for the PLAAF, it also created a myth. During the last fifty years, there has been no shortage of Chinese literature about the PLAAF in general, and in Korea, particularly. However, Chinese military historians and writers prefer to write of the Korean War in heroic terms, so none of the accounts emerged in coherent, coordinated, well-documented form, or were realistic accounts of life and battle in Korea. A deeply ingrained tradition of military secrecy and suspicion of Westerners has resulted in little access to PLAAF documents concerning operations in Korea. Consequently, information released about the role of the Chinese air force and the performance of Chinese pilots during the Korean War has given legitimacy to an obviously biased and slanted version of the PLAAF's history. The most popular and widely accepted myth coming out of the Korean War is that although Chinese pilots were young and inexperienced, they bravely challenged their much more experienced American counterparts and defeated them. Stories about young Chinese pilots shooting down American aces like George Davis and Harold Fischer made Zhang Jihui and Han Dechai household names in China, and Wang Hai and his squadron are representative of the PLAAF's collective glory in Korea. General Hoyt Vandenberg's press statement that "Communist China had become one of the major air powers of the world" almost overnight has been widely cited in PLAAF literature as further evidence supporting the myth of the Chinese air force in Korea.[36] For too many Chinese air force veterans, the PLAAF's role in Korea nestled in their memories as an unbroken string of victories and heroism. Few have dared question the legitimacy of their records and stories, and indeed, these have become important components of the national military myths. As a result, the accounts not only lead to distortions, but to a self-delusion that perpetuated misunderstanding and ignorance about the role of airpower for more than forty years.

Because of the 1991 Gulf War, in which modern technology played a more dominant, effective, and visible role than in past military conflicts, China, like many other nations, has increased its emphasis on air and naval power. The PLAAF's leaders came to realize that the air force must play a major, rather than a supportive, role in warfare in a high-tech age. They thus began formulating an air strategy requiring the air force to conduct offensive and defensive missions, and emphasizing the use of the air force to seize the initiative at the beginning of a war. The serious problem with this strategy has been, however, that China does not have the necessary weapons and support systems needed to conduct effective offensive operations. Since the early 1990s, sustained efforts have been made at home and abroad to modernize the Chinese air force, including the solicitation of new-generation fighters and sophisticated antiaircraft missile systems, as well as their technology, from Russia so they can be manufactured in China. Between 1994 and 1999, a number of military exercises were conducted aimed at transforming the Chinese air force from primarily a defensive force to an independent arm. Today, the Chinese air force is at last turning its back on its Korean War experience, which has limited it to defensive missions for the past half-century.[37]

Today's Chinese military thinkers believe war could easily stem from unification quarrels over Taiwan, ethnic tension on the borders, or territorial disputes over the islands in the South China Sea. The PLAAF is now determined to make airpower a strategic deterrent by intimidating potential enemies while preparing to launch strikes deep into enemy territory in conflict. According to Western standards, the PLAAF may yet remain far from being a modern force. Still, questions remain. Is the PLAAF's Korean War experience relevant to contemporary discussions of China's growing military and economic capacities? What is the role of airpower in maintaining the future security environment of the Asia-Pacific region?

The Korean War is the only war the Chinese air force has fought in its fifty-year history, and as such the experience may be irrelevant to today's concept of modern war. Will China's inferior military capacities again restrain leaders in Beijing from acting if China's national security and pride are perceived to be at stake? What matters is not so much the growth of China's military capacity, but rather *how* Beijing will use its newfound military strength, especially its air and naval power. About a half-century ago, Korea, as Chinese leaders discerned, posed a serious threat to international peace and security. Although the Chinese military was an anachronism with no air or navel power, the CCP's leaders decided to intervene. The U.S. military paid scant attention to the strategic thinking of the Chinese Communists. This lack of interest in developing an understanding of a "non-Western" military philosophy, or the tactics of "an irregular army," as a Chinese historian correctly points out, may have been contributing factors to the fatal clash between China and the United States in Korea.[38] From a future perspective, the Korean War also demonstrated that China can be counted on to fight valiantly, despite military insufficiencies, by drawing on pride and the need to protect national security. Taking into account the historical experience of the Korean War, it must be recognized that the will of the Chinese people, not the nation's military capabilities, will likely continue to play a vital role in China's national security decision making.

Perhaps even more relevant is the positive self-perception the PLAAF derived from its Korean War experience. It may also have had a significant effect on how Chinese leaders will use airpower in future conflicts. As the Chinese air force moves into the twenty-first century, continuing to develop and expand its capabilities, anyone hoping to understand the PLAAF must begin by considering its Korean War experience.

APPENDIX A

PLAAF Aviation Troops, 1950–51

DIVISIONS	AIRCRAFT	DATE OF CREATION	LOCATION
2d	MiG-15/La-11	November, 1950	Shanghai
3d	MiG-15	October, 1950	Shenyang
4th	MiG-15	October, 1950	Liaoyang, Liaoning
5th	Il-10	December, 1950	Kaiyuan, Liaoning
6th	MiG-9/15	November, 1950	Anshan, Laioning
7th	MiG-9/15	December, 1950	Dongfeng, Jinin
8th	Tu-2	December, 1950	Siping, Jilin
9th	La-9	December, 1950	Jilin, Jinlin
10th	Tu-2	January, 1951	Nanjing, Jiangsu
11th	Il-10	February, 1951	Xuzhou, Jiangsu
12th	MiG-9/15	December, 1950	Xiaoshan Xian, Zhejiang
13th	Il-12	December, 1950	Xinjin Xian, Sichuan
14th	MiG-9/15	February, 1951	Beijing
15th	MiG-15	May, 1951	Huaide Xian, Jilin

DIVISIONS	AIRCRAFT	DATE OF CREATION	LOCATION
16th	MiG-9/15	February, 1951	Qingdao, Shandong
17th	MiG-9/15	April, 1951	Tangshan, Hebei
18th	MiG-15	May, 1951	Guangzhou, Guangdong
19th	MiG-15	November, 1951	Wuhan, Hubei
20th	Tu-2	November, 1951	Bengbu, Anhui

Units Organized after November, 1951

1. Between November, 1951, and May, 1952, the 21st and 24th Fighter Divisions, 23d and 25th Bomber Divisions, 22d Ground-Attack Division, and 1st and 2d Independent Reconnaissance Regiments were organized.

2. Between December, 1952, and March, 1953, the 26th and 27th Fighter Divisions, 28th Ground-Attack Division, 3d Independent Transport Regiment, and 4th Independent Bomber Regiment were organized.

3. Between December, 1953, and early 1954, the 29th Fighter Division and 5th Independent Reconnaissance Regiment were organized.

APPENDIX B

Soviet VVS/POV Forces in China, 1950–51

Independent Aviation Divisions

UNIT	AIRCRAFT	DATE OF ARRIVAL	LOCATION
17th GIAD[1]	62 MiG-9	November 20, 1950	Shenyang
20th IAD	62 MiG-9	November 19, 1950	Tangshan
65th IAD	62 MiG-9	November 19, 1950	Guangzhou
	40 MiG-1/40-La-11		Shanghai
106th IAD	26 Il-10/10 Tu-2	March 7, 1950	Xuzhou
	26 Il-10/10 Tu-2		Nanjing
144th IAD	62 MiG-9	November 19, 1950	Shanghai
151st GIAD	120 MiG-15	August 4, 1950	Shenyang
297th IAD	62 La-9	November 19, 1950	Jilin
309th IAD	62 MiG-9	December 10, 1950	Gongzhulin
328th IAD	62 MiG-9	November 14, 1950	Beijing

UNIT	AIRCRAFT	DATE OF ARRIVAL	LOCATION
186th SHAD	62 Il-10	November 25, 1950	Kaiyuan
846th SHAP	30 Il-10	November 20, 1950	Xuzhou
162d BAD	62 Tu-2	November 21, 1950	Siping

64th Fighter Aviation Corps

UNIT	AIRCRAFT	DATE OF ARRIVAL	LOCATION
303d IAD	91 MiG-15	April 1, 1951	Shenyang
324th IAD	62 MiG-15	December 23, 1950	Dongfeng

67th Fighter Aviation Corps

UNIT	AIRCRAFT	DATE OF ARRIVAL	LOCATION
50th IAD	62 MiG-15	December, 1950	Anshan
151st GIAD	62 MiG-15	November, 1950	Shenyang

Soviet PVO Forces on Liaodong Peninsula

83d Independent Fighter Aviation Corps: 28th IAD and 153d IAD.
55th Independent Fighter Aviation Corps: 149th IAD.

[1] One source refers to the 17th as the 15th GIAD.

APPENDIX C

Soviet PVO Forces in Korea, November 1, 1950–July 27, 1953

Flying Elements of the 64th Fighter Aviation Corps

Division	Regiment	Period of Service	Claims of Enemy Aircraft Destroyed	Friendly Losses Aircraft	Friendly Losses Pilots
28th IAD	67th IAP	11, 1950 | 2, 1951	6	Unknown	Unknown
	139th GIAP	11, 1950 | 2, 1951	23	1	1
50th IAD	29th GIAP	12, 1950 | 2, 1951	36	5	4
	177th IAP	11,1950 | 2, 1951	24	2	1
151st GIAD	28th GIAP	11, 1950 | 3, 1951	23	Unknown	Unknown
	72d GIAP	11, 1950 | 3, 1951	13	3	3

Division	Regiment	Period of Service	Claims of Enemy Aircraft Destroyed	Friendly Losses Aircraft	Friendly Losses Pilots
324th IAD	176th GIAP	4, 1951 | 2, 1952	107	Unknown	5
	196th IAP	4, 1951 | 2, 1952	108	24	5
303d IAD	17th IAP	8, 1951 | 12, 1951	108	Unknown	4
	18th GIAP	8, 1951 | 12, 1951	92	18	8
	523d IAP	8, 1951 | 12, 1951	102	17	5
32d IAD	224th IAP	9, 1952 | 7, 1953	33	22	6
	535th IAP	9, 1952 | 7, 1953	19	16	5
	913th IAP	9, 1952 | 7, 1953	29	20	5
97th IAD	16th IAP	1, 1952 | 8, 1952	26	12	4
	148th GIAP	1, 1952 | 8, 1952	41	2	2

Division	Regiment	Period of Service	Claims of Enemy Aircraft Destroyed	Friendly Losses Aircraft	Friendly Losses Pilots
133d IAD	147th GIAP	7, 1952 | 8, 1953	21	4	4
	415th IAP	7, 1952 | 8, 1953	28	12	4
	578th IAP	8, 1952 | 4, 1953	4	10	4
	726th IAP	7, 1952 | 8, 1953	39	12	7
190th IAD	256th IAP	1, 1952 | 8, 1952	16	16	5
	494th IAP	1, 1952 | 8, 1952	23	20	6
	821st IAP	1, 1952 | 8, 1952	44	Unknown	Unknown
216th IAD	676th IAP	7, 1952 | 8, 1953	33	14	4
	781st IAP	1, 1952 | 7, 1953	11	9	3
	878th IAP	7, 1953 | 8, 1953	38	17	6

Division	Regiment	Period of Service	Claims of Enemy Aircraft Destroyed	Friendly Losses Aircraft	Friendly Losses Pilots
282d IAD	518th IAP	3, 1952 | 7, 1953	31	19	6
37th IAD	236th IAP	7, 1953			
	282d IAP	|			
	940th IAP	12, 1954			
100th IAD	9th GIAP	7, 1953			
	731st IAP	|			
	735th IAP	12, 1954			

INDEPENDENT REGIMENTS UNDER 64TH
FIGHTER AVIATION CORPS

	351st IAP	3, 1951 | 1, 1953	10	2	2
	298th IAP	1, 1953 | 1, 1954	4	1	1

NONFLYING ELEMENTS OF THE 64TH
FIGHTER AVIATION CORPS

87th AAD		3, 1951 | 1, 1953			
92d AAD					

Division	Regiment	Period of Service	Claims of Enemy Aircraft Destroyed	Friendly Losses Aircraft	Friendly Losses Pilots
28th AAD 35th AAD		1, 1951 | 12, 1953			
18th ATD		3, 1953 | 8, 1953			
16th ATD		7, 1953 | 12, 1954			
	10th SAP	3, 1951 | 1, 1953			
	20th SAP	1, 1953 | 12, 1954			

1404th Hospital for Infectious Diseases
8th Mobile Field Hospital

APPENDIX D

CPV Air Forces in Korea, December, 1950–July, 1953

Division	Regiment	Period of Service	Claims of Enemy Aircraft Destroyed	Friendly Losses Aircraft
2d FAD		Dec., 1951 | Jan., 1952	4	
3d FAD		Oct., 1951 | Jan., 1952 May, 1952 | Jan., 1953	87	43
4th FAD		Dec., 1950 | July, 1951 Jan., 1952 | May, 1952 Dec., 1952 | July, 1953	64	55

Division	Regiment	Period of Service	Claims of Enemy Aircraft Destroyed	Friendly Losses Aircraft
6th FAD		Nov., 1951 | Mar., 1952 Dec., 1952 | July, 1953	26	
12th FAD		Mar., 1952 | Mar., 1953	57	
14th FAD		Nov., 1951 | Feb., 1952 Apr., 1953 | July, 1953	10	
15th FAD		Jan., 1952 | May, 1952 Oct., 1952 | July, 1953	51	41
16th FAD		Jan., 1953 | July, 1953	1	
17th FAD		Mar., 1952 | July, 1953	23	

Division	Regiment	Period of Service	Claims of Enemy Aircraft Destroyed	Friendly Losses Aircraft
18th FAD		May, 1952 | Dec., 1952	6	
8th BAD		Dec., 1950 | Mar., 1952	1	4
10th BAD		Oct., 1951 | Mar., 1952		

Notes

Introduction

1. People's Liberation Army leaders allegedly were shocked to learn how significant the role played by airpower was in the Gulf War. Subsequently, Jiang Zemin, president of the PRC, gave instructions for the future development of the Chinese air force. See Wang Jinna, Zhang Nongke, and Weng Huainan, "The Chinese Air Force Took Historical Strides in Fifty Years," *Zhongxin she,* Nov. 2, 1999; Kong Yun, "Revealing the Real Air Combat Strength of the Chinese Air Force," *Zhongxin she,* Jan. 6, 2000; Zhang Nongke, "China's Air Force Is Transforming from an Air Defense Force to an Air Offense and Defense Force: An Interview with Air Force Commander Lt. Gen. Liu Shunyao and Political Commissar Lt. Gen. Qiao Qingchen," *Zijing,* Nov., 1999, 4–9.

2. Only three books about the PLAAF have been published in the West. More than half of Richard M. Bueschel's *Communist Chinese Airpower* deals with PLAAF aircraft. Kenneth W. Allen's *People's Republic of China, People's Liberation Army Air Force* is a handbook on the organization of the PLAAF. Kenneth W. Allen, Glenn Krumel, and Jonathan D. Pollack's *China's Air Force Enters the 21st Century* provides an overview and assessment of the PLAAF.

3. Conrad C. Crane, *American Airpower Strategy in Korea, 1950–1953,* 46.

4. For recent diplomatic and political analysis of the events leading up to China's intervention, see Sergei N. Goncharov, John W. Lewis, and Xue Litai, *Uncertain Partners: Stalin, Mao, and the Korean War;* and Chen Jian, *China's Road to the Korean War: The Making of the Sino-American Confrontation.* For the most recent and thorough account of Chinese military participation in the Korean War, see Shu Guang Zhang, *Mao's Military Romanticism, China, and the Korean War, 1950–1953.* Because these books were published before 1995, they do not include the more recently released Chinese and Russian archival materials.

5. For older American studies on the air war in Korea, see Robert F. Futrell, *The United States Air Force in Korea, 1950–1953;* Richard P. Hallion, *The Naval Air War in Korea;* Robert Jackson, *Air War over Korea;* Stewart, ed., *Airpower: The Decisive Force in Korea.*

6. The best example is Allen et al., *China's Air Force.* The authors show their suspicion and criticism of Chinese records and use American sources to depict PLAAF's involvement in the air war in Korea.

7. John R. Bruning, *Crimson Sky: The Air Battle for Korea,* xiv; Crane, *American Airpower Strategy in Korea,* 107.

8. Robert F. Futrell, interview with author, Montgomery, Ala., May 27, 1997.

9. These earlier accounts are Steven J. Zaloga, "The Russians in MiG Alley," *Air Force Magazine,* Feb., 1991, 74–77; Jon Halliday, "Air Operations in Korea: The Soviet Side of the Story," in *A Revolutionary War: Korea and the Transformation of the Postwar World,* ed.

William J. Williams, 149–70; Yefim Gordon and Vladimir Rigmant, *MiG-15: Design, Development, and Korean War Combat History.*

10. Askold Andreyevich German and Igor Atayevich Seidov, *Krasnye D'yavoly na 38-y Paralleli* (*Red Devils on the 38th Parallel*); Vitaliy Petrovich Naboka, *NATOvskiye Yastreby v Pritselye Stalinskikh Sokolov: Sovetskiye Letchiki na zashchite neba Kitaya i Korei, 1950–1951* (*NATO's Hawks in the Sights of Stalin's Falcons: Soviet Pilots Protecting the Skies of China and Korea, 1950–1951*). I greatly appreciate Stephen L. Sewell, a Defense Department Russian expert, for kindly supplying me with this information, and for translating parts of these books for me.

11. Naboka plans to produce a three-volume set that is chronologically arranged: June, 1950–July, 1951; August, 1951–July, 1952; and August, 1952–July, 1953. Only the first volume has thus far been published.

12. Mark A. O'Neill, "The Other Side of the Yalu: Soviet Pilots in the Korean War, Phase One, 1 November 1950–12 April 1951" (Ph. D. diss., Florida State University, 1996). I am indebted to O'Neill for supplying me a copy of his dissertation and allowing me to share his sources.

13. Wang Dinglie et al., *Dangdai Zhongguo kongjun* (*China Today: The Air Force*); Air Force Headquarters Editorial and Research Office, *Kongjun shi.*

14. See Mao Zedong, *Jianguo yilai Mao Zedong wengao* (*Mao Zedong's Manuscripts Since the Founding of the People's Republic*), and *Mao Zedong junshi wenji* (*A Collection of Mao Zedong's Military Papers*).

15. Evgeniy P. Bajanov and Natalia Bajanova, "The Korean Conflict, 1950–1953: The Most Mysterious War of the 20th Century," unpublished manuscript, 51–52. I am grateful to William Stueck for supplying me with this essay.

16. Kathryn Weathersby, "New Russian Documents on the Korean War," *Cold War International History Project Bulletin*, nos. 6 and 7 (winter, 1995–96): 30–84; and Alexander Y. Mansourov, "Stalin, Mao, Kim, and China's Decision to Enter the Korean War, Sept. 16–Oct. 15, New Evidence from the Russian Archives," ibid., 94–119; *Guanyu Chaoxian zhanzheng de Eguo dangan wenjian* (*Russian Archival Documents on the Korean War*). The latter is a collection of documents on the Korean War from the Archives of the President of the Russian Federation (APRF), translated into Chinese and published by the Military Science Academy for internal use. Hereafter it will be cited as APRF (Chinese). I am grateful to Chen Jian for cordially providing me with a copy.

17. Zhou Enlai, *Zhou Enlai junshi wenxuan* (*Selected Military Works of Zhou Enlai*).

18. CCP Central Archives and Studies Office, ed., *Zhou Enlai nianpu, 1949–1976* (*The Chronicle of Zhou Enlai, 1949–1976*).

19. The most important are two volumes of *Lantian zhi lu* (*The Road to the Blue Sky*), compiled by the Political Department of the Air Force.

20. This database is compiled with information drawn from the kill list the Soviets presented to the Defense POW/MIA Office (DPMO)/Task Force Russia in early 1993, the Naboka and German/Seidov books, and the USAF's POW/MIA/KIA list. However, the USAF database only covers aviators who were (a) killed in action, (b) missing in action/body not returned, (c) died of wounds, (d) died in captivity, or (e) died while missing. The list does not include those who returned from captivity or were shot down over the Gulf of Korea or land and picked up by search and rescue teams.

Chapter 1. Aviation and the Chinese Revolution

1. Futrell, *United States Air Force in Korea*, 412; Austin Stephens, "Reds in Korea Challenge U.N. in Air, Vandenberg Declares," *New York Times*, Nov. 22, 1951, 1–2.

2. James C. Thomson Jr., Peter W. Stanley, and John Curtis Perry, *Sentimental Imperialists: The American Experience in East Asia*, 14. For a more analytical study of the American view of China in the nineteenth century, see Akira Iriye, *Across the Pacific: An Inner History of American-East Asian Relations*, 3–32.

3. Basil Collier, *A History of Airpower*, 1.

4. *Mo Zi xian gu* (*Mencius Chat*), vol. 13, *Zhuzi jicheng* (*Collections of Various Biographies*), pt. 4, 292.

5. For example, *Han shu*, 2467, tells of a young Chinese who used two bird wings and feathers to cover his body and head and was able to glide for a hundred feet. These examples are also cited in the PLAAF's official histories. See Wang Dinglie et al., *Dangdai Zhongguo kongjun*, 2; *Dangdai Zhongguo de minhang shiye* (*China Today: Civil Aviation Industry*), 1–3.

6. In 1970, the International Association of Astronomy recognized this incident as the first human attempt at powered flight. See Wang Suhong and Wang Yubing, *Xuese tiankong: Zhongguo kongjun kongzhan shilu* (*Crimson Sky: A True Account of Air Operations by China's Air Force*)., 11–12.

7. See Ma Yufu, *Zhongguo junshi hangkong* (*China's Military Aviation*), 14–15,

8. Western scholars, for example, point out that the Chinese abacus, a primitive calculator, prevented China from embracing advanced mathematical innovations like algebra (John King Fairbank and Merle Goldman, *China: A New History*, 3).

9. For Sun's view, see Sun to Homer Lee, Nov. 7, 1910, letter, in *Sun Zhongshan quanji* (*Completed Works of Sun Yat-sen*), 1:290–300; Sun to Li Jian, May 31, 1911, letter, in History Research Division of Guangdong Provincial Philosophy and Social Science Institute, ed., *Sun Zhongshan nianpu* (*The Chronicle of Sun Yat-sen*), 118.

10. Wang Suhong and Wang Yubing, *Xuese tiankong*, 24–26. For details, see Xiao Qiang and Li Debiao, *Guofu and kongjun* (*The Founding Father and the Air Force*).

11. Sun's activities related to aviation can also be seen in Chen Xiqi, ed., *Sun Zhongshan nianpu changbian* (*A Long Edition of the Chronicle of Sun Yat-sen*).

12. Ma Yufu, *Zhongguo junshi hangkong*, 363–64; Xiao Qiang and Li Depiao, *Guofu and Kongjun*, 39.

13. Guan Songru. "Liu Zuochen: Pioneer of China's Aviation Undertaking," *Junshi lishi*, no. 3 (1998): 39.

14. See Wang Dinglie et al., *Dangdai Zhongguo kongjun*, 4; Wang Suhong and Wang Yubing, *Xuese tiankong*, 24–26.

15. For more on the international arms embargo against China in the 1920s, see Stephen J. Valone, *"A Policy to Benefit China": The United States and the China Arms Embargo, 1919–1929*. See also Xiaoming Zhang, "Toward Arming China: United States Arms Sales and Military Assistance to China, 1921–1941" (Ph.D. diss., University of Iowa, 1994).

16. Tang Duo's recollections in *Lantian zhi lu*, 1:15–16; Ma Yufu, *Zhongguo junshi hangkong*, 314–15. These two trainers were sold to China as commercial aircraft. For details, see Zhang, "Toward Arming China," 24.

17. During the embargo, the supply of military aircraft depended on smuggling efforts, and only a handful of aircraft actually found the way to GMD's control. See Zhang, "Toward Arming China," 30. After entering an alliance with Moscow, the Nationalist government in Guangzhou began to receive arms supplies, including military aircraft, from the Soviet Union, which was not a party to the international embargo. More than sixty advisers served in China during 1925 and 1926. See Wang Zhenghua, *Kangzhan shiqi waiguo duihua junshi yuanzhu* (*Foreign Military Assistance to China during the Resistance War*), 97.

18. Ma Yufu, *Zhongguo junshi hangkong*, 314–16.

19. Several of these graduates later played a vital role in either the Nationalist or Communist air forces. For example, Wang Shuming and Mao Bangchu served as commander of the Nationalist air force in the 1940s and 1950s, respectively, while Chang Qiankun became deputy commander of the PLAAF in 1949 (*Dangdai Zhongguo de minhang shiye*, 2–3; Wang Dinglie et al., *Dangdai Zhongguo kongjun*, 6).

20. One Chinese study says the GMD air fleet at the time consisted of thirteen British-built DeHavillands. Because Great Britain was a signatory to the international arms embargo, the aircraft were most likely supplied by the Soviets. In late 1927, the Nationalists bought twelve British- and French-made aircraft from the Soviet Union (Ma Yufu, *Zhongguo junshi hangkong*, 381, 612). Beginning in 1925, the Russians started to make their own versions of the DeHavilland. See John T. Greenwood, "The Designers: Their Design Bureaux and Aircraft," in *Russian Aviation and Airpower in the Twentieth Century*, ed. by Robin Higham, John T. Greenwood, and Von Hardesty, 164.

21. "General Report on Politics of the Nationalist Government at the Fourth National Congress of the Guomindang, November 1931," in *Zhonghua minguo zhongyao shiliao: DuiRi kangzhan shiqi, xubian* (*Important Historical Documents on the Republic of China: The Anti-Japanese War, Supplementary Part*), 3:217–19.

22. These Nationalist strategists include Jiang Jieshi, Jiang Baili (senior adviser of the Nanjing government), and Yang Jie (deputy chief of the General Staff). See Liu Ziming, *Zhongguo jindai junshi sixiang shi* (*History of Modern China's Military Thoughts*), 319–57.

23. John H. Jouett, "War Planes Over China," *Asia* 37 (1937): 828.

24. *Kangzhan shengli sishi zhounian lunwenji* (*Essays on the Fortieth Anniversary of Resistant War Victory*), 1:262–66; Zhang, "Toward Arming China," 127–35.

25. Most aircraft in the GMD air force were U.S.-made Curtiss Hawk II and III fighters, Douglas O-38 bombers, Northrop 2-E bombers, Vaught V-65 light bombers, along with a few U.S.- and Italian-made long-range bombers such as the Martin B-10 and Savoia S81 (Zhang, "Toward Arming China," 317, *Kangzhan shengli sishi zhounian lunwenji*, 1:266). For the total strength of the GMD air force at this time, see Wang Daoping, *Zhongguo kangRi zhanzheng shi* (*The History of the War of Resistance Against Japanese Aggression*), 1:510–11.

26. For example, in mid-1936, the Guangdong-Guangxi leaders openly defied the central authority in Nanjing. After the entire Guangdong air force defected to Nanjing, the Southwest insurrection collapsed and the Nanjing government reclaimed control of the two revolting provinces without firing a shot (Lloyd Eastman, *The Abortive Revolution: China and Nationalist Rule, 1927–1937*, 259–60).

27. By the end of 1937, the Chinese air force had only eighty combat planes left (Wang Daoping, *Zhongguo kangRi zhanzheng shi*, 3:282).

28. Between October, 1937, and June, 1941, the Soviet Union outfitted China with 885 aircraft, including 222 I-15 biplane fighters, 197 I-16 fighters (monoplane), 75 I-153 fighters (biplane), 279 SB-2 light bombers, 24 DB-3 medium bombers, and 18 TB-3 heavy bombers (Wang Zhenghua, *Kangzhan shiqi waiguo duihua junshi yuanzhu*, 114, 118–21). From 1942 to the end of the war, the U.S. supplied the Nationalist air force with 1,394 aircraft, including 1,038 fighters, 244 bombers, 15 reconnaissance aircraft, and 97 transports (*Kangzhan shengli sishi zhounian lunwenji*, 1:312–13).

29. E. R. Hooton, *The Greatest Tumult: The Chinese Civil War, 1936–1949*, 75.

30. More than three thousand Communists trained at the Huangpu Military Academy between 1924 and 1927 (Xu Yan, *Junshijia Mao Zedong* [*Mao Zedong: A Military Strategist*], 10).

31. Chang studied flying and aviation engineering, then served in the Red Army air force until 1938. Wang Bi went to Moscow in 1927 and studied aviation engineering in a Soviet air force academy, then worked as an air force engineer there until 1940 (Wang Dinglie et al., *Dangdai Zhongguo kongjun*, 40–41).

32. Ibid., 5–7.

33. During this battle, the Red Army captured more than five thousand Nationalist troops, including the commander of the Nationalist 69th Division (ibid., 8).

34. Guo Shushen's recollections in *Lantian zhi lu*, 1:22–26.

35. Wang Dinglie et al., *Dangdai Zhongguo kongjun*, 9.

36. For the Sino-Soviet alliance during the war, see John W. Carver, *Chinese-Soviet Relations, 1937–1945: The Diplomacy of Chinese Nationalism*.

37. Wang Dinglie et al., *Dangdai Zhongguo kongjun*, 9–10.

38. Yang Jun, chief ed., *Gongheguo buzhang dangan* (*The Biographic Archives Concerning the Ministers of the Republic*), 2:501–506.

39. Lü Liping, *Tongtian zhi lu* (*The Road to the Sky*), 4.

40. Yang Jun, chief ed., *Gongheguo buzhang dangan*, 2:505. See also Lü Liping's recollections in *Lantian zhi lu*, 1:29.

41. One candidate from Yan'an failed the physical examination before the training program started. See Lü Liping's recollections in *Lantian zhi lu*, 1:29–31.

42. Lü Liping, *Tongtian zhi lu*, 4–5.

43. The U-2 entered service in 1927, and from 1929 on more than thirty thousand were built. It was redesignated Po-2 in 1944, and then used as a night bomber, earning notorious names like "Washing-Machine Charlie" and "Bed-Check Charlie" when harassing UN forces during the Korean War (Greenwood, "Designers," 165).

44. The I-15 biplane and I-16 monoplane fighters were N. N. Polikarpov designs, and first appeared in 1934–35. The I-16 was the first mass-production low-wing monoplane equipped with retractable landing gear, and was the fastest fighter in the world in 1935. Beginning in 1940, the Soviet air force began to equip with three new fighters: the MiG-3, LaGG-3, and Yak-1. At the start of the war, there were still more than three thousand obsolete fighter aircraft in the western military districts (Reina Pennington, "From Chaos to the Eve of the Great Patriotic War, 1922–41," in *Russian Aviation and Airpower*, ed. by Higham et al., 41, 54).

45. Lü Liping's recollections in *Lantian zhi lu*, 1:27–49.

46. Ibid., 36–37.

47. Lü Liping, *Tongtian zhi lu,* 5.

48. Wang Dinglie et al., *Dangdai Zhongguo kongjun,* 14; Zhong Zhaoyun, *Baizhan jiangxing Liu Yalou (Biography of Gen. Lin Yalou),* 145.

49. When Chang Qiankun was sent to establish an aviation school in northeast China, Liu went along with him and began his flying career. From 1988–94, Liu was commander of the Beijing Military Region Air Force (Liu Yüti's recollections in *Lantian zhi lu,* 1:50–55).

50. For more on the Dixie mission, see David D. Barrett, *Dixie Mission: The United States Army Observer Group in Yenan, 1944.*

51. They were Chen Yun, Peng Zhen, Wu Xiouquan, and Ye Jizhuan (You Jiang's recollections in *Lantian zhi lu,* 1:56–65).

52. Wang Dinglie et al., *Dangdai Zhongguo kongjun,* 17; Liu Shanben's recollections in *Lantian zhi lu,* 1:119–33.

53. According to Lü Liping, the Japanese had three hundred combat planes and seven hundred trainers in Manchuria (*Tongtian zhi lu,* 48).

54. Wang Dinglie et al., *Dangdai Zhongguo kongjun,* 17–18; Liu Chongwen and Chen Shaochou, chief eds. *Liu Shaoqi nianpu (The Chronicle of Liu Shaoqi),* 1:479.

55. Chang Qiankun's and Huang Naiyi's recollections in *Lantian zhi lu,* 1:86–87, 97–98.

56. Wang Dinglie et al., *Dangdai Zhongguo kongjun,* 19–20; Zeng Kelin's recollections in *Lantian zhi lu,* 1:81–85; Lü Liping, *Tongtian zhi lu,* 49.

57. This Japanese unit consisted of forty-six aircraft and more than three hundred people, including seventeen pilots, ninety-six ground maintenance crews, and 188 other ground support personnel (Lü Liping, *Tongtian zhi lu,* 46–47).

58. Wang Dinglie et al., *Dandai Zhongguo kongjun,* 20–24.

59. Chang Qiankun's recollections in *Lantian zhi lu,* 1:86–96; Wang Dinglie et al., *Dangdai Zhongguo kongjun,* 27; Lü Liping, *Tongtian zhi lu,* 74–75, 79.

60. Korean War pilots frequently told me this during my research trip in China in 1999. See also Geng Longwu, *Zhongguo wangpai feixingyuan (China's Ace Pilots),* 208.

61. Lü Liping, *Tongtian zhi lu,* 68–85.

62. Ibid., 67.

63. Chen Xi and Li Dongliu's recollections in *Lantian zhi lu,* 1:222.

64. See, e.g., Xu Yan, *Junshijia Mao Zedong;* Liu Ziming, *Zhongguo jindai junshi shixiang shi;* and Liao Guoliang et al., *Mao Zedong junshi sixiang fazhan shi (History of Mao Zedong's military Thought Development).*

65. See Shu Guang Zhang, *Mao's Military Romanticism.*

66. *Mao Zedong Junshi wenji (A Collection of Mao Zedong's Military Papers),* 1:342.

67. *Mao Zedong Xuanji (Selected Works of Mao Zedong),* 2:511; *Mao Zedong Junshi wenji,* 4:424.

68. Liao Guoliang et al., *Mao Zedong junshi sixiang fazhan shi,* 476.

69. According to Shi Zhe, Mao's Russian-language translator, Mao was never willing to do anything unrealistic. This is probably why Mao was less vocal on aviation issues before 1949. See Shi Zhe, *Zai lishi juren shenbian Shi Zhe huiyilu (Beside Great Historical Figures: Shi Zhe's Memoirs),* 237–38.

70. Lü Liping, *Tongtian zhi lu,* 4; Lü Liping's recollections in *Lantian zhi lu,* 1:38.

71. Lü Liping, *Tongtian zhi lu,* 9; Li Chuangeng, *Feijiangjun Liu Shanben (Flying General Liu Shanben),* 178.

72. Military Historical Research Division of Military Science Academy, ed., *Zhongguo renmin jiefangjun de qishi nian* (*The Seventy Years of the People's Liberation Army*), 252, 274.

73. *Mao Zedong junshi wenxuan* (*Selected Military Works of Mao Zedong*), 4.

74. Lü Liping, *Tongtian zhi lu*, 12–13.

75. Zhou Enlai to the CCP Northeast Bureau, Dec. 5, 1947, telegram, in *Mao Zedong junshi wenji*, 4:340.

76. See Shi Zhe, *Zai lishi juren shenbian* (*Beside Great Historical Figures*), 350–51, 375–87.

77. After the founding of the People's Republic, the CCP leadership showed no hesitation to use airpower to achieve national unity and consolidate control. For example, when the PLA marched into Tibet in early 1950, the PLAAF sent transport aircraft with ground troops, flying 1,282 sorties and dropping 2,236 tons of materials between April, 1950, and November, 1952. The air force also employed bombers and fighters in Sichuan Province, and transport aircraft in Gansu Province to support bandit suppression campaigns in July and December, 1952, respectively (Wang Dinglie et al., *Dangdai Zhongguo kongjun*, 114–25).

78. *Mao Zedong junshi wenji*, 5:471–77.

Chapter 2. Fledgling Years

1. This squadron initially had six P-51s, two British-built Mosquito bombers, and two PT-19 trainers. In October, 1949, its aircraft inventory increased to nineteen P-51s, three Mosquitoes, one B-25, two C-47s, and three C-46s. In August, 1950, it switched to Soviet-built La-9 fighters, and disbanded in November, 1950, after one Soviet MiG-9 division arrived to assist with the air defense of Beijing (Wang Dinglie et al., *Dangdai Zhongguo kongjun*, 40–41; and Yang Peiguang and Yan Lei's recollections in *Lantian zhi lu*, 1:206–15).

2. Fang Huai's recollections in *Lantian zhi lu*, 1:139–51.

3. Liu Chongwen and Chen Shaochou, chief eds, *Liu Shaoqi nianpu*, 2:215.

4. Division of CCP Central Historical Documents, *Zhu De nianpu* (*The Chronicle of Zhu De*), 330.

5. Wang Dinglie et al., *Dangdai Zhongguo kongjun*, 35.

6. CMC to Fourth Field Army, July 26, 1949, telegram, in Zhong Zhaoyun, *Baizhan jiangxing Liu Yalou*, 144.

7. This information is from Lü Liping's recollections in *Tongtian zhi lu*, 137, but the recently released Russian document indicates this telegram was sent on July 25, 1949, and contained other Chinese messages but made no mention that Liu Yalou would be sent over for further negotiations. See "Mao Zedong's Telegram to Liu Shaoqi to Be handed to Joseph Stalin," in Andrei Ledovsky's "The Moscow Visit of a Delegation of the Communist Party of China in June to August 1949," *Far Eastern Affairs* (Moscow), no. 5 (1996): 84–97.

8. The Soviet leaders initially wanted to set up the school in Dalian, but later realized that it would be too crowded to conduct flight training there as the Liaodong Peninsula already housed a complete Soviet air force corps (Lu Liping, *Tongtian zhi lu*, 137, 156).

9. Ibid., 139–45.

10. Lü Liping's recollections in *Lantian zhi lu*, 1:187–98.

11. The La-9 was the last piston-engined fighter the Soviet Union developed in World War II and went into service in 1946. It had a top speed of 690 kilometers per hour, a ceiling of 11,300 meters, a maximum range of 1,735 kilometers, and was equipped with two 23-mm cannons. The P-51's technical characteristics were: speed, 426 miles per hour; ceiling, 41,900 feet; range, 1,539 miles; and it was armed with six .50-cal. wing-mounted machine guns.

12. See Lü Liping, *Tongtian zhi lu*, 161.

13. Ibid., 169.

14. At the time, the General Staff Department also recommended to Mao the name "Chinese People's Air Force" (He Tingyi's recollections in *Lantian zhi lu*, 1:201).

15. Wang Dinglie et al., *Dangdai Zhongguo kongjun*, 43–45.

16. Ibid., 219–23; He Tingyi's recollections in *Lantian zhi lu*, 2:105–108. See also Zhang Aiping, chief ed. *Zhongguo renmin jiefangjun (The Chinese People's Liberation Army)*, 274–85.

17. For a discussion of Soviet air doctrine in World War II, see John T. Greenwood, "Soviet Frontal Aviation during the Great Patriotic War, 1941–45," in *Russian Aviation and Airpower*, ed. Higham et al., 62–90.

18. Yang Wanqin and Qi Chunyuan, *Liu Yalou jiangjun zhuan (Biography of General Liu Yalou)*, 1, 28.

19. Ibid., 75, 79, 131, and 161–72.

20. During the 1920s and 1930s, the CCP was a branch of the Soviet-controlled Comintern, and there was sharp disagreement among the party leadership between the native faction headed by Mao and the international faction headed by Wang Ming, a Soviet-trained orthodox Communist, who was supported by Stalin. After Mao emerged as the top CCP leader after the Long March, he attributed CCP's earlier defeats to the mistakes made by Wang Ming, but the Comintern continued to suspect his true Communist identity.

21. Yang Wanqing and Qi Chunyuan, *Liu Yalou Jiangjun zhuan*, 173–75, 178–87, 194, 204.

22. Ibid., 258–59.

23. This article was published in *People's Air Force*, Aug. 1, 1951. See also Wang Dinglie et al., *Dangdai Zhongguo kongjun*, 47; Yang Wanqing and Qi Chunyuan, *Liu Yalou jiangjun zhuan*, 283.

24. On October 18, 1949, after listening to Liu's report about his negotiations for Soviet assistance for the PLAAF, Mao promised Liu he would have direct contact with him about air force matters (Lü Liping, *Tongtian zhi lu*, 171–72).

25. Zhu Hong's recollections in *Lantian zhi lu*, 1:269.

26. According to Liu, "elimination of the remnant enemy" was the PLAAF's contemporary mission, while "the consolidation of national defense" was its future one (Mao's message to the air force, April, 1950, in Yang Wanqing and Qi Chunyuan, *Liu Yalou jiangjun zhuan*, 284.

27. At the time, the 7th Aviation School was the only training facility that continued to rely on Japanese and former GMD instructors, and use U.S.-made PT-19s and ex-Japanese type 99 advanced trainers for flight training.

28. Wang Dinglie et al., *Dangdai Zhongguo kongjun*, 58, 62.

29. Ibid., 60; Lü Liping, *Tongtian zhi lu*, 195.

30. Wang Dinglie et al., *Dangdai Zhongguo kongjun*, 67–69; Chen Xi and Li Dongliu's recollections in *Lantian zhi lu*, 1:220.

31. During interviews with former PLAAF pilots, I was told that examinations on theoretical courses were given orally and students often were assisted by Chinese translators and teaching assistants.

32. Wang Dinglie et al., *Dangdai Zhongguo kongjun*, 63–64.

33. Wei Bihai, "Rememberance of the Air War during the War to Resist U.S. Aggression and Aid Korea: An Interview with Wang Bingzhang," *Junshi lishi*, no. 6 (2000): 31.

34. Ibid., 66; Lü Liping, *Tongtian zhi lu*, 241.

35. Unless otherwise cited, the information in this paragraph and those following is from Lü Liping, *Tongtian zhi lu*, 189, 192, 197, 217–32.

36. Chen Xi, then commander of the 3d Aviation School, recalled that the Soviet Union dispatched a complete set of aviation school personnel to China, including school commander, political commissar, chief engineer, flight instructors, maintenance crews, and even typists (Chen Xi and Li Dongliu's recollections in *Lantian zhi lu*, 1:217). See also Li Chuangeng, *Feijiangjun Liu Shanben*, 283.

37. Xiaoming Zhang, "China and the Air War in Korea, 1950–1953," *Journal of Military History* 62 (Apr., 1998): 347. In addition, during my research in the Jiangsu Provincial and Dalian City Archives in China, I came across several documents asking local governments to use the same supply system for Soviet troops and military personnel as the PLA, and that the central government would bear the costs. See, e.g., Ministry of Finance to People's Government of Lüda City, Apr. 28, 1953, cable, vol. 542, Dalian City Archives.

38. According to Lü Liping, Soviet advisers received double salaries (one from China, and the other from their own country), had a higher meal standard than at home, lived in the best housing facilities, and enjoyed other preferential treatment.

39. Lü Liping, *Tongtian zhi lu*, 199–200; Zhao Jianguo and Ma Yuan, *Chaoxian da kongzhan* (*The Great Air War in Korea*), 50–51.

40. Lü Liping, *Tongtian zhi lu*, 218.

41. For Russian complaints, see Boris Sergeyevich Abakumov, "Soviet Fliers in the Skies of Korea," *Voprosy Istorii*, no. 1 (Jan., 1993): 129–39. I saw a number of reports concerning Chinese complaints about the behavior of Soviet troops in the Dalian City Archives.

42. Lü Liping, as a former commander of the 4th Aviation School, recalled later that he had no idea how many Russian advisers served at his school.

43. Zhou Zhaoping's recollections in *Lantian zhi lu*, 1:232.

44. Many Soviet advisers, anxious to get the training completed and return home, rushed Chinese student pilots to solo, which often led to accidents.

45. For example, on April 15, 1950, an incompetent Chinese student pilot was urged to solo for aerobatics in an La-9. Due to lack of confidence, he damaged the plane during the landing. Soviet advisers suggested that there was no need to report the incident to Beijing because the damaged plane could still be used for groundcrew training. The Chinese, however, declined to follow this advice.

46. When Chinese commanders refused to accept a washout decision made by the Russians, they would use Chinese instructors to continue the pilot's training. For example,

three student pilots washed out by the Russians at the 4th Aviation School later graduated after being trained by Chinese instructors. One died in the Korean War as a hero with five kills, and the other two became high-ranking Chinese air force commanders in the 1980s (Lü Liping, *Tongtian zhi lu,* 223–28).

47. Former North Korean pilot No Kum-Sok notes that Russian advisers were often "pulling strings behind the scenes," and such an accusation seems consistent with Lü Liping's account about Russian advisers (*A MiG-15 to Freedom,* 87).

48. Liu Yalou's comment was made after the senior Soviet adviser at the 4th Aviation School wrongly accused the Chinese commander of being responsible for the death of a Russian technician due to a lack of medical care in May, 1950.

49. Zhou Zhaoping's recollections in *Lantian zhi lu,* 1:234.

50. No Kum-Sok, *MiG-15 to Freedom,* 87–93.

51. On December 16, 1952, at the air force party committee meeting, Peng Dehuai criticized the air force's unwillingness to study Soviet experiences, reminding the air force leadership that without the Soviet Union, China could not build a strong air force within a short period of time. See Wang Yan, chief ed. *Peng Dehuai nianpu* (*The Chronicle of Peng Dehuai*), 538.

52. Although the PLAAF was officially established in November, 1949, it consisted of no combat air units until June, 1950, and people joked that it should be called "Kongjun," a name that literally means it was a skeleton force (Wang Hai, *Wo de zhandou shengya* [*My Combat Career*], 48).

53. According Zhou Enlai's report to Mao Zedong on September 3, 1950, this plan projected to create eleven regiments (330 planes) in 1950, twelve regiments (480 planes) in 1951, and thirty one regiments in 1952, a total of fifty four air regiments (including six transport regiments) and 1,560 planes. See Zhou to Mao, Sept. 3, 1950, memorandum, Zhou Enlai, *Zhou Enlai junshi wenxuan,* 4:52–53.

54. Wang Dinglie et al., *Dangdai Zhongguo kongjun,* 77.

55. Ibid., 49, 75.

56. Ibid., 76. In 1950, PLA leaders gave high priority to the development of the PLAAF over other military needs. For example, on November 4, the CMC ordered the East China Military Region to transfer four army divisions slated for the development of new artillery forces to the air force for the immediate formation of six air force divisions (Zhou to Chen Yi, Rao Shushi, Tang Liang, and Zhang Aiping, telegram, Nov. 4, 1950 in *Zhou Enlai nianpu,* 1:92).

57. Duan underwent flight training on only the Yak-18 before being appointed commander of the 2d Air Army. Zeng finished his flight training on the Tu-2 in April, 1952, and became commander of the 1st Navy Aviation Division five months later (Li Jie, "General Takes Wing to Blue Sky," *Xinhua wenzhai,* no. 12 [1994]: 128–33). See also Zhou Zhaoping's recollections in *Lantian zhi lu,* 1:231.

58. In September, 1971, when Lin Biao, vice chairman of the CCP, allegedly failed to use the air force to launch a military coup against Mao, the central leadership again sent army officers to take control of the PLAAF.

59. Lü Liping, *Tongtian zhi lu,* 144.

60. Air Force Headquarters Editorial and Research Office, *Kongjun shi,* 36; Wang Dinglie et al., *Dangdai Zhongguo kongjun,* 77. For additional information, see Liu Zhen,

Liu Zhen huiyilu (*Liu Zhen's Memoirs*); Nie Fengzhi, *Zhanchang: Jiangjun de yaolan* (*Battle-fields: The Cradle of Generals*); Yang Shilu's recollections in *Lantian zhi lu*, 1:302–13.

61. Li Shi'an's recollections in *Lantian zhi lu*, 1:273–84.

62. In October, 1950, the 3d Fighter Brigade was established in Shenyang, consisting of 7th, 8th, and 9th Regiments. The 4th Fighter Brigade was formed in Liaoyang, Liaoning Province, using the 4th Mixed Brigade's 10th Regiment and the 3d Fighter Brigade's 7th Regiment (which became the 12th Regiment). At almost the same time, the 3d and 4th Fighter Brigades were renamed the PLAAF 3d and 4th Divisions and reduced from three regiments to two each. In November, the 4th Mixed Brigade's 11th Regiment became the PLAAF 2d Division, consisting of the 4th and 6th Regiments (Wang Dinglie et al., *Dangdai Zhongguo kongjun*, 87–88).

63. By May, 1951, the PLAAF order of battle included the 5th Attack Division at Kaiyuan, Liaoning Province; 6th Fighter Division at Anshan, Liaoning Province; 7th Fighter Division at Dongfeng Xian, Jilin Province; 9th Fighter Division at Jilin, Jilin Province; 8th Bomber Division at Siping, Jilin Province; 10th Bomber Division (formed from the 4th Mixed Brigade's bomber regiment) at Nanjing, Jiangsu Province; 12th Fighter Division at Xiaoshan Xian, Zhejiang Province; 14th Fighter Division at Beijing; 15th Fighter Division at Huaide Xian, Jilin Province; 16th Fighter Division at Qingdao, Shandong Province; 17th Fighter Division at Tangshan, Hebei Province; 18th Fighter Division at Guangzhou, Guangdong Province; 11th Attack Division (formed from the 4th Mixed Brigade's attack regiment) at Xuzhou, Jiangsu Province; and 13th Transport Division at Xinjin Xian, Sichuan Province.

64. Wang Dinglie et al., *Dangdai Zhongguo kongjun*, 89–108.

65. Shi Zhonghan's recollections in *Lantian zhi lu*, 1:260.

66. Wang Dinglie et al., *Dangdai Zhongguo kongjun*, 91.

67. Ibid., 92–97.

68. The P-3 was a copy of a U.S. Army radar the Soviets obtained via lend-lease in World War II. See Alfred Price, *The History of U.S. Electronic Warfare*, vol. 2.

69. The lack of a radar early-warning system and poor coordination between ground radar control and interceptors continued to annoy CCP leaders until 1957 (Zou Guang's recollections in *Lantian zhi lu*, 2:396–97). See also Wang Dinglie et al., *Dangdai Zhongguo kongjun*, 92–96.

70. Wang Dinglie et al., *Dangdai Zhongguo kongjun*, 98–99.

71. Liu Yalou, "The First Seven Years of the People's Air Force," *Lantian zhi lu*, 2:38.

72. Air Force Headquarters Editorial and Research Office, *Kongjun shi*, 96–97. See also Shi Zhonghan's recollections in *Lantian zhi lu*, 2:255–56.

73. The Soviets agreed to supply China with 20,011 tons of various fuels for training pilots in 1950. See the minutes of a conversation between Mao and A. Yvshiskiy, Jan. 6, 1950. A copy translated in Chinese is found in Shen Zhihua, *ZhongSu tongmeng yu Chaoxian zhanzheng yanjiu* (*Study of the Sino-Soviet Alliance and the Korean War*), 333–35.

74. Wang Dinglie et al., *Dangdai Zhongguo kongjun*, 103–105.

75. For the English text of this agreement, see Goncharov et al., *Uncertain Partners*, 263–64. For minutes of the conversation between Stalin and Mao on this matter, see "Stalin's Conversation with Chinese Leaders: Talks with Mao Zedong, December 1949–

January 1950, and with Zhou Enlai, August–September 1952," trans. Danny Rozas, *Cold War International History Project Bulletin*, nos. 6 and 7 (winter 1995–96): 9.

76. Mao to Li Fuchun, Wang Jiaxiang, and Liu Yalou, Mar. 2, 1950, telegram, in *Zhou Enlai nianpu*, 1:26.

77. These orders were placed on February 11 and 15, March 8, and April 13. Zhou Enlai to Ambassador Wang (Jiaxiang), May 6, 1950, telegram, in *Zhou Enlai junshi wenxuan*, 4:2–3.

78. Wang Dinglie et al., *Dangdai Zhongguo kongjun*, 78; Han Huaizhi, chief ed., *Dangdai Zhongguo jundui de junshi gongzuo* (*The Military Affairs of China Today: Army*), 2:160–61.

79. On April 13, 1950, China asked the Soviet Union to send forty-three advisers to help organize and train the first air force division, scheduled for activation in May. See Zhou to Ambassador Wang, May 6, 1950, telegram.

80. Han Huaizhi, chief ed., *Dangdai Zhongguo jundui de junshi gongzuo*, 2:161.

81. Shi Zhonghan's recollections in *Lantian zhi lu*, 1:259.

82. Air Force Headquarters Editorial and Research Office, *Kongjun shi* (*History of Air Force*), 86; Xiao Jingguang, *Xiao Jingguang huiyilu* (*Memoirs of Xiao Jingguang*), 2:29. Probably as compensation, the PLAAF later transferred two aviation divisions (two regiments each from the 9th Division, and 17th Division) to navy aviation, including 175 MiG-15bis jet fighters and twenty-one La-9 piston-engined fighters (Yang Guoyu et al., *Dangdai Zhongguo haijun* [*China Today: The Navy*], 73–74).

83. Zhou Keyu, *KangMei yuanChao zhanzheng* (*The War to Resist America and Assist Korea*), 351–53.

84. Wang Dinglie et al., *Dangdai Zhongguo kongjun*, 105–106.

Chapter 3. Promise, Decision, and the Airpower Factor

1. Alexander Y. Mansourov, "Stalin, Mao, Kim, and China's Decision to enter to the Korean War, September 16–October 15, 1950: New Evidence from the Russian Archives," *Cold War International History Project Bulletin*, nos. 6 and 7 (winter, 1995–96): 103; O'Neill, "Other Side of the Yalu," 31.

2. Goncharov et al., *Uncertain Partners*, 187–92; Chen Jian, *China's Road*, 196–200.

3. Stalin to Zhou, July 5, 1950, telegram, cited in Weathersby, "New Russian Documents," 43.

4. Goncharov et al., *Uncertain Partners*, 145.

5. As early as the spring of 1949, Mao had expressed his disagreement with North Korea's proposal for military action on the Korean Peninsula (Dunkin to A. R., Sept. 14, 1949, telegram, cited in APRF (Chinese), 82–83).

6. In early 1950, China placed a number of orders for Soviet arms and ammunition destined for the scheduled military campaign against Taiwan and other GMD controlled islands. See Zhou to Ambassador Wang, May 6, 1950, telegram, *Zhou Enlai junshi wenxuan*, 4:2–3.

7. For China's plan to seize Taiwan, see Xu Yan, *Jinmen zhi zhan* (*The Battles for Jinmen*), 124; Zhou Jun, "A Preliminary Exploration of Reasons for the People's Liberation

Army's Abortive Plan to Attack Taiwan after the Formation of the People's Republic," *Zhonggong dangshi yanjiu*, no. 1 (1991): 72; Chen Jian, *China's Road*, 87–88.

8. For details on the transfer of Korean PLA soldiers, see Chen Jian, *China's Road*, 110. See also Bruce Cumings, *The Origins of the Korean War*, 2:363.

9. Shen Zonghong et al, *Zhongguo renmin zhiyuanjun kangMei yuanChao zhan shi* (*A History of the War to Resist America and Assist Korea*), 8; Du Ping, *Zai zhiyuanjun zongbu: Du Ping huiyilu* (*My Days at the Headquarters of the Chinese People's Volunteers: Du Ping's Memoirs*), 17.

10. Before visiting Beijing, Kim Il Sung told the Soviet ambassador to Pyongyang, T. F. Shtykov, that he had no need for Chinese aid because Moscow had already satisfied all of his requests (Shtykov to Stalin, May 12, 1950, telegram, cited in Weathersby, "New Russian Documents," 39).

11. According to Lei Yingfu, director of the Operations Office of the General Staff, Chinese leaders had no knowledge of the NKPA's war plan when the crisis erupted (Chen Xianyi and Lie Yingfu, *Zai zuigao tongshuaibu dang canmo: Lei Yingfu jiangjun huiyilu* [*My Services in the Supreme Command: General Lei Yingfu's Memoirs*], 144). For Kim's attitude toward China's assistance, see T. F. Shtykov, Soviet ambassador to the DPRK, to A. Ya. Vyshinskiy, USSR minister of foreign affairs, May 12, 1950, telegram, cited in Weathersby, "New Russian Documents," 38–39. For a secondary account of this, see Goncharov et al., *Uncertain Partners*, 153.

12. See Chen Jian, *China's Road*, 112.

13. Roshchin to Stalin, May 16, 1950, telegram, cited in Bajanov and Bajanova, "Korean Conflict," 53.

14. According to recently available Russian archival sources, Mao did not offer China's support for North Korea's invasion plan until he received a personal explanation from Stalin on the issue. See Roshchin to Stalin, May 13, 14, 15, and 16, 1950, telegrams, cited in ibid., 51–52. The correspondence between Mao and Stalin on May 13 and 14, 1950, can also be found in "More Documents from the Russian Archives," trans. Vladislav M. Zubok and Kathryn Weathersby, *Cold War International History Project Bulletin*, no. 4 (fall, 1994): 61.

15. Chen Feng et al., *ZhongMei jiaoliang da xiezheng* (*A True Description of the Trial of Strength between China and the United States*), 1:6.

16. Ibid.

17. Stalin to Shtykov, July 1, 1950, and Shtykov to Stalin, July 1, 1950, telegrams, cited in Bajonov, "Assessing the Politics," 40, 42.

18. Deng Lifeng, *Xin Zhongguo junshi huodong jishi, 1949–1959* (*The True Records of the New China's Military Affairs*), 110. For Mao's plan to reduce the PLA, see Mao to Deng Zhihui, Tan Zhen, Zhao Erlu, Tao Zhu, etc., Apr. 21, 1950, telegram, in *Mao Zedong junshi wenji*, 6:78–79.

19. According to Xiao Jinguang, commander of the PLA navy in 1950, China's plans to cope with the situation would be "to continue the demobilization of our land forces while at the same time strengthening the construction of our naval and air forces. And the Taiwan campaign will be postponed." Xiao Jinguang, *Xiao Jinguang huiyilu*, 2:8, 20.

20. On July 8, 1950, after receiving a complaint from Kim Il Sung, Stalin urged Chinese leaders to send their representatives to Korea in order to cooperate with the North Koreans (Weathersby, "New Russian Documents," 44). Chai Chengwen and seven other

Chinese military intelligence officers arrived in Pyongyang on July 10. See Chai Chengwen and Zhao Yongtian, *Banmendian tanpan* (*The Panmunjom Negotiations*), 35–36.

21. On July 12, 1950, Kim Il Sung sent the NKPA's deputy chief of staff to Beijing to inform Chinese leaders that North Korea needed only military supplies. Chinese leaders thus believed the war would end before the United States could assemble a major force to conduct an amphibious assault on the Korean Peninsula (*Zhou Enlai nianpu*, 1:55; *Zhou Enlai junshi wenxuan*, 4:44).

22. On July 6, 1950, an editorial in the *People's Daily* claimed the increase of U.S. military forces in Korea meant victory would be delayed, and that the Korean people must prepare for a long, hard struggle. See Chen Xiaowei and Huang Xiaoqin, "On China's Decision-making in the Korean War," *Junshi lishi*, no. 2 (2000): 10.

23. *Zhou Enlai junshi wenxuan*, 4:44–45.

24. Roshchin to Moscow, July 2, 1950, telegram, cited in Bajanov and Bajanova, "Korean Conflict," 86. See also Evgeniy P. Bajanov, "Assessing the Politics of the Korean War, 1949–51." *Cold War International History Project Bulletin*, nos. 6 and 7 (winter, 1995–96): 89.

25. Since some participants had to travel to Beijing from Shenyang and Wuhan, there is no doubt that the meeting on July 7 was a response to Stalin's July 5 cable. For participants, see Zhang, *Mao's Military Romanticism*, 58.

26. The best record of this resolution is summarized in a footnote to Mao's letter to Nie Rongzhen, acting chief of the General Staff, July 7, 1950, in *Mao Zedong jianguo yilai wengao*, 1:428.

27. On July 10, Zhou held another meeting to discuss the details of force deployment with several regional commanders (Du Ping, *Zai zhiyuanjun zongbu*, 14). Zhou revised the draft of the CMC "Resolution on Defending the Northeast Border Security" before sending for Mao's approval (Yang Shengqun and Tien Shongnien, eds., *Gongheguo zhongda juece de lailong qumai* (*The Origin and Development of Important Decision by the People's Republic*), *1949–1965*, 56).

28. All Chinese sources seem inconsistent and unclear about the sequence of events. See, e.g., Shen Zonghong et al., *Zhongguo renmin zhiyuanjun kangMei yuanChao zhan shi* (*A History of the War to Resist America and Assist Korea by the Chinese People's Volunteers*), 8; Du Ping, *Zai zhiyuanjun zongbu*, 17; Yang Di, *Zai zhiyuanjun zongbu de suiyue li: xianwei renzhi de zhenqing shikuang* (*During the Years of the CPV's Headquarters: Rarely Known True Accounts*), 6–7.

29. Stalin to Zhou Enlai or Mao Zedong, July 13, 1950, telegram, in Weathersby, "New Russian Documents," 44.

30. Mao to Stalin, July 22, 1950, telegram, in APRF (Chinese), 82–83.

31. A. Ya. Vyshinskiy, minister of foreign affairs, to N. V. Roshchin, ambassador to the PRC, July 25, 1950, telegram, in Weathersby, "New Russian Documents," 45.

32. Vasiliyevskiy and Malandin to Bulganin, Aug. 29, 1950, telegram, cited in O'Neill, "Other Side of the Yalu," 21.

33. Du Ping, *Zai zhiyuanjun zongbu*, 73. See also Jiang Yonghui, *Sanshibajun zai Chaoxian* (*The Thirty-Eighth Army in Korea*), 28–29.

34. Jiang Yonghui, *Sanshibajun zai Chaoxian*, 21.

35. The initial deadline was the end of August (Mao to Gao Gang, commander of the Northeast Military Region, Aug. 5, 1950, telegram, in *Mao Zedong jianguo yilai wengao*, 1:454).

36. Mao to Gao, Aug. 18, 1950, telegram, in ibid., 469.

37. Stalin to Zhou, Aug. 27, 1950, telegram, in Weathersby, "New Russian Documents," 45.

38. For an American version of the incident, see Futrell, *United States Air Force in Korea,* 148–49. For the Chinese side of the story, see Xie Lifu, *Chaoxian zhanzheng shilu* (*Historical Records of the Korean War*), 1:140. See also *Zhou Enlai nianpu,* 1:71. For a detailed record, see Zhang Ye, "Records of American Planes Invading Chinese Territorial Air Space in the Fifties and Sixties," *Junshi lishi,* no. 3 (2001): 62–63.

39. A. M. Vasiliyevskiy and German Malandin to N. A. Bulganin, Aug. 27, 1950, report, cited in O'Neill, "Other Side of the Yalu," 24.

40. Vasiliyevskiy to Belov, Aug. 27, 1950, telegram. A copy of this order supplied by O'Neill reads:

> (1) The 151st GIAD will carry out its task to retrain Chinese pilots, by 1 September it will organize, in coordination with AAA PVO, cover for the troops of the PLA's 13th Army Group, located in the area Tonghua, Tieling, Liaoyang, and Andong; (2) While conducting air cover, aircraft of the 151st GIAD will not fly across the state border with the Korean People's Democratic Republic; (3) Together with the staff of the 13th Army Group (Andong), develop a plan of cooperation with the AAA PVO of the PLA. The Division's plan of action regarding air cover is to be presented to the General Staff of the Soviet Army by the next diplomatic post via Shenyang General Consul; (4) Submit by ciphered direct line, in the name of the Chief of the General Staff of the Soviet Army, an operational summary every day at 20:00 hours. Report air battles at once; (5) Acknowledge the receipt of the directives and report readiness to carry out the combat tasks.

A summary of this order can be found in O'Neill, "Other Side of the Yalu," 24–25. It is necessary to note that despite the pressure on Belov to retrain Chinese pilots at once, the Chinese air unit that was supposed to be trained by the 151st had not been formed and thus no Chinese pilots would embark on such training until late October. This will be discussed separately.

41. Weathersby, "New Russian Documents," 31.

42. According to a Chinese document, the Russian plane was shot down thirty miles off Haiyang Island, and Soviet authorities asked local Chinese fishermen to help rescue its crewmen (Han Guang to Zhou Meixing, Sept. 4, 1950, telegram, in People's Government of Lüda City, vol. 69, Dalian City Archives). Soviet sources state that on September 4, 1950, a lend-lease A-20 bomber from the 36th Naval Torpedo Bomber Aviation Regiment, 589th Naval Torpedo Bomber Aviation Division, based out of Port Arthur was shot down on a reconnaissance mission that encountered eleven F4U Corsairs from the USS *Valley Forge.* Three crewmen were killed. See Aleksandr V. Kotlobovskiy and Igor Seidov, "The Hot Skies of the 'Cold War,'" *Mir Aviatsiya* (*World of Aviation*), no. 2 (1995): 21. See also Crane, *American Airpower Strategy in Korea,* 44–45.

43. Vasiliyevskiy to Stalin, Sept. 21, 1950 and Sept. 23, 1950, memorandums, in Mansourov, "Stalin, Mao, Kim," 108.

44. Du Ping, *Zai zhiyuanjun zongbu,* 21–22.

45. Chen Jian, *China's Road,* 150–51.

46. Zhu Jianrong, *Mo Takuto no chosen senso: Chugoku ga Oryokko o wataru made* (*Mao Zedong's Korean War: China Crosses the Yalu*), 264. For identification of Lt. Gen. P.

Kotov-Legon'kov, see V. A. Zolotarev, chief ed., *Rossiya (SSSR) v Lokal'nykh Voynakh i Voyennykh Konfliktakh Vtoroy Poloviny XX Veka* (*Russia [USSR] in Local Wars and Regional Conflicts in the Second Half of the 20th Century*), 63.

47. Chen Jian, *China's Road,* 177.

48. M. V. Zakharov to Stalin, Sept. 26, 1950, telegram, in Mansourov, "Stalin, Mao, Kim," 110.

49. Stalin to Mao and Zhou, Oct. 1, 1950, telegram, in ibid., 114.

50. Mao to Stalin, Oct. 2, 1950, telegram, in *Mao Zedong jianguo yilai wengao,* 1:539–41.

51. Roshchin to Stalin, Oct. 3, 1950, telegram, in Mansourov, "Stalin, Mao, Kim," 114–15.

52. For details about China's decision making in early October, see Chen Jian, *China's Road,* 171–85; and Goncharov et al., *Uncertain Partners,* 176–79.

53. This explanation was offered by Chinese scholar Shen Zhihua in the spring, 1996, issue of *Dangshi yanjiu ziliao* (*Party History Research Materials*) and then translated by Chen Jian as "The Discrepancy between the Russian and Chinese Versions of Mao's 2 October 1950 Message to Stalin on Chinese Entry into the Korean War: A Chinese Scholar's Reply," in the *Cold War International History Project Bulletin,* nos. 8 and 9 (winter, 1996–97): 237–42. Shen declares that the Chinese version was "in Mao's own handwriting," but does not bear Mao's office staff's signature as other telegrams do. Thus, he believes that this might not have been sent to Stalin.

54. Mansourov, "Stalin, Mao, Kim," 100.

55. Stalin to Kim Il Sung, Oct. 8, 1950, telegram, in Bajonov, "Assessing the Politics," 116. Russian researcher Alexander Mansourov notes that this letter was sent on October 5, following a Soviet Politburo meeting in Moscow that day (ibid., 100–101).

56. Chen Jian, *China's Road,* 181–82; Goncharov et al., *Uncertain Partners,* 179–83.

57. Stalin to Kim Il Sung, Oct. 8, 1950, telegram.

58. Hong Xuezhi, *KangMei yuanChao zhanzheng huiyi* (Recollections of the War to Resist America and Assist Korea), 24–25; Xie Lifu, *Chaoxian zhanzheng shilu,* 1:178. Yao Xu, *Cong Yalujiang dao Banmendian* (*From the Yalu River to Panmunjom*), 25; Zhang Xi, "Peng's Appointment to Command of Troops to Resist America and Aid Korea," *Zhonggong dangshi ziliao,* no. 31 (1989): 142, 147–48; Hao Yufan and Zhao Zhihai, "China's Decision to Enter the Korean War: History Revisited," *China Quarterly,* no. 121 (Mar., 1990): 100.

59. Shi Zhe, *Zai lishi juren shenbian,* 497–98.

60. Between July and October, 1950, Mao sent some forty-six telegrams to Stalin discussing China's military intervention. However, few have been made available so far, so any current argument will remain inconclusive.

61. According to the U.S. Joint Chiefs of Staff's estimation, in July 1950, the Soviet air force in the Far East had a total of 5,300 aircraft, including 2,200 fighters, 600 attack aircraft, 1,100 light bombers, 600 bombers, 500 transports, and 300 surveillance aircraft (Paul Kesaris, ed., *Records of the Joint Chiefs of Staff,* pt. 2, *The Far East, 1946–1953,* reel 9).

62. For insight into the mentality of Chinese leaders, see Zhou Enlai, "International Situation and Diplomatic Tasks after the Signing of the Sino-Soviet Treaty," in *Zhou Enlai waijiao wenxuan* (*Selected Diplomatic Works of Zhou Enlai*), 11–17; and Mao Zedong's address to the sixth session of the Central People's Government Council, Apr. 11, 1950, *Mao Zedong jianguo yilai wengao,* 1:291.

63. According to Wu Xinquan, former commander of the Thirty-ninth Army, the NBDA commanders wanted to learn how to fight with air and tank support, and how to communicate between ground troops and the air force. See Wu Xinquan, *Chaoxian zhanchang 1000 days: Sanshijiu jun zai Chaoxian* (*One Thousand days in the battlefield of the Korean War: The Thirty-ninth Army in Korea*), 24; Wang Bo, *Peng Dehuai ruchao zuozhan jishi* (*A True Record of Peng Dehuai in the Korean War*), 57–58. Wang's information is drawn from his interview with Hong Xuezhi, deputy commander of the CPV; Zhang Yangwu, Peng's political secretary; and Yang Feng'an, Peng's military secretary. The summary here is based on Zhang Xi, "Peng's Appointment," 144.

64. Peng and Gao to Mao, Oct. 9, 1950, telegram, in *Mao Zedong junshi wenji*, 6:114–15. According to one Chinese source, Peng drafted this telegram himself (Wang Bo, *Peng Dehuai*, 58).

65. Peng to Mao, Oct. 10, 1950, telegram, in *Mao Zedong junshi wenji*, 6:115.

66. By September, 1950, the PLA had only sixteen antiaircraft artillery regiments, with five deployed in the Shanghai-Nanjing area, five in the Beijing-Tianjin area, and four in the Guangzhou-Wuhan area. There were only two in the Northeast Military Region (Wang Dinglie et al, *Dangdai zhongguo kongjun*, 221). See also Chen Zhonglong et al., eds., *Zhongguo renmin zhiyuanjun renwu zhi* (*Biographies of the Chinese People's Volunteers*), 117.

67. Peng to Mao, Oct. 10, 1950, telegram, in *Mao Zedong junshi wenji*, 6:114.

68. Goncharov, Lewis, and Xue interpret wrongly that the Chinese word *kongjun* [air force] in Mao's cable to Peng referred to the Soviet air force, because at the time China had no air force. However, Mao made it very clear that this cable was in response to Peng's telegram of October 9. See Goncharov et al., *Uncertain Partners*, 188, 343.

69. According to Zhang Xi, Zhou took a Soviet-made Il-14 plane to Irkutsk on October 8, then to Omsk on October 9, and finally arrived in Moscow on the tenth (Zhang Xi, "On the Eve of Entering Korea: Zhou Enlai's Secret Visit to the Soviet Union," in *Da chubing* (*The Great Dispatch of Troops*), ed. Xiao Yunbin, 20–21). Chen Jian notes that Zhou continued on to Stalin's Black Sea villa on October 10 and met with Soviet leaders from 7 P.M. to five the next morning. For more on this controversy, see Chen Jian, *China's Road*, 284–85. The recently published chronicle biography of Zhou reveals that the Zhou-Stalin talks were held October 11 (*Zhou Enlai nianpu*, 1:85).

70. Goncharov et al., *Uncertain Partners*, 187–92; Chen Jian, *China's Road*, 196–200; Shu Guang Zhang, *Mao's Military Romanticism*, 83–84.

71. Shi Zhe, *Zai lishi juren shenbian*, 496–98.

72. "Kang Yinmin's Recollections on Zhou Enlai's Secret Visit to the Soviet Union in October 1950," cited in Qi Dexue, *Chaoxian zhanzheng juece neimu* (*The Inside Story of Decision Making during the Korean War*), 62–63.

73. Mansourov, "Stalin, Mao, Kim," 103.

74. See Chen Jian, *China's Road*, 285.

75. Zhang served on the General Staff for more than forty years. Since 1983, he has been involved in compiling Peng Dehuai's official biography and thus received special access to the party's classified archives.

76. Mao to Zhou, Oct. 13, 1950, telegram, in Zhang Xi, "On the Eve of Entering Korea," 21–22. Part of this telegram (items 1 and 2) is in *Mao Zedong junshi wenji*, 6:117, and

items 3 and 4, cited here, have been sanitized. Part of this telegram also appears in Shi Zhe, *Zai lishi juren shenbian,* 502. See also *Zhou Enlai nianpu,* 1:85–86.

77. See Shi Zhe's *Zai lishi juren shenbian,* 498–501.

78. Mao to Peng and Gao, Oct. 12, 1950; Mao to Rao Shushi and Chen Yi, Oct. 12, 1950, Mao to Zhou, Oct. 13, 1950, telegrams, in *Mao Zedong jianguo yilai wengao,* 1:552–53, 556.

79. This part is not included in Mao's October 13 telegram published in ibid., but is in the original text cited in Yang Shengqun and Tien Shongnien, eds., *Gongheguo zhongda juece de lailong qumai,* 62. A reference to this Chinese ciphered telegram can be found in Roshchin's telegram to Stalin. According to the Soviet ambassador, Mao said: "The main thing that we need is airpower which shall provide us with air cover. We hope to see its arrival as soon as possible, but not later than in two months in any case" (Rushchin to Stalin, Oct. 13, 1950, in APRF [Chinese], 103). See also, Bajanov, "Assessing the Politics," 118–19.

80. Yang Shengqun and Tien Shongnien, eds., *Gongheguo zhongda juece de lailong qumai,* 62; Zhang Xi, "On the Eve of Entering Korea," 21–22.

81. The content of Stalin's telegram to Zhou on October 14 is not available. See *Zhou Enlai nianpu,* 1:86.

82. "Mao Zedong and Zhou Enlai's Conversations with Kim Il Sung," Oct. 10, 1970, minutes, cited in Xiong Huayuan, "Zhou Enlai's Secret Visit to the Soviet Union on the Eve of the War to Resist U.S. and Aid Korea," *Dang de wenxian,* no. 3 (1994): 85. See also *Zhou Enlai nianpu,* 1:87.

83. Ibid., 87.

84. O'Neill, "Other Side of the Yalu," 31–36.

85. Zhu Jianrong, *Mo Takuto no chosen senso,* 243–47.

86. Mao to Zhou, Oct. 14, 1950, telegram, in *Mao Zedong jianguo yilai wengao,* 1:560–61. However, the phrase "waiting for the arrival of the Soviet air force" is cut out in the published text of the telegram in *Mao Zedong jianguo yilai wengao.* For reference, see Xiong Huayuan, "Zhou Enlai's Secret Visit," 87.

87. Wang Bo, *Peng Dehuai,* 77–78.

88. The information in this paragraph is from Peng Dehuai's speech at the CPV commanders' meeting, Oct. 14, 1950, in Peng Dehuai, *Peng Dehuai junshi wenxuan (Selected Military Writings of Peng Dehuai),* 320–25. Peng probably drafted this speech on October 14, then delivered it on October 16 at Andong. See Chinese Academy of Military Science, *Zhongguo renmin zhiyuanjun kangMei yuanChao zhan shi,* 15.

89. Jiang Yonghui, *Sanshibajun zai Chaoxian,* 8; Wang Bo, *Peng Dehuai,* 55, 93.

90. Jiang Yonghui, *Sanshibajun zai Chaoxian,* 28–29.

91. Luo Yinwen, *Deng Hua jiangjun zhuan (Biography of General Deng Hua),* 198–99.

92. Heng Xueming, *Shengsi sanbaxian: Zhongguo zhiyuanjun zai Chaoxian zhanchang shimo (Life and Death on the 38th Parallel: The Whole Story of the Chinese Volunteer Army in the Korean War),* 71. Zhang Xi, "Peng's Appointment," 157.

93. Luo Yinwen, *Deng Hua jiangjun zhuan,* 198.

94. Wang Yazhi, "Some Information before and after Mao Zedong Decided to Send Troops to Korea," *Dang de wenxian,* no. 6 (1995): 87.

95. Mao to Deng Hua, Hong Xuezhi, Han Xianchu, and Xie Fang, Oct. 18, 1950, telegram, in *Mao Zedong jianguo yilai wengao,* 1:568.

96. *Mao Zedong junshi wenxuan*, 650; Tang Jingqiao, ed., *KangMei yuanChao zhanzheng* (*The War to Resist America and Aid Korea*), 21; Heng Xueming, *Shengsi sanbaxian* (*Life and Death on the 38th Parallel*), 79.

97. Mao to Peng, Oct. 23, 1950, telegram, in *Mao Zedong jianguo yilai wengao*, 1:588–89.

Chapter 4. From Defending China to Intervention in Korea

1. For American accounts, see Futrell, *United States Air Force in Korea*, 219, 244.

2. Jiang Tianran, "Air Defense of Great Shanghai: A Real Account of the Defeat of Jiang Jieshi's Air Force by Chinese and Soviet Air Defense Forces," *Zhongguo guofang bao*, Feb. 28, 2001, 6. The author was the chief of staff when the Shanghai air defense headquarters was established on March 1, 1950.

3. Shanghai party authorites cabled the central leadship for assistance with air defense five times: on January 25 and 29, February 7 and 18, and March 9, 1950 (Zhu Bingxiu, "Air Defense of Shanghai during the Initial Post-liberation Period," *Junshi lishi*, no. 3 (1994): 51).

4. Ibid., 51–54; Wang Dinglie et al., *Dangdai Zhongguo kongjun*, 99–100.

5. Mao Zedong to Liu Shaoqi, July 25, 1949, cited in Andrei Ledovsdky, "The Moscow Visit of a Delegation of the Communist Party of China in June to August 1949," *Far Eastern Affairs*, no. 5 (1996): 89–91. See also Goncharov et al., *Uncertain Partners*, 69, 312 n 130.

6. Conversation between Stalin and Mao, Moscow, Dec. 16, 1949, memorandum, in "Stalin's Conversation," 6.

7. Mao to Liu Shaoqi, Feb. 17, 1950, telegram, in *Mao Zedong junshi wenji*, 6:76.

8. One Chinese source identifies Lt. General Slyusarev as the deputy of Lt. General Batitskiy, but one Russian source claims that he was in charge of air operations and succeeded Lt. General Batitskiy in commanding the units after the latter returned home in September 1950. Wang Suhong and Wang Yubing, *Kongzhan zai Chaoxian* (*The Air War in Korea*), 100; Leonid Krylov and Yuriy Chepsurkayev, "An Unpublicized Mission by the Government," *Aviamaster*, no. 4 (1997): 34, and no. 5 (1997): 50; Zolotarev, chief ed., *Rossiya (SSSR)*, 62.

9. Unless otherwise cited, the information in this paragraph and the ones that follow is from Leonid Krylov and Yuriy Chepsurkayev, "An Unpublicized Mission by the Government," 34–39. The mission was restricted seventy kilometers northeast of Shanghai, and more to the south of Hensha Island, off the north coast of the Gulf of Hangzhou, and to the city of Hangzhou (Zolotarev, chief ed., *Rossiya [SSSR]*, 64).

10. According to one Russian pilot's recollections, the 133d Fighter Aviation Division did not begin to fly MiG-15s until mid-1951. Leonid Krylov and Yuriy Chepsurkayev, "Nikolay Ivanovich Ivanov," *Mir Aviatsiya*, no. 2 (1997): 21.

11. Besides these three air regiments, there was an independent air transport group, three independent aircraft maintenance battalions, a communications company, and several other support units.

12. Their MiG-15s were the third production series built at Factory 153 at Novosibirsk (Ye. Arsen'yev and Leonid Krylov, *Istrebitel' MiG-15* [*The MiG-15 Fighter*], 57). Stephen L. Sewell of the Department of Defense supplied me with a translated copy of this publication.

13. For details about the involvement of the Soviet air force beyond Soviet territory from 1950–89, see Mark O'Neill, "Air Combat on the Periphery: The Soviet Air Force in Action during the Cold War, 1945–89," in *Russian Aviation and Airpower*, ed. Higham et al., 208–32.

14. According to Russian sources, Batitskiy arrived in Beijing on February 25. He was met by Zhu De, to whom he reported the composition and missions of the force. They decided to include four Chinese antiaircraft regiments in Shanghai (Zolotarev, chief ed., *Rossiya [SSSR]*, 65).

15. Jiang Tianran, "Air Defense of Great Shanghai," 7.

16. Chen Yi reported this problem to Beijing on March 11, and Zhou Enlai ordered the railroad minister to transship all Soviet equipment and supplies out of Manchuria for Shanghai immediately (Zhu Bingxiu, "Air Defense of Shanghai," 52).

17. Mark O'Neill claims that the Soviet kill was a Nationalist B-26 shot down by P. F. Dushin and V. D. Sidorov over Xuzhou in March (O'Neill, "Other Side of the Yalu," 17). See also Liu Wen-hsiao, ed., *Zhonggong kongjun shi* (*History of Chinese Communist Air Force*), 67. People's Liberation Army Air Force sources recorded the shootdown of a B-25 on March 14. See Zhu Bingxiu, "Air Defense of Shanghai," 53–54.

18. Kelenichkov was credited with the kill based on pilot observations, gun camera evidence, and enemy radio communications. After the PLA occupied the Zhoushan Islands, the wreckage of a P-38 that crashed before landing also verified this claim (Krylov and Chepsurkayev, "An Unpublicized Mission by the Government," 47).

19. Nationalist records admit the losses of two P-51s on April 2 and a B-24 on May 11, 1950. See Liu Wen-hsiao, ed., *Zhonggong kongjun shi*, 67.

20. Chinese sources indicate that the fighter and attack aircraft regiments logged about fourteen hundred flying hours, with an average of eleven to thirteen flying hours per pilot (Li Shi'an's recollections in *Lantian zhi lu*, 1:279–81).

21. These included one B-24 by Chinese antiaircraft artillery units on March 14 and two P-51 Mustangs downed by Captain I. Guzhev on April 2 (Zolotarev, chief ed., *Rossiya* [SSSR], 65).

22. The 29th GIAP lost one pilot and MiG-15 in an accident in Shanghai. See Aleksandr V. Kotlobovskiy, "Twenty Years in Combat: A History of MiG-15 Fighters in Combat," pt. 1, *Aehrokhobbi* (*Aerohobby*), no. 2, (1994): 25.

23. Arsen'yev and Krylov, *Istrebitel' MiG-15*, 9.

24. The 29th GIAP arrived at a Soviet base, Sanshilibao, on the Liaodong Peninsula on October 3, and the 351st IAP returned to Dalian on October 20.

25. The National Air Defense Preparatory Committee was established at this meeting to take charge of this matter. In the meantime, four armies were deployed to Fujian and Guangdong Provinces to prepare for attacks on the coastal area by the U.S. Navy or Nationalist troops from Taiwan. See *Zhou Enlai nianpu*, 1:90, 95–96; Zhou to Mao, Liu Shaoqi, and Chen Yun, Oct. 31, 1950, letter, in *Zhou Enlai junshi wenxun*, 4:84–85; Shen Zonghong et al., *Zhongguo renmin zhiyuanjun zhan shi*, 13.

26. A Russian study claims that it would have been unwise to deploy larger, more bulky units in such a small area of operation (Oleg Sarin and Lev Dvoretsky, *Alien Wars: The Soviet Union's Aggressions Against the World, 1919–1989*, 74).

27. Halliday, "Air Operations in Korea," 152.

28. For more details about this deployment, see O'Neill, "Other Side of the Yalu," 31–39.

29. Mark O'Neill cordially supplied me with this document. For more details about this deployment, see his "Other Side of the Yalu," 104–105.

30. Ibid., 105, 107.

31. Xia Zhenduo, "Ten Years of the Soviet Red Army Garrison in Lüda," *Zhonggong dangshi ziliao*, no. 43 (1992): 126.

32. The MiG-9 units were the 17th, 20th, 65th, 144th, 309th, and 328th IADs; the MiG-15 units were the 28th and 324th IADs; the La-9 unit was the 297th IAD; the Il-10 unit was the 186th SHAD; and the Tu-2 unit was the 162d BAD (O'Neill, "Other Side of the Yalu," 31–39). The Chinese source claims that there were two SHADs. According to Soviet sources, the three regiments of the 186th SHAD split into two regiments to assist with the training of two Chinese SHADs (the 5th and 11th) at Kaiyuan, Jilin Province, and Xuzhou, Jiangsu Province, respectively.

33. Yang Wanqing and Qi Chunyuan, *Liu Yalou jiangjun zhuan*, 298; Gordon and Rigmant, *MiG-15*, 111. One Russian source I received from Stephen L. Sewell indicates that the 67th IAK possessed only two IADs (the 50th and 151st Guards), while making MiG-9 and La-9 divisions (15th Guards, 65th, 144th, 309th, and 328th), and one MiG-15 division, the (106th) independent. Another questionable disparity between the Pentagon's sources and the schedule of troop deployments from the former Soviet Central Archives of the Ministry of Defense I received from Mark O'Neill is whether the 15th GIAD should be the 17th. For a brief account of Krasovskiy's role in World War II, see Greenwood, "Soviet Frontal Aviation," 72.

34. *Dangdai zhongguo kongjun*, 78–79, 86–88.

35. For example, when the 809th IAD was transferred to China from Baku, its replacement, the 216th IAD, began to rearm with MiG-15s (O'Neill, "Other Side of the Yalu," 100).

36. Bulganin to Stalin, Oct. 24, 1950, memorandum, cited in O'Neill, "Other Side of the Yalu," 34.

37. Even after Stalin's intervention, the Soviets continued to persuade the Chinese to purchase the remaining MiG-9 engines in stock from them. Based on the consideration that MiG-9s still could be used for training and against Taiwan's piston aircraft, as well as friendship, the Chinese agreed to this Soviet request (Wang Yazhi, "Some Information," 88). See also Xu Yan, *Diyici jiaoliang: KangMei yuanChao zhanzheng de lishi huigu yu fansi* (*The First Test of Strength: A Historical Review and Evaluation of the War to Resist America and Assist Korea*), 31–32.

38. Robert Futrell, "USAF Intelligence in the Korean War," in *The Intelligence Revolution: Historical Perspective*, ed. Walter T. Hitchcock, 285.

39. Yang Shengqun and Tien Shongnien ed., *Gongheguo zhongda juece de lailong qumai*, 62; Zhang Xi, "On the Eve of Entering Korea," 21–22.

40. O'Neill, "Other Side of the Yalu," 35, 38.

41. Ibid., 59–60. In the after-action ciphered telegram to Moscow, Zakharov erroneously reported that Soviet MiGs shot down two F-82s, the "Twin Mustang" piston-engined fighter (Zakharov to Stalin, Nov. 2, 1950, telegram, in Weathersby, "New Russian Documents," 48).

42. Futrell, *United States Air Force in Korea*, 219; Gordon and Rigmant, *MiG-15*, 111–15; Sarin and Dvoretsky, *Alien Wars*, 70.

43. The 151st GIAD assumed its training duties with the PLAAF's 3d Fighter Aviation Division and was scheduled to be completed on January 25, 1951. The 28th IAD was

responsible for training the PLAAF's 4th Fighter Aviation Division, followed by the 15th Fighter Aviation Division by October, 1951 (O'Neill, "Other Side of the Yalu," 39. See also Zhui Wenbing's recollections in *Lantian zhi lu*, 1:421.

44. Futrell, *United States Air Force in Korea*, 223, 307.

45. Leonid Krylov and Yuriy Chepsurkayev, "Combat Episodes of the Korean War: Three out of One Thousand," *Mir Aviatsiya*, no. 1 (1997): 38–40. The sources the authors cite draw from the combat logs of the 72d GIAP.

46. FEAF Intelligence Weekly Roundup, no. 9, Nov. 4, 1950, U.S. Air Force Historical Research Agency, Montgomery, Ala. (Hereafter USAFHRA.)

47. O'Neill notes that the 64th IAK's monthly report awarded credit for three F-80s shot down on November 7, 1950. This record appears questionable not only because the FEAF acknowledged no losses that day but also because in their initial reports, Soviet airmen misidentified the Mustangs as F-84s, which were not actually sent into combat in Korea until December, 1950 (O'Neill, "Other side of the Yalu," 77). See also FEAF Weekly Intelligence Roundup, no. 10, Nov. 12, 1950, USAFHRA.

48. Hallion, *Naval Air War in Korea*, 72–75.

49. Yang Wanqing and Qi Chunyuan, *Liu Yalou jiangjun zhuan*, 289. Krasovskiy's entourage might have included Lt. Gen. Georgiy A. Lobov, commander of the 303d IAD, who recalled that he went to Andong as an observer "literally the day after a huge U.S. air raid" on Sinuiju (Halliday, "Air Operations in Korea," 152, 163 n 3).

50. O'Neill, "Other Side of the Yalu," 78–79.

51. General Zakharov, Stalin's personal military envoy, forwarded this proposal to Zhou in Beijing on the evening of November 15 (*Zhou Enlai nianpu*, 1:97). See also Zhang, "China and the Air War in Korea, 1950–1953," 348; O'Neill, "Other Side of the Yalu," 106.

52. Joseph C. Goulden, *Korea: The Untold Story of the War*, 298–300; Futrell, *United States Air Force in Korea*, 221–22; Crane, *American Airpower Strategy in Korea*, 46–47.

53. Memorandum by the Northeast People's Government, Nov. 13, 1950. A copy of the memorandum is located in People's Government of Lüda City File, vol. 69, Dalian City Archives.

54. O'Neill, "Other Side of the Yalu," 73.

55. Ibid., 77–78.

56. According to UN pilots' observations, in early November, 1950, the Russians often flew "uncoordinated passes" and demonstrated "lack of concentrated firepower" during their attacks on UN aircraft (FEAF Weekly Intelligence Roundup, no. 10). This problem is also discussed in Krylov and Chepsurkayev, "Combat Episodes," 39, 40.

57. Cited from Japanese Society for Ground War Studies, ed., *Chaoxian zhanzheng* (*The Korean War*), 2d ed., 1:704.

58. Weathersby, "New Russian Documents," 32.

59. Mao to Stalin, Nov. 15, 1950, telegram, in ibid., 49. See also *Zhou Enlai nianpu*, 1:97.

60. Pashkevich was allegedly an intimate friend of V. Stalin, commander of the Moscow Military District Air Force, since their days at the Odessa Flying School. See Hans D. Seidl, *Stalin's Eagles: An Illustrated Study of the Soviet Aces of World War II and Korea*, 163.

61. The 177th IAP was separated from the 303d IAD in August, 1950, and then deployed to the Liaodong Peninsula. This regiment was named after Soviet hero V. V.

Talalikhin, a squadron leader, who ran into a German bomber during a night raid on Moscow, August 8, 1941. See Igor A. Seidov, "The Korean Score of the Talalikhins," *Aviatsiya i Vremya*, no. 6 (1995): 38.

62. Xu Yan, *Diyichi jiaoliang*, 52–59.

63. Futrell, *United States Air Force in Korea*, 254–60.

64. FEAF Weekly Intelligence Roundup, no. 13, Dec. 3, 1950, USAFHRA.

65. Peng to Mao, Dec. 8, 1950, telegram, and Zhou to Mao, Dec. 12, 1950, memorandum, in *Zhou Enlai junshi wenxuan*, 4:127–30.

66. O'Neill, "Other Side of the Yalu," 134.

67. The combat diaries of the 151st indicate that on December 4, the 50th IAD flew combat missions out of Andong (ibid., 92, 133). See also, Fang Ziyi's recollections, *Lantian zhi lu*, 1:329.

68. Futrell, "USAF Intelligence in the Korean War," 285.

69. FEAF Intelligence Weekly Roundup, no. 16, Dec. 23, 1950, USAFHRA. American intelligence accounts appear correct about the number of Soviet aircraft in the airfields in the Dalian-Lüda area. Soviet troops turned over almost four hundred planes to the Chinese when they withdrew from northeast China in 1954 (Xia Zhenduo, "Ten Years of the Soviet Red Army Garrison in Lüda," 151). The navy took over 78 Il-28 torpedo bombers, 12 Il-28UT bomber trainers, and 2 Li-2 navigation trainers from the Soviet navy troops at Lüda (Yang Guoyu et al., *Dangdai Zhongguo haijun*, 74).

70. Futrell, *United States Air Force in Korea*, 246.

71. Ibid., 222, 246–48, 250–51.

72. By December 17, the 29th GIAP had lost three MiG-15s. Besides the one lost to an F-86 on December 17, it also lost two other MiGs on December 4 and 6, respectively. Far East Air Forces records claimed no enemy aircraft destroyed from December 1–7, but credited three aircraft damaged (O'Neill, "Other Side of the Yalu," 135, 137–38). It is also interesting to note that although U.S. and Soviet records seldom match, Soviet sources do acknowledge the loss of a MiG-15 by the 29th GIAP on December 17 (Aleksandr V. Kotlobovskiy, "Twenty Years in Combat: A History of MiG-15 Fighters in Combat," pt. 1, *Aehrokhobbi*, no. 2 [1994]: 26).

73. Seidov, "Korean Score of the Talalikhins," 38–39. The FEAF acknowledged the loss of only one F-86, while claiming to have brought down six MiGs and damaged one (FEAF Weekly Intelligence Roundup, no. 16).

74. Ibid., Futrell, *United States Air Force in Korea*, 252.

75. O'Neill, "Other Side of the Yalu," 124–78.

76. FEAF Intelligence Weekly Roundup, no. 16.

77. O'Neill, "Other Side of the Yalu," 81.

78. Shen Zonghong et al., *Zhongguo renmin zhiyuanjun kangMei yuanChao zhan shi*, 94.

79. Peng to Mao, Dec. 8, 1950, and Mao to Peng, Dec. 13, 1950, telegrams, in *Mao Zedong junshi wenji*, 6:239–40.

80. Peng to Gao Gang, Li Fuchun, as well as to Mao and Zhou, Dec. 23, 1950, telegrams, in Wang Yan, chief ed., *Peng Dehuai nianpu*, 458.

81. Shen Zonghong et al., *Zhongguo renmin zhiyuanjun kangMei yuanChao zhan shi*, 94; Xu Yan, *Diyici jiaoliang*, 68.

82. Sarin and Dvoretsky, *Alien Wars*, 69.

83. Futrell, *United States Air Force in Korea*, 289, 317.

84. Stalin to Mao, Mar. 3, 1951, telegram, in APRF (Chinese), 141. See also *Zhou Enlai nianpu*, 1:140.

Chapter 5. Months of Frustration

1. Zhong Zhaoyun, *Baizhan jiangxing Liu Yalou*, 184; Wang Bo, *Peng Dehuai*. See also Zhao Jiangou and Ma Yuan, *Chaoxian da kongzhan*, 82–83.

2. Futrell notes that the United States had an average of 1,248 aircraft in the theater at any one time. Also, according to U.S. records, these units were the 4th, 35th, and 51st Fighter-Interceptor Wings; 8th, 18th, and 49th Fighter-Bomber Wings; 3d Light Bombardment Wing; 452d Light Bombardment Group; 19th, 22d, and 92d Medium Bombardment Groups; 1st Marine Air Wing; and three navy carriers of Task Force 77. However, this Chinese estimate failed to include the 27th Fighter-Escort Wing. For details, see Futrell, *United States Air Force in Korea*, and Hallion, *Naval Air War in Korea*.

3. Wang Dinglie et al., *Dangdai Zhongguo kongjun*, 127.

4. It is interesting to note that in order to give the CPVs division commanders some kind of perceptual knowledge about flying in mid-October they all took a half-hour flight in Yak-18 trainers (Lü Liping, *Tongtian zhi lu*, 245).

5. Wang Dinglie et al., *Dangdai Zhongguo kongjun*, 127–29; Liu Zhen, *Liu Zhen huiyilu*, 341–44.

6. Zhou to Mao, Dec. 12, 1950, memorandum, in *Zhou Enlai junshi wenxuan*, 4:128–29.

7. According to Russian sources, at the beginning of the war North Korea had one mixed air division (consisting of an attack regiment with ninety-three Il-10s, a fighter regiment with seventy-nine Yak-9s, a training regiment with sixty-seven trainers, and communication aircraft), and air logistic service brigades, totaling 2,829 troops. By November, 1951, North Korea had only twenty-eight aircraft. See V. Morosov and S. Uskov, "Defending Peace and Labor: A Brief Account of the People's Democratic Republic of Korean Air Force, 1948–1996," *Mir Aviatsiya*, no. 2 (1997): 30; S. E. Zakharov to Stalin, Nov. 2, 1950, telegram, in Weathersby, "New Russian Documents," 48. See also Futrell, *United States Air Force in Korea*, 244.

8. Wang Dinglie et al., *Dangdai Zhongguo kongjun*, 129.

9. Yang Wanqing and Qi Chunyuan, *Liu Yalou jiangjun zhuan*, 292; Zhong Zhaoyun, *Baizhan jiangxing Liu Yalou*, 184–85; Zhao Jianguo and Ma Yuan, *Chaoxian da kongzhan*, 84.

10. Chen Zhonglong et al., eds., *Zhongguo renmin zhiyuanjun renwu zhuan*, 244; Ma Jinhai and Hou Yunli, eds., *Zhonggong hujiang yu mingzhan* (*The CCP's Generals and Battles*), 339–40.

11. Duan Suquan, who at the time was the air force commander in the Northeast Military Region, did not serve in the Fourth Field Army, to which the 13th Army Group belonged. See Wang Dinglie et al., *Dangdai Zhongguo kongjun*, 43.

12. Ibid., 134.

13. Zhou Enlai to Stalin, Feb. 12, 1951, telegram, in APRF (Chinese), 135–36. In this telegram, Zhou requested one adviser each for the commanders of the CPV Air Force, the chief of staff, chief of operations, chief of intelligence, engineering specialists, and every other important command or administrative post.

14. Stalin to Zhou Enlai via Zakharov, Feb. 16, 1951, telegram, in Weathersby, "New Russian Documents," 59, and Zakharov to Stalin, Feb. 17, 1951, telegram, in APRF (Chinese), 136.

15. Zhou to Kim Il Sung via Chai Junwu, Jan. 7, 1951, telegram, in *Zhou Enlai nianpu,* 1:114. The CPV's joint command with the NKPA was established on December 4, 1950, with Peng Dehuai as its commander and political commissar. Two North Korean generals, Kim Ung and Pak Il Yu, served as deputy commander and deputy political commissar, respectively (Xu Yan, *Diyici jiaoliang,* 58–59).

16. Wang Yong was also a Russian-trained pilot, and a staff member of old Northeast Aviation School (Nie Fengzhi, *Zhanchang,* 194).

17. *Zhou Enlai nianpu,* 1:135; Qi Dexue, *Chaoxian zhanzheng juece neimu,* 185; Shen Zonghong et al., *Zhongguo renmin zhiyuanjun kangMei yuanChao zhan shi,* app. 2.

18. Author interview with the former deputy chief of staff of the CPV Air Force, 1999.

19. Li Xueyan's recollections in *Lantian zhi lu,* 1:480–81.

20. Wang Dinglie et al., *Dangdai Zhongguo kongjun,* 134–35.

21. The information in this and the following paragraphs is from Fang Ziyi's recollections in *Lantian zhi lu,* 1:326–39.

22. Ibid., 330–31.

23. For Soviet accounts about the air war in late December, 1950, and early January, 1951, see O'Neill, "Other Side of the Yalu," 149–51, 185–88.

24. The Americans admitted that one Thunderjet went down, but they also claimed a kill during the battle (Futrell, *United States Air Force in Korea,* 287). The pilots of the 50th IAD claimed eight Thunderjets were shot down that morning (O'Neill, "Other Side of the Yalu," 196).

25. Wang Dinglie et al., *Dangdai Zhongguo kongjun,* 131.

26. FEAF Weekly Intelligence Roundup, no. 22, Feb. 4, 1951, USAFHRC.

27. Wang Dinglie et al., *Dangdai Zhongguo kongjun,* 132–33; Liu Zhen, *Liu Zhen huiyilu,* 347–49.

28. See Liu Yalou, "Founding of the People's Air Force during the First Seven Years," in *Lantian zhi lu,* 2:22.

29. Two days before this fatal morning, the Chinese had already lost one MiG in a crash landing.

30. Fang Ziyi's recollections in *Lantian zhi lu,* 1:327.

31. O'Neill, "Other Side of the Yalu," 239–41, 246–47, 250.

32. Wang Dinglie et al., *Dangdai Zhongguo kongjun,* 87–88.

33. At the time, most of the Chinese pilots had received only initial flight training, with an average of about sixty flying hours from aviation schools, including twenty-seven hours in the Yak-18 and thirty hours in the Yak-11 (Lü Liping, *Tontian zhi lu,* 241).

34. Mao to Peng, Jan. 14, 1951, telegram, cited in Shen Zonghong et al., *Zhongguo renmin zhiyuanjun kangMei yuanChao zhan shi,* 92–93. See also Qi Dexue, *ChaoXian zhanzheng juece neimu,* 117–18; Xu Yan, *Diyici jiaoliang,* 69.

35. By late February, 1951, the PLAAF had reduced its earlier projected number of air force units to ten regiments, with only four MiG regiments and three Tu-2 regiments (Zhou to Stalin, Feb. 23, 1951, telegram, in APRF [Chinese], 137).

36. Wang Dinglie et al., *Dangdai Zhongguo kongjun,* 135–36.

37. The MiG-15 did not have an automatic gun sight linked with ranging radar, as did the F-86. The pilot had to put the target into his ASP sight, estimate the lead and range, and then fire. This proved to be troublesome for inexperienced Chinese pilots to master during the war. See Tang Jihan's recollections in *Lantian zhi lu*, 1:497.

38. Wang Dinglie et al., *Dangdai Zhongguo kongjun*, 136–38.

39. According to Gao Houliang, political commissar of the 3d Aviation Division, the PLAAF conducted two additional similar exercises in August and September, hoping to improve the young Chinese air force's performance (quoted in *Lantian zhi lu*, 1:370).

40. For Beijing's air force plan, see Zhou to Mao, Dec. 12, 1950, memorandum, in *Zhou Enlai junshi wenxuan*, 4:128–29.

41. Zhou to Chai Junwu, Dec. 13, 1950, telegram, in *Zhou Enlai nianpu*, 1:105.

42. For North Korean airfields, see Futrell, *United States Air Force in Korea*, 19.

43. Wang Dinglie et al., *Dangdai Zhongguo kongjun*, 138.

44. Mao to Stalin, Mar. 1, 1951, telegram, in APRF (Chinese), 141. See also *Zhou Enlai junshi wenxuan*, 4:164.

45. Stalin to Mao, Mar. 3, 1951, telegram, in APRF (Chinese), 142.

46. *Zhou Enlai nianpu*, 1:137.

47. Zhou to Peng and Gao, Mar. 11, 1951, telegram, in *Zhou Enlai nianpu*, 1:138–39; Zhou to Peng and Gao, Mar. 22, 1951, telegram, in *Zhou Enlai junshi wenxuan*, 4:176.

48. Zhou to Peng and Gao, Mar. 28, 1951, telegram, in *Zhou Enlai nianpu*, 1:143.

49. Zhou to Kim Il Sung via Chai Junwu, Feb. 27, 1951, telegram, ibid., 134; Zhou to Peng Dehuai, Mar. 11, 1951, telegram, in Wang Yan, chief ed., *Peng Dehuai nianpu*, 484.

50. These individual names do not match the Western spellings of Korean locations. Futrell gives two airfield locations as Pyong-ni and Kangdong, which are likely Sunchon and Namyong-ni, as the Chinese called them. See Wang Dinglie et al., *Dangdai Zhongguo kongjun*, 139, and Futrell, *United States Air Force in Korea*, 407.

51. Zhou to Peng, Mar. 22, 1951, telegram, in *Zhou Enlai junshi wenxuan*, 4:175–78; Zhou to Peng, Mar. 25 and 28, 1951, telegrams, in *Zhou Enlai nianpu*, 1:141–43; Peng to CMC, Mar. 26, 1951, and Peng to Zhou and Nie Rongzhen, Mar. 28, 1951, telegrams, in Wang Yan, chief ed., *Peng Dehuai nianpu*, 486–87.

52. The Fiftieth Army was formerly the GMD Sixtieth Army, which defected to the PLA in 1948.

53. Zhou to Stalin, Apr. 1, 1951, telegram, in APRF (Chinese), 146; Zhou to Kim Il Sung via Li Zhiliang, Chinese ambassador to Pyongyang, Mar. 31, 1951, telegram, in *Zhou Enlai nianpu*, 1:144.

54. Li Xueyan, "Recollections of Logistics Work for the CPV's Air Force," in *Lantian zhi lu*, 1:483; Wang Dinglie et al., *Dangdai Zhongguo kongjun*, 140.

55. See FEAF Weekly Intelligence Roundup, nos. 31–37, USAFHRC.

56. According to Zhou's telegram to Peng on March 22, 1951, the Soviet Union agreed to send eight antiaircraft artillery regiments to defend the four airfields being built for the Soviet air force (*Zhou Enlai junshi wenxuan*, 1:177). See also Zhou to Stalin, Mar. 23, 1951, telegram, in APRF (Chinese), 143; Zhou Keyu, *KangMei yuanChao zhanzheng*, 201.

57. Wang Dinglie et al., *Dangdai Zhongguo kongjun*, 141.

58. Zhou to Mao, Liu Shaoqi, and Chen Yun, Aug. 6, 1951, letter, *Zhou Enlai nianpu*, 1:167.

59. Du Ping, *Zai zhiyuanjun zongbu*, 204.

60. Peng to the CMC and each army command, Feb. 17, 1951, in *Peng Dehuai junshi wenxuan*, 373–74; Wang Yan, chief ed., *Peng Dehuai zhuan* (*Biography of Peng Dehuai*), 451.

61. Wang Yan, chief ed., *Peng Dehuai zhuan*, 451; Mao to Stalin, Mar. 1, 1951, telegram, in APRF (Chinese), 140–41. See also *Zhou Enlai junshi wenxuan*, 4:164.

62. Wang Yan, chief ed., *Peng Dehuai nianpu*, 480.

63. Ibid., 454. See also Zhong Zhaoyuan, *Baizhan jiangxing*, 187–88.

64. Wang Yan, chief ed., *Peng Dehuai nianpu*, 480.

65. Mao to Stalin, Mar. 1, 1951, telegram, in *Zhou Enlai junshi wenxuan*, 4:164.

66. Liu Pushao et al., "A Biography of Zhu Guang," in *Zhongguo renmin zhiyuanjun renwu zhuan*, ed. Chen Zhonglong et al., 309.

67. Stalin to Mao, Mar. 3, 1951, telegram, in APRF (Chinese), 141. See also *Zhou Enlai nianpu*, 1:140.

68. Stalin to Mao, Mar. 15, 1951, telegram, in APRF (Chinese), 141. See also, Weathersby, "New Russian Documents," 59. The size of the Soviet air division was mentioned in Zhou's telegram to Peng, on March 22, 1951 (*Zhou Enlai junshi wenxuan*, 4:175). For U.S./UN actions against these bridges, see Futrell, *United States Air Force in Korea*, 321–22.

69. Peng to Zhou, Mar. 11, 1951, telegram, in Wang Yan, chief ed., *Peng Dehuai nianpu*, 483. See also Wang Yan, chief ed., *Peng Dehuai zhuan* (*Biography of Peng Dehuai*), 456.

70. By that time, the North Korean Air Force had two combat-ready regiments: one with twenty La-9 and Yak-9 fighters at Sinuiju, and one with twenty La-9s at Yanji, Jilin Province (Zhou to Kim Il Sung via Li Ziliang, Apr. 5, 1951, telegram, in *Zhou Enlai junshi wenxuan*, 4:187).

71. Hong Xuezhi, *KangMei yuanChao zhanzheng huiyi* (*Recollections of the War to Resist America and Assist Korea*), 173.

72. This was Zhou's response to Zakharov's criticism that Chinese leaders were too cautious about sending their air force to Korea, and that there would always be casualties in war, and that they would have to sacrifice some planes and pilots (Wei Bihai, "Remembrances of the Air War," 32). In addition, North Korean leaders did not want to risk their propeller-driven aircraft and pilots unless Soviet MiGs would be available to shield them from the lethal Sabres. See Zhou and Nie Rongzhen to Peng and Gao, Apr. 16, 1951, in *Zhou Enlai junshi wenxuan*, 4:189–90; Zhou to Kim Il Sung via Li Zhiliang, Apr. 23, 1951, telegram, in *Zhou Enlai nianpu*, 1:150.

73. Peng Dehuai hastily launched the fifth offensive campaign based on a mistaken intelligence analysis that the UN command would conduct another Inchon-type amphibious assault on the North Korean coast. Fearing he would have to fight a two-front war if he did not act quickly, the CPV commander decided to move up the planned attack from early May to April 22 even before receiving approval from Beijing. Peng submitted a report four days after the CPV started the attack, and received a response on April 28 (Peng to the CMC and Mao, Apr. 26, 1951, and the CMC to Peng and Gao, Apr. 28, 1951, in *Zhou Enlai junshi wenxuan*, 4:193–95). See also Xu Yan, *Diyici jiaoliang*, 86; Du Ping, *Zai zhiyuanjun zongbu*, 238.

74. For the CPV's fifth offensive campaign, see Shu Guang Zhang, *Mao's Military Romanticism*, 149–53.

75. Xu Yan, *Diyici jiaoliang*, 96.

76. Wang Yan, chief ed., *Peng Dehuai zhuan,* 457; Heng Xueming, *Shengsi sanbaxian,* 302.

77. Xu Yan, *Diyici jiaoliang,* 97.

78. Mao to Liu Yalou, Wu Faxian, and Wang Bingzhang, June 24, 1951, telegram, *Mao Zedong jianguo yilai wengao,* 2:369.

79. Sarin and Dvoretsky, *Alien Wars,* 76.

80. Peng to Mao, June 4, 1951, telegram, in APRF (Chinese), 153.

81. Wei Bihai, "Air War Decision Making at the Highest Level during the War to Oppose America and Aid Korea: An Interview with Wang Bingzhang," *Guangming ribao,* Nov. 8, 2000.

82. Stalin to Mao via Krasovskiy, May 22 and 26, 1951, telegrams, in APRF (Chinese), 149–50.

83. Mao to Stalin, May 25, 1951, telegram, Ibid., 150.

84. The MiG-15bis had a new engine, the VK-1, rated at 2,700 kilograms of thrust. The older RD-45F engine was rated at only 2,270 kilograms of thrust. The rate of climb and maximum speed increased from 1,050 to 1,076 kilometers per hour. A reversible hydraulic booster was introduced in the control system.

85. More than four thousand MiG-15bis were built in 1951. See Ye. Arsen'yev and Krylov, *Istrebitel' MiG-15,* 50–57.

86. The F-80C, for example, had a top speed of 967 kilometers per hour, a ceiling of 14,265 meters, and a maximum range of 1,328 kilometers. The MiG-9's specifications, on the other hand, were 920 kilometers per hour, 13,000 meters, and 1,100 kilometers. The 37-mm and two 23-mm automatic cannon mounted in the aircraft's nose caused problems for the engine's air intake, which could cause them to stop running during firing (ibid., 3).

87. Stalin to Mao via Krasovskiy, May 22, 1951, telegram, in APRF (Chinese), 149.

88. Stalin to Mao via Roshchin, June 13, 1951, telegram, in Weathersby, "New Russian Documents," 60–61. See also APRF (Chinese), 159–60.

89. Stalin to Krasvoskiy, June 13, 1951, telegram, in Weathersby, "New Russian Documents," 60. See also APRF (Chinese), 160.

90. Mao to Stalin, June 13, 1951, telegram, in Weathersby, "New Russian Documents," 61. See also APRF (Chinese), 158–59.

91. Cited in Yang Wanqing and Qi Chunyuan, *Liu Yalou jiangjun zhuan,* 304.

92. Krasvoskiy to Stalin, June 15, 1951, telegram, in APRF (Chinese), 161–62.

93. Mao to Liu Yalou, Wu Faxian, and Wang Bingzhang, June 24, 1951, telegram, *Mao Zedong jianguo yilai wengao,* 2:369. I have no access to the PLAAF's report; however, a recent interview with Wang Bingzhang offers some highlights of its content. See Wei Bihai, "Remembrances of the Air War," 32. For Chinese accounts, see Xu Yan, *Diyici jiaoliang,* 31.

94. This view can be found in his earlier telegram to Mao on May 22. See note 82.

95. Stalin to Krasovskiy, June 26, 1951, and Krasovskiy to Stalin, June 28, 1951, telegrams, in Bajonov, "Assessing the Politics," 62–63. See also APRF (Chinese), 164, 166–67.

96. The official PLAAF history includes no record of this period of Chinese air operations in Korea. For information, see Fang Ziyi and Gao Houliang's recollections in *Lantian zhi lu,* 1:338–37, 371.

97. Wei Bihai, "Remembrances of the Air War," 32.

98. Xu Yan, *Diyici jiaoliang,* 106–107; Yang Di, *Zai zhiyuanjun zongbu de suiyue li,* 156–57; Meng Zhaohui, "On the Sixth Campaign in the War to Resist U.S. Aggression and Aid Korea," *Junshi lishi,* no. 6 (1998): 37–39.

99. Peng to Mao, Aug. 8, 1951, telegram, in Wang Yan, chief ed., *Peng Dehuai nianpu,* 512–13.

100. Zhou to Mao, Aug. 11, 1951, memorandum, in *Zhou Enlai junshi wenxuan,* 4:211–12.

101. CMC to Peng, Aug. 19, 1951, telegram, in *Zhou Enlai nianpu,* 1:173; Mao to Peng, Aug. 21, 1951, Peng to CMC, Aug. 21 and 22, 1951, telegrams, in Wang Yan, chief ed., *Peng Dehuai nianpu,* 513–15.

102. Soviet Communist Party Central Committee to Mao, Aug. 17, 1951, telegram, in APRF (Chinese), 228.

103. Zhou to Peng, Mar. 3, 1951, and Peng to CMC, Sept. 27, 1951, telegrams, in Wang Yan, chief ed., *Peng Dehuai nianpu,* 481, 518; Zhou to Peng and Gao, Mar. 22, 1951, telegram, in *Zhou Enlai junshi wenxuan,* 4:175–76. See also Shen Zonghong et al., *Zhongguo renmin zhiyuanjun kangMei yuanChao zhan shi,* 162–65; Liu Zhen, *Liu Zhen huiyilu,* 351; Wang Dinglie et al., *Dangdai Zhongguo kongjun,* 205–206.

Chapter 6. Soviet Air Operations in Korea

1. Futrell, *United States Air Force in Korea,* 692; Stewart, ed., *Airpower,* 286; Jackson, *Air War over Korea,* 105.

2. Morosov and Uskov, "Defending Peace and Labor," 31–32.

3. Gordon and Rigmant, *MiG-15,* 111. Mark O'Neill divides the three phases of Soviet air involvement in Korea as follows: the first phase was November, 1950–July, 1951; the second phase ran from August, 1951, to July, 1952; and the third phase began in August, 1952, and lasted until the armistice in July, 1953. The author does not explain why Soviet participation in the Korean War should be divided along this time line.

4. Futrell, *United States Air Force in Korea,* 279, 281. For Chinese accounts about the third phase offensive, see Shu Guang Zhang, *Mao's Military Romanticism,* 130–31. See also Mao to Stalin, Jan. 15, 1951, telegram, in Weathersby, "New Russian Documents," 55–56.

5. Peng to Mao, Jan. 1, 1951, telegram, in *Peng Dehaui nianpu,* 463; Yang Di, *Zai zhiyuanjun zongbu de suiyue li,* 93–96. See also Shu Guang Zhang, *Mao's Military Romanticism,* 132.

6. Sarin and Dvoretsky, *Alien Wars,* 69.

7. For Soviet accounts of operations in January, 1951, see O'Neill, "Other Side of the Yalu," chap. 4. See also Seidov, "Korean Score of the Talalikhins," 38–40. For U.S. accounts, see Futrell, *United States Air Force in Korea,* 287–89.

8. For a Chinese account of events on January 23, 1951, see Fang Ziyi's recollections in *Lantian zhi lu,* 1:334. For U.S. accounts, see Futrell, *United States Air Force in Korea,* 287–89.

9. The main requests included: improved air brakes, flight endurance, and ammunition load; improved visibility to the rear and controllability at high speed and high altitude; and the addition of the SPO-1 Bariy-M IFF radio transponder (Arsen'yev and Krylov, *Istrebitel' MiG-15,* 58–59).

10. Evgeniy Pepelyaev's recollections in Gordon and Rigmant, *MiG-15,* 134.

11. Stalin to Mao, Mar. 3, 1951, telegram, in APRF (Chinese), 142.

12. Evgeniy Pepelyaev's recollections in Gordon and Rigmant, *MiG-15,* 135. For the number of MiGs, see Zhou to Peng and Gao, Mar. 22, 1951, telegram, in *Zhou Enlai junshi*

wenxuan, 4:175. For the regiments attached to the 303d, see Kotlobovskiy, "Twenty Years in Combat," pt. 1, 28.

13. Stalin to Mao, Mar. 15, 1951, telegram, in Weathersby, "New Russian Documents," 59.

14. Seidov, "Korean Score of the Talalikhins," 38; Grigory Okhay's recollections in Gordon and Rigmant, *MiG-15*, 125.

15. Sarin and Dvorestsky, *Alien Wars*, 71–73; Seidov, "Shield of the Night: An Unknown Chapter in the Korean War, 1950–1953," *Mir Aviatsiya*, no. 1 (1993): 29.

16. FEAF Weekly Intelligence Roundup, no. 38, Apr. 8, 1951, USAFHRA; Kotlobovskiy, "Twenty Years in Combat," pt. 1, 34; Boris Sergeyevich Abakumov's recollections in Gordon and Rigmant, *MiG-15*, 131.

17. O'Neill, "Other Side of the Yalu," 273.

18. V. V. Gagin, "Air Operations in Korea, 1950–1953," *Poligraf* (Voronezh), Aug., 1997, 47. For the American side of story, see Futrell, *United States Air Force in Korea*, 297–300.

19. Conrad Crane provides better-researched and more detailed descriptions of the FEAF Bomber Command's disaster in October (*American Airpower Strategy in Korea*, 85–92). See also Bruning, *Crimson Sky*, 127–64.

20. Futrell, *United States Air Force in Korea*, 411–12; Gagin, "Air Operations in Korea," 47; Lobov's, Sergey Kramarenko's, and Abakumov's recollections in Gordon and Rigmant, *MiG-15*, 122, 127–28, 131–32.

21. American records show that Captain Jabara shot down one MiG each day on April 3, 10, 12, and 22, 1951, and destroyed two MiGs on May 20. Russian sources dispute the U.S. claims. The Russians acknowledged losing three MiGs on April 3, which matches U.S. claims, but they admitted no losses on April 10. Despite U.S. claims of shooting down eleven MiGs on April 12, the Russians reported only one loss that day. On April 22, the Russians reported only one loss, while Jabara and three other American pilots all claimed to have shot down one MiG each. As for the battle on May 20, Capt. Victor A. Nazarkin, a pilot with the 196th IAP, was shot down and forced to bail out. According to Russian records, even if Jabara were credited with both of the Soviet losses on April 12 and 22, he would only have scored four victories by May 20 (Krylov and Chepsurkayev, "Combat Episodes," 43).

22. Ibid., 38–40.

23. Vasiliyevskiy and Shtemenko to Belov, Aug. 30, 1951, telegram, in APRF (Chinese), 231.

24. Zolotarev, chief ed., *Rossiya (SSSR)*, 69–70; Gordon and Rigmant, *MiG-15*, 113.

25. Futrell, *United States Air Force in Korea*, 402–403.

26. Lobov's recollections in Gordon and Rigmant, *MiG-15*, 122; Futrell, *United States Air Force in Korea*, 404–405.

27. Lobov erroneously states that "Black Tuesday" was October 30 (Gordon and Rigmant, *MiG-15*, 121).

28. Igor A. Seidov, "The Meteors Suffer a Fiasco," *Mir Aviatsiya*, no. 2 (1995): 40; FEAF Weekly Intelligence Roundup, no. 60, Oct. 21 and 27, 1951, USAFHRA. For the fate of the B-29s, see Bruning, *Crimson Sky*, 161.

29. Bruning, *Crimson Sky*, 149.

30. Morosov and Uskov, "Defending Peace and Labor," 31; Fang Ziyi's recollections in *Lantian zhi lu*, 1:342.

31. Seidov, "Meteors Suffer a Fiasco," 40. The FEAF listed this Meteor as damaged (FEAF Weekly Intelligence Roundup, no. 60).

32. For U.S. losses, see FEAF Weekly Intelligence Roundup, no. 60, as well as no. 61, Oct. 28 and Nov. 4, 1951, USAFHRA. Futrell does not include such losses (*United States Air Force in Korea*, 411).

33. Lobov's recollections in Gordon and Rigmant, *MiG-15*, 122, 123; Seidov, "Meteors Suffer a Fiasco," 42–44; Halliday, "Air Operations in Korea," 158.

34. Gordon and Rigmant, *MiG-15*, 112.

35. Kotlobovskiy, "Twenty Years in Combat," pt. 1, 27–28; Gordon and Rigmant, *MiG-15*, 113–14; Futrell, *United States Air Force in Korea*, 411–13; Halliday, "Air Operations in Korea," 159–60.

36. Futrell, *United States Air Force in Korea*, 419–20, 482.

37. Kotlobovskiy, "Twenty Years in Combat," pt. 1, 27–28; Krylov and Chepsurkayev, "Nikolay Ivanovich Ivanov," 21.

38. Abakumov's recollections in Gordon and Rigmant, *MiG-15*, 134.

39. The authors also point out that the older hands had learned how to account for it, but the new replacements had no idea and suffered badly. See Leonid Krylov and Yuriy Chepsurkayev, "The Hunt for A Sabre," *Mir Aviatsiya*, no. 2 (1998): 39–44.

40. Halliday, "Air Operations in Korea," 153; Abakumov's recollections in Gordon and Rigmant, *MiG-15*, 134.

41. Stalin to Mao, Mar. 12, 1952, telegram, in *Zhou Enlai nianpu*, 1:222. For Chinese allegations about U.S. bacteriological warfare, see Shu Guang Zhang, *Mao's Military Romanticism*, 181–86.

42. Krylov and Chepsurkayev, "Nikolay Ivanovich Ivanov," 21; Igor A. Seidov, "Single Combat," *Mir Aviatsiya*, no. 1 (1995): 35. Nikolay Zameskin claims that he, as a member of the 216th, arrived China in July 1952. See Gordon and Rigmant, *MiG-15*, 126. The 216th IAD started its tour of duty in China in February, 1952 (Kotlobovskiy, "Twenty Years in Combat," pt. 1, 29).

43. Futrell, *United States Air Force in Korea*, 497–98, 512.

44. Seidov, "Single Combat," 34.

45. Krylov and Chepsurkayev, "Nikolay Ivanovich Ivanov," 22–23; FEAF Weekly Intelligence Roundup, no. 100, Aug. 2, 1952, USAFHRA.

46. Halliday, "Air Operations in Korea," 155.

47. Sarin and Dvoretsky, *Alien Wars*, 76.

48. Krylov and Chepsurkayev, "Nikolay Ivanovich Ivanov," 23.

49. Soviet sources wrongly claim three B-29s were shot down on July 10, 1952 (Seidov, "Shield of the Night," 29–31). For American accounts, see Futrell, *United States Air Force in Korea*, 512.

50. Seidov, "Shield of the Night," 31.

51. Gagin, "Air Operations in Korea," 43–47; Kotlobovskiy, "Twenty Years in Combat," pt. 1, 28–29.

52. Futrell, *United States Air Force in Korea*, 653; Jackson, *Air War over Korea*, 153; Halliday, "Soviet Operations in Korea," 163.

53. The FEAF did not report the loss of any F-86s to MiGs on July 19, 1953, while acknowledging the loss of two Sabres the next day (Fifth Air Force Intelligence Summary,

no. 2, July 16–31, 1953, USAFHRA). Crane offers a detailed account about how Maj. Thomas Sellers was shot down over the Yalu on July 20 (*American Airpower Strategy in Korea*, 166).

54. Lt. Gen. Sidor. V. Slyusarev, who succeeded Lobov as commander of the 64th IAK, recommended Lobov for the title "Hero of the Soviet Union." Moscow, however, did not award him this honor (Seidov, "Single Combat," 34–37).

55. Zolotarev, chief ed., *Rossiya (SSSR)*, 68.

56. Morosov and Uskov, "Defending Peace and Labor," 31–32; Kotlobovskiy, "Twenty Years in Combat," pt. 2, *Aehrokhobbi*, no. 3 (1994): 34.

57. Halliday, "Air Operations in Korea," 150.

58. In 1996, a Russian military historian published an article that implied Russian pilots were required to disguise themselves as Chinese when conducting air operations. See Vasiliy Golotyuk, "Chinese in the Air, Russians on the Ground," *Aremisky Sbornik*, June, 1996, 80–84. A copy of this article was translated and supplied to me by Stephen L. Sewell of the Department of Defense.

59. Halliday, "Air Operations in Korea," 151–52; Xu Yan, *Diyici jiaoliang*, 199; Zhang, "China and the Air War in Korea," 349.

60. For Soviet post–World War II military doctrine, see Joseph P. Mastro, "The Lessons of World War II and the Cold War," in *Soviet Aviation and Airpower: A Historical View*, ed. Robin Higham and Jacob W. Kipp, 195–201.

61. Mao to Stalin, Oct. 4, 1951, telegram, in APRF (Chinese), 235–36.

62. Gordon and Rigmant, *MiG-15*, 121, 124; Halliday, "Air Operations in Korea," 153.

63. Krylov and Chepsurkayev, "Combat Episodes," 43.

64. Sarin and Dvoretsky, *Alien Wars*, 72.

65. According to Col. Boris S. Abakumov, an element leader in the 196th IAP, the only measure taken as a result of the inspection was to delay conferring decorations upon pilots of Kozhedub's 324th IAD, so the performance of the two units would not be strikingly in contrast (Gordon and Rigmant, *MiG-15*, 114, 120, 134, 138; Krylov and Chepsurkayev, "Nikolay Ivanovich Ivanov," 21; Halliday, "Air Operations in Korea," 153).

66. Georgiy Lobov, "The Blank Spots of History: In the Skies of North Korea," *JPRS Report*, JPRS-UAC-91-003, June 28, 1991, 30.

67. According to Wang Bingzhang's recall, the Chinese air force had suggested the creation of a single command under the Soviet control, but Chairman Mao disagreed with this idea, insisting on Chinese air force's independence. Wei Bihai, "Remembrances of the Air War," 32.

68. For coordination between the Soviet air command and the Chinese–North Korean command, see Zhou to Peng and Gao, Mar. 22, 1951, telegram, in *Zhou Enlai junshi wenxuan*, 1:178; Wang Yan, chief ed., *Peng Dehuai nianpu*, 536.

69. Wei Bihai, "Remembrances of the Air War," 32–33. There were even incidents involving the accidental shooting of surviving Russian pilots by Chinese soldiers who mistook them as Americans after they landed by parachute (Chen Shijian, "Encounters with the Soviet Army on the Battlefield of Korea," *Junshi lishi*, no. 5 [2000]: 66–71). For Russian views, see Halliday, "Air Operations in Korea," 154; Sarin and Dvoretsky, *Alien Wars*, 74.

70. Sarin and Dvoretsky, *Alien Wars*, 76.

71. Gordon and Rigmant, *MiG-15*, 121–23; Sarin and Dvoretsky, *Alien Wars*, 70.

72. Halliday, "Air Operations in Korea," 155.

73. Gordon and Rigmant, *MiG-15*, 114; Krylov and Chepsurkayev, "Nikolay Ivanovich Ivanov," 21.

74. According to Nikolay Ivanov, who went to Korea with the 133d IAD in April, 1952, those who were married and had children were much less spirited in combat (Krylov and Chepsurkayev, "Nikolay Ivanovich Ivanov," 21).

75. According to Ivanov, a squadron leader in the 133d IAD, pilots were given 1,500 rubles for shooting down an enemy plane (ibid., 23).

76. Kotlobovskiy, "Twenty Years in Combat," pt. 1, 27. Not all Soviet jet aces received the title "Hero of the Soviet Union." Lobov earned the title in World War II, flying 346 combat sorties, shooting down nineteen aircraft, and sharing in the destruction of eight more. See Georgiy Lobov, "The Blank Spots of History," *JPRS Report,* JPRS-UAC-92-001, Jan. 21, 1992, 2–3.

77. Minutes of Conversation between Stalin and Zhou Enlai, Sept. 3, 1952, in "Stalin's Conversation," 16.

Chapter 7. China Enters the Air War

1. Futrell, *United States Air Force in Korea,* 433.

2. Nie Rongzhen, acting chief of staff, to Peng Dehuai, Sept. 15, 24, and 26, 1951, telegrams, cited in Qi Dexue, *Chaoxian zhanzheng juece neimu,* 228–29.

3. Liu Zhen, *Liu Zheng huiyilu,* 344–45; Wang Dinglie et al., *Dangdai Zhongguo kongjun,* 205.

4. Fang Ziyi's recollections in *Lantian zhi lu,* 1:340; Wang Dinglie et al., *Dangdai Zhongguo kongjun,* 143; Liu Zhen, *Liu Zhen huiyilu,* 351.

5. Combat Diary of the 4th Division, Sept. 26, 1951, PLAAF Archives; Li Yongtai's recollections in *Lantian zhi lu,* 1:357–58.

6. Wang Dinglie et al., *Dangdai Zhongguo kongjun,* 145–46. FEAF records also claim five MiGs destroyed and five damaged that day (FEAF Weekly Intelligence Roundup, no. 56, Sept. 30, 1951, USAFHRA).

7. Liu Zhen, *Liu Zhen huiyilu,* 353. See also Fang Ziyi's recollections in *Lantian zhi lu,* 1:342.

8. Combat Diary of the 4th Division, Oct. 12, 1951, PLAAF Archives.

9. For example, see FEAF Weekly Intelligence Roundup, nos. 57 and 58, Oct. 7 and 14, 1951, USAFHRA.

10. Fang Ziyi's recollections in *Lantian zhi lu,* 1:342.

11. Bruning wrongly claims that on October 23, 1951, thirty-two Chinese MiGs flew a cover mission for Soviet units while the latter were striking the B-29s. But, the 3d Division was not ready for combat missions as it had just deployed to the front (*Crimson Sky,* 140).

12. Gao Houliang and Yuan Bing's recollections in *Lantian zhi lu,* 1:370–72; Wang Dinglie et al., *Dangdai Zhongguo kongjun,* 147.

13. The material in this and following paragraphs is drawn from Zhao Baotong's recollections in *Lantian zhi lu,* unless otherwise indicated.

14. "Pictorial Volume of the CPV Air Force in the War to Resist America and Assist Korea," *Junshi shijie huakan,* no. 2 (1992): 16.

15. Guo Guibao, "Mao Zedong's Congratulations to the 3d Aviation Division," in *Junshi lishi*, no. 5 (1995): 57–59; Wang Hai's recollections in *Lantian zhi lu*, 1:387–95.

16. Wang Hai's recollections in *Lantian zhi lu*, 1:389–90.

17. Ibid., 390–91. The FEAF's records acknowledge the destruction of one F-84 and damage to another, and the same MiG's tactics against the F-84s' Lufbery circle (FEAF Weekly Intelligence Roundup, no. 64, Nov. 24, 1951, USAFHRA).

18. Bruning, *Crimson Sky*, 183.

19. Liu's recollections in *Lantian zhi lu*, 1:406–409.

20. For FEAF records, see FEAF Weekly Intelligence Roundup, no. 64.

21. During an interview in 1999, I learned that Liu Yüti was not credited with his claims until 1954. My informant said this was largely due to the skeptical attitude of PLAAF leaders toward pilot claims. For official sources, see Wang Dinglie et al., *Dangdai Zhongguo kongjun*, 149.

22. Liu's recollections in *Lantian zhi lu*, 1:409.

23. Wang Dinglie et al., *Dangdai Zhongguo kongjun*, 147.

24. Gao Houliang's recollections in *Lantian zhi lu*, 1:375.

25. Wang Suhong and Wang Yubing, *Kongzhan zai Chaoxian* (*The Air War in Korea*), 146.

26. Wang Dinglie et al., *Dangdai Zhongguo kongjun*, 150. See also Gao Houliang's recollections in *Lantian zhi lu*, 1:378.

27. Li Chuangeng, *Feijiangjun Liu Shanben*, 336.

28. For the air force war plan, see Zhou to Peng, Gao, and Mao, Mar. 22, 1951, in *Zhou Enlai junshi wenxuan*, 4:175–76.

29. Wang Dinglie et al., *Dangdai Zhongguo kongjun*, 151; Liu Zhen, *Liu Zhen huiyilu*, 358.

30. Wang Dinglie et al., *Dangdai Zhongguo kongjun*, 151; Wu Kai's and Ge Zhenyue's recollections in *Lantian zhi lu*, 1:412.

31. Miao Deliang, "A Short Biography of Zeng Zesheng" in *Zhongguo renmin Zhiyuanjun renwu zhuan*, ed. Chen Zhonglong et al., 957–63.

32. Wu Kai's and Ge Zhenyue's recollections in *Lantian zhi lu*, 1:415.

33. Gao Yueming, group leader of the second raid on Taehwa-do, interview with author, June 10, 1999.

34. FEAF Weekly Intelligence Roundup, no. 65, Dec. 1, 1951, USAFHRA.

35. Bruning, *Crimson Sky*, 167–68.

36. Wu Kai's and Ge Zhenyue's recollections in *Lantian zhi lu*, 1:416; Wang Suhong and Wang Yubing, *Kongzhan zai Chaoxian*, 167–68.

37. Bruning, *Crimson Sky*, 172.

38. Wang Dinglie et al., *Dangdai Zhongguo kongjun*, 154. For the pilot Winton W. Marshall's story, see Bruning, *Crimson Sky*, 177.

39. PLAAF Headquarters Combat Report, Dec. 1, 1951, PLAAF Archives. See also Wu Kai's and Ge Zhenyue's recollections in *Lantian zhi lu*, 1:417–18.

40. Bruning, *Crimson Sky*, 175.

41. Zhao Baotong's recollections in *Lantian zhi lu*, 1:398.

42. Wang Dinglie et al., *Dangdai Zhongguo kongjun*, 154; Wu Kai's and Ge Zhenyue's recollections in *Lantian zhi lu*, 1:418.

43. Futrell, *United States Air Force in Korea*, 415; Bruning, *Crimson Sky*, 179.

44. Futrell, *United States Air Force in Korea*, 415–16.

45. Fang Ziyi's recollections in *Lantian zhi lu,* 1:344.

46. Kotlobovskiy, "Twenty Years in Combat," pt. 1, 27.

47. For the official account, see Futrell, *United States Air Force in Korea,* 421.

48. Bruning, *Crimson Sky,* 186.

49. "Top U.S. Jet Ace Lost in Korean Air War," *New York Times,* Feb. 12, 1952, 1–2.

50. The information in this and the following paragraphs is drawn from John Bruning, *Crimson Sky,* 181–88.

51. "Sabres Fight MiGs Five Times in Day," *New York Times,* Feb. 11, 1952, 2; FEAF Weekly Intelligence Roundup, no. 76, Feb. 16, 1952, USAFHRA.

52. Liu Yalou to Liu Zhen, Feb. 15, 1952, telegram, cited in Fang Ziyi's recollections in *Lantian zhi lu,* 1:344.

53. For Chinese losses, see Liu Yalou to Mao Zedong, Feb. 23, 1952, report, PLAAF Archives.

54. Zhang Jihui's recollections in *Lantian zhi lu,* 1:363–64.

55. Ibid., 364–66.

56. Liu Yalou to Mao Zedong, Feb. 23, 1952, report, PLAAF Archives.

57. Halliday, "Air Operations in Korea," 154.

58. German and Seidov, *Krasnye D'yavoly na 38-y Paralleli,* 178.

59. Besides three kills claimed by the 148th's pilots, Capt. V. F. Shulev of the 17th IAP was also credited with one kill on February 10, 1952 (ibid.).

60. At the time, Chinese leaders saw great possibilities for successful peace talks. It is unclear what led to such a view (Mao to Peng, Nov. 11, 1951, telegram, in *Jianguo yilai Mao Zedong wengao,* 2:497).

61. Wang Dinglie et al., *Dangdai Zhongguo kongjun,* 155; Xu Yan, *Diyici jiaoliang,* 203, 232–33.

62. Wang Dinglie et al., *Dangdai Zhongguo kongjun,* 206.

63. Ibid., 156–57.

64. FEAF Weekly Intelligence Roundup, no. 68, Dec. 22, 1951, USAFHRA.

65. Wang Dinglie et al., *Dangdai Zhongguo kongjun,* 158–59.

66. Ibid., 159.

67. Xu Yan, *Diyici jiaoliang,* 201.

68. Mao to Su Yu (deputy chief of staff of the PLA), June 11, 1952, telegram, *Mao Zedong jianguo yilai wengao,* 3:470. For the losses, see Gao Houliang's recollections in *Lantian zhi lu,* 1:379.

69. Li Xueyan's recollections in *Lantian zhi lu,* 1:489.

70. Wang Dinglie et al., *Dangdai Zhongguo kongjun,* 141, 205; Qi Dexue, *Chaoxian zhanzheng juece neimu,* 236–37.

Chapter 8. From MiG Alley to Panmunjom

1. Wang Dinglie et al., *Dangdai Zhongguo kongjun,* 166; Liu Zhen's recollections in *Lantian zhi lu,* 1:458.

2. Quan Yanchi and Du Weidong, *Kongheguo mishi (A Secret Mission of the Republic),* 53–55.

3. Zhou to Kim, Feb. 3, 1952, telegram, in *Zhou Enlai nianpu,* 1:213–14.

4. Wang Dinglie et al., *Dangdai Zhongguo kongjun*, 166–67.

5. Ibid., 162–65.

6. Liu Zhen's recollections in *Lantian zhi lu*, 1:461–64.

7. Wang Dinglie et al., *Dangdai Zhongguo kongjun*, 192–94.

8. Ibid.

9. Mao's remarks on the General Staff Department's report, Aug. 16, 1952, in *Mao Zedong jianguo yilai wengao*, 2:408–409.

10. Wang Dinglie et al., *Dangdai Zhongguo kongjun*, 194–95.

11. For a detailed discussion of the PLA's views on spirit power over technological strength in Korea, see Shu Guang Zhang, *Mao's Military Romanticism*, 188–215.

12. The material in this subsection draws from Political Department of the CPV Air Force, "Air Force's Political Work during Wartime," in *KangMei yuanChao zhanzheng zhengzhi gongzou jingyan huibian* (*Collections of Political Work Experience in the War to Resist America and Assist Korea*), ed. Editorial Committee for the CPV's Political Work Experience in the Resistance of America and Assistance of Korea War, 2:645–54.

13. Report by the 4th Air Division Political Department, ibid., 2:659.

14. Gordon and Rigmant, *MiG-15*, 141.

15. Wang Dinglie et al., *Dangdai Zhongguo kongjun*, 170.

16. Report by the 4th Air Division Political Department, 2:659.

17. "Air Force's Political Work during Wartime," 2:645–53.

18. Wang Suhong and Wang Yubing, *Kongzhan zai Chaoxian*, 150.

19. American records acknowledge the loss of one F-86 that afternoon; a Soviet pilot in the 17th IAP claimed the kill. The information used here comes from a database compiled by Stephen L. Sewell of the Department of Defense.

20. Air Force Political Department's report in *KangMei yuanChao*, ed. Editorial Committee of the CPV, 2:667.

21. Wang Suhong and Wang Yubing, *Kongzhan zai Chaoxian*, 200.

22. Li Xueyan's recollections in *Lantian zhi lu*, 1:488–89.

23. Pepelyaev's recollections in Gordon and Rigmant, *MiG-15*, 137.

24. Liu Yüti's recollections in *Lantian zhi lu*, 1:406; Han Decai's Diary, Feb. 28, 1953, cited in *Chaoxian tongxun baogaoxuan sanji* (*Three Volumes of Collected News Reports from Korea*), ed. Editorial Department of People's Literature Press, 174–75.

25. Air Force Political Department's report, 2:663–64. In fact, Liu Yalou determined that in this institutional culture the political commissar was the head of air units and the commander was responsible only for flying. See Yang Wanqing and Qi Chunyuan, *Liu Yalou jiangjun zhuan*, 357.

26. Report by the 4th Air Division's Political Department, 2:654–58.

27. Li Shi'an's recollections in *Lantian zhi lu*, 1:472.

28. Report by the 4th Air Division's Political Department, 2:654–58.

29. Wang Dinglie et al., *Dangdai Zhongguo kongjun*, 171–72.

30. *Zhou Enlai nainpu*, 1:238; Wei Bihai, "Remembrances of the Air War," 33.

31. Xu Yan, *Deyici jiaoliang*, 127. See also Shu Guang Zhang, *Mao's Romanticism*, 224. For the number of CPV artillery pieces, see Mao to Stalin, Dec. 17, 1952, telegram, in APRF (Chinese), 299–300.

32. Wang Dinglie et al., *Dangdai Zhongguo kongjun*, 173–74; Wei Bihai, "Remembrances of the Air War," 33.

33. Stalin to Krasovskiy, Apr. 9, 1952, and Mao to Stalin, Apr. 22, 1952, telegrams, in APRF (Chinese), 273–75; Wei Bihai, "Remembrances of the Air War," 35.

34. "Pictorial Volume of the CPV's Air Force in the War to Resist America and Assist Korea," *Junshi shijie huakan*, no. 2 (1992): 33.

35. For Chinese attitude toward their negotiations with the Soviets for assistance, see Wei Bihai, "Remembrances of the Air War," 35.

36. This kind of sentiment can be seen in Xu Xiangqian, *Lishi de huigu* (*Remember the History*), 2:797–805; Nie Rongzhen, *Nie Rongzhen huiyilu* (*Nie Rongzhen's Memoirs*), 757–58; Shu Guang Zhang, *Mao's Romanticism*, 222.

37. Li Chuangeng, *Feijiangjun Liu Shanben*, 344–45.

38. Nie Fengzhi, *Zhanchang*, 194–95; Xu Yan, *Diyici jiaoliang*, 206.

39. Peng to the Air Force Joint Command, June 11, 1952, telegram, and Deng Hua to Peng, July 1, 1952, telephone memorandum, in Wang Yan, chief ed., *Peng Dehuai nianpu*, 528–29; Li Chuangeng, *Feijiangjun Liu Shanben*, 346.

40. Li Chuangeng. *Feijiangjun Liu Shanben*, 344.

41. Crane, *American Airpower Strategy in Korea*, 156–59.

42. Futrell, *United States Air Force in Korea*, 479.

43. Halliday, "Air Operations in Korea," 170.

44. Lobov, "Blank Spots of History," Jan. 21, 1992, 2; Liu Zhen, *Liu Zhen huiyilu*, 370.

45. Mao to Kim, July 18, 1952, telegram, in Weathersby, "New Russian Documents," 78.

46. Kim to Mao, July 15, 1952, telegram, in ibid., 79.

47. Kim to Stalin, July 17, 1952, telegram, in APRF (Chinese), 277.

48. Memorandum of conversation between Stalin and Zhou Enlai, Aug. 20, 1952, in "Stalin's Conversation," 13.

49. Memorandum of conversation between Stalin and Zhou Enlai, Sept. 3, 1952, ibid., 16.

50. Deng Hua to Peng Dehuai, July 1, 1952, telephone memorandum, in Wang Yan, chief ed., *Peng Dehuai nianpu*, 529. See also Yang Wanqing and Qi Chunyuan, *Liu Yalou jiangjun zhuan*, 314; Wang Dinglie et al., *Dangdai Zhongguo kongjun*, 225; Tian Xuan, "Biography of Nie Fengzhi," in *Zhongguo renmin zhiyuanjun renwu zhuan*, ed. Chen Zhonglong et al., 783. See also Zhang, "China and the Air War in Korea," 363.

51. Wei Bihai, "Remembrances of the Air War," 34.

52. Nie Fengzhi, *Zhanchang*, 194; Wei Bihai, "Remembrances of the Air War," 34.

53. Wang Dinglie et al., *Dangdai Zhongguo kongjun*, 180–81.

54. Ibid., 178–79, 184–85; Air Force Headquarters Editorial and Research Office, *Kongjun shi*, 74–75.

55. Futrell, *United States Air Force in Korea*, 525–25.

56. Tian Xuan, "Biography of Nie Fengzhi," 784. No Kum-Sok claims he saw a North Korean pilot shoot down an F4U5 Corsair by over the sea (*MiG-15 to Freedom*, 132).

57. Shen Zonghong et al., *Zhongguo renmin zhiyuanjun kangMei yuanChao zhan shi*, 257–63.

58. Wang Dinglie et al., *Dangdai Zhongguo kongjun*, 183–86; Air Force Headquarters Editorial and Research Office, *Kongjun shi*, 79, 81.

59. For example, at one point the 3d Aviation Division had only eight pilots capable of flying combat missions, and the 12th Aviation Division started its tour of duty in Korea with some sixty pilots, but had only twelve pilots able to fly when it returned home (Wang Hai, *Wo de zhandou shengya*, 119; Nie Fengzhi, *Zhanchang*, 199).

60. Peng Dehuai to the Air Force, Dec. 7, 1952, memorandum, *in* Wang Yan, chief ed., *Peng Dehuai nianpu*, 537.

61. Ma Hongjiao and Liang Zhanfang, "Brilliant Victory of Air Battle of General Nie Fengzhi in the Korean War," *Junshi lishi*, no. 1 (1998): 37.

62. Simultaneously, Liu Yalou also recommended the CMC select combat experienced pilots from those units to study at Soviet air force's War College (Yang Wanqing and Qi Chunyuan, *Liu Yalou jiangjun zhuan*, 315). See also Yang Weiqun's recollections in *Lantian zhi lu*, 2:55–64.

63. Wang Dinglie et al., *Dangdai Zhongguo kongjun*, 183; Tian Xuan, "Biography of Nie Fengzhi," 787; Fang Ziyi's recollections in *Lantian zhi lu*, 1:346.

64. Hagerstrom, a "fighter jock," allegedly was unhappy over his transfer from the 4th Fighter-Interceptor Wing to the 18th Fighter-Bomber Wing and wanted to go shoot down more MiGs. As a result, he taught his pilots to quickly dump their bombs, with no concern for what they hit, and then go chasing after MiGs. Hagerstrom wound up shooting down 6.5 MiGs in his F-86F-30 fighter-bomber, making him the highest scoring fighter-bomber ace of the Korean War. American records show that Hagerstrom was credited with shooting down two MiGs from Wang's flight, and his wingman, Metten, destroyed one. Stephen L. Sewell supplied the author with this information. Chinese records, on the other hand, account for one MiG lost and one damaged (the latter was the wingman in the second pair of MiG's in Wang's formation). According to Wang, his plane was damaged during the initial encounter, and then was hit again when he tried to make an emergency landing on Dabao Airfield. That may explain why the U.S. pilots claimed three MiGs destroyed. See Wang Hai, *Wo de zhandou shengya*, 141–48.

65. According to a Russian source, Capt. K. V. Ugryumov of the 224th IAP, 32d IAD, piloted this Soviet aircraft, which suffered twenty-two hits from Fischer's .50-caliber machine guns but landed safely at the airfield (German and Seidov, *Krasnye D'yavoly na 38-y Paralleli*, 272–73).

66. That afternoon, twelve MiGs from the 43d Regiment, 15th Division, were sent to intercept enemy planes over the mouth of the Yalu. After encountering no enemy planes, the first flight, according to Han Dechai's recollections, was ordered to fly a cover mission over Dabao Airfield while the others came in to land. After circling the southern end of the airfield nine or ten times, Han and his leader were low on fuel and prepared to land, descending from an altitude of three thousand to four hundred meters. All of a sudden, Han heard the ground controller call for him to pull up because an enemy aircraft was blasting at them from behind. Han checked his tail and saw nothing, then looked down and forward, spotting an F-86 chasing another MiG flying underneath and behind his leader. The Sabre suddenly pulled up to shoot at the lead Chinese MiG and smoke poured from its engine. Realizing that his leader was hit, Han dropped down and closed on the Sabre. As soon as he had the target framed in his gunsight, he squeezed off a long burst that caused the F-86 to burst into flames. After Fischer bailed out, Han radioed the ground to prepare to take him prisoner (Huai Decai's recollections in *Lantian zhi lu*, 1:432–37).

67. Fischer offered an account about his own experience on April 7, 1953, in *Hot Shots*, ed. Jennie Ethell Chancey and William B. Forstchen, 173–76. According to Fischer, after engaging several MiGs over MiG Alley close to the border, he decided to press attacks across the Yalu. After seeing three aircraft, "one straggler behind the two in front," he dropped down and got off a shot at the former, then "rolled over on the number two MiG in the

formation." This time, Fischer claimed, his guns were "calibrated" and he let the MiG have "a long burst." He continued the attack on the lead aircraft, alleging that his six .50 calibers "literally tore the aircraft apart." At that moment, Fischer noticed his own aircraft was stalling and that flames had erupted in the cockpit. He said he had no choice but to bail out.

68. Fischer allegedly refused to accept the fact he had been shot down by an inexperienced young Chinese pilot until he met his opponent during his captivity (Wang Dinglie et al., *Dangdai Zhongguo kongjun*, 187–89; Huai Decai's recollections in *Lantian zhi lu*, 1:432–37).

69. The Soviet pilot credited with shooting Fischer down was Grigoriy N. Berelidze of the 224th IAP. According to his recollections, Berelidze was paired with Lev P. Kolesnikov flying at an altitude of nine thousand meters above Dabao Airfield as cover for the returning MiGs. Just as the wheels of the last planes in his group touched down, an F-86 appeared out of nowhere at low altitude and began to attack the MiGs. In response to a radio call for help, he spotted the silhouette of an aircraft below them. Sure enough, it was an enemy plane. Berelidze made a turn and dove to low altitude. After recovering from the pressure of g forces, he found that his MiG was about three kilometers behind the Sabre. As soon as he was within firing range, Berelidze blasted the Sabre out of the sky (German and Seidov, *Krasnye D'yavoly na 38-y Paralleli*, 271–73).

70. Deng Hua to Mao, Apr. 20, 1953, telegram, *Mao Zedong jianguo yilai wengao*, 4:201–202.

71. Wei Bihai, "Remembrances of the Air War," 35.

72. Tian Xuan, "Biography of Nie Fengzhi," 787; Futrell, *United States Air force in Korea*, 654.

73. Wei Bihai, "Remembrances of the Air War," 35.

74. Ibid.

75. Wang Dinglie et al., *Dangdai Zhongguo kongjun*, 190–91; Zhao Jianguo and Ma Yuan, *Chaoxian da kongzhan*, 320.

76. For this information, see the official USAF and U.S. Navy KIA/MIA listings on the DPMO website.

77. Wang Dinglie et al., *Dangdai Zhongguo kongjun*, 195–98. In fact, the 15th Division lost a regimental commander on June 22, 1953, the last PLAAF casualty in the air war. See Cui Wenbing's recollections in *Lantian zhi lu*, 1:430.

78. Futrell, *United States Air Force in Korea*, 653; Jackson, *Air War over Korea*, 153. Halliday, "Air Operations in Korea," 163.

79. Futrell, *United States Air Force in Korea*, 653–56, 666–72.

80. Bulganin's response was made in October, 1951, when he met Kim Il Sung, Gao Gang, head of the Northeast Bureau of the CCP, and Xu Xiangqian, chief of the PLA General Staff, who were negotiating for military assistance in Moscow. See Xu Xiangqian, *Lishi de huigu* (*Remember History*), 797–805; Zhang Lin and Ma Changzhi, *Zhongguo yuanshuai Xu Xiangqian* (*Chinese Marshal Xu Xiangqian*), 448.

81. Mao to Stalin, Mar. 28, 1952, telegram, in APRF (Chinese), 270–72.

82. Shen Zhihua, *Mao Zedong, Stalin yu Hanzhan* (*Mao Zedong, Stalin and Korean War: Highest Secret Archives from China and Soviet Union*), 302.

83. Stalin's hard line position was best revealed in his conversation with Zhou Enlai on Aug. 20, 1952, in "Stalin's Conversation," 12–13. Evidence of Chinese requests for assistance that exceeded Soviet ability can be found in Stalin to Mao, Dec. 27, 1952, and Jan. 15, 1953, telegrams, and Report from A. M. Vasilevsky and S. M. Shtemenko to Stalin, Jan. 12, 1953, in APRF (Chinese), 303–308.

84. William W. Stueck Jr., *The Korean War: An International History,* 327.

85. Council of Ministers of the USSR Resolution, Mar. 19, 1953, in Weathersby, "New Russian Documents," 80–82; *Zhou Enlai nianpu,* 1:291.

86. Shu Guang Zhang, *Mao's Military Romanticism,* 245.

87. See, e.g., Crane, *American Airpower Strategy in Korea;* Futrell, *United States Air Force in Korea;* Hallion, *Naval Air War in Korea.*

88. Crane, *American Airpower Strategy in Korea,* 164.

89. James Sheply, "How Dulles Averted War," *Life,* Jan. 16, 1956, 70–72; Dwight D. Eisenhower, *The White House Years: Mandate for Change, 1953–1956,* 179–80. For discussion of the debate over the utility of nuclear threats in the Korean War, see Roger Dingman, "Atomic Diplomacy During the Korean War," *International Security* 13, no. 3 (winter, 1988-89): 50–91; and Rosemary Foot, "Nuclear Coercion and the Ending of the Korean Conflict," *International Security* 13, no. 3 (winter, 1988-89): 92–112. Based on a study of Chinese press reaction to possible American use of nuclear weapons, one historian notes that there is no evidence indicating the Chinese leadership "caved in and agreed to an armistice out of fear of U.S. nuclear attacks." The Chinese leadership, he argues, actually continued "to view a U.S. recourse to nuclear weapons as relatively unlikely . . . even if the weapons were used, Chinese forces in Korea," and "the Chinese mainland itself, would be able to withstand the impact" (Mark A. Ryan, *Chinese Attitudes Toward Nuclear Weapons: China and the United States during the Korean War,* 163–64).

90. See Robert Futrell's unpublished article, "The Korean War Reexamined," 14.

91. For example, on November 25, 1950, Zhou Enlai held a meeting with representatives of non-Communist parties in Beijing, trying to eliminate their fears of U.S. nuclear power. He was confident the United States would not use nuclear weapons because the Soviet Union also possessed atomic bombs (*Zhou Enlai junshi wenxuan,* 4:116). Lei Yingfu, Zhou's military secretary, also recalled when he reported to Mao and Zhou in December, 1950, that the United States had threatened to use nuclear weapons in Korea. The chairman said the threat was blackmail. Zhou responded by saying that the other Western allies would never support Truman in such an action (Chen Xianyi and Lie Yingfu, *Zai zuigao tongshuaibu dang canmo,* 167–68). Furthermore, at a foreign affairs conference on June 5, 1953, Zhou Enlai proclaimed that the new U.S. president had talked big, making five threats that were clearly bluffs: (1) to strike the Communist position from the flank, (2) to extend the bombing campaign into northeastern China, (3) to harass the coast from the sea, (4) to possibly employ nuclear weapons, and (5) to attack the Chinese mainland. Zhou declared that China was ready to deal with the first three threatened actions, and added that "the allies of the American imperialists would not support the latter two because they were afraid of being involved in a bigger war" (*Zhou Enlai junshi wenxuan,* 4:321–32).

92. American military leaders were concerned about the repercussions of attacks against those irrigation dams during the last stage of the UN air campaign. However, neither public opinion nor the media at home or abroad paid much attention to the U.S. bombardment of civilian targets (Crane, *American Airpower Strategy in Korea,* 160, 162).

93. Kuznetsov and Fedorenko to Molotov, Mar. 29, 1953, telegram, in Weathersby, "New Russian Documents," 83.

94. *Peng Dehuai nianpu*, 553; Mao to Peng, June 21, 1953, telegram, in *Mao Zedong junshi wenji*, 6:350.

95. Tan Jingqiao, ed., *KangMei yuanChao zhanzheng*, 289, 325–26; Chai Chengwen and Zhao Yongtian, *Banmendian tanpan*, 261–62.

96. Tan Jingqiao, ed., *KangMei yuanChao zhanzheng*, 298–305; Shen Zongzhong et al., *Zhongguo renmin zhiyuanjun kangMei yuanChao zhan shi*, 283–91.

97. Xu Yan, *Diyici jiaoliang*, 146, 169–70.

98. Mao Zedong, *Mao Zedong Xuanji*, 5: 102. See also the July 29, 1953, telegram from Kuznetsov to Foreign Ministry in Moscow, in which the Soviet ambassador to China reported his conversations with Mao on July 28 (in Weathersby, "New Russian Documents," 83).

99. The first episode of MiG defection to the West did not occur until September 21, 1953, when North Korean pilot No Kum-Sok landed his MiG-15bis at Kimpo Air Base in South Korea. However, he claims that he had never heard of Project Moolah's offer for a MiG. (No Kum-Sok, *MiG-15 to Freedom*, 2). The first Chinese defector was a naval pilot, Liu Chengze (Liu Cheng-sze), who landed his MiG-15bis at Taoyuan Air Base on Taiwan in March, 1962 (Bueschel, *Communist Chinese Airpower*, 78).

100. Wang Dinglie et al., *Dangdai Zhongguo kongjun*, 183. See also Liu Yalou's report on May 28, 1956, in *Lantian zhi lu*, 2:27.

101. For example, Wei Bihai gives monthly kill ratios from January to May, 1953, as 1.64:1, 2.5:1, 1:1, 1:1.4, and 1:1.5 ("Remembrances of the Air War," 35). Wang Dinglie et al., *Dangdai Zhongguo kongjun*, 186, and Tian Xuan, "Biography of Nie Fengzhi," 787, cite a claim of 70 kills between January and April and 18 kills in May. An inference can be drawn to show the PLAAF's total losses for the five months were about 81. However, one Chinese military historian notes that the CPV Air Force lost 84 during the last seven months of the war. See Qi Dexue, "The Imposing Appearance of Young Pilots: A Brief Historical Account of the CPV Air Force," *Junshi lishi*, no. 5 (1995): 19. The Soviets lost 47 during the same period. The Americans recorded claims of 193 kills. This information is drawn from a database compiled by Stephen L. Sewell of the Department of Defense.

102. Golotyuk, "Chinese in the Air," 80–84.

103. Tang Jihan's recollections in *Lantian zhi lu*, 1:501–502. See also No Kum-Sok, *MiG-15 to Freedom*, 142.

104. For the best analysis of UN interdiction campaigns that failed in Korea, see Crane, *American Airpower Strategy in Korea*. For problems on UN interdiction efforts against Communist supply lines, see Charles R. Shrader, *Communist Logistics in the Korean War*.

Chapter 9. Conclusion

1. Wang Dinglie et al., *Dangdai Zhongguo kongjun*, 200–201; Deng Lifeng, *Jianguohou junshi xingdong quanlu* (*A Complete Record of Military Operations since the Founding of State*), 313.

2. Kotlobovskiy, "Twenty Years in Combat," pt. 2, 34; Golotyuk, "Chinese in the Air," 83; Arsen'yev and Krylov, *Istrebitel' MiG-15*, 69; Zolotarev, chief ed., *Rossiya (SSSR)*, 73–74.

3. Morosov and Uskov, "Defending Peace and Labor," 31.

4. FEAF Intelligence Roundup, no. 145, Dec., 1953, USAFHRA.

5. Futrell (*United States Air Force in Korea*, 692) says FEAF, Marine Corps, and friendly foreign units sustained 147 air-to-air losses. Halliday ("Air Operations in Korea," 167) adds five naval planes lost in aerial combat, and his quote is cited on page 157 in the same source.

6. American pilots believed that enemy MiGs did not burst into flames "in the thin air at high altitudes but would go down later" (Crane, *American Airpower Strategy in Korea,* 167). Stephen L. Sewell informed me that the "USAF was getting ridiculous toward the end," and recent reports indicate that "as little as three bullet strikes on a MiG in gun-camera film" were credited as a kill.

7. For example, U.S/UN pilots claimed four MiGs destroyed on April 3 and 4, 1951. Soviet records indicate, however, that all but one MiG from the 176th GIAP, including three that were damaged, returned to base safely (Kotlobovskiy, "Twenty Years in Combat," pt. 2, 33–34). For the U.S. account of the battle on April 3 and 4, see Futrell, *United States Air Force in Korea, 297.*

8. Bruning, Crimson Sky, ix. I was also informed of this unfortunate situation through my E-mail communications with Stephen L. Sewell.

9. Bruning's *Crimson Sky,* xiv.

10. Gordon and Rigmant, *MiG-15,* 114.

11. Duan Suquan to Peng Dehuai, May 8, 1953, letter, in Li Jie, "General Takes Wing to Blue Sky," 130–31. In early November, 1953, PLAAF leaders allegedly met to reexamine Chinese victory claims and subsequently made an adjustment.

12. Futrell, *United States Air Force in Korea,* 689–90; Hallion, "Naval Air Operations in Korea," in *A Revolutionary War: Korea and the Transformation of the Postwar World,* ed. William J. Williams, 144–45; Shen Zonghong et al., *Zhongguo renmin zhiyuanjun kangMei yuanChao zhan shi,* 319.

13. The Fifth Air Force wings had only 132 F-86 fighter-bombers and 165 F-86 fighter-interceptors in July, 1953 (Futrell, *United States Air Force in Korea,* 645).

14. Xu Yan, *Diyici jiaoliang,* 207. See also Qi Dexue et al, "Enlightenment on Defeating a Strong Enemy with Inferior Weapons and Equipment in the Korean War," *Junshi lishi,* no. 6 (1999): 33.

15. Wang Dinglie et al., *Dangdai Zhongguo kongjun,* 207.

16. Ibid., 204.

17. Ibid., 208–209.

18. Ibid., 210.

19. Allen et al., *China's Air Force,* 52.

20. Wang Dinglie et al., *Dangdai Zhongguo kongjun,* 207.

21. According to Chinese sources, the Soviet Union supplied China with arms and equipment for ten divisions in 1951, then continued to deliver one and one-half divisions a month beginning in January, 1952, through the first half of 1954 (Mao to Xu Xiangqian, July 29, 1951, telegram, in *Zhou Enlai nianpu,* 1:164–65). See also Zhang Lin and Ma Changzhi, *Zhongguo yuanshuai Xu Xiangqian,* 404.

22. Zhang Yutao, *Xin Zhongguo junshi dashi jiyao* (*The Records of Major Events in New China's Military*), 53. Xu Yan claims that in 1950–54, China received enough Soviet arms and equipment to outfit 107 army divisions (Xu Yan, *Diyici jiaoliang,* 186).

23. According to Xu Yan, China owed a war debt of 3 billion Chinese *yuan*, plus 1 billion *yuan* worth of weapons and equipment China received from the Soviet forces when they evacuated from Lüshun and Andong for home—equivalent to $1.3 billion. China paid off the debt plus interest in 1964. Compare that with the $10 billion lend-lease war debt the Soviet Union owed the United States, its World War II ally. Xu Yan points out the Soviets made only a symbolic payment of $300 million until the 1970s (ibid., 32). See also Pei Jianzhang, chief ed., *Zhonghua renmin gongheguo waijiaoshi, 1949–1969* (*Diplomatic History of the People's Republic of China, 1949–1969*), 2:257–58; Shen Zhihua, *Mao Zedong, Stalin yu hanzhan*, 302. In a letter to CCP leaders on December 3, 1953, Zhou attached an initial ten-year payment schedule for Soviet war debts (*Zhou Enlai nianpu*, 1:336–37).

24. Mao's son, Mao Anying, served as Peng Dehuai's secretary and Russian-language interpreter, and was killed on the morning of November 25, 1950, when four UN aircraft dropped incendiary bombs on the CPV headquarters (CPV Headquarters to CMC, Nov. 25, 1950, telegram, in Wang Yan, chief ed., *Peng Dehuai zhuan*, 428).

25. Liu Pushao et al., "A Biography of Zhu Guang," in *Zhiyuanjun renwu zhi*, 309. For the story of Mao's son, see Shu Guang Zhang, *Mao's Military Romanticism*, 193–94.

26. Wang Yan, chief ed., *Peng Dehuai zhuan*, 502, 506.

27. Mastro, "Lessons of World War II," 195–201.

28. Wang Dinglie et al., *Dangdai Zhongguo kongjun*, 87–88, 110.

29. Liu Yalou, "To Build An Air Force on the Basis of the Army," *Lantian zhi lu*, 1:3.

30. The CMC's Instruction, July 23, 1954, telegram, *Mao Zedong jianguo yilai wengao*, 4:516–17.

31. Liao Guoliang et al., *Mao Zedong junshi sixiang fazhan shi*, 459–60; Li Ke and Hao Shengzhang, *Wenhua dageming zhong de renminjiefangjun* (*The People's Liberation Army in the Cultural Revolution*), 341. See also Xiaoming Zhang, "The Vietnam War, 1964–1969: A Chinese Perspective," *Journal of Military History* 60 (Oct., 1996): 743–45.

32. The PLAAF lost 168 planes to noncombat causes during the Korean War (Deng Lifeng, *Jianguohou junshi xingdong quanlu*, 313).

33. These problems were summarized in Liu Yalou's 1956 report, *Lantian zhi lu*, 2:28.

34. Ibid., 28–29.

35. See Shen Weiping, *8.23 paoji Jinmen* (*Shelling Jinmen on August 23*), 143–44. Lin Hu served as a deputy regiment commander in the 3d Aviation Division in Korea and claims to have shot down one F-86 and damaged an F-84. During the 1958 Taiwan Strait crisis, he was commander of the 18th Air Division in Shantou, Guangdong Province (Geng Longwu, *Zhongguo wangpai feixingyuan*, 30–44).

36. Futrell, *United States Air Force in Korea*, 414.

37. See, e.g., Chang Qing and Zhang Nongke, "'Bearing the Brunt' in Future War: An Outlook of the Chinese Air Force's Modernization from Major Military Exercises," *Zijing*, Nov., 1999, 32–35; Kong Yun, "Revealing the Real Air Combat Strength of the Chinese Air Force."

38. Shu Guang Zhang, *Mao's Military Romanticism*, 261.

Bibliography

Published and Unpublished Documents, Papers, and Dissertations

Bajanov, Evgeniy P., and Natalia Bajanova. "The Korean Conflict, 1950–1953: The Most Mysterious War of the 20th Century." Unpublished manuscript based on secret Soviet archives.

Dalian City Archives

Editorial Committee for the CPV's Political Work Experience in the War of Resisting America and Assisting of Korea ed. *KangMei yuanChao zhanzheng zhengzhi gongzou jingyan huibian* (*Collections of Political Work Experience in the War to Resist America and Assist Korea*). 2 vols. Beijing: People's Liberation Army Political Department, 1958.

FEAF Weekly Intelligence Roundup. United States Air Force Historical Research Agency, Montgomery, Alabama.

Fifth Air Force Intelligence Summary. United States Air Force Historical Research Agency, Montgomery, Alabama.

Futrell, Robert F. "The Korean War Reexamined." Unpublished paper.

Guanyu Chaoxian zhanzheng de Eguo dangan wenjian (*Russian Archival Documents on the Korean War*). Beijing: Second Division of the Military History Research Department of the Military Science Academy, 1996.

Jiangsu Provincial Archives.

Kesaris. Paul ed., *Records of the Joint Chiefs of Staff.* Pt. 2: *The Far East 1946–1953,* reel 9, Washington: A Microfilm Project of University Publication of America, Inc, 1979.

Mansourov, Alexander Y. "Stalin, Mao, Kim, and China's Decision to enter to the Korean War, September 16-October 15, 1950: New Evidence from the Russian Archives." *Cold War International History Project Bulletin,* nos. 6 and 7 (winter 1995–96): 94–119.

Mao Zedong. *Mao Zedong junshi wenxuan* (*Selected Military Works of Mao Zedong*) Internal ed. Beijing: People's Liberation Army Soldiers' Press, 1981.

———. *Jianguo yilai Mao Zedong wengao* (*Mao Zedong's Manuscripts Since the Founding of the People's Republic*). 13 vols. Beijing: the Central Historical Materials Press, 1987–98.

———. *Mao Zedong xuanji* (*Selected Works of Mao Zedong*). 5 vols. Beijing: People's Press, 1991.

———. *Mao Zedong junshi wenji* (*A Collection of Mao Zedong's Military Papers*). 6 vols. Beijing: Military Science Press and the Central Historical Materials Press, 1993.

O'Neill, Mark A. "'The Other Side of the Yalu': Soviet Pilots in the Korean War, Phase One, 1 November 1950–12 April 1951." Ph.D. Diss., Florida State University, 1996.

Peng Dehuai. *Peng Dehuai junshi wenxuan* (*Selected Military Writings of Peng Dehuai*). Beijing: Central Historical Materials Press, 1988.

"Stalin's Conversation with Chinese Leaders: Talks with Mao Zedong, December 1949–January 1950, and with Zhou Enlai, August–September 1952." Translated by Danny

Rozas. *Cold War International History Project Bulletin,* nos. 6 and 7 (winter 1995–96): 4–20.

Weathersby, Kathryn. "New Russian Documents on the Korean War." *Cold War International History Project Bulletin,* nos. 6 and 7 (winter 1995–96): 30–86.

Xu Xiangqian. *Xu Xiangqian junshi wenxuan (Selected Works of Xu Xiangqian).* Beijing: People's Liberartion Army Press, 1993.

Zhang Xiaoming. "Toward Arming China: United States Arms Sales and Military Assistance to China, 1921–1941." Ph.D. Diss., University of Iowa, 1994.

Zhonghua minguo zhongyao shiliao: duiRi kangzhan shiqi, xubian (Important Historical Documents on the Republic of China: The Anti-Japanese War, Supplementary Part). Taibei: Guomindang Press, 1981.

Zhou Enlai. *Zhou Enlai waijiao wenxuan (Selected Diplomatic Works of Zhou Enlai).* Beijing: The Central Historical Materials Press, 1991.

———. *Zhou Enlai junshi wenxuan (Selected Military Works of Zhou Enlai).* 4 vols. Beijing: People's Press, 1997.

Periodicals and Newspapers

Aehrokhobbi (Aerohobby) (Ukraine)
Air Force Magazine
Aremisky Sbornik (Army Digest)
Asia
Aviamaster
Aviatsiya i Kosmonavtika (Aviation and Cosmonautics)
Aviatsiya i Vremya (Aviation and Time) (Kiev)
Dang de wenxian (Party's Historical Documents)
Dangdai Zhongguo shi yanjiu (Research of Contemporary China History)
Guangming ribao (Guangming Daily)
JPRS Report
Junshi lishi (Military History)
Junshi lishi yanjiu (Studies on Military History)
Junshi shijie huakan (Military World Pictorial Issue)
Junshi shilin (Military History Circles)
Krasnaya Zvezda (Red Star)
Life
Mir Aviatsiya (World of Aviation)
New York Times
Poligraf (Polygraph) (Voronezh)
Voprosy Istorii (Questions of History)
Xinhua wenzhai (New China Digest)
Zijing (Lily) or *Bauhinia Monthly* (Hong Kong)
Zhonggong dangshi yanjiu (CCP History Studies)
Zhongguo guofang bao (China Defense Gazette)
Zhonggong dangshi ziliao (CCP Historical Materials)
Zhongxinshe (China News Agency)

Books and Articles

Abakumov, Boris Sergeyevich. *Neizvestnaya Voyna* (*The Unknown War*). Kursk, Russia: Raduga, 1997.

———. "Soviet Fliers in the Skies of Korea." *Voprosy Istorii*, no. 1 (1993): 129–39.

Air Force Headquarters Editorial and Research Office. *Kongjun shi* (*History of the Air Force*). Beijing: People's Liberation Army Press, 1989.

Allen, Kenneth W. *People's Republic of China, People's Liberation Army Air Force.* Washington, D.C.: Defense Intelligence Agency, 1991.

———, Glenn Krumel, and Jonathan D. Pollack. *China's Air Force Enters the 21st Century.* Santa Monica, Calif.: RAND, 1995

Appleman, Roy E. *Disaster in Korea: The Chinese Confront MacArthur.* College Station: Texas A&M University Press, 1989.

Arsen'yev, Ye., and Krylov, A. *Istrebitel' MiG-15* (*The MiG-15 Fighter*). Armanda no. 10, Moscow: Ehksprint, 1999.

Babich, Vladimir. "MiG Against Sabre." *Krasnaya Zvezda,* October 14, 1995.

Bajanov, Evgeniy. "Assessing the Politics of the Korean War, 1949–51." *Cold War International History Project Bulletin,* nos. 6 and 7 (winter 1995–96): 54, 87–91.

Barrett, David D. *Dixie Mission: The United States Army Observer Group in Yenan, 1944.* Berkeley: University of California Press, 1970.

Bo Yibo. *Ruogan zhongda juece yu shijian de huigu* (*Recollections of Several Important Decisions and Events*). 2 vols. Beijing: CCP Central Academy Press, 1991, 1993.

Borowski, Harry R. *A Hollow Threat: Strategic Air Power and Containment Before Korea.* Westport, Conn.: Greenwood Press, 1982.

Bruning, John R., Jr. *Crimson Sky: The Air Battle for Korea.* Dulles, Va.: Brassey's, 1999.

Bueschel, Richard M. *Communist Chinese Air Power.* New York: Frederick A. Praeger, 1968.

Cai Renzhao. *Zhongguo yuanshuai Nie Rongzhen* (*Chinese Marshal Nie Rongzhen*). Beijing: CCP Central Academy, 1994.

CCP Central Archives and Studies Office, ed. *Zhou Enlai nianpu, 1949–1976* (*The Chronicle of Zhou Enlai, 1949–1976*). 3 vols. Beijing: Central Historical Material Press, 1997.

Chai Chengwen and Zhao Yongtian. *Banmendian tanpan* (*The Panmunjom Negotiations*). Beijing: People's Liberation Army Press, 1989.

Chancey, Jennie Ethell, and William R. Forstchen, eds. *Hot Shots: An Oral History of the Air Force Combat Pilots of the Korean War.* New York: HarperCollins, 2000.

Chang Qing and Zhang Nongke. "'Bearing the Brunt' in Future War: The Outlook of the Chinese Air Force's Modernization from Major Military Exercises." *Zijing,* November, 1999, 32–35.

Chen Feng et al. *ZhongMei jiaoliang da xiezheng* (*A True Description of the Trial of Strength between China and the United States*). 2 vols. Beijing: China Human Affairs Press, 1996.

Chen Hongyou. "On Historical Experiences of Air Force's Air Defense Operations." *Junshi lishi yanjiu* (*Studies on Military History*), no. 1 (1992): 53–62.

Chen, Jian. *China's Road to the Korean War: The Making of the Sino-American Confrontation.* New York: Columbia University Press, 1994.

Chen Xiqi, ed. *Sun Zhongshan nianpu changbian* (*A Long Edition of the Chronicle of Sun Yat-sen*). Beijing: China Book Bureau, 1991.

Chen Xianyi and Lie Yingfu. *Zai zuigao tongshuaibu dang canmo: Lei Yingfu jiangjun huiyilu* (*My Services in the Supreme Command: General Lei Yingfu's Memoirs*). Nanchang: Bahuazhou Art Press, 1998.

Chen Zhonglong et al. *Zhongguo renmin zhiyuanjun renwu zhuan* (*Biographies of the Chinese People's Volunteers*). Nanjing: Jiangsu People's Press, 1996.

Chinese Social Science Academy and Central Archives, eds. *Zhonghua renmin gongheguo jingji dangan ziliao xuanbian* (*A Collection of Economic Documents of the People's Republic of China, 1949–1952*). Comp. vol. Beijing: China's Urban Economic Society Press, 1990.

Chinese Social Science Academy and Central Archives, eds. *Zhonghua renmin gongheguo jingji dangan ziliao xuanbian* (*A Collection of Economic Documents of the People's Republic of China, 1949–1952*). Foreign trade vol. Beijing: Economic Management Press, 1994.

City Historical Record Office of Dalian, ed. *Sulian hongjun zai Lüda* (*Soviet Red Army in Port Arthur*). Dalian: 1995.

Collier, Basil. *A History of Air Power.* New York: Macmillan, 1974.

Crane, Conrad C. *American Airpower Strategy in Korea, 1950–1953.* Lawrence: University Press of Kansas, 2000.

Cumings, Bruce. *The Origins of the Korean War.* Vol. 2. Princeton, N.J.: Princeton University Press, 1990.

Dangdai Zhongguo de minhang shiye (*China Today: Civil Aviation Industry*). Beijing: China Social Science Press, 1989.

Deng Lifeng. *Xin Zhongguo junshi huodong jishi, 1949–1959* (*The True Records of the New China's Military Affairs*). Beijing: CCP Historical Materials Press, 1989.

———. *Jianguo hou junshi xingdong quanlu* (*A Complete Record of Military Operations since the Founding of State*). Taiyuan: Shanxi People's Press, 1991.

Dingman, Roger. "Atomic Diplomacy during the Korean War." *International Security* 13, no. 3 (winter, 1988–89): 50–91.

Division of Central Historical Documents. *Zhu De nianpu* (*The Chronicle of Zhu De*). Beijing: People's Press, 1986.

Dokuchayev, Anatoliy. "Aces of the Unknown War." *Krasnaya Zvezda,* December 28, 1991.

———. "The Secret Valor of Nikolay Sutyagin." *Krasnaya Zvezda,* September 14, 1993.

———. "Aces of Jet Wars." *Krasnaya Zvezda,* March 11, 1995.

Dorr, Robert F., and Warren Thompson. *The Korean Air War.* Osceola, Wisc.: Motorbooks International, 1994.

Du Ping. *Zai zhiyuanjun zongbu: Du Ping huiyilu* (*My Days at the Headquarters of the Chinese People's Volunteers: Du Ping's Memoir*). Beijing: People's Liberation Army Press, 1988.

Eastman, Lloyd. *The Abortive Revolution: China and Nationalist Rule, 1927–1937.* Cambridge, Mass.: Harvard University Press, 1974.

Editorial Committee for the Summarization of Logistics Experience in the War to Resist America and Assist Korea, ed. *KangMei yuanChao zhanzheng houqin jingyan zonjie jiben jingyan* (*Summarization of Logistics Experience in the War to Resist America and Assist Korea: Basic Experience*). Beijing: Gold Shield Press, 1987.

Editorial Department of People's Literature Press, ed. *Chaoxian tongxun baogaoxuan sanji* (*Three Volumes of Collected News Reports from Korea*). Beijing: People's Literature Press, 1953.

Editorial Department of *Xinghuo liaoyuan*, ed. *Jiefangjun jiangling zhuan* (*A Collection of Biographies of PLA Generals*). 13 vols. Beijing: People's Liberation Army Press, 1987–88.

Eisenhower, Dwight D. *The White House Years: Mandate for Change, 1953–1956*. Garden City, N.Y.: Doubleday, 1963.

Fairbank, John King, and Merle Goldman. *China: A New History*. Cambridge, Mass.: Harvard University Press, 1998.

Foot, Rosemary. "Nuclear Coercion and the Ending of the Korean Conflict." *International Security* 13, no. 3 (winter, 1988–89): 92–113.

Foss, Joe, and Brennan, Mathew. *Top Guns: America's Fighter Aces Tell Their Stories*. New York: Simon and Schuster, 1991.

Futrell, Robert F. *The United States Air Force in Korea, 1950–1953*. Rev. ed. Washington, D.C.: Office of Air Force History, 1983.

———. "USAF Intelligence in the Korean War." In *The Intelligence Revolution: A Historical Perspective*, ed. Walter T. Hitchcock. Washington, D.C.: Office of Air Force History, 1988.

Gagin, V. V. "Air Operations in Korea, 1950–1953." *Poligraf* (Voronezh), August, 1997, 40–47.

Garver, John W. *Chinese-Soviet Realtions, 1937–1945: The Diplomacy of Chinese Nationalism*. New York: Oxford University Press, 1988.

Ge Longwu. *Zhongguo wangpai feixingyuan* (*China's Ace Pilots*). Beijing: National Defense University Press, 1998.

German, Askold Andreyevich, and Igor Atayevich Seidov. *Krasnye D'yavoly na 38-y Paralleli* (*Red Devils on the 38th Parallel*). Kiev, Ukraine: OOO Ruslan, 1998.

Golotyuk, Vasiliy. "Chinese in the Air, Russians on the Ground." *Aremisky Sbornik*, June, 1996, 80–84.

Goncharov, Sergei N., John W. Lewis, and Xue Litai. *Uncertain Partners: Stalin, Mao, and the Korean War*. Stanford, Calif.: Stanford University Press, 1993.

Gordon, Yefim, and Vladimir Rigmant. *MiG-15: Design, Development, and Korean War Combat History*. Osceola, Wisc.: Motorbooks International, 1993.

Goulden, Joseph C. *Korea: The Untold Story of the War*. New York: Times Books, 1982.

Guan Songru. "Liu Zuochen: Pineer of China's Aviation Undertaking." *Junshi lishi*, no. 3 (1998): 37–39.

Guo Guibao. "Mao Zedong's Congratulations to the 3d Air Division." *Junshi lishi*, no. 5, (1998): 57–59.

Halliday, Jon. "Air Operations in Korea: The Soviet Side of the Story." In *A Revolutionary War: Korea and the Transformation of the Postwar World*, ed. William J. Williams. Chicago: Imprint, 1993.

Hallion, Richard P. *The Naval Air War in Korea*. Baltimore: Nautical and Aviation, 1986.

———. "Naval Air Operations in Korea." In *A Revolutionary War: Korea and the Transformation of the Postwar World*, ed. William J. Williams. Chicago: Imprint, 1993.

Han Huaizhi et al. *Dangdai Zhongguo jundui de junshi gongzuo* (*China Today: The Military Affairs of the Army*). 2 vols. Beijing: Chinese Social Science Press, 1989.

Han shu (*History of Han*). Shanghai: Commercial Press, 1958.

Hao Yufan and Zhai Zhihai. "China's Decision to Enter the Korean War: History Revisited." *China Quarterly*, no. 121 (March, 1990): 94–115.

Heng Xueming. *Shengsi sanbaxian: Zhongguo zhiyuanjun zai Chaoxian zhanchang shimo* (*Life and Death on the 38th Parallel: The Whole Story of the Chinese Volunteer Army in the Korean War*). Hefei: Anhui Literature and Arts Press, 1992.

Higham, Robin, John T. Greenwood, and Von Hardesty, eds. *Russian Aviation and Air Power in the Twentieth Century.* London: Frank Cass, 1998.

Higham, Robin and Kipp, Jacob W. eds. *Soviet Aviation and Air Power: A Historical View.* Boulder, Colo.: Westview Press, 1977.

History Research Division of Guangdong Provincial Philosophy and Social Science Institute, ed. *Sun Zhongshan nianpu* (*The Chronicle of Sun Yat-sen*). Beijing: China Book Bureau, 1980.

Hong Xuezhi. *KangMei yuanChao zhanzheng huiyi* (*Recollections of the War to Resist America and Assist Korea*). Beijing: People's Liberation Army Literature Press, 1990.

Hooton, E. R. *The Greatest Tumult: The Chinese Civil War, 1936–1949.* London: Brassey's, 1991.

Hu Guangzheng and Ma Shanyin, eds. *Zhongguo renmin zhiyuanjun xulie* (*The Organizations of the Chinese People's Voulnteers*). Beijing: People's Liberation Army Press, 1987.

Hu Qiaomu. *Hu Qiaomu huiyi MaoZedong* (*Hu Qiaomu's Recollections of Mao Zedong*). Beijing: People's Press, 1994.

Iriye, Akira. *Across the Pacific: An Inner History of American-East Asian Relations.* Rev. ed. Chicago: Imprint, 1992.

Jackson, Robert. *Air War over Korea.* London: Ian Allan, 1973.

Japanese Society for Ground War Studies, ed. *Chaoxian zhanzheng* (*The Korean War*). 2 vols Changsha: University of National Defense Press, 1996.

Jiang Jianxiong. "Survey of the Development of the PLA Air Force through the Founding of the Air Force and the Two Wars." *Junshi lishi,* no. 6 (1999): 21–24.

Jiang Tianran. "Air Defense for Great Shanghai: A Real Account of Defeating Jiang Jieshi's Air Force by Chinese and Soviet Air Defense Forces." *Zhongguo guofang bao,* February 28 and March 7, 2001.

Jiang Yonghui. *Sanshibajun zai Chaoxian* (*The Thirty-eighth Army in Korea*). Shenyang: Liaoning People's Press, 1989.

Jouett, John H. "War Planes Over China." *Asia,* no. 37 (1937): 827–30.

Kangzhan shengli sishi zhounian lunwenji (*Essays on the Fortieth Anniversary of Resistance War Victory*). 2 vols. Taibei: History Office of the Defense Ministry, 1985.

Kim, Chullbaum, ed. *The Truth about the Korean War: Testimony 40 Years Later.* Seoul: Eulyoo, 1991.

Kong Yun. "Revealing the Real Air Combat Strength of the Chinese Air Force." *Zhongxin she,* January 6, 2000.

Kotlobovskiy, Aleksandr V. "Yevgeniy Pepelyayev." *Mir Aviatsiya,* no. 2 (1993): 25–26.

———. "Twenty Years in Combat: A History of MiG-15 Fighters in Combat" Pt. 1. *Aehrokhobbi* (*Aerohobby*), no. 2 (1994): 25–29.

———. "Twenty Years in Combat: A History of MiG-15 Fighters in Combat." Pt. 2. *Aehrokhobbi* (*Aerohobby*), no. 3 (1994): 33–37.

———.(Kiev), and Igor Seidov (Ashkhabad). "The Hot Skies of the 'Cold War.'" Pt. 1. *Mir Aviatsiya,* no. 2 (1995): 19–2.

———. "The Hot Skies of the 'Cold War.'" Pt. 2. *Mir Aviatsiya*, no. 1 (1996): 31–45.

Krylov, Leonid and Yuriy Chepsurkayev. "Combat Episodes of the Korean War: Three Out of One Thousand." *Mir Aviatsiya*, no. 1 (1997): 38–44.

———. "Nikolay Ivanovich Ivanov." *Mir Aviatsiya*, no. 2 (1997): 18–24.

———. "An Unpublicized Mission by the Government." Pt. 1. *Aviamaster*, no. 4 (1997): 34–39.

———. "An Unpublicized Mission by the Government." Pt. 2. *Aviamaster*, no. 5 (1997): 46–51.

———. "The Hunt for A Sabre." *Mir Aviatsiya*, no. 2 (1998): 39–44.

———. "The Soldier Airplane." *Mir Aviatsiya*, no. 2 (1998): 44–46.

Ledovsky, Andrei. "The Moscow Visit of a Delegation of the Communist Party of China in June to August 1949." Pt. 1. *Far Eastern Affairs* (Moscow), no. 4 (1996): 64–80.

———. "The Moscow Visit of a Delegation of the Communist Party of China in June to August 1949." Pt. 2. *Far Eastern Affairs* (Moscow), no. 5 (1996): 84–97.

Li Cheng, Xiao Ji and Wang Libing, chief eds. *Jianguo yilai junshi baizhuang dashi (One Hundred Important Events in Military History since the Founding of State)*. Beijing: Knowledge Press, 1992.

Li Chuangeng. *Feijiangjun Liu Shanben (Flying General Liu Shanben)*. Beijing: CCP History Press, 1995.

Li Jie. "General Takes Wing to Blue Sky." *Xinhua wenzhai*, no. 12 (1994): 128–33.

Li Ke and Hao Shengzhang. *Wenhua dageming zhong de renmin jiefangjun (The People's Liberation Army in the Cultural Revolution)*. Beijing: Central Historical Materials Press, 1989.

Liao Guoliang et al. *Mao Zedong junshi sixiang fazhan shi (History of Mao Zedong's military Thought Development)*. Beijing: People's Liberation Army Press, 1991.

Liu Chongwen and Chen Shaochou, chief eds. *Liu Shaoqi nianpu (The Chronicle of Liu Shaoqi)*. Beijing: Central Historical Materials Press, 1996.

Liu Wen-hsiao, ed. *Zhonggong kongjun shi (The History of the Chinese Communist Air Force)*. Taibei: Wing of China Press, 1993.

Liu Zhen. *Liu Zhen huiyilu (Liu Zhen's Memoirs)*. Beijing: People's Liberation Army Press, 1990.

Liu Ziming. *Zhongguo jindai junshi sixiang shi (History of Modern China's Military Thoughts)*. Nanchang: Jiangxi People's Press, 1997.

Lobov, Georgiy. "Blank Spots of History: In the Skies of North Korea." *JPRS Report*. JPRS-UAC-91-003, June 28, 1991.

———. "Blank Spots of History: In the Skies of North Korea." *JPRS Report*. JPRS-UAC-91-004, July 2, 1991.

———. "Blank Spots of History: In the Skies of North Korea." *JPRS Report*. JPRS-UAC-92-001, January 21, 1992.

Luo Yinwen. *Deng Hua jiangjun zhuan (Biography of General Deng Hua)*. Beijing: CCP Central Academy Press, 1995.

Lü Liping. *Tongtian zhi lu (The Road to the Sky)*. Beijing: People's Liberation Army Press, 1989.

Lyman, Flt. Lt. B. *The Significance of Australian Air Operations in Korea*. Fairbairn: Royal Australian Air Force Air Power Studies Centre, 1992.

Ma Hongjiao and Liang Zhanfang. "Brilliant Victory of Air Battle of General Nie Fengzhi in the Korean War." *Junshi lishi,* no. 1 (1998): 35–37.

Ma Jinhai and Hou Yunli, eds. *Zhonggong hujiang yu mingzhan* (*The CCP's Generals and Battles*). Beijing: China Social Science Press, 1995.

Ma Yüfu. *Zhongguo junshi hangkong* (*China's Military Aviation*). Beijing: Aviation Industry Press, 1994.

Mark, Eduard. *Aerial Interdiction: Air Power and the Land Battle in Three American Wars: A Historical Analysis.* Washington, D.C.: Center for Air Force History, 1994.

Mastro, Joseph P. "The Lessons of World War II and the Cold War." In *Soviet Aviation and Air Power: A Historical View,* ed. Robin Higham and Jacob W. Kipp. Boulder, Colo.: Westview Press, 1977.

Meng Xianzhang, chief ed. *ZhongSu maoyi shi ziliao* (*Historical Materials of Sino-Soviet Trade*). Beijing: China Foreign Economic and Trade Press, 1991.

———. *ZhongSu maoyi shi* (*History of Sino-Soviet Trade*). Harbin: Heilongjiang People's Press, 1992.

Meng Zhaohui. "On the Sixth Campaign in the War to Resist U.S. Aggression and Aid Korea." *Junshi lishi,* no. 6 (1998): 37–40.

Military Historical Research Division of Military Science Academy, ed. *Zhongguo renmin jiefangjun de qishi nian* (*The Seventy Years of the People's Liberation Army*). Beijing: Military Science Press, 1997.

Morosov, V., and S. Uskov. "Defending Peace and Labor: A Brief Account of the People's Democratic Republic of Korean Air Force, 1948–1996" *Mir Aviatsiya,* no. 2 (1997): 29–39.

Mo Zi xian gu (*Mencius Chat*). Vol. 13, *Zhuzi jicheng* (*Collections of Various Biographies*), pt. 4. Beijing: China Books, 1954.

Naboka, Vitaliy Petrovich. *NATOOvskiye Yastreby v Pritselye Stalinshikh Sokolov: Sovetskiye Letchiki na zashchite neba Kitaya Korei, 1950–1951* (*NATO's Hawks in the Sights of Stalin's Falcons: Soviet Pilots Protecting the Skies of China and Korea, 1950–1951*). Krasnodar, Russia: Sovetskaya Kuban Publishing, 1999.

Nie Fengzhi. *Zhanchang: Jiangjun de yaolan* (*Battlefields: The Cradle of Generals*). Beijing: People's Liberation Army Press, 1989.

Nie Rongzhen. *Nie Rongzhen huiyilu* (*Nie Rongzhen's Memoirs*). Beijing: People's Liberation Army Press, 1986.

No, Kum-Sok. *A MiG-15 to Freedom.* Jefferson, N.C.: McFarland, 1996.

Pang Xianzhi and Li Jie. *Mao Zedong yu kangMei yuanChao* (*Mao Zedong and the War of Resisting America and Aiding Korea*). Beijing: Central Historical Materials Press, 2000.

Pei Jianzhang, cheif ed. *Zhonghua renmin gongheguo waijiao shi, 1949–1969* (*Diplomatic History of the People's Republic of China, 1949–1969*). Beijing: World Knowledge Press, 1998.

Petrov, Vladimir. "Mao, Stalin, and Kim Il Sung: an Interpretative Essay." *Journal of Northeast Asian Studies* 113, no. 2 (summer, 1994): 3–30.

———, and N.V. Yakubovich. *Istrebiteli La-9 i La-11* (*The La-9 and La-11 Fighters*). Armada no. 11. Moscow: M-Khobbi (Ehksprint), 1999.

"Pictorial Volume of the CPV's Air Force in the War to Resist America and Assist Korea." *Junshi shijie huakan,* no. 2 (1992): 1–48.

Political Department of the Air Force, ed. *Lantian zhi lu* (*The Road of the Blue Sky*). Internal ed. 2 vols. Beijing: Political Department of Air Force, 1992.

Price, Alfred. *The History of U.S. Electronic Warfare.* Vol. 2. Arlington, Va.: Association of Old Crows, 1989.

Qi Dexue. *Chaoxian zhanzheng juece neimu (The Inside Story of Decision Making during the Korean War).* Shenyang: Liaoning University Press, 1991.

———. "The Imposing Appearance of Young Pilots: A Brief Historical Account of CPV's Air Force." *Junshi lishi,* no. 5 (1995): 14–19.

———. "The Major Experience and Significance for Winning the War to Resist US and Aid Korea." *Dangdai Zhongguo shi yanjiu,* no. 5 (1995): 44–52.

———. "A Few Questions Concerning the Korean War and How to Treat and Use the Recently Declassified Russian Korean War Archives." *Zhonggong dangshi yanjiu,* no. 1 (1998): 74–88.

——— et al. "Enlightenment on Defeating a Strong Enemy with Inferior Weapons and Equipment in the Korean War." *Junshi lishi,* no. 6 (1999): 33–35.

Qing Mu. *Zhongguo yuanshuai Zhu De (Chinese Marshal Zhu De).* Beijing: CCP Central Academy Press, 1995.

Quan Yanchi and Du Weidong. *Kongheguo mishi (A Secret Mission of the Republic).* Beijing: Guangming Daily Press, 1991.

Ryan, Mark A. *The Chinese Attitude Toward Nuclear Weapons: China and the United States during the Korean War.* New York: M. E. Sharpe, 1989.

Sarin, Oleg, and Lev Dvoretsky. *Alien Wars: The Soviet Union's Aggressions Against the World, 1919–1989.* Novato, Calif.: Presidio Press, 1996.

Seidl, Hans D. *Stalin's Eagles: An Illustrated Study of the Soviet Aces of World II and Korea.* Atglen, Pa.: Schiffer Military History, 1998

Seidov, Igor A. "Shield of the Night: an Unknown Chapter in the Korean War, 1950–1953." *Mir Aviatsiya,* no. 1 (1993): 29–34.

———. "Single Combat." *Mir Aviatsiya,* no. 1 (1995): 34–37.

———. "The Meteors Suffer a Fiasco." *Mir Aviatsiya,* no. 2 (1995): 38–45.

———. "The Korean Score of the Talalikhins." *Aviatiya i Vremya* (Kiev), no. 6 (1995): 38–40.

Shen Weiping. *8.23 paoji Jinmen (Shelling Jinmen on August 23).* Beijing: China Art Press, 1998.

Shen Zhihua. *ZhongSu tongmeng yu Chaoxian zhanzheng yanjiu (Study of the Sino-Soviet Alliance and the Korean War).* Guilin: Guangxi Teacher's University Press, 1999.

———. *Mao Zedong, Sidalin yu Hanzhan: ZhongSu zuigao jimi dangan (Mao Zedong, Stalin and Korean War: Highest Secret Archives from China and Soviet Union).* Hong Kong: Tiandi Books, 1998.

———. *Chaoxian zhanzheng jiemi (Revealing the Secrets of the Korean War).* Hong Kong: Tiandi Books, 1994.

———. "The China-Soviet Alliance and the Decision to Send Chinese Troops to Korea." *Dangdai Zhongguo shi yanjiu,* no. 6 (1997): 14–22.

———. "The Discrepancy between the Russian and Chinese Versions of Mao's 2 October 1950 Message to Stalin on Chinese Entry into the Korean War: A Chinese Scholar's Reply." *Cold War International History Project Bulletin,* nos. 8 and 9 (winter, 1996–97): 237–42.

———. "The Factors of the Soviet Union in Making Policy about the War to Resist U.S. Aggression and Aid Korea." *Dangdai Zhongguo shi yanjiu,* no. 1 (2000): 28–39.

Shen Zonghong et al. *Zhongguo renmin zhiyuanjun kangMei yuanChao zhan shi* (*A History of the War to Resist America and Assist Korea by the Chinese People's Volunteers*). Beijing: Military Science Press, 1988.

Sheply, James. "How Dulles Averted War." *Life,* January 16, 1956, 70–72.

Sherwood, John Darrell. *Officers in Flight Suits: The Story of American Air Force Fighter Pilots in the Korean War.* New York: New York University Press, 1996.

Shi Zhe. *Zai lishi juren shenbian Shi Zhe huiyilu* (*Beside Great Historical Figures: Shi Zhe's Memoirs*). Beijing: Central Historical Materials Press, 1991.

Shrader, Charles R. *Communist Logistics in the Korean War.* Westport Conn.: Greenwood, 1995.

Stewart, James T. *Airpower: The Decisive Force in Korea.* Princeton, N.J.: D. Van Nostrand, 1957.

Stueck, William. *The Korean War: An International History.* Princeton, N.J.: Princeton University Press, 1995.

Sun Kejia. "The New Development of Mao Zedong's Thought of People's War during the War to Resist America and Assist Korea." *Junshi lishi,* no. 5 (1990): 3–7.

Sun Xiao and Zuo Dong. *Paobing chuanqi* (*The Legend of the Artillery Force*). Jinan: Yellow River Press, 1997.

Sun Yaoshen. "General Xie Fang in the War to Resist U.S. Aggression and Aid Korea." *Junshi lishi,* no. 4 (1990): 43–44.

Sun Yat-Sen. *Sun Zhongshan quanji* (*Complete Works of Sun Yat-sen*). 3 vols. Beijing: China Book Bureau, 1981.

Tan Jingqiao, ed. *KangMei yuanChao zhanzheng* (*The War to Resist America and Aid Korea*). Beijing: Chinese Social Science Press, 1990.

Tan Zheng. *Zhongguo renmin zhiyuanjun renwu lu* (*Biographic Records of Members of the Chinese People's Volunteers*). Beijing: CCP History Press, 1992.

Thomson, James C., Jr., Peter W. Stanley, and John Curtis Perry. *Sentimental Imperialists: The American Experience in East Asia.* New York: Harper and Row, 1981.

Valone, Stephan J. *"A Policy to Benefit China": The United States and China Arms Embargo, 1919–1929.* New York: Greenwood, 1991.

Wang Bo. *Peng Dehuai ruChao zouzhan jishi* (*A True Record of Peng Dehuai in the Korean War*). Shijiazhuang: Huashan Art Press, 1992.

Wang Daoping. *Zhongguo kangRi zhanzheng shi* (*The History of the War of Resistance Against Japanese Aggression*). 3 vols. Beijing: People's Liberation Army Press, 1991.

Wang Dinglie et al. *Dangdai Zhongguo kongjun* (*China Today: The Air Force*). Beijing: China Social Science Press, 1989.

Wang Hai. *Wo de zhandou shengya* (*My Combat Career*). Beijing: the Central Historical Materials Press, 2000.

Wang Suhong and Wang Yubing. *Xuese tiankong: Zhongguo kongjun kongzhan shilu* (*Crimson Sky: A True Account of Air Operations by China's Air Force*). Chengdu: Sichuan People's Press, 1996.

———. *Kongzhan zai Chaoxian* (*The Air War in Korea*). Beijing: People's Liberation Army Art and Literature Press, 1992.

Wang Zhenghua. *Kangzhan shiqi waiguo duihua junshi yuanzhu* (*Foreign Military Assistance to China during the Resistance War*). Taibei: Around the World Book Bureau, 1987.

Wang Yan, chief ed. *Peng Dehuai nianpu* (*The Chronicle of Peng Dehuai*). Beijing: People's Press, 1998.

———. *Peng Dehuai zhuan* (*Biography of Peng Dehuai*). Beijing: Today's China Press, 1993.

Wang Yazhi. "Some Information Before and After Mao Zedong Decided to Send Troops to Korea." *Dang de wenxian*, no. 5 (1995): 84–89.

———. "Peng Dehuai and Nie Rongzhen during the War to Resist U.S. Aggression and Aid Korea: A Recollection of a Staff Member." *Junshi shilin*, no. 1 (1994): 9–15.

Weathersby, Kathryn. "The Soviet Role in the Early Phase of the Korean War: New Documentary Evidence." *Journal of American-East Asian Relations* 12, no. 4 (winter, 1993): 425–58.

———. "Soviet Aim in Korea and the Origins of the Korean War, 1949–50: New Evidence from Russian Archives." Working Paper no. 8, Cold War International History Project, Woodrow Wilson Center for Scholars, Washington, D.C., November, 1993.

———. "Korea, 1949–50: To Attack, or Nor to Attack? Stalin, Kim Il Sung, and the Prelude to War." *Cold War International History Project Bulletin*, no. 5 (spring, 1995): 1–9.

Wei Bihai. "Remembrances of the Air War to Resist U.S. Aggression and Aid Korea: An Interview with Wang Bingzhang." *Junshi lishi*, no. 6 (2000): 30–35.

———. "Air War Decision Making at the Highest Level during the War to Oppose America and Aid Korea: An Interview of Wang Bingzhang." *Guangming ribao*, November 8, 2000.

Whiting, Allen A. *China Crosses the Yalu: The Decision to Enter the Korean War*. New York: Macmillan, 1960.

Wu Chunguang. *Zhongguo kongjun shilu* (*The True Account of the Chinese Air Force*). Shenyang: Chunfeng Arts Press, 1997.

Wu Xinquan. *Chaoxian zhanchang 1000 days: Sanshijiu jun zai Chaoxian* (*One Thousand days in the battlefield of the Korean War: The Thirty-ninth Army in Korea*). Shenyang: Liaoning People's Press, 1995.

Wu Xiuguan. *Huiyi yu huainian* (*Remembering and Cherishing the Memory*). Beijing: Central Party Academy Press, 1991.

Xia Zhenduo. "Ten Years of the Soviet Red Army Garrison in Lüda." *Zhonggong dangshi ziliao*, no. 43 (1992): 125–53.

Xiao Jingguang. *Xiao Jingguang huiyilu* (*Memoirs of Xiao Jingguang*). 2 vols. Beijing: People's Liberation Army Press, 1988.

Xiao Qiang and Li Debiao. *Guofu and kongjun* (*The Founding Father and the Air Force*). Taibei: Huata Press, 1983.

Xiao Yunbin, ed. *Da chubing* (*The Great Dispatch of Troops*). Beijing: Tuanjie Press, 1993.

Xie Lifu. *Chaoxian zhanzheng shilu* (*Historical Records of the Korean War*). 2 vols. Beijing: World Knowledge Press, 1993.

Xiong Huayuan. "Zhou Enlai's Secret Visit to the Soviet Union on the Eve of the War to Resist U.S. Aggression and Aid Korea." *Dang de wenxian*, no. 4 (1994): 83–87.

Xu Xiangqian. *Lishi de huigu* (*Remember the History*). 2 vols. Beijing: People's Liberation Army Press, 1987.

Xu Yan. *Junshijia Mao Zedong* (*Mao Zedong: A Military Strategist*). Beijing: Party Central Historical Materials Press, 1995.

———. *Jinmen zhi zhan* (*The Battles for Jinmen*). Beijing: Chinese Broadcasting and Television Press, 1992.

———. *Diyici jiaoliang: kangMei yuanChao zhanzheng de lishi huigu yu fansi* (*The First Test of Strength: A Historical Review and Evaluation of the War to Resist America and Assist Korea*). Beijing: Chinese Broadcasting and Television Press, 1990.

Yang Di. *Zai zhiyuanjun zongbu de suiyue li: xianwei renzhi de zhenqing shikuang* (*During the Years of the CPV's Headquarters: Rarely Known True Accounts*). Beijing: People's Liberation Army Press, 1998.

Yang Fengan and Wang Tiancheng. *Jiayu Chaoxian zhanzheng de ren* (*The People Who Dominated the Korean War*). Beijing: CCP Central Academy Press, 1993.

Yang Guoyu et al. *Dangdai Zhongguo haijun* (*China Today: The Navy*). Beijing: Chinese Social Sciences Press, 1987,

Yang Jun, chief ed. *Gongheguo buzhang dangan* (*The Biographic Archives Concerning the Ministers of the Republic*). 2 vols. Wulumuqi: Xinjiang Youth Press, 1998.

Yang Shengqun and Tien Shongnien eds. *Gongheguo zhongda juece de lailong qumai, 1949–1965* (*The Origin and Development of Important Decisions by the People's Republic, 1949–1965*). Nanjing: Jiangsu People's Press, 1996.

Yang Wanqing. "Liu Yalou: The First Commander of the People's Air Force." *Zhonggong dangshi ziliao*, no. 42 (1990): 215–58.

——— and Qi Chunyuan. *Liu Yalou jiangjun zhuan* (*Biography of General Liu Yalou*). Beijing: CCP History Press, 1995.

Yang Zhen et al. *Kongjun chuanqi* (*The Legend of the Air Force*). Jinan: Yellow River Press, 1997.

Yang Zhongyi et al. "Vanguard of Race to Control the Northeast China: An Interview with Zeng Kelin." *Junshi lishi*, no. 6 (1998): 2–7.

Yao Jun. *Zhongguo hangkong shi* (*The History of Chinese Aviation*). Zhengzhou: Henan Education Press, 1998.

Yao Xu. *Cong Yalujiang dao Banmendian* (*From the Yalu River to Panmunjom*). Beijing: People's Press, 1985.

Zaloga, Steven J. "The Russians in MiG Alley." *Air Force Magazine,* February, 1991.

Zhang Aiping, chief ed. *Zhongguo renmin jiefangjun* (*The Chinese People's Liberation Army*). Beijing: Today's China Press, 1994.

Zhang Lin and Ma Changzhi. *Zhongguo yuanshuai Xu Xiangqian* (*Chinese Marshal Xu Xiangqian*). Beijing: CCP Central Academy Press, 1995.

Zhang Nongke. "China's Air Force Is Transforming from an Air Defense Force to an Air Offense and Defense Force: An Interview with Air Force Commander Lt. General Liu Shunyao and Political Commissar Lt. General Qiao Qingchen." *Zijing,* November, 1999, 4–9.

Zhang Shu Guang. *Mao's Military Romanticism: China and the Korean War, 1950–1953.* Lawrence: University Press of Kansas, 1995.

Zhang Xi. "Peng's Appointment to Command of Troops to Resist America and to Aid Korea." *Zhonggong dangshi ziliao*, no. 31 (1989): 111–59.

Zhang Xiaoming. "The Vietnam War, 1964–1969: A Chinese Perspective." *Journal of Military History* 60 (October, 1996): 731–62.

———. "China and the Air War in Korea, 1950–1953." *Journal of Military History* 62 (April, 1998): 335-70.

Zhang Yutao. *Xin Zhongguo junshi dashi jiyao* (*The Records of Major Events in New China's Military*). Beijing: Military Science Press, 1998.

Zhao Dexin et al. *Zhonghua renmin gongheguo jingji shi* (*An Economic History of the People's Republic of China, 1949-1966*). Zhengzhou: Henan People's Press, 1989.

Zhao Jianguo and Ma Yuan. *Chaoxian da kongzhan* (*The Great Air War in Korea*). Beijing: China Personnel Press, 1996.

Zhong Zhaoyun. *Baizhan jiangxing Liu Yalou* (*Biography of General Liu Yalou*). Beijing: People's Liberation Arts Press, 1996.

Zhonghua renmin gongheguo jingji dangan ziliao xuanbian (*A Collection of Economic Documents of the People's Republic of China, 1949-1952*). Comp. Vol. Beijing: China's Urban Economic Society Press, 1990.

Zhonghua renmin gongheguo jingji dangan ziliao xuanbian (*A Collection of Economic Documents of the People's Republic of China, 1949-1952*). Foreign trade vol. Beijing: Economic Management Press, 1994.

Zhou Jun. "A Preliminary Exploration of Reasons for the People's Liberation Army's Abortive Plan to Attack Taiwan after the Formation of the People's Republic." *Zhonggong dangshi yanjiu*, no. 1 (1991): 67-74.

Zhou Junlun, chief ed. *Nie Rongzhen nianpu* (*The Chronicle of Nie Rongzhen*). Beijing: People's Press, 1999.

Zhou Keyu. *KangMei yuanChao zhanzheng* (*The War to Resist America and Assist Korea*). Beijing: China Social Science Press, 1990.

Zhu Bingxiu. "Air Defense of Shanghai during the Initial Post-liberation Period." *Junshi lishi*, no. 3 (1994): 51-54.

Zhu Jianrong. *Mo Takuto no chosen senso: Chugoku ga Oryokko o wataru made* (*Mao Zedong's Korean War: China Crosses the Yalu*). Tokyo: Iwanami Book Store, 1991.

Zhu Yuanshi. "Liu Shaoqi's 1949 Secret Visit to the Soviet Union." *Dang de wenxian*, no. 3 (1991): 74–89.

Zolotarev, A. V., chief ed. *Rossiya (SSSR) v Lokal'nykh Voynakh i Voyennykh Konfliktakh Vtoroy Poloviny XX Veka* (*Russia [USSR] in Local Wars and Regional Conflicts in the Second Half of the 20th Century*). Moscow: Kuchkovo Polye, 2000.

Index

Note: References to illustrations appear in *italics*.

CPSIA information can be obtained at www.ICGtesting.com
Printed in the USA
LVOW042126190212

269433LV00004B/13/P